THE THERAPEUTIC POWERS OF PLAY

Edited by
Charles E. Schaefer, Ph.D.

JASON ARONSON INC.
Northvale, New Jersey
London

Production Editor: Judith D. Cohen

This book was set in Schneidler by Lind Graphics of Upper Saddle River, New Jersey, and printed and bound by Haddon Craftsmen of Scranton, Pennsylvania.

The editor gratefully acknowledges permission to reprint "The Maligned Wolf" by Dr. Uvaldo Palomares from *A Curriculum on Conflict Management*, copyright © 1984 by Magic Circle Publishing Company, P.O. Box 4270, San Clemente, CA 92672, telephone (714) 366-0564.

Library of Congress Cataloging-in-Publication Data

The therapeutic powers of play / edited by Charles E. Schaefer.
    p. cm.
    Includes bibliographical references and indexes.
    ISBN 0-87668-454-1 (hard cover)
    1. Play therapy. I. Schaefer, Charles E.
    [DNLM: 1. Play Therapy – in infancy & childhood.   WS 350.2 T3977].
RJ505.P6T47 1992
618.92' 891653 – dc20
DNLM/DLC
for Library of Congress   92-2849

Manufactured in the United States of America. Jason Aronson Inc. offers books and cassettes. For information and catalog write to Jason Aronson Inc., 230 Livingston Street, Northvale, New Jersey 07647.

Contents

Contributors

Allyson I. Aborn, M.S.W.
Department of Psychiatry
New York Hospital–Cornell Medical Center
White Plains, NY

James N. Bow, Ph.D.
Hawthorn Center and Wayne State University School of Medicine
Department of Psychiatry
Detroit, MI

JoAnn L. Cook, Ed.D.
Private Practice
Winter Park, FL

Nancy E. Curry, Ph.D.
Professor, Program in Child Development and Child Care
School of Social Work
University of Pittsburgh
Pittsburgh, PA

Diane E. Frey, Ph.D.
Professor of Counseling Psychology
Wright State University
Dayton, OH

Barry G. Ginsberg, Ph.D.
Director, Center of Relationship Enhancement
Doylestown, PA

Louise F. Guerney, Ph.D.
Professor of Human Development and Counseling Psychology
The Pennsylvania State University
University Park, PA

Diane M. Horm-Wingerd, Ph.D.
University of Rhode Island
Kingston, RI

Eleanor C. Irwin, Ph.D.
Department of Psychiatry
Clinical Assistant Professor of Child Psychiatry
University of Pittsburgh
Pittsburgh, PA

Ann M. Jernberg, Ph.D.
Founder and Director of The Theraplay Institute
Chicago, IL

Garry L. Landreth, Ed.D.
Professor of Counseling Education
Director of Center for Play Therapy
University of North Texas
Denton, TX

D'Arcy Lyness, Ph.D.
Department of Family Medicine
The Reading Hospital and Medical Center
Reading, PA

Evelyn K. Oremland, Ph.D.
Director, Child Life Program
Mills College
Oakland, CA

Steven Reid, Ph.D.
Director, Early Intervention Program
Herbert G. Birch Children's Center
Brooklyn, NY

Janet K. Sawyers, Ph.D.
Virginia Polytechnic Institute and State University
Blacksburg, VA

Charles E. Schaefer, Ph.D.
Professor of Psychology and
Director, Psychological Services Center
Fairleigh Dickinson University
Teaneck, NJ

Dorothy G. Singer, Ed.D.
Research Scientist, Psychology Department
Yale University
Co-Director, Yale University Family Television Research and Consultation Center
New Haven, CT

Mary Sinker, M.A.
Child Development Consultant
Private Practice
Evanston, IL

Preface

Although play therapy is a well-established and popular mode of treatment for children, the fundamental question of how it works has seldom been raised or addressed. For example:

- Is it the ability of the child and therapist to communicate better with each other through play interactions than in words?
- Is it the miniaturization of experiences in play that leads to mastery of stresses and traumas?
- Is it the motoric release of feelings in play actions?
- Is it the special relationship and rapport that develops with the therapist in the play room?

The goal of this book is to address these questions by presenting a comprehensive account of how play therapy works, and by specifically highlighting those elements of the play process likely to be responsible for its most beneficial effects. The basic premise of this volume is that play is not just a medium for applying other interventions such as positive reinforcement or reframing, but that play itself has a number of therapeutic elements that produce behavior change. A deeper understanding of the elements of change should lead to improvement in play therapy effectiveness based on an integrative approach to the field.

There are numerous theories of how play therapy works and empirical research on the subject is just starting to appear. The therapeutic factors in this volume were selected by the editor and contributors based upon their clinical experiences and a review of the play therapy literature.

Since this is the first book to focus on the curative properties of play, the factors presented must be considered preliminary and tentative. Clearly there is a need for more systematic studies of the therapeutic elements of play in terms of their clinical effectiveness, applicability to certain disorders, and power when combined.

In the course of time, other therapeutic components undoubtedly will emerge, and some of the factors in this book may prove rather weak in comparison. Nevertheless, we believe that a description of specific therapeutic factors as currently recognized will be of particular value to clinicians and trainees as they struggle with the complexities of play interactions. These factors can be matched with the goals of an individual case and can prove to be invaluable guidelines in formulating a play intervention.

The contents of this book should be useful to child therapists in such fields as psychology, psychiatry, clinical social work, counseling, nursing, child life, therapeutic recreation, and occupational therapy.

A Word about Pronouns

Both boys and girls play and benefit from play interventions. The information in this book on therapeutic factors applies equally to all children regardless of gender; however, in the interest of simplicity and uniformity we have decided to avoid the awkward and confusing reference to "he and she" and "him and her." Therefore, in this book all children are referred to as "he."

1

What Is Play and Why Is It Therapeutic?

Charles E. Schaefer

What Is Play?

Play, like love, happiness, and other psychological constructs, is easier to recognize than to define. Although there are many different definitions of play, there has been an emerging consensus of late on the common characteristics of play behaviors. First, play is characterized by intrinsic versus extrinsic motivation. Activities performed for their own sake are intrinsically motivated because pleasure is inherent in the activity itself. One does not have to pressure or motivate a child to play by giving external rewards. Rather, play seems to satisfy an inner desire in the child.

Second, the player is more concerned about the play activity itself than the outcome or successful completion of the activity. In other words, the play process is more important than the end result. Third, positive feelings accompany play. These pleasurable feelings are derived from the play activity itself and are a result of the play. Such feelings of enjoyment are evident in the smiles, laughter, and joy exhibited by children during and just following the play. Fourth, the child is actively involved and often becomes so engrossed in play as to lose awareness of time and surroundings. Fifth, play has an "as if" or nonliteral quality, which means it is carried out as if it is not real life. Sixth, play gives one freedom to impose novel meaning on objects and events. This is seen in the fact that there is always some variation in play, and often creativity and innovation result. Seventh, play is different from exploratory behavior that seeks to determine "what is this object and what can it do?" Play tries to answer the question, "What can I do with this object?"

These specific behaviors make it easier for observers to recognize behavior as playful than to define play in the abstract. The more these seven characteristics are present, the more likely the behavior is playful.

Developmental Stages

One reason play is difficult to define is because it changes its form as young children mature. Four stages of cognitive development in play have been distinguished by

Piaget (1951) and others: Practice play, construction play, symbolic play, and games with rules. Practice play refers to the sensorimotor play seen in infants during the first year of life. This involves non-goal oriented actions with objects, stemming from the infant's pleasure in having actions and objects under his own control, for example, repetitively banging and dropping a rattle.

Construction or combinatorial play begins at 15 to 24 months and entails putting things together such as shapes into a shape box, stacking blocks on top of one another, grouping objects by function or shape, and putting blocks together to construct something.

Symbolic or pretend play, most common from 2 to 6 years, is perhaps the most interesting and creative form of play. Using fantasy, children change themselves into people, objects, or situations other than themselves, as evident in their verbal expressions and/or motor movements. Piaget considered pretend play as primarily assimilative rather than accommodative in that the player adapts reality to his own needs. Examples of pretend play or "acting as if" include pretending to feed a doll, using a block as a hairbrush, and acting out a pretend sequence (putting a doll to bed). Games with rules, such as chess and checkers, are a mature form of play common in older children (ages 5 and up) and adults. Adult recreation often involves team games with rules, such as volleyball, basketball, and baseball.

In regard to social development in play, Parten (1932) identified six categories: unoccupied behavior, onlooker, solitary or independent play, parallel activity, associative play, and cooperative play. Unoccupied behavior is a type of play in which children look around the play room and perform some simple movements that are not goal directed, for example, stroking their bodies. An onlooker watches others at play and may talk with them but is unable or unwilling to join in. Solitary or independent play occurs when a child plays alone without concern for the activities of others nearby. During parallel play, which is common among 2-year-olds, the child plays independently but with toys that are similar to those used by children in close proximity. During this stage, children play next to other children but not with them. Associative play is typical of preschoolers who are actively involved with one another but they cannot sustain these interactions. They seem more interested in socializing with their peers than in the play activities. There is a flightiness to their play and social interactions. Finally, cooperative play emerges in the later part of the preschool stage and continues into middle childhood. This type of play consists of group play, playing specific roles, and active cooperation for sustained intervals of time. Numerous studies have confirmed Parten's observation that as children develop, the amount of their social play increases. Their attention spans also lengthen, allowing them to sustain their social interactions for longer periods.

Play and Normal Development

Play is a universal behavior in children. By the time they reach the age of 6, children are likely to have spent more than 15,000 hours playing. What are the benefits of this play activity? Child development researchers over the past twenty years have produced evidence that play facilitates a child's gross and fine motor development, cognitive and language development, and social adjustment (Smith 1982). The physical benefits of play are most obvious. Throwing a ball helps strengthen muscles and improves eye-hand coordination. Socially, play provides an opportunity to practice sharing and other social skills. As previously mentioned, play becomes more cooperative with age.

Over the centuries, philosophers, poets, psychologists and others have speculated on the reasons why play is helpful to man. Herbert Spencer, a nineteenth century British philosopher, proposed the "surplus energy" theory of play. According to this theory, children are likely to have extra energy (beyond what is needed for survival), and this surplus energy will build up and exert internal pressure on the child, unless it is released by such activity as play. The "recreation theory" delineated by the German poet Moritz Lazarus suggests that we play to restore energy expended in work. Energy is regenerated by doing an activity very different from the work that used it up. Play, which is the opposite of work, is an ideal way to restore this lost energy. The Dutch philosopher Karl Groos (1901) advanced the "practice theory" of play, which states that play gives children the opportunity to practice and develop skills needed for the future. The psychoanalytic approach stresses that play allows a child to actively relive stresses and traumas that were experienced passively (Waelder 1979). Cognitive theorists suggest that play promotes a child's creativity and flexible thinking, while arousal theorists (Ellis 1973) contend that we all seek an optimum level of arousal through play. All of these theories seem to have some validity, but we are still awaiting an elegant, unifying "grand" theory of play that integrates all its positive qualities.

Recently, however, children's right to play is being questioned as segments of our society are calling for more structure, more work, and more adult-directed activity for children. There is increasing pressure for more academic work by preschoolers. The attitude of many adults to child's play is reflected in the comment, "Oh, he's just playing"–a comment that suggests play is a trivial activity. Another trend in our society is for children to spend more time watching television than engaged in active play. Thus, although the universal and enduring nature of play suggests it satisfies some basic inner needs in the child, there are several competing forces in our society that seek to reduce children's play time.

Uses of Play Therapy

Play has the power not only to facilitate normal child development but also to alleviate abnormal behavior. Play therapy can be defined as an interpersonal process wherein a trained therapist systematically applies the curative powers of play to help clients resolve their psychological difficulties. In the 1940s and '50s, play therapy was the major form of child psychotherapy. As newer approaches appeared (behavior therapy, family therapy), play therapy faded into the background. Like business cycles, there are inevitable cycles of interest in major schools of psychotherapy. According to Allport (1968) the average life of most theoretical concepts is about two decades. It seems time, then, for play therapy to be viewed as new and exciting again.

Several schools of play therapy have been developed that use play as a therapeutic process rather than simply as a medium for applying other interventions. Behavioral play therapists use play for its relaxation properties as well as for helping clients role-play more adaptive behaviors. Psychoanalytic play therapists use interpretations to give clients insight into their unconscious conflicts. These conflicts may be revealed symbolically in a child's play. Child-centered and existential play therapists use play to establish a therapeutic relationship. Family play therapists use play for diagnostic purposes and as a way to alter dysfunctional family interaction patterns. Eclectic play therapists borrow ideas and techniques from the various schools so as to individualize treatment for the child.

In the past, play therapists have paid much more attention to understanding and developing a particular theoretical approach, such as cognitive-behavioral principles, rather than to identifying discrete elements of the play process that seem to account for clinical improvement. Advocates of the diverse schools of play therapy have largely ignored the possibility that underlying their theoretical beliefs there might exist a core of common therapeutic components. Play therapists of these diverse orientations are believed to achieve approximately the same proportion of successful outcomes, which implies that various play therapies are more similar than commonly believed.

Although each school of play therapy has its unique theories and special techniques, they share a number of common factors that reduce their differences. Frank (1979) delineated a basic set of general, nonspecific factors in psychotherapy. Yalom (1975) described a list of twelve therapeutic factors common to group psychotherapy: altruism, cohesiveness, universality, interpersonal learning-input, interpersonal learning-output, guidance, catharsis, identification, family reenactment, self-understanding, instillation of hope, and existential factors. A clearer knowledge of the array of therapeutic factors underlying play therapy will allow child clinicians to borrow flexibly from available theoretical positions and practical techniques. The most helpful play therapy theories are those that detail processes of change. Prochaska and Di Clemente (1982) maintain that without processes to implement change, systems of psychotherapy are merely theories of personality and psychotherapy. Process, then, highlights what exactly therapists do to effect change.

Therapeutic Factors

A therapeutic factor is an element in the play process that exerts a beneficial effect on clients. The basic premise of determining therapeutic factors is that the play therapy process contains a limited number of elements that are differentiated from each other by their specific effects on a child. If a factor results in clinical improvement of some sort, it is therapeutic. This improvement can be either a decrease in symptoms or an increase in desired behaviors. A therapeutic factor, then, is an element of play that contributes to a positive outcome. Other names for an element or factor are force, dynamic, mechanism, power, and component.

To understand therapeutic factors we must understand that they are not conditions for change, techniques, or beneficial outcomes. Conditions for change refer to the place, space, and play materials involved in the play. These conditions for change are necessary for the therapeutic factors to operate, but do not have intrinsic therapeutic effects. Techniques are procedures that specify how to use the play materials. There are numerous play therapy techniques, including the Color-Your-World technique and the Two-Houses technique (Schaefer and O'Connor 1983). Beneficial outcomes refer to desired changes that occur in the client because of the effectiveness of the therapeutic factors.

Group therapists have long been active in their search for therapeutic forces in the group process. Corsini and Rosenberg (1955) proposed a unifying classification of the therapeutic elements underlying group therapy. Yalom (1975) extended the work of Corsini and Rosenberg by adding interpersonal dimensions. Block and Crouch (1985) updated the knowledge that has accumulated on how group therapy works, in particular those elements of the group process likely to be responsible for its positive effects. Recently, psychoanalysts have attempted to define their conceptions of the effective ingredients of psychoanalysis and psychoanalytic psychotherapy (Rothstein 1988).

Play Therapy Factors

By what mechanisms do clients benefit from play therapy? Table 1–1 presents a proposed taxonomy together with the therapeutic benefits likely to be produced by each of fourteen factors. A brief description of these factors follows, and an in-depth discussion is presented in the fourteen chapters of the book. In clinical practice, therapeutic factors are typically intertwined. To facilitate understanding, we will discuss the factors as if they were completely distinct entities.

Overcoming Resistance

The first goal in child therapy is to draw the child into a working alliance. Most children do not come voluntarily to therapy, deny they have problems, and are wary of talking to a strange adult in an unfamiliar office. Typically, children come to therapy because their parents or teachers want them to be there. Usually they do not feel troubled, but they are troublesome to those around them. They tend to view therapy as a punishment and expect criticism from the therapist rather than support.

Table 1-1.   Therapeutic Factors of Play

Therapeutic Factor	Beneficial Outcome
Overcoming Resistance	Working Alliance
Communication	Understanding
Competence	Self-Esteem
Creative Thinking	Innovative Solutions to Problems
Catharsis	Emotional Release
Abreaction	Adjustment to Trauma
Role-Play	Practice and Acquiring of New Behaviors, Empathy
Fantasy/Visualization	Fantasy Compensation
Metaphoric Teaching	Insight
Attachment Formation	Attachment
Relationship Enhancement	Self-Actualization, Self-Esteem, Closeness to Others
Positive Emotion	Ego Boost
Mastering Developmental Fears	Growth and Development
Game Play	Ego Strength, Socialization

Play seems to be the best way of establishing rapport and alliance with a child since it is a behavior that is interesting, enjoyable, and natural to children. Once rapport is established the child will be more likely to commit to therapy and agree to work towards needed change. Poor progress in psychotherapy has been found to be associated with a lack of rapport and a problematic therapeutic relationship (Colson et al. 1991).

Communication

Play is to the child what verbalization is to the adult – the most natural medium for self-expression. Before reaching junior high level, children have difficulty using words to fully communicate their feelings, needs, and thoughts. Toys are a young child's words, and play is his natural language. According to Piaget (1951) fantasy play "provides the child with the live, dynamic, individual language indispensable for the expression of his subjective feelings for which collective language alone is inadequate" (p. 166). For example, a 4-year-old boy whose parents were separated recently had developed an underlying fear of total abandonment. In play, he buried the adult dolls in the sand, while the child dolls sailed away in a toy boat calling for help since there was no one left to rescue them.

Play is a special form of communication. It is primarily nonverbal and constitutes a language quite different from verbal language. Play is a more fantastic, drive-dominated form of communication that is full of images and emotions. It seems more right-brain oriented than the logical, sequential, and analytic thought expressed in words, which seems more left-brain centered.

The communication process in play operates on two levels. On the conscious level, play allows children to enact those thoughts and feelings of which they are aware but can't express in words. For example, sexually abused children may be able to express themselves better using puppets and anatomically correct dolls than they can in words.

In addition to expressing conscious thoughts and feelings, children use play to express their unconscious wishes and conflicts. Through play, children often reveal thoughts, feelings, and conflicts of which they are totally unaware. Sigmund Freud was the first therapist to realize the value of play in uncovering a child's unconscious conflicts. In his classic study of Little Hans, Freud asked the boy's father to observe Hans's play, dreams, and talk. Freud then interpreted the meanings of these expressions to the father. Similarly, by closely tuning in to children's play and interpreting its symbolic content, clinicians report that they are better able to understand the emotional problems of children. Clearly, play provides a window into the otherwise invisible inner world of the child.

Mastery

Play is a self-motivated activity that satisfies a child's innate need to explore and master his environment (Berlyne 1960). Apart from play, there are few areas in a child's life that produce a sense of efficacy, the feeling that the behaviors in which one engages make a difference in the world. The infant notices the mobile attached to his crib, hits the mobile, and it moves. These play experiences contribute to a sense of power, control, and mastery of the environment.

White (1959) described the child's motivation toward competence as "effectance." Effectance motivation helps a child learn about the world and acquire skills. This inner drive impels a child to become competent, and is satisfied by a feeling of efficacy. When children are engaged in an activity that is enjoyable they tend to persist at it longer. Such persistence is likely to produce success in mastering the task. Play is also characterized by the qualities of novelty, variability, and challenge, which further strengthen the child's engrossment in the task.

Creative Thinking

Play encourages children to improve their problem-solving skills. It promotes creativity and flexibility because it allows children to experiment with new options without fear of negative consequences. Pretend play in childhood has been linked to adult creativity and innovative problem solving (Sherrod and Singer 1989). Creative adults report higher levels of childhood imaginative play than do less creatively oriented adults (Singer 1973). Several studies (Dansky and Silverman 1973) have found a relationship between play and innovative behavior. Moreover, numerous studies have indicated that prior play with certain materials improved children's problem solving with those materials later (Sylva et al. 1976). It seems that the flexible and original thinking inherent in play can help children find alternate and more effective solutions to real life social and emotional problems.

Catharsis

Catharsis is a core therapeutic factor shared by many schools of psychotherapy (Greencavage and Norcross 1990). It provides clients comfort through the release of tension and affect on such inanimate objects as punching bags, pillows, and bobo dolls. The safety of the playroom allows children the opportunity for emotional release without fear of retaliation or censure.

Catharsis refers to the arousal and discharge of strong emotions (positive and negative) for therapeutic relief. It seems related to but different from ventilation. Ventilation refers to the open expression of one's innermost thoughts and secrets. Catharsis is the release of feelings associated with the ventilated thought or secret. In Aristotle's time, catharsis meant the purifying and release of emotions in art, and was first used to describe the emotional impact of tragic drama. Breuer and Freud introduced the concept of catharsis in psychotherapy at the turn of the last century. Both primal scream and Gestalt therapy consider catharsis a primary therapeutic element.

In play therapy, clients can release intense feelings of anger, grief, or anxiety that have been difficult or impossible to ventilate before. This discharge of pent-up affect usually results in a sense of relief. The ensuing feeling of ease and comfort is seen in such comments as "blowing off steam," "getting it off my chest," and "loosening up."

Some clinicians believe catharsis should combine two distinct processes: the release of feelings with accompanying relief, and the expression of ideas (often unconscious) about the feelings. Thus, after the motoric expression of the feelings and resultant relief, a therapist may help the client appraise the personal significance of the feelings. The motoric release tends to free up the child for ventilation, that is, verbal release of inner thoughts. For example, a girl who plays out the scene of an older doll beating a baby doll in the doll house may then be able to talk about how she resents her new baby sister. Unless a client feels better after the ventilation or achieves a greater understanding of self, the experience is unlikely to be therapeutic.

To date, research on catharsis has been sparse. If handled inappropriately, it is possible for catharsis to have adverse clinical effects. For example, encouraging ventilation of aggressive feelings to other play group members may lead to hurt feelings and open warfare among group members. Also, intense catharsis by a borderline or psychotic child may result in the child's fragile ego being over-whelmed.

Abreaction

Abreaction is the reliving of past stressful events and the emotions associated with them. It is a more heightened process than catharsis in that the discharge of affect is greater. In play, children can slowly mentally digest and assimilate traumatic experiences by reliving them with an appropriate release of affect. Children deal with stresses and traumas by playing out similar situations and gradually achieving mastery over them. In play, the child is in control of the events and there is less anxiety because it is just pretend. The assimilation model draws on the conceptual work of Piaget (1951). The model proposes that a traumatic experience must be gradually assimilated into a schema (frame of reference, script) that is developed by the therapist–client interaction.

According to Piaget (1951), as young children make dolls relive their own unpleasant past experiences, they gain a sense of mastery over a world that they tend to experience passively in real life. Erikson (1940) stated that playing out troublesome situations is the most natural self-therapeutic process that childhood offers. Terr (1983) noted that the children who experienced the Chowchilla bus kidnapping subsequently engaged in secret repetitive play centered on their experience of the incident.

In play therapy, the therapist can set up play situations that allow the child to reexperience an event or a relationship in a different way, and with a more positive outcome than that of the original event. The child can re-create in play those events over which he needs to gain mastery so as to proceed with his development.

Role-play

Pretend play offers children the opportunity to try out alternative behaviors through role-playing. The ability to take part in sociodramatic play – requiring the creation and maintenance of interactive fantasy play – is widely regarded as an advanced form of pretend play. Role-play begins as children reach their third birthday. In play therapy, children are encouraged to role-play new behaviors they may never have considered before, to experience what it feels like to behave this way, and to consider the pros and cons of the new behaviors.

According to Garvey (1976), the major roles assumed by children in play are:

1. *Functional roles* (unnamed roles represented by the actions of the players, e.g., driver–passenger).
2. *Relational roles* (such as family roles of mommy, daddy, baby).
3. *Occupational roles* (including doctor, teacher, policeman).
4. *Fantasy roles* (which encompass fantastic characters, e.g., Superman, and TV characters, e.g., Flintstones).

Mead (1967) concluded that children's pretend role-play contributes to the development of the self as a separate identity by allowing the child to step outside of himself and view himself from another's perspective. By playing the roles of others, children gain a reflected view of their own identity from the perspective of those identities whose roles they enact (Stone 1971). Through role-playing, children also develop their powers of empathy, that is, the ability to put themselves in others' shoes and thereby understand other people's thoughts, feelings, and actions. The more children experience situations from the perspective of others, the less egocentric they become. Social pretend play has been found to be positively related to teacher ratings of social competence, peer popularity, and conflict resolution skills (Rubin et al. 1983). In a recent study of 6-year-old children by Strayer and Roberts (1989), empathy and role taking were found to be related, and both were associated with imaginative play. Role taking was also associated with ego resiliency. Children's empathy was positively correlated with reported prosocial behavior in the family, while role taking was associated with teacher reports of prosocial behavior.

Fantasy

One of the major therapeutic functions of play is that it enhances the flexible and varied use of one's imagery capacities. Children learn about themselves and enlarge their world by fantasizing. In the world of imagination, children do not have to be satisfied with current realities or their own limitations. Fantasy or make-believe play allows children to create characters, place setting, and events that are not immediately part of their environment. The child might say, for instance, "Pretend this block is a spaceship with aliens inside." Ole Kirk Christiansen, the inventor of Lego toys, said that the world of the child is as infinite as his imagination is. If you give a child's creativity free rein, the child can build a richer and more imaginative world than any adult can conceive.

Pretending gives a child power over the world, even when he does not have much control in real life. It is one area in which children can make reality conform to their wishes. This power and control is ego-boosting and augments an inner locus of control. In their fantasy play, children can compensate for their real life weaknesses, hurts, and losses, and satisfy unmet needs. Imagination can be the cure for a child's boredom, loneliness, anxiety, jealousy, and fearfulness.

By pretending to be a Bengal tiger or a black panther, children can learn to conquer their real life timidity and fears. Imagination can also help a child overcome impulsivity, poor planning, and weak empathic tendencies (Singer 1961, 1973, 1974). Singer and Singer (1976), after reviewing the literature on children's fantasy play, concluded that skill in imaginative play is positively correlated with the ability to tolerate repetitive stimulation, the ability to regulate affect (to reduce aggression and generate positive affect), the ability to separate reality and pretense, and the lack of psychopathology. Moreover, White (1959) and Saltz and Johnson (1974) observed that make-believe play helps children develop feelings of mastery over their environments.

Metaphoric Teaching

Humans are myth-making beings who create reality by belief in stories they have told about it. Myths help shape belief systems that structure, energize, and give meaning to life. The power of a myth is partly due to the fact that it goes directly through to the right side of the brain (Watzlawick 1978). Messages can be directly communicated to the child's unconscious by stories, fantasy play, and drawings.

Children in play therapy can be provided with new myths that address the sources of conflicts, fears, and hostilities in their lives and offer more adaptive solutions for consideration. New myths can tone down unrealistic expectations by the child (e.g., "everyone is against me") and diminish aggressive solutions to problems.

Mills and Crowley (1986) suggest that it is therapeutic to develop a shared phenomenological reality by use of metaphor. By identification with the story's characters, the child's feelings of isolation and hopelessness can be replaced by a sense that the problem is shared by others and is solvable.

By observing a child's fantasy play, a therapist often can discover a child's current concerns, such as goals that have not yet been realized but that elicit strong affects (Klinger 1971). If the concern is repeatedly experienced in play without resolution, the therapist can replay the situation in a way that suggests new options or solutions. Even though these solutions seem obvious to adults, young children who are overcome with strong emotion about a situation may need help to recognize them.

Attachment Formation

One way to establish feelings of secure attachment in children is to replicate the positive parent–infant relationship through sensorimotor play, for instance, patty cake and itsy-bitsy spider. Playful interactions involving touch and smiling are perhaps the most natural and enjoyable ways to form an attachment with a child in the playroom. Austin DesLauriers and others concluded that, without this basic attachment in infancy, children are prone to emotional problems later in life (Jernberg 1979). The Theraplay technique developed by Jernberg and her associates seeks to provide children with the positive infantile sensory experiences that they lacked in early life. There is little discussion in the Theraplay process. Rather, the procedure focuses on pleasurable activities, such as tickling children's feet, carrying them piggyback, and playing with them in a variety of other physical ways that are so pleasurable to a 1-year-old.

As is characteristic of parent–infant play, the therapy is fun filled and includes such elements of surprise as putting a shoe on a child's head and a hat on his feet. Through this intense, enjoyable experience, the child gains a sense of self as someone whose skills and body boundaries he knows well and who can have fun with another person. Viola Brody, at the University of South Florida, works with children experiencing school difficulties using a similar developmental play approach, which can provide a corrective emotional experience for children (O'Connor 1991).

Relationship Enhancement

The theoretical basis for relationship play therapy evolved from the writings of Allen (1934), Rank (1936), and Axline (1950). They deemphasized the importance of uncovering past conflicts and highlighted the therapist–child relationship as being crucial for the child to gain a more adequate acceptance of himself.

All clinical interactions with a child are inextricably bound to the relational context in which they are applied. The role of play in facilitating a positive relationship is related to the nature of playful interactions that are fun filled and concerned with enjoyment rather than achievement. Mutual feelings of liking between therapist and child are fostered by playing together. Through play, a pleasure bond is formed that makes each party more attractive to the other. Once formed, mutual feelings of warmth and closeness between therapist and child contribute to the child's sense of well being. Also, when a child likes the therapist, he is more likely to identify with the therapist's behaviors and values. The child will also be more apt to want to please the therapist by complying with the therapeutic tasks.

A warm, accepting, respectful therapist creates a playroom atmosphere of safety, devoid of threat. Within such a climate the child can examine and solidify his sense of self. Self-realization (Rogers 1951) comes from feeling accepted, respected, and esteemed. Children who feel rejected, on the other hand, tend to respond to the lack of a warm relationship with defiance, aggression, and withdrawal (Wolberg 1967). A number of studies have connected an affiliative therapeutic relationship with improved clinical outcomes (Sachs 1983).

Enjoyment

The most apparent and fundamental aspect of play is that children enjoy it. All the current definitions of play list enjoyment or positive affect as a basic attribute. Children do not need incentives to play, since it is a behavior pleasurable in its own right. Children play because it is fun.

The positive affect accompanying play has two strong therapeutic advantages. First, it contributes to a sense of happiness or well-being. Second, enjoyment is a powerful antidote to the stresses of living. The more stress and tension in our lives, the more we need the refuge afforded by play. Play is free from external demands, obligation, and serious intent. It gives us relief from the "oughts" and anxieties of life (Groos 1901). Having fun and enjoyment in play is uplifting and restores the spirit when we are weighed down with feelings of anxiety, bleakness, or boredom. Moreover, research indicates that children do better work under the influence of strong emotion, that enjoyment of a task enhances striving and persistence at it, and joy provides motivation in unrelated activities (Reichenberg 1939).

Mastering Developmental Fears

Systematic desensitization is a technique designed by Wolpe (1958) to treat such maladaptive emotional behaviors as anxiety, irrational fears, and phobias. Systematic desensitization basically uses the processes of counterconditioning, wherein a client learns a new response that is incompatible with a previous response, but is elicited by the same stimulus. On the basis of extensive clinical and experimental work, Wolpe made the process of counterconditioning adaptable for clinical practice with his principle of reciprocal inhibition: "If a response inhibitor of anxiety can be made to occur in the presence of anxiety–evoking stimuli, it will weaken the bond between these stimuli and the anxiety" (p. 15). One response that physiologically inhibits anxiety is the enjoyment a child feels in play. Barnett and Storm (1981) found physiological evidence linking play with anxiety reduction.

Play can reduce anxiety by the process of systematic desensitization. By exposing a child to a fearful situation while the child is relaxed in play, the pleasure of play can counteract and neutralize the fearfulness so the child can perform the desired behavior. Fear of the dark, for example, can be overcome by repeatedly playing games with the child in a dark room. Initially the child is asked to play with the adult in the dark room for only a brief time period. In subsequent sessions the time intervals in the room are gradually extended. Through repeated play experiences, the strange and scary become familiar and no longer frightening.

Game Play

The development of a wide variety of therapeutic board games in the past ten years has opened up the field of play therapy for use with older children, adolescents, and adults (Schaefer and Reed 1986). Games are a primary way for children to become socialized, because the players must agree upon a set of prearranged rules. The rules of games prepare children for the rules of life, that is, fair play, taking turns, and gracious winning and losing (Salamone 1978). The meaning of a rule becomes evident in a game – that a rule must be obeyed by all players or else the game does not function.

Children begin playing board games at about age 5 or 6, and this interactive play increases in frequency during elementary school years and remains stable during the adult years. Game play contributes to a child's cognitive, emotional, and social development. Since games involve rule-governed behavior, ego control must be stronger than impulse-driven behavior. Game play also prepares children for their roles in the social world, including both competitive and cooperative roles. Among other ego-enhancing powers of games are: (1) helping distractible children focus and sustain their attention, (2) seeing the immediate consequences of one's actions in a game develops a sense of an inner locus of control of the environment; the challenge inherent in games helps overcome feelings of boredom and dullness.

References

Allen, F. (1934). Therapeutic work with children. *American Journal of Orthopsychiatry* 4:193–202.

Allport, G. W. (1968). *The Person in Psychology: Selected Essays.* Boston: Beacon Press.

Axline, V. (1950). Entering into the child's world via play experiences. *Progressive Education* 27:68–75.

Barnett, L. A., and Storm, B. (1981). Play, pleasure, and pain: the reduction of anxiety through play. *Leisure Sciences* 4:161–175.

Berlyne, D. E. (1960). *Conflict, Arousal and Curiosity.* New York: McGraw-Hill.

Block, S., and Crouch, E. (1985). *Therapeutic Factors in Group Psychotherapy.* New York: Oxford University Press.

Colson, D. B., Cornsweet, C., Murphy, T., et al. (1991). Perceived treatment difficulty and therapeutic alliance on an adolescent psychiatric hospital unit. *American Journal of Ortho-psychiatry* 61:221–229.

Corsini, R., and Rosenberg, B. (1955). Mechanisms of group psychotherapy: processes and dynamics. *Journal of Abnormal and Social Psychology* 51:406–411.

Dansky, J. L., and Silverman, I. W. (1973). Effects of play on associative fluency in preschool children. *Developmental Psychology* 9:38–43.

Ellis, M. J. (1973). *Why People Play.* Englewood Cliffs, NJ: Prentice Hall.

Erikson, E. H. (1940). Studies in the interpretation of play. *Genetic Psychology Monographs* 22:559–671.

Frank, J. D. (1979). Therapeutic components of psychotherapy. *Journal of Nervous and Mental Disease* 159:325–342.

Garvey, C. (1976). Some properties of social play. In *Play,* ed. J. Bruner, A. Jolly, and K. Sylva, pp. 570–583. New York: Basic Books.

Greencavage, L. M., and Norcross, J. C. (1990). Where are the commonalities among the therapeutic common factors? *Professional Psychology* 21:372–378.

Groos, K. (1901). *The Play of Man.* London: Heinemann.

Jernberg, A. M. (1979). Theraplay technique. In *The Therapeutic Use of Child's Play,* ed. C. E. Schaefer, pp. 345–349. New York: Jason Aronson.

Klinger, E. (1971). *Structure and Functions of Fantasy.* New York: Wiley.

Mead, G. H. (1967). *Mind, Self, and Society.* Chicago: University of Chicago Press.

Mills, J. C., and Crowley, R. J. (1986). *Therapeutic Metaphors for Children and the Child Within.* New York: Brunner/Mazel.

O'Connor, K. J. (1991). *The Play Therapy Primer.* New York: Wiley.

Parten, M. B. (1932). Social participation among preschool children. *Journal of Abnormal and Social Psychology* 27:243–269.

Piaget, J. (1951). *Play, Dreams and Imitation in Childhood.* London: Routledge & Kegan Paul.

Prochaska, J. O., and Di Clemente, C. C. (1982). Transtheoretical therapy: toward a more integrative model of change. *Psychotherapy: Theory, Research & Practice* 19:276–288.

Rank, O. (1936). *Will Therapy.* New York: Knopf.

Reichenberg, W. (1939). An experimental investigation of the effect of gratification upon effort and orientation to reality. *American Journal of Orthopsychiatry* 9:186–204.

Rogers, C. R. (1951). *Client-Centered Therapy.* Boston: Houghton Mifflin.

Rothstein, A. (1988). *How Does Treatment Help? On the Modes of Therapeutic Action of Psychoanalytic Psychotherapy.* Madison, CT: International Universities Press.

Rubin, K. H., Fein, G. G., and Bandenberg, B. (1983). Play. In *Handbook of Child Development,* ed. E. Hetherington, pp. 693–775. New York: Wiley.

Sachs, H. (1983). Negative factors in brief psychotherapy: An empirical assessment. *Journal of Consulting and Clinical Psychology* 51:557–564.

Salamone, F. A. (1978). Children's games. *Ethnicity* 5:208–212.

Saltz, E., and Johnson, J. (1974). Training for thematic-fantasy play in culturally disadvantaged children: preliminary results. *Journal of Educational Psychology* 66:623–630.

Schaefer, C. E., and O'Connor, K. J. (1983). *Handbook of Play Therapy.* New York: Wiley.

Schaefer, C. E., and Reid, S. E. (1986). *Game Play: Therapeutic Use of Childhood Games.* New York: Wiley.

Sherrod, L. R., and Singer, J. L. (1989). The development of make-believe play. In *Sports, Games and Play,* ed. J. Goldstein, pp. 1–38. Hillsdale, NJ: Lawrence Erlbaum.

Singer, J. L. (1961). Imagination and waiting ability in young children. *Journal of Personality* 29:396–413.

—— (1973). *The Child's World of Make-Believe: Experimental Studies of Imaginative Play,* New York: Academic Press.

—— (1974). Day dreaming and the stream of thought. *American Scientist* 2:417–425.

Singer, J. L., and Singer, D. G. (1976). Imaginative play and pretending in early childhood: some experimental approaches. In *Child Personality and Psychopathology,* vol. 3, ed. A. Davids, pp. 419–444. New York: Wiley.

Smith, P. K. (1982). Does play matter? Functional and evolutionary aspects of animal and human play. *Behavioral and Brain Sciences* 5:139–184.

Stone, G. R. (1971). The play of little children. In *Child's Play,* ed. R. E. Herron and B. Sutton-Smith, pp. 4–14. New York: Wiley.

Strayer, J., and Roberts, W. (1989). Empathy and role taking behavior in children. *Journal of Applied Developmental Psychology* 10:227–239.

Sylva, K., Bruner, J. S., and Genova, P. (1976). The role of play in the problem-solving of children 3–5 years old. In *Play,* ed. J. Bruner, A. Jolly, and K. Sylva, pp. 244–257. New York: Basic Books.

Terr, L. (1983). Play therapy and psychic trauma: a preliminary report. In *Handbook of Play Therapy,* ed. C. Schaefer and K. O'Connor, pp. 79–93. New York: Wiley.

Waelder, R. (1979). Psychoanalytic theory of play. In *Therapeutic Use of Child's Play,* ed. C. E. Schaefer, pp. 79–93. New York: Jason Aronson.

Watzlawick, P. (1978). *The Language of Change: Elements of Therapeutic Communication.* New York: Basic Books.

White, R. W. (1959). Motivation reconsidered: the concept of competence. *Psychological Review* 96:297–333.

Wolberg, L. R. (1967). *The Technique of Psychotherapy.* New York: Grune & Stratton.

Wolpe, J. (1958). *Psychotherapy by Reciprocal Inhibition.* Stanford, CA: Stanford University Press.

Yalom, I. D. (1975). *The Theory and Practice of Group Psychotherapy.* New York: Basic Books.

2

Overcoming Resistance

James N. Bow

Overcoming resistance to the therapeutic process is a difficult task. Children often present as angry, upset, frightened, withdrawn, shy, or inhibited when initially entering therapy. This may surface as refusing to talk, hiding from the therapist, running around the lobby or office in an uncontrollable manner, or throwing temper tantrums. These situations create a frustrating and challenging scenario for child psychotherapists. Although therapy books deal with the theoretical aspects of treatment, they rarely address practical ways of overcoming initial resistance. This chapter will focus on this topic, with an emphasis on the seductive power of play in engaging children in the treatment process. Also addressed will be related topics and issues such as the factors underlying resistance, engaging children in the therapeutic process, and innovative play techniques. Case illustrations will also be provided.

Dynamics Underlying Resistance to Therapy

Many dynamics underlie initial resistance to the treatment process. Developing an awareness of these dynamics is critical in understanding and overcoming resistance. Six major dynamics will be briefly reviewed. Markowitz (1959) notes that, first, many children are fearful when entering a therapeutic situation. New situations commonly create anxiety and a sense of unpredictability. In such situations children will use their limited coping skills in an effort to reduce their anxiety and gain a sense of control. Second, children are often ill-prepared for the initial therapeutic encounter. Parents may provide false information, sometimes blatantly, resulting in the child making statements, such as, "I thought I was going to the dentist," or "My mom said we were going shopping and next thing I know I'm here." The result of such misinformation is mistrust, which commonly surfaces as anger and resentment. Furthermore, since the parent made the appointment, it appears that the therapist is aligned with the parent in the deception. Third, children rarely initiate treatment on their own. Referrals for children are almost exclusively made by the parent, school, or court. Since children have little control over the process, they often respond in an uncooperative manner as a way of gaining power or control. In addition, since they did not initiate the referral, they commonly view their behavior as ego-syntonic, that is, acceptable and normal, and show little motivation for change or treatment (Gardner 1979). Fourth is the "why me" syndrome (Bow 1988), most apparent in highly dysfunctional families, in which the child is the identified client. Although on closer examination it becomes apparent that the child's behavior is a means of drawing attention to family problems, the child resents being singled out and resists involvement in the therapeutic process. He may respond with, "Why me? My dad's a drunk, my mother is depressed and suicidal, and my brother is in jail. My problems are minor in comparison to theirs." Fifth, children who have been traumatized by abuse or neglect sometimes avoid therapeutic involvement for fear of being further victimized. They feel powerless and vulnerable, and fear additional physical and emotional harm. They may also resent another professional asking "the same old" questions, thereby recreating terrible memories. Another area of concern for these children is the possible outcome of providing such information because they have often been victimized by the system in terms of court and placement decisions. Lastly, the sixth dynamic, children involved with the court and/or child protection agencies sometimes resist involvement in therapy because of loyalty issues. In most cases, parents oppose the involvement of the court or protection agencies. Children are aware of this attitude and act out the parents' feelings as a way of maintaining a sense of loyalty. Cooperating with the system would cause guilt because the child has gone against the parents' wishes.

The child's manifestation of these dynamics during the initial contact is important to evaluate. Are they externalized through verbal aggression, temper outbursts, and destructive behaviors, or are they internalized in the form of withdrawn, shy, and inhibited behaviors? The type of resistance reveals pertinent information about the child's ways of dealing with environmental stressors, along with signs of possible psychopathology. The quantity and intensity of the negative attitudes are also an important index in differentiating well-adjusted from disturbed children (Moustakas 1982). Negative attitudes are expressed more frequently and intensely among disturbed children, and they are also less focused (Moustakas 1982).

The next step in overcoming resistance involves engaging children in the therapeutic process. Four major factors play a role: the therapist's personality, establishing the relationship, the initial contact, and combining play and therapy. Each factor will be addressed individually.

Therapist's Personality

The therapist's personality is one of the most important factors in engaging clients (Gardner 1975, Wolberg 1977). Many characteristics are involved. First and foremost, child therapists need to enjoy children. Most child therapists enter the field because they like the spontaneous, vivacious, unpredictable, and constantly changing nature of children. Each week brings a new experience and potential for growth. Being part of this can be a very rewarding experience for the child therapist. Another important characteristic is the ability of the child therapist to create an atmosphere of warmth, concern, and acceptance. This type of atmosphere allows the child to express feelings and thoughts freely without rejection or humiliation. The therapist also needs to be flexible and innovative, constantly adjusting and adapting to the child's needs and using creative ideas to gain the attention and interest of the child.

Self-projection is another important virtue (Gardner 1975). This is the ability of therapists to place themselves in the child's situation as a means of understanding what he is experiencing, even though few therapists have faced the traumas experienced by their clients. Self-projection allows the therapist to identify with the client, enhancing empathy. However, overidentification with the client's problems and needs should be avoided because it enmeshes the therapeutic boundaries and reduces objectivity.

An awareness of child/adolescent trends and interests is also important. This does not mean the therapist attempts to imitate clothing styles or jargon. To do so would be contraindicated because it would enmesh the separation-individuation process. The purpose of this awareness of trends and interests is to understand the child's expression of his culture, which reveals significant information about the child's self-identity.

Another important trait for therapists is patience. Developing a therapeutic alliance is not a process that can be rushed, nor can progress be forced. It is usually a slow, unfolding process that has peaks and valleys. For beginning therapists, this is often a difficult concept to grasp. They expect immediate and positive results. When this does not occur, they show impatience and disappointment, which the client perceives as another failure. This tendency of the therapist to personalize interactions with clients can lead to many pitfalls. Insight is critical at this juncture. The client–therapist relationship is influenced by many factors, including transference and countertransference issues. How the client deals with a therapist is greatly affected by past experiences with adults, especially parental figures. This is critical to remember when the child expresses unprovoked rage and hostility. Therapeutically, the key is to find the source of these displaced feelings and to make the necessary interventions depending upon the stage of therapy. The therapist's ability to evaluate his own interactions with children and parents is paramount. This allows the therapist to avoid certain antitherapeutic roles, such as rescuer, perfect parent, and enabler.

Establishing a Relationship

A therapeutic relationship thrives in a comfortable, safe, and nonthreatening setting where the therapist and child have time alone together to address relevant problems and issues. The child's time with the therapist should be uninterrupted and regularly scheduled. This allows predictability, and creates a special time for the child. In this way, the therapist gives the child a sense of importance and self-worth.

A child's social, emotional, and cognitive abilities need to be considered when developing a therapeutic relationship. The level of conversation and selection of play activities are very different for a mentally retarded child than for a gifted child of the same age. Also, the types of strategies and play activities utilized vary depending on the type of psychopathology. Children who externalize their symptomology need structured activities, whereas internalizers need play activities that encourage spontaneity and freedom.

The ability of children to view their therapists as ego ideal is a major factor in establishing and maintaining a therapeutic relationship. Child therapists play an important role as models and teachers. They model and teach children appropriate ways of handling interpersonal conflicts and intrapsychic problems. It is hoped that as a result of this modeling, the child will introject positive aspects of the relationship and of the therapist.

The therapeutic relationship is also enhanced by showing appropriate affection, such as a pat on the back or a hug, but the child's readiness for and possible acceptance of such affection need to be considered beforehand. Abused children are often fearful of further sexual or physical harm and initially maintain physical distance as a safeguard. Oppositional, defiant children also avoid close contact or affection because it causes them to feel smothered or controlled. With these types of children such behavior would be contraindicated. However, when affection is possible it should be shown because it gives children a sense of warmth and acceptance. One final note on affection: it should never have a sexual connotation. When it does, it violates the therapeutic relationship and harms the mental health of the child.

Another important factor in establishing the relationship involves the issue of confidentiality. Children are often suspicious about what information will and will not be revealed to their parent(s). It is critical for the therapist to address this issue, even if it is not directly mentioned by the child. The information exchanged between the child and therapist should remain confidential, except in three incidences. They are (1) the child reveals suicidal/self-abusive ideation or behavior, (2) the child reveals homicidal/dangerous ideation or behavior toward others, or (3) the child reveals that he is being abused or neglected. Children should be told that these exceptions are necessary for ethical, legal, and moral reasons.

Initial Contact

Adequately preparing the child for the therapy appointment is critical in reducing resistance. When children are ill-prepared, much anxiety, mistrust, and anger are created. To avoid this it is important that the therapist or designated person in charge of scheduling appointments provide the parent(s) with suggestions on preparing the child for the first appointment. The following suggestions may be helpful: (1) Be honest and open. (2) Inform the child at least three days before the appointment of the day, time, length, and place. This provides the child enough time to prepare, but limits the amount of time anxiety can be generated. (3) Discuss the reasons for the appointment. (4) Inform the child that the therapist will talk to both the child and parent and the child will also play with some toys. (5) Tell the child that no medical procedures will be performed, such as blood work or shots. It is hoped that by utilizing these suggestions initial resistance can be prevented or minimized.

The saying, "First impressions make lasting impressions," sums up the importance of the initial therapy contact with a child and his parent(s). Furthermore, the first few minutes of the interaction can be critical in preventing resistance or overcoming it. The therapist must present as friendly, self-confident, and in control. When approaching the child and parent, the therapist must be aware of nonverbal cues, such as the child's seating location in relation to the parent's, the type and level of interaction between child and parent, and parent and child body language. These cues provide valuable information about the parent–child relationship. During the introduction process, the therapist should be aware of interpersonal space and distance. The therapist should avoid being either too close to the child, which may create anxiety, or too distant, which may indicate a cold, detached atmosphere. It is a good idea to be situated at the level of younger children so as not to tower over them.

The therapist should introduce himself to the child first, then to the parent. Addressing the child first signals to the child that he is an important person and that his input is important. The child should be asked by what name he would like to be called. When the therapist invites the child and parent to his office and notes that it is hard to talk in the lobby with other people around, he shows the child that he is concerned about the child's privacy. Having the parent initially accompany the child to the office rather than seeing the child individually has the following advantages: (1) it reduces the child's anxiety about being separated from the parent and seeing a stranger, (2) it allows further evaluation of the parent–child relationship, (3) it affords the opportunity to clarify the presenting problem and treatment issues, and (4) it allows the therapist to explain to the parent the purpose and use of play therapy. This last advantage is important because many parents have misconceptions about the value of play therapy.

In the therapy office, the next step involves clarifying the purpose of the session (e.g., evaluative) and how the therapist became involved, that is, who made the referral. This in itself may reduce resistance, especially if the child has misconceptions. At this point, it is also worth finding out what the parent told the child about the appointment. This reflects on the parent–child relationship. The reasons for the referral need to be reviewed with the parent and child, along with other pertinent historical information. During this process, verbal and nonverbal cues should be assessed. The purpose and role of therapy also need to be addressed, such as increasing self-understanding, working through past traumas, eliminating emotional problems, and/or decreasing family conflict, along with the role of play therapy in this process. After between twenty and thirty minutes, the parent(s) will be asked to return to the lobby and the therapist will see the child for the remainder of the therapy hour. At this point, it is prudent to show the child around the office, introducing him to the different types of toys available. Allowing the child to choose toy activities provides diagnostic information, and gives the child a sense of control.

Resistant children frequently test limits to exert control and/or to avoid engagement in therapy. Limits are a necessary part of therapy because they encourage catharsis through symbolic channels. Other rationales for limits outlined by Ginott (1982a) include the following: (1) Limits allow the therapist to maintain an empathetic and accepting attitude. It is hard to maintain such an attitude if the child is hurting the therapist or breaking toys; (2) limits assure physical safety for both the child and therapist; and (3) limits strengthen the child's ego control by providing structure and supervision. Limits should only apply to behavior, never to words. Furthermore, the focus should be on the reason(s) the child is testing or violating a limit.

Four steps are involved in setting limits (Ginott 1982a). First, recognize the child's feelings and wishes and help him experience them. Second, state clearly the limit on a specific act. Third, point out channels through which feelings and wishes can be appropriately expressed. Last, help the child bring out feelings that arise from the limit. When establishing rules and limits for resistant children it is important to set priorities because the therapist will be unable to enforce every possible limit/rule. The most widely used limits pertain to the child's and therapist's safety, protection of play materials, and socially unacceptable behavior, for example, urinating on the floor, or yelling profanities out the window.

When used appropriately, humor is another vehicle to reduce tension and resistance. Salameh (1986) discusses the power of humor in therapy in distracting clients from areas of struggle or conflict. Magic has also been used in therapy to overcome resistance (Bow 1988, Howard 1977, Moskowitz 1973). Children love magic; a few tricks are a great way to gain their attention. Diagnostic information is gained by analyzing their reaction to the tricks. Furthermore, magic can symbolically represent therapeutic issues. Magic can be used with most children, except those who are psychotic, paranoid, or intellectually limited.

Combining Play and Therapy

Play, in itself, is not therapy. For play to be therapeutic it needs to have definite qualities. Amster (1982) defines six therapeutic uses of play. First, play provides opportunities for diagnostic assessment. Valuable information about a child's social and emotional functioning is gained through play. An inability to play suggests severe emotional disturbance (Schaefer 1980). Second, play helps develop a working relationship between the child and the therapist. It provides an enjoyable and natural setting that affords intense interpersonal interaction. Third, play assists in breaking down defenses. Children lack the defense mechanisms present in adults, and their egos easily regress, thereby allowing their rich fantasy life to surface. Fourth, play facilitates verbalization. It creates the distance necessary so that children can talk about traumatic events. Fifth, play provides a cathartic release for children. It enables them to deal with emotionally charged material, by providing an outlet for emotional discharge. In addition, it lets children act out unconscious material through symbolism. Last, play has a developmental significance in preparing children for future life events.

Toy selection is critical in overcoming resistance. Ginott (1982b) outlines the following rationale for toy selection. Toys should facilitate contact with the child by gaining his interest and attention. Toys should also permit reality testing and yield a chance to explore self and others. In addition, toys should permit children to express their needs symbolically, allowing them to deal with feelings that are difficult to address in real life. Toys should also yield an opportunity for emotional release, along with a medium for sublimation. In the end, it is hoped that the selected toys will provide opportunities for insight.

Role of Therapist in Play

The role of the child therapist encompasses a wide range of functions and duties. First and foremost is engaging the child in therapy. This occurs when the child becomes invested and is committed to change. The key to working with resistant children is establishing this alliance.

A second function involves observing the child's play and assessing the underlying themes and dynamics. Many different types of themes will surface, such as abandonment, rejection, aggression, power/control, and loneliness. The difference between well-adjusted and disturbed children is not in the content of themes, but in the quality of the play and intensity of the themes (Schaefer 1979). Disturbed children are unable to modulate emotion, and become highly aroused. In addition, the play of disturbed children is much more variable and unreliable than that of well-adjusted children (Schaefer 1979).

A third function of the therapist is to help the child develop greater awareness and insight. This is done by helping the child understand the relationship between feelings and behavior and appropriate ways of expressing affect and needs. In play therapy, the key to this process is increasing self-observation by making the child aware of his play behavior. This can be done by encouraging the child to talk during his play or by the therapist reflecting on the child's play. The next step involves interpreting. This technique involves making the child aware of feelings, attitudes, and the relationships between events in his life that he is unaware of at the present time (Dodds 1987). Harter (1983) identifies a four-level interpretive hierarchy. The first level involves interpreting through a toy/object that has some meaning to the child. For example, "This boy (doll) is fighting because he is angry at his father for leaving the family." The next level consists of interpreting through the toy/object as in level one, but making a direct connection to the child, such as "I wonder if you feel like the boy (doll)?" The third level involves indirect interpretations, discussing a friend or anonymous client who has a similar problem to the child's. For example, "I have another child in therapy whose father left the family. He is very angry about his father leaving and sometimes loses control of his anger and gets into fights." The fourth level is made up of direct interpretations, such as "It appears you are angry at your father for leaving, which results in your taking out your anger on others by fighting."

The following guidelines may be helpful in using interpretations. Before making interpretations, a relationship between the child and therapist needs to be established. This is critical because the therapist must know the child fairly well to make a valid interpretation and the child needs to know and trust the therapist to pay attention to the interpretation (Dodds 1987). The child's psychological readiness and stage of therapy should also be considered. Interpreting before a child reaches some level of self-observation would be futile. Also, the child's defenses need to be worked through before interpretations can be assimilated. It is critical to remember that there is no urgency in making interpretations. If interpretations are made too soon, the child's defenses will reemerge, and resistance will surface. Beginning therapists often express much regret over missing the ideal opportunity for an interpretation. However, if it is truly an important dynamic, many more interpretive opportunities will arise. Furthermore, the child may be even more able to deal with the interpretation at a later point. Last, consider the levels of interpretations outlined by Harter (1983). Resistant children are more willing to initially accept interpretations at the first two levels because they are less threatening.

Developmental Perspective

It is critical to consider developmental factors in treating children. This is especially true when working with resistant children, because unrealistic expectations can cause resistance. Children vary widely in their social, emotional, and cognitive development. Many factors have to be considered in assessing their play and degree of psychopathology. The following section will focus on analyzing children's play and making a diagnostic assessment according to developmental perspectives.

In analyzing children's play, it is always important to consider their chronological and mental ages in terms of the developmental line of play. Piaget (1962) discusses how sensorimotor play occurs from infancy through 18–24 months. The assimilation of sensory information into the child's cognitive processes is the primary function of play during this period. Repetition and imitation are major components, along with practice and mastery. Symbolic and pretend play become the primary type of play behavior for children approximately 2 to 6 years of age. The conscious and unconscious assimilation of symbols occurs during this period. Around age 6, play consists of games with rules. The function of games takes on many roles, from having fun, to cooperating with peers, to competition. Games have strong interpersonal and social components, whereas the prior two stages of play focus on intrapersonal development.

Another important aspect to assess is the choice of play activities. During infancy, autoerotic pleasure is gained from the child's own body or mother's body. Around 1 year of age the development of transitional objects occurs, such as a blanket or stuffed animal. The representational use of toys happens around 18 months. About a year later, toys lose their object status and begin to have symbolic meaning. As a result, fantasy and pretend activities become popular, such as puppets, drawing, and play acting. Around age 6, games become a major interest area because of their social and competitive characteristics.

In addition to assessing the choice of play activities, it is important to analyze the specific types of toys, fantasy materials, and games the child chooses. Each has a symbolic meaning and dynamic underlying its choice. The themes that surface are also important, especially in regard to their quality and intensity.

The continuity of play is also important to evaluate. Normal children have a smooth unfolding of play reality, whereas disturbed children have disjointed and erratic play. Another area to assess is the balance between drives and instincts and ego material. This is reflected in the spontaneity of the child, along with the capacity of the ego to regress. Disturbed children will present as overcontrolled, that is, inhibited, rigid, and compulsive, or undercontrolled, that is, impulsive and driven. The play of well-adjusted children is characterized by age-appropriate spontaneity, self-control, and ego resilience.

The child's sense of reality, his ability to temporarily suspend reality and differentiate between reality and fantasy boundaries, is also critical to analyze. Normal play should involve an ability to move between internal and external realities, while maintaining clear reality ties. Psychotic children are consumed with fantasy play and deny external reality. On the other hand, obsessive-compulsive children are bound to external reality without elaboration of their internal world. Also, the emotional reactions exhibited by children during play provide valuable information about their perception of the environment and reality ties. Psychotic children are frightened by their play because internal and external realities are enmeshed. Depressed children will often show indifference, with a view of life as hopeless and gloomy. Healthy play is characterized by emotional pleasure.

Another important area to evaluate in play is the child's level of interaction and degree of responsiveness to the therapist. Social play becomes increasingly complex with age, with children going through the following stages: solitary, parallel, associative, and cooperative play (Parten 1932). Solitary play involves the child playing by himself, whereas parallel play consists of playing in the vicinity of other children, but without any meaningful interaction. Associative play involves inter-acting with other children in a play setting, but without a common goal. Coopera-tive play occurs when both social interaction and a common goal are apparent. The child's level of social play is important to assess because it reflects the degree of social development, along with potential for attachment. The latter is further indicated by the child's responsiveness to the therapist, which is shown through the child's willingness to engage in a therapeutic relationship and accept intervention.

Through analyzing these different aspects of play, a diagnostic formulation can be made. This is important with resistant children because significant psychopathology is often present. The following section will review how different types of psychopathology may present in play therapy.

Autism. This is probably the most apparent and easiest disorder to diagnose in a play setting. Rutter (1985) discusses how autistic children are unable to initiate or organize play in a meaningful manner. Repetitive and ritualistic play, along with emotional detachment, are also characteristic of this group (Schaefer 1979).

Borderline Personality Disorder. Chethik (1979) reports that these children have primary process thinking, which is characterized by magical thinking and a rich narcissistic fantasy life filled with rage and aggression. They also perceive the world as malevolent and have fears of annihilation. Rituals and obsessions are common. Splitting of good and bad characters occurs frequently, reflecting the defense mechanism of *splitting*. Chronic problems with impulse control are also evident.

Neurosis. Schaefer (1979) notes that these anxious and fearful children show less activity, vigor, and creativity in their play than do well-adjusted children. They are also constricted, inhibited, and compulsive (Murphy and Krall 1960).

Conduct Disorder, Aggressive Type. Willock (1983) writes that these children lack self control and are primary process driven. The latter is reflected in their raw enactment of sex and violence in play. There is little disguise from the primary object because these children have difficulty communicating their concerns symbolically. They have little capacity for reflective verbalizations and are threatened by any therapeutic observation or intervention. Imaginative play tends to be barren and stereotyped.

Attention Deficit Hyperactivity Disorder (ADHD). Roberts (1987) summarizes her research and the research of others and concludes that ADHD signs are more evident in restricted play than during free play. In restricted settings, ADHD children are less attentive, less productive, and more active. In comparison to aggressive children without ADHD, the best discriminate was the poor on-task behavior of the ADHD children.

Gender Identity Disorder. Rekers's (1983) review of the literature found that boys in this group chose feminine sex-typed play activities more often, such as playing with baby and female dolls, cosmetic sets, feminine jewelry, and female attire. Feminine behavioral characteristics, such as effeminate gestures and speech, were also more apparent during role playing, along with the choice of female roles in fantasy play. In general, masculine sex-typed play was avoided. Girls with this disorder rejected stereotypic feminine toys and dress and were preoccupied with masculine sex-typed toys and clothing.

Abused and Neglected. Mann and McDermott (1983) describe how the play of abused and neglected children is inhibited, unimaginative, and confused. These children are often fixated or regressed at a primitive level. Initially they are distrustful of the therapist, but once the alliance is established they become very dependent. Themes of stealing, hiding, and hoarding are common.

Therapeutic Techniques for Clinical Practice

Play varies on a continuum from unstructured to structured. Exactly where play falls on the continuum depends on the following factors: the setting (office vs. play-room), the therapist's role (passive vs. active), the limits (none vs. many), and goal directedness (no goal vs. specific goal). In terms of resistant children, in most cases a structured play setting is necessary. The therapist needs to be an active participant who is goal directed and establishes necessary limits. Furthermore, the play activities must gain the attention and interest of children, thereby luring them into the therapeutic process. The play activities discussed below fulfill these criteria.

Hidden Puppet

Children are curious and fascinated by the unknown, which can be used as an asset in overcoming their resistance. The hidden puppet technique involves placing a puppet in a suitcase or large closed paper bag and presenting it to the child. The therapist explains to the child that he has a friend he wants him to meet. However, he never knows if his friend will cooperate. The therapist then looks into the bag and politely asks his friend to come out. The friend states "No!" It is important to note that the therapist's friend can be as resistant as any child. Furthermore, he is in control because the child is fascinated by what is in the bag and will go to great lengths to satisfy his curiosity. The therapist provides encouragement to his friend, but with no success. Next, he suggests that his friend may feel more at ease if the child tells him his name and age. After this is done the therapist again asks his friend to come out, but to no avail. At this point, the therapist asks the child, "What do you think is happening?" or "Why is he uncooperative?" The child will then project his own feelings and thoughts about the situation, which reflect his own resistance. The next step involves problem-solving about ways to reduce resistance and increase cooperation. Then, the puppet finally agrees to meet the child. This technique is especially effective with shy, quiet, and anxious children below the age of 10. A number of factors underlie the success of this technique. First, the resistance is dealt with through a third person. This creates personal distance and allows the child to project his own feelings and thoughts on the puppet. Second, the therapist's concern and empathy in dealing with the puppet's resistance creates a safe, non-threatening atmosphere that is conducive to therapy. Third, the therapist and child are aligned together trying to overcome the puppet's resistance. They are working together toward a common goal rather than in opposite directions.

Puppetry and Ventriloquist Figures

Both of these techniques have great projective value and provide opportunities for diagnostic and therapeutic work. Woltmann (1940) was one of the first to discuss the use of puppets with children. He used them widely with individuals and groups in formal and informal settings on the children's ward of Bellevue Hospital (New York). Woltmann found puppets useful because of their ease of manipulation, rich symbolism, and opportunity for spontaneity. Puppet play creates an unrealistic and nonthreatening atmosphere that assists in the identification process, thereby encouraging the projection of emotional aspects and interpersonal relationships through the characters (Haworth 1968). When utilizing puppetry, a wide selection of puppets and materials should be provided. The format can take many avenues, with the child telling a spontaneous make-believe story or the therapist providing a specially selected script. The latter can be performed by the child, therapist, or both. In dealing with resistant children, it is sometimes better for the therapist to perform the puppet script, while having the child comment on the action and content.

Another form of puppetry that is rarely mentioned in the literature on child psychotherapy is ventriloquism. This may be due to the skill and practice involved in learning the technique, along with the expense of the figures. The technique is highly effective because children are intrigued and fascinated by ventriloquist figures. They view the figures as lifelike, age-appropriate pals. As a result, therapy is made congruent with the child's level of development. The relationship between the child and ventriloquist figure is further enhanced by the ventriloquist figure having similar problems. The child feels comfortable discussing his problems with the figure because it acts as a misdirection. It takes attention away from the therapist and places it on the figure, creating distance between the child and the therapist. The child becomes so absorbed with the figure and its lifelike quality that he forgets about the therapist's presence. This is best reflected by comments from resistant children such as, "I will tell Chester Lester (the figure), but not you!" The therapeutic value of this technique lies in engaging children in therapy, gathering sensitive information concerning issues such as sexual abuse, evaluating ways of dealing with behavioral problems (e.g., lying, stealing), coping with difficult situations such as divorce or adoption, and social skill training.

Storytelling Techniques

Gardner (1971) developed the mutual storytelling technique. This technique involves having a child tell a make-believe story. The therapist surmises the psychodynamic meaning and tells a story with a similar setting and characters, but with a healthier resolution. Each story is analyzed in terms of how needs are attained, the symbolic significance of each character, types of themes, and emotional climate. A drawback to this technique is that resistant children often refuse to tell stories because they feel self-conscious. To minimize this drawback, Bow (1988) developed a technique called balloon animal storytelling. This technique uses balloon animals to represent characters in the story. Children are fascinated by balloon animals, and the use of concrete objects to represent figures in the story reduces resistance. The child's selection of balloon animals also reveals diagnostic information. For example, a family of alligators is considerably different than a family of mice. Another advantage of balloon animals is that they can be taken home at the end of the session to represent symbolically what was discussed. Learning to make balloon animals is easy, and balloons are readily available and inexpensive.

Another way of facilitating storytelling is through a technique called the Radio Talk Show. Radio stores sell a microphone (e.g., "Mr. Mike") that will broadcast over the office radio when properly adjusted. The signal is not strong enough to transmit to other radios in the vicinity; therefore, confidentiality is not violated. The technique involves having the therapist play the role of a radio host who interviews different guests. Since the conversation is transmitted over the office radio it creates for the child a realistic sense of being a radio star. Children get a real thrill from this experience. The following is a sample of an interview format:

> This is Dr. Bow's Radio Talk Show and we have a very special guest today. His name is John. John, tell the people in radio land how old you are and what town you come from. As people in radio land know, each week our special guest tells the world's greatest story. Following our guest's story, Dr. Bow will tell his own story. So people in radio land, listen carefully. Here's John!

A third storytelling technique is the Squiggle Drawing Game developed by Winnicott (1971). This technique involves having both the child and therapist draw a squiggle on a piece of paper. A squiggle is any variation of a straight, curved, or wavy line. The child and therapist then exchange papers and make a drawing out of each other's squiggle. A story about the drawing follows.

Another storytelling technique developed by Gardner (1975) is called the Bag of Objects. This technique is geared toward younger children, ages 4 through 8. The child and therapist take turns removing objects and toys from a grab bag. One chip is received for identifying the object or toy and two chips for a story about it. The winner is the person with the most chips at the end of the game. The competitive nature of this technique motivates children to tell stories. Its therapeutic value lies in analyzing the stories.

Color-Your-Life Technique

This technique, recommended for children ages 6 through 12, was developed by O'Connor (1983). It helps bridge the gap between action and verbalization. The goals of the technique are to enhance the child's awareness of affective states, encourage discussion of events on an affective level, encourage a verbal rather than action orientation, and reveal an affective self-image. Younger players must be able to recognize colors and feeling states in order to use the technique, which involves pairing each feeling with a color. O'Connor recommends the following equations:

red = angry	gray = lonesome
purple = very angry	yellow = happy
blue = sad	orange = excited
black = very sad	violet = scared
green = jealous	brown = bored

These should be actively discussed with the child. O'Connor suggests using a maximum of eight or nine color equations, displayed on a color code sheet showing each color and its corresponding feeling. Children view this as fun because they are intrigued by secret symbols or codes. The next step is to give the child a blank piece of 8½ × 11 paper and crayons, and ask him to fill the paper with colors to show the feelings he has experienced throughout his life. The colors can be completed in whatever way the child chooses. Squares, circles, or designs may be used.

When the drawing is completed, each equation is reviewed, with an emphasis on experiences underlying that feeling state. Other important factors to consider are the relative quantity of each color, the style of the drawing, and the amount of paper used. The quantity of each color reflects the amount that corresponding feeling was experienced. In terms of style, strips and blocks are most commonly used. Scribbles suggests impulsivity. Heavy lines indicate psychic tension and anger. Faintly drawn lines suggest insecurity and inadequacy. Most children use the whole front side of the paper. Using less than this may suggest affective constrictedness, whereas using the front and back suggests a loss of affective control.

An adaptation of this technique, Color-Your-Shape, involves having the child draw an outline of his body shape on a large piece of paper. Using the same feeling-color equations, the child draws the feelings he is currently experiencing. The quantity and location of the colors, along with verbalizations about the affective experiences, provide much diagnostic information.

Another adaptation, called Feeling Balloons, consists of drawing a series of different sized balloons on a sheet of paper. The number of balloons should approximately equal the number of feeling-color equations. The child is asked to color the balloons with the feelings he has experienced. Again, the quantity of each color and verbalizations about those affective states provide worthwhile information.

The Bottle of Feelings is a third adaptation of O'Connor's technique. The therapist draws the shape of a pop bottle on a sheet of paper. The child is asked to fill the bottle with the feelings he has experienced throughout his life using the feeling-color equations. In addition to analyzing the quantity of each color and verbalizations, the location of the feelings—that is, at the top, middle or bottom of bottle – reveals how the child deals with that feeling state, so to speak letting it out or burying it.

Family Word Association Game

This technique was developed by Bow (1988) to assist in analyzing family roles, dynamics, and interaction patterns. The first part of the technique involves administering the Kinetic Family Drawing (Burns and Kaufman 1972, p. 5). The instructions are: "Draw a picture of everyone in your family, including yourself, doing something. Try to draw a whole person, not cartoons or stick people. Remember, make everyone doing something, some kind of action." A blank sheet of white paper (8½ × 11) is provided, along with a pencil. The drawing will reveal pertinent projective information. However, it does not provide objective information about how the child views each family member. Then, the child is given a stack of cards with the descriptors listed in Table 2-1. The child is asked to place each card on the person it best describes. For nonreaders, the words can be read aloud and explained. The child may complain that a descriptor does not apply to anyone in his family. In that case, he may place the card in a discard pile. However, it is stressed to the child that in the end no more than ten cards should be placed in that pile. Otherwise, with resistant children, most of the cards will find their way to the discard pile. When the child has completed the task of assigning all the cards to an appropriate pile, each pile is reviewed. Further explanations are gathered about each descriptor, along with an analysis of the pattern of responses.

Table 2-1. Family Word Association Game

Descriptive Words			
clown	lies	soft	moody
gentle	happy	boring	handsome
crazy	cheats	small	gets mad easily
failure	weird	fun	person in charge
bossy	silent	mild	not around much
nasty	pretty	distant	can't be trusted
perfect	dumbest	wild	I'm closest to
spiteful	mouthy	kind	easy to push around
loving	steals	bad	mother's pet
sneak	cool	angry	father's pet
cruel	sad	protective	tells stories
weak	strict	mean	trouble maker
lonely	rude	colorful	easy to fool
aggressive	ugly	passive	changes mind
friendly	cheerful	quiet	cries a lot
fighter	dirty	smartest	independent
strong	ambitious	outgoing	name caller
loud	uptight	good	dependent
good	rough	active	spoiled
big	pushy	bratty	clean

Clinical Case Illustrations: Overcoming Anger, Silence, and Aggression in Children

Case 1

Ronnie was a 10-year-old boy referred for outpatient treatment because of oppositional-defiant behavior at home and school. He and his mother arrived on time for the appointment. As the therapist approached the waiting area, he noticed Ronnie was seated a good distance from his mother, staring out the window. After introductions, Ronnie and his mother accompanied the therapist to his office. Ronnie presented as nonverbal and angry. The therapist reviewed the purpose of the session, noting it was to evaluate the child's and parent's worries and concerns and determine if therapy was necessary on an ongoing basis. The therapist inquired about what Ronnie was told prior to today's session. The mother said little information was given, other than telling him it was a doctor's appointment. The mother apologetically said she forgot to review the suggestions given during the intake/scheduling call. The mother was evasive about family history. She reported Ronnie refuses to listen or obey at home or school and she and her husband were frustrated. Ronnie refused to talk or contribute to the discussion. After thirty minutes, the mother was asked to wait in the lobby while Ronnie and the therapist met alone. Ronnie continued to refuse to talk; however, he seemed fascinated by the toys in the room. He picked up a small basketball water toy and played with it. The therapist discussed how other children feel about coming to the evaluation, trying to normalize his negative feelings. Confidentiality issues were also reviewed. Ronnie continued to be nonverbal. The therapist showed him around the office, pointing out different play activities. After doing this it was suggested that he meet Chester Lester, a friend of the therapist. Ronnie looked somewhat puzzled as a suitcase was presented, with the name Chester Lester on it. The therapist explained how Chester is usually cooperative, but at times he is negative and resistant. Ronnie seemed interested in the suitcase and amused by the therapist's description. The therapist knocked on the suitcase, opened it slightly and asked Chester to come out and meet someone. Chester adamantly stated, "No, leave me alone!" The therapist acted puzzled and suggested that maybe if Ronnie told Chester his name, Chester would feel more comfortable and would possibly come out of his suitcase. Ronnie said "Yes," his first word to the therapist. The therapist again knocked on the suitcase and informed Chester that his friend wanted to tell him his name. Chester said "Okay" and Ronnie proceeded to tell his name. Chester asked a few more questions about Ronnie's age and school, but refused to leave the suitcase. The therapist then turned to Ronnie and inquired about the possible reasons Chester was so resistant. Ronnie said that Chester probably did not want to be at the clinic; he probably had a baseball game, which the therapist found out later was a reflection of Ronnie's own situation. Ways of reducing Chester's resistance were reviewed. Ronnie suggested we all play a game, with the winner getting a piece of candy. This was proposed to Chester, who agreed. Chester finally left his suitcase and Ronnie warmly greeted him. He was fascinated by the ventriloquist figure and they became pals.

During the next session, Ronnie immediately asked to see Chester Lester. He wanted to tell Chester about a school problem. He had been accused of stealing from other children. The two reviewed the situation and Ronnie acknowledged stealing some toys from another child. Chester explored the reasons underlying this behavior. Ronnie displayed little insight into his behavior. Chester discussed possible reasons for stealing and ways of handling the situation. Following this discussion, Chester suggested they do a play activity, with Ronnie choosing the activity. Ronnie decided to do the Squiggle Drawing Game. Chester watched as the therapist and Ronnie made squiggles on a blank sheet of paper. They exchanged papers and Ronnie made the drawing seen in Figure 2–1.

He told the following story: "These are mountains. This guy up here is hang gliding back and forth on this side of the mountains. He cannot get to the other side. It is cold and lonely on this side. On the other side, it is beautiful and sunny. The beach is over there and everyone is swimming and laying in the sun." This story revealed Ronnie's loneliness, isolation, lack of affection, and sense of instability.

During the third session, Ronnie again requested some drawing activities. Ronnie chose the Bottle of Feelings and Family Word Association Game. For the Bottle of Feelings Activity, a sheet of paper with the shape of a bottle was produced. The feeling/color equations were reviewed: red = angry, black = sad, brown = lonely, green = jealous, yellow = happy, and orange = excited. Ronnie was asked to fill the bottle with the feelings he was presently experiencing. Only negative equations were used, with red the dominant color. Furthermore, the red was drawn oozing from the top of the bottle, which suggests that the anger was overflowing. The bottom of the bottle consisted of black. Above this were small amounts of brown and green. Inquiries revealed much anger about family life. Feelings of jealousy were expressed toward his brother. He said he felt lonely at home because nobody paid attention to him. Underneath all this he felt sad. The sadness (black) at the bottom of the bottle suggests a need to mask this feeling.

Ronnie's Kinetic Family Drawing, from the Family Word Association Game, is shown in Figure 2–2.

FIGURE 2–1. Ronnie's Squiggle Drawing Mountain Scene

FIGURE 2-2. Ronnie's Kinetic Family Drawing (L to R: Ronnie hang gliding, mother, father, and brother)

All family members are included, but Ronnie was drawn hang gliding above the other three family members, who were also outside. Facial features were missing on all figures. The mother was described as flying a kite, while the stepfather was raking leaves. The younger brother was playing on the slide. An Air Force bomber was flying above, along with four black birds. Clouds were drawn, with one partially blocking the sun. A transparent sketch of the house was also included. Clinical indicators reveal Ronnie's desire to escape from a gloomy family setting, lack of interaction and warmth, and rage toward family members, including a wish for them to be annihilated. Also, the mother flying a kite may suggest her attempt to make a connection with Ronnie.

The word association task was done next. Examples of words used to describe the mother included: easy to fool, passive, doesn't stay mad, silent, mild, and weak. The following words were used for the stepfather: moody, strict, uptight, bossy, pushy, crazy, and aggressive. The younger brother was described as dumbest, ugly, spoiled, small, mother's pet, and father's pet. Ronnie described himself as a trouble maker, mouthy, sad, cries a lot, lonely, and distant. Further questioning about the descriptors revealed marital problems due to the stepfather's low frustration tolerance and temper. Ronnie also described the stepfather as verbally and physically aggressive toward the mother, but not toward the children. The pattern of responses also suggested this, with the stepfather seen in a very negative light, while the mother was viewed as helpless. Much hostility was expressed toward the brother, especially in regard to being the favored child. As in other play activities, Ronnie viewed himself as sad, lonely, and distant from the family. At this point, interpretations were provided about his view of himself and his family.

This case illustrates how play techniques played a major role in overcoming Ronnie's resistance and identifying factors underlying his anger. Much of his anger was related to his dysfunctional family. Even though family problems were evident from the first interview (stepfather's absence, the mother not fully informing Ronnie about the evaluation, and the mother being evasive and guarded concerning the family history), it was Ronnie's play that clearly identified the specific dynamics and allowed opportunities for intervention. In addition, play helped establish the treatment alliance. Ronnie continued to receive play therapy to help him deal with his anger and hostility toward the family and to develop better ways of adapting and coping. However, family therapy was also instituted to deal directly with family problems.

Case 2

Tom was a 7-year-old boy seen in an outpatient clinic. He was referred by the school because he refused to talk to peers or teachers. As the therapist approached the waiting room, he noticed Tom sitting on his mother's lap. At the time of the introduction, the mother stated, "Tom won't talk to strangers!" They were asked to accompany the therapist to his office. The mother carried Tom, as she stated, "He won't come otherwise." While in the office, Tom continued to sit on his mother's lap. The purpose of the session was discussed, along with how the therapist got involved. The mother said she reviewed with Tom the suggestions about preparing him for his first session, but that he is scared of anything outside the home. She elaborated, noting he talks freely at home, but refuses to talk outside the home. After about thirty minutes, the mother was asked to leave the session. Tom clung onto his mother even more, screaming. It was decided the mother would stay for the remainder of this session. At this point Tom calmed down. He and his mother were shown the different toys in the office. It was then suggested he meet Chester Lester. The suitcase with Chester in it was produced. Tom's interest perked up. He was informed that sometimes Chester is cooperative and other times he is very uncooperative. The therapist knocked on the suitcase and asked Chester to come out. Chester asked who was there. The therapist replied, "A friend and his mother." Chester said, "No parents, only kids!" Tom was informed that Chester would not leave his suitcase with his mother in the room. Tom shook his head no. As the therapist was putting the suitcase away he mentioned he was hoping Tom would meet Chester because he was such a nice guy.

When the therapist went to the lobby to get Tom for the second session, his mother said Tom decided he would go alone with the therapist because he wanted to meet Chester. On the way to the office and once in the office, the therapist tried to make conversation, but to no avail. Confidentiality issues were briefly reviewed. The suitcase with Chester Lester was produced again. Chester was asked to leave the suitcase, at which point he wanted to know who was in the office. The therapist replied, "Just me and a friend, no parents." Chester wanted to know the kid's name. Tom was told to tell Chester his name. He hesitated. Chester said, "No name, no Chester." With encouragement, Tom finally said his name. Chester immediately left his suitcase. Gradually, with continued encouragement over a number of sessions, Tom spoke more and more with Chester and the therapist.

Another technique used with Tom was the Bag of Objects. Tom was fascinated by the objects and toys, and with choosing an unknown object/toy. Initially he only identified the object/toy, but after awhile, and with encouragement, he started using short sentences. This was partly due to the setup of a paradoxical situation, with Chester playfully telling him he could not do it and the therapist providing encouragement that he could. Tom developed a strong desire and need to prove Chester wrong.

The Feeling Balloons exercise was also used. The different feeling/color equations were explained: black = sad, red = angry, yellow = happy, violet = scared, brown = lonely, and orange = excited. Most of Tom's balloons were colored violet, brown, and black. As expected, Tom was reluctant to elaborate on factors underlying these feelings, but he did state he was scared of dogs, people, and water, and that he was sad about not talking at school.

In an attempt to generalize his verbalization to school, Chester provided a challenge. Chester bet him that he would be unable to talk to one kid in school during the next week. Tom adamantly stated he could. The therapist provided encouragement and agreed to provide the winner with a treat. The teacher would be contacted at the end of the week to verify the outcome. Tom won the first week, showing much pleasure with his success. The next week he had to talk with two children, and so forth. Each week Tom won the little bet, gradually increasing the number of verbalizations in the school setting.

During sessions, attempts were also made to broaden his verbalizations. Tom once saw a balloon animal on the therapist's desk and showed much interest in it. The therapist explained that the balloon animals were for storytelling. Tom said he wanted to make some balloon animals. He was told he would also have to tell a story. Tom reluctantly agreed. He requested four mice. He described the family of mice as living together, alone in the woods. They just wanted to be left alone. The world out there was big and bad. This story reflected Tom's own family, which was very withdrawn and isolated, and viewed the outside world as malevolent. The therapist's story focused on a close-knit family who initially saw the world as big and bad. But as they got to know others, and good places to go, they developed friendships and attempted to visit fun places. The family found they could have fun with others in addition to their own family members. As they interacted with others, they felt less frightened.

This case shows how play was effective again in overcoming resistance and developing an alliance with a child. Furthermore, it directly addressed his elective mutism and dramatically increased his verbalizations over time. Tom continued in play therapy for approximately two years. Family intervention was also utilized to provide parental guidance.

Case 3

Tim is an 8-year-old child who arrived with his mother early for his appointment. About ten minutes before the scheduled appointment, the receptionist called the therapist to say that Tim was destroying the lobby and intimidating the other children and parents. As the therapist entered the waiting area, Tim was running wildly around the lobby, while the mother was looking helpless. Short introductions were made, and then Tim and his mother were taken to the therapist's office. When questioned about his behavior in the lobby, Tim stated he was bored and needed some action. Limits, expectations, and confidentiality issues were briefly reviewed. The mother said this is the type of behavior that the school complains about. It also occurs at home, more around her than her husband. The mother provided further familial and developmental information before returning to the lobby. While in the office, Tim's behavior was very driven. He looked around the room and started rummaging through the cabinet drawers, yelling "Where is the toy gun?" The therapist called a time out, to settle and review the rules again. Tim's interest in the gun was also explored. It was then decided that each play item would be reviewed and at the end Tim would choose one to play with. Tim decided he wanted to try the Radio Talk Show. The format for Dr. Bow's Radio Talk Show was reviewed, along with his role. He requested an interview format, rather than a storytelling one. This was agreed upon and the talk show proceeded. Tim told about his family and school history, placing blame on the outside world for his problems. Profanities were used throughout in expressing his anger and hostility toward his parents. He noted his father drinks too much and has a temper, while his mother just watches television. When asked about family rules or expectations, he replied, "What rules? I do anything I want, as long as Dad's not home."

During the next session, Tim asked to do some drawing. After reviewing different types of drawing activities, he chose the Color-Your-Life Technique. Feeling/color equations were reviewed: red = angry, black = sad, violet = scared, yellow = happy, orange = excited, brown = bored. He used the full sheet of paper. Half the paper was red, while the remaining half was almost equally divided among black, violet, and brown. All drawing was very heavy. Tim described himself as sad and angry about family life, noting his parents fight a lot and his dad is mean. When requested to elaborate on this, Tim refused, other than stating that he is scared of his father. Tim described feeling bored because he has no siblings or friends.

During the third session, Tim requested to see Chester Lester. The therapist went through the routine with the suitcase. As Chester came out of the suitcase, Tim grabbed him and hit him smack in the nose, stating, "Hey sucker, you don't mess with me!" Chester returned to his suitcase, saying he wasn't going to get hit anymore. Tim's behavior was discussed, along with the previously established rules. Tim impulsively stated, "That's what my father does to me when I mess with him. See, here's a bruise on my arm." Further specific information was gathered and the mother was requested to join the session. Concerns about possible physical abuse were reviewed with the mother. She verified that her husband is often verbally and physically aggressive toward her and Tim. The mother and Tim were informed that the therapist must make a Protective Services referral because of the reported abuse. The mother understood and seemed somewhat relieved.

This case illustrates the effectiveness of play therapy with conduct-disordered children in gathering pertinent information and providing therapeutic intervention. Tim remained in play therapy for a number of years. Day treatment school services were also pursued, along with family intervention, to improve parent management skills. Furthermore, the father was referred for substance abuse treatment.

Case 4

Sally was a 7-year-old girl in foster care because of abuse and neglect. She was brought to the outpatient clinic to assist in working through past trauma and to alleviate conduct problems, such as stealing and lying. Sally was initially guarded, but with support she accompanied her foster parents to the therapist's office. Normal introductory information was reviewed, such as the purpose of the session, the referral source, and confidentiality issues. The foster parents briefly reviewed Sally's history and their involvement during the past two years. Sally added comments in a silly and immature manner. After thirty minutes, the foster parents were asked to return to the lobby so the therapist and Sally could spend time alone. After the foster parents left, Sally seemed even more reserved and distant. She was shown the different play activities and was asked to choose an activity. She chose to play with the puppets. Sally played out a skit about a girl lost from her mother. The mother had left her outside so she could go in the house to get some "stuff." The girl waited and waited, but the mother never returned. This story reflected Sally's own experiences with her drug-abusing mother.

During the second session, Sally was cooperative but quiet and reserved. She wanted to do some coloring and chose the Color–Your–Shape activity. A large piece of paper was placed on the floor and Sally's body shape was outlined. Feeling/color equations were reviewed: red = angry, black = sad, orange = excited, yellow = happy, and brown = lonely, and instructions were provided. Sally drew the outline of the body shape in black, with the head region colored red. This suggests pervasive feelings of sadness, with angry thoughts. Yellow and brown circles were included in the torso area. Inquiries about the drawing revealed much sadness over being separated from her biological mother and anger over the court's removing her from the home. Sally said she is lonely because she is separated from her siblings, who live with an aunt. She expressed happiness about having nice foster parents.

The dynamics revealed during the first two sessions provided the basis for therapeutic work during subsequent sessions. Sally used puppets to play out different skits about her upcoming court dates and the possible termination of parental rights. During the course of therapy, she changed from a quiet, suspicious child to a clingy, talkative one. Again, play was an excellent pathway in overcoming resistance and exploring the underlying dynamics.

Summary: Resolving Resistance by Structured Play Activities

Children often initially resist involvement in the therapeutic process by presenting as angry, upset, negative, withdrawn, frightened, and/or inhibited. Overcoming this resistance is a difficult task for child therapists. The first step in treating these children involves understanding some of the factors that may create their resistance, such as fear of new encounters, feelings of being the scapegoat for family problems, concerns about further victimization, inadequate preparation for the initial session by the parent(s), loyalty issues, and lack of motivation due to viewing the presenting problem as ego-syntonic, that is, viewing behavior and attitudes as acceptable and normal. Developing an awareness of these dynamics is critical in understanding the types of worries children have about entering therapy. Furthermore, by analyzing the type, quantity, and intensity of the resistance the therapist is able to formulate initial impressions about the child's social-emotional functioning.

The next steps involve engaging resistant children in therapy. Four factors are involved: the therapist's personality, establishing a relationship, the initial contact, and combining play and therapy. Warmth, concern, self-projection, flexibility, patience, and empathy are important characteristics of a child therapist. An enjoyment of children and an awareness of their interests/trends is also necessary. In terms of the therapeutic relationship, it thrives in a safe, nonthreatening environment where the child and therapist have special time together. In developing this relationship the child's social, emotional, and cognitive abilities need to be considered. Confidentiality issues also should be addressed to safeguard privacy and reduce suspicion. The initial contact is critical because impressions about others are quickly formulated and hard to undo. The child therapist's ability to present as friendly, self-confident, and in control plays a major role in conveying a positive impression. Proper introductions make the child feel respected and important. Once in the office, the purpose of the evaluation needs to be reviewed, along with pertinent background information. The style of interaction between the child and parent should be analyzed, because it reflects the child–parent relationship. After basic background information is gathered, the child should be seen alone. Play is then introduced to the child with a review of different play activities. Play acts as a symbolic channel of self-expression for the child as well as a diagnostic and therapeutic tool for the child therapist.

In working with resistant children, structured play is usually preferred, with an emphasis on gaining their attention and involvement. Opportunities for symbolic expression, emotional release, sublimation, and reality testing are also important aspects of play selection. A child's choice of toys, along with the quality and intensity of the themes, reveals much diagnostic information. By increasing the child's self-observation skills and providing appropriate interpretations, the child is able to develop insight and make therapeutic gains.

In these cases, a variety of play activities fulfilling the above criteria are reviewed, including the hidden puppet, puppetry and ventriloquism, storytelling, affective coloring exercises, and the family drawing/word game. Case illustrations are used to show the power of play in overcoming resistance, exploring dynamics, and creating opportunities for intervention.

References

Amster, F. (1982). Differential uses of play in treatment of young children. In *Play Therapy: Dynamics of the Process of Counseling with Children,* ed. G. L. Landreth pp. 33–42. Springfield, IL: Charles C Thomas.

Bow, J. N. (1988). Treating resistant children. *Child and Adolescent Social Work* 5:3–15.

Burns, R. C., and Kaufman, S. H. (1972). *Action, Style, and Symbols in Kinetic Family Drawings.* New York: Brunner/Mazel.

Chethik, M. (1979). The borderline child. In *Basic Handbook of Child Psychiatry,* vol. II, ed. J. D. Noshpitz, pp. 304–321. New York: Basic Books.

Dodds, J. B. (1987). *A Child Psychotherapy Primer.* New York: Human Sciences.

Gardner, R. A. (1971). *Therapeutic Communication with Children: The Mutual Storytelling Technique.* New York: Jason Aronson.

_____ (1975). *Psychotherapeutic Approaches to the Resistant Child.* New York: Jason Aronson.

_____ (1979). Helping children cooperate in therapy. In *Basic Handbook of Child Psychiatry,* vol. II, ed. J. D. Noshpitz, pp. 414–433. New York: Basic Books.

Ginott, H. G. (1982a). Therapeutic intervention in child treatment. In *Play Therapy: Dynamics of the Process of Counseling with Children,* ed. G. L. Landreth, pp. 160–172. Springfield, IL: Charles C Thomas.

———— (1982b). A rationale for selecting toys in play therapy. In *Play Therapy: Dynamics of the Process of Counseling with Children,* ed. G. L. Landreth, pp. 145–159. Springfield, IL: Charles C Thomas.

Harter, S. (1983). Cognitive-developmental considerations in the conduct of play therapy. In *Handbook of Play Therapy,* ed. C. E. Schaefer and K. J. O'Connor, pp. 95–127. New York: Wiley.

Haworth, M. R. (1968). Doll play and puppetry. In *Projective Techniques in Personality Assessment,* ed. A. I. Rabin, pp. 327–365. New York: Springer.

Howard, T. W. (1977). *How to Use Magic in Psychotherapy with Children.* Long Beach, MS: Emerald Press.

Mann, E., and McDermott, J. F. (1983). Play therapy for victims of child abuse and neglect. In *Handbook of Play Therapy,* ed. C. E. Schaefer and K. J. O'Connor, pp. 283–307. New York: Wiley.

Markowitz, J. (1959). The nature of the child's initial resistance to psychotherapy. *Social Work* 4:46–51.

Moskowitz, J. A. (1973). The sorcerer's apprentice or the use of magic in child psychotherapy. *International Journal of Psychotherapy* 2:138–162.

Moustakas, C. E. (1982). Emotional adjustment and the play therapy process. In *Play Therapy: Dynamics of the Process of Counseling with ·Children,* ed. G. L. Landreth, pp. 217–230. Springfield, IL: Charles C Thomas.

Murphy, L. B., and Krall, V. (1960). Free play as a projective tool. In *Projective Technique with Children,* ed. A. I. Rabin and M. R. Haworth, pp. 290–304. New York: Grune & Stratton.

O'Connor, K. J. (1983). The color-your-life technique. In *Handbook of Play Therapy,* ed. C. E. Schaefer and K. J. O'Connor, pp. 251–258. New York: Wiley.

Parten, M. B. (1932). Social participation among preschool children. *Journal of Abnormal and Social Psychology* 27:243–269.

Piaget, J. (1962). *Play, Dreams, and Imitation in Childhood.* New York: Norton.

Rekers, G. A. (1983). Play therapy with cross-gender identified children. In *Handbook of Play Therapy,* ed. C. E. Schaefer and K. J. O'Connor, pp. 369–385. New York: Wiley.

Roberts, M. A. (1987). How is playroom behavior observation used in the diagnosis of attention deficit disorder? In *The Young Hyperactive Child,* ed. J. Loney, pp. 65–74. New York: Haworth.

Rutter, M. (1985). Infantile autism. In *The Clinical Guide to Child Psychiatry,* ed. A. A. Ehrhardt and L. L. Greenhill, pp. 48–78. New York: Free Press.

Salameh, W. A. (1986). The effective use of humor in psychotherapy. In *Innovations in Clinical Practice: A Source Book,* vol. 5, ed. P. A. Keller and L. G. Ritt, pp. 157–175. Sarasota, FL: Professional Resource.

Schaefer, C. E., ed. (1979). *The Therapeutic Use of Child's Play.* New York: Jason Aronson.

———— (1980). Play therapy. In *Emotional Disorders in Children and Adolescents,* ed. G. P. Sholevar, R. M. Benson, and B. J. Blinder, pp. 95–105. New York: Spectrum.

Willock, B. (1983). Play therapy with aggressive, acting-out children. In *Handbook of Play Therapy,* ed. C. E. Schaefer and K. J. O'Connor, pp. 387–411. New York: Wiley.

Winnicott, D. W. (1971). *Therapeutic Consultation in Child Psychiatry.* New York: Basic Books.

Wolberg, L. R. (1977). *The Technique of Psychotherapy.* New York: Grune & Stratton.

Woltmann, A. G. (1940). The use of puppetry in understanding children. *Mental Hygiene* 24:445–458.

3

Self-Expressive Communication

Garry L. Landreth

There are over 4,000 languages communicated throughout the world (Comrie 1987), and although play is not listed anywhere as one of these languages, it should be. Children from all parts of the world use play to express themselves. Their efforts to communicate are facilitated by the use of toys as their words and play as their language. During play, children can express what they want to express in any way they wish. Verbal words are sometimes used in addition to the child's play, but are not necessary for the child's communication to be complete. Free play interaction serves as the child's vocabulary and thus can be viewed as a limitless language of self-expression because of the unlimited subtle nuances possible in play and the absence of specific rules of meaning found in verbal communication.

Many adults think of play as something fun children do to pass the time or as a waste of time. However, adults who understand children and know about their world view play as a time of creative self-expression, a valuable part of each child's life. Self-expression of children, as viewed here, is the expression of all parts of self that exist and are experienced at the moment. Expression of only a part of self would not be self-expression. Play enables children to express themselves completely. Nothing is held back, because the self the child is can be expressed safely through the natural facilitative dimensions of play. Play does not require translation from one language to another or from one mind to another; it simply exists as self-expression.

Play is the most natural thing children do and yet may be the least understood of all their behaviors. Could there be more to play than meets the casual observer's eye? Surely this activity, which captivates children so and through which they expend so much emotional and physical energy, has significance other than as an activity for spending time.

Play is the singular central activity of childhood, occurring at all times and in all places. Seldom do children sit down and talk to each other for very long periods of time without doing anything active. Children do not need to be taught how to play, nor must they be made to play. Play is spontaneous, enjoyable, voluntary, and non-goal directed. In order to make children's play more acceptable, some adults have invented a meaning for play by defining it as work. The attitude is that

41

children must be accomplishing something or working toward some important goal acceptable to adults; that play can only be important if it somehow fits what adults consider important in their world. It is regrettable that play has been identified by many writers as children's work. Just as childhood has intrinsic value and is not merely preparation for adulthood, so too, play has intrinsic value and is not dependent on what may follow for importance. In contrast to work, which is goal focused and directed toward accomplishment or completion of a task by accommo-dating to the demands of the immediate environment, play is intrinsically complete, does not depend on external reward, and assimilates the world to match the individual's concepts as in the case of a child pretending a block of wood is an airplane (Landreth 1991).

Definition of Play

Play is an integral part of childhood, a unique medium that facilitates the develop-ment of expressive language, communication skills, emotional development, social skills, decision-making skills, and cognitive development in children. Play is also a medium for exploration and discovery of interpersonal relationships, experimenta-tion with adult roles, and understanding of one's own feelings. Play is the most complete form of self-expression developed by the human organism.

Play is a complex multidimensional series of behaviors that change significantly as children grow and develop, and we have yet to fully describe what play is and what it is not. Play is often easier to recognize and observe than it is to define. A problem that arises when attempting to derive an acceptable definition is that there is no single set of behaviors that includes the many types of play. Bergen (1988) summarizes definitions of play as they relate to self-expression, drawing from the works of several child development specialists: Seashore–"free self-expression for the pleasure of expression" (p. 10); Dulles–"an instinctive form of self-expression and emotional escape valve" (p. 10); Hall–"the motor habits and spirit of the past persisting in the present" (p. 10); and Froebel–"[an expression of] the natural unfolding of the germinal leaves of childhood" (p. 10).

Erikson (1977) defines play as a situation in which the ego can deal with experiences by creating model situations and can also master reality by experi-menting and planning. Moustakas (1981) describes play as "a form of letting go, merging freely into experience, immersing oneself totally in the moment so that there is no distinction between self and object or self and other. Energy, life, spirit, surprise, fusion, awakening, renewal are all qualities of play . . . it is free flowing form, opening and expanding in unexpected and unpredictable ways" (p. 20).

Coleman and Skeen (1985) define play as free of space, time, and role limitations; self-directed and spontaneous; and involving internal rewards of self-expression and self-discovery of one's capabilities. Following the suggestions of various authors, play can be defined as an activity that is intrinsically motivating, bringing pleasure and gratification simply for the joy of doing it. The play activity is voluntarily chosen, and an activity in which the child asks, "What can I do with this object?" (Ellis 1984, Guerney 1984, Tegano et al. 1989).

Characteristics of Play

There are six characteristics that distinguish children's play from other pursuits (Almy 1984, Monighan et al. 1987, Rubin et al. 1983). The first characteristic is intrinsic motivation – the genuine desire to be doing what one is doing. The activity is participated in freely and openly. New experiences are often chosen because they offer a different perspective on a familiar experience. Play, therefore, facilitates children's understanding of what they have experienced.

A second characteristic of play is attention to the means or process rather than the end goal. The goals of play often change during the activity and are less important than the experiences and interactions of the moment, which are spontaneous expressions of the self. A third characteristic of play is nonliteral behavior or make-believe, in which children pretend to be other characters and act out any variety of pretend scenes through which they express themselves in ways that are psychologically safe. A fourth characteristic of play is freedom from external rules. The rules come from the children themselves. Children may have some implicit rules that regulate how certain roles are played, but these directions are arranged by the participants and not by anyone outside their play. Therefore, the boundaries of self-expression are determined by the participants.

The fifth characteristic of play is freedom of exploration of new items or environments. Children feel, smell, touch, and look at new items as they begin to play with them. This experienced freedom allows children to express themselves more fully. The sixth characteristic of play is active engagement. Children are often intently involved in their play and resist distraction. This kind of intensity allows fullness of self-expression at the felt moment.

Types of Play

Sensorimotor play, which functions as a means of assimilation of sensory information into the child's cognitive processes, begins at birth and continues until approximately 18 to 24 months of age. According to Piaget (1962), the child initially engages in reflexive behavior and then begins to repeat movements for their own sake, thus demonstrating that these reflexive behaviors are now under conscious control. This type of play is engaged in because it feels good. In the beginning the child observes, then is able to manipulate objects, and finally is able to maneuver objects to view them in different ways (Jernberg 1983). "Looking and touching have become coordinated and the child learns that to push the toy hanging from its cot will make it swing or rattle. Once learned the action will be repeated again and again. This is play" (Millar 1968, p. 54). Sensorimotor play, therefore, initiates the process of communication of self.

The second stage of development in children's play proposed by Piaget (1962) is symbolic or pretend play, which is the primary type of play between 2 and 6 years of age. Symbolic play emerges at approximately 2 years of age and involves the child being able to conjure up mental images and to utilize them in play. According to Monighan, Scales, and Van Hoorn (1987), children begin to develop abstract generalizations of objects. Examples of symbolic play include pretending to build a skyscraper, prepare a meal, or drive a truck. The ability to participate in symbolic play has been said to facilitate development in adaptability, flexibility, and divergent thinking (Guddemi 1987), all of which are important for later cognitive development and thus self-expression.

Games with rules play develops at approximately age 6 and is the last stage of play to develop. In this most complex stage, children can accept rules, they can assume the perspective of others, they are able to remain attentive, and they can control their behavior, actions, and reactions. At this age, cognitive abilities to comprehend rules and requirements have developed, enabling children to participate successfully in organized sports and board games and to express self in more socially acceptable ways.

Significance of Play in Self-Expression

White (1960) maintains that play may be fun, but it is also a serious business in childhood. During play, children build up confidence in dealing with their environment. Bruner (1986) believes play gives children their first and most crucial opportunity to have the courage to think, to talk, and to be themselves. According to Amster (1982), play is an activity children comprehend and in which they are comfortable – their method of communication, and their means of testing, partly incorporating and mastering external realities. Since play provides a nonthreatening environment and a flexible atmosphere, creative thoughts are encouraged as children explore and experiment with a variety of solutions to different problems (Tegano et al. 1989). Play allows this process to proceed on a scale controllable by the child. It is through the process of play that children can consider new possibilities not possible in reality, thus greatly expanding the expression of self.

Through play, children find out what the world is like, try on different roles, and cope with conflicting emotions (Papalia and Olds 1986). The urge to play is universal, and when thwarted can hamper the joyful path of development and self-discovery that is the calling of every child (Bettelheim 1987a). Only through engaging in the process of play can children express and use the totality of their personality. Thus, children extend the person they are, the self, into the creative expression of play. As children develop an appreciation for their play, they begin to discover and accept self. Frank (1952) enumerated the ways in which play facilitates these discoveries: children express emotions in play, they express their thoughts in play, they rehearse behaviors in play, they exert their will in play, they move through developmental stages with play, and they learn with play. Everything the child is, does and becomes may at one time or another be demonstrated through play.

Play is a vital component of healthy development, for it is through play that the total self of the child is created, expressed, and re-created. Play provides a medium through which children's interpretations, wishes, needs, experiences, feelings, and perceptions of self are expressed and explored. Children live in the world of the present; yet, many of the experiences they encounter in the adult world are future oriented and abstract. In order to translate these experiences into terms they can understand, children reenact them through play, enabling them to gain a better understanding of the experiences. Through the process of play, children explore the unfamiliar and develop knowledge that is both experiential/feeling and cognitive. It can then be said that through play the unfamiliar becomes familiar. For the child, then, the unfamiliar takes on new meaning and the child's expression of self is enhanced. According to Lee (1969), a child has to experience a thing before he or she can understand it. Play, therefore, facilitates understanding and understanding thus facilitates children's self-expression.

Play provides healing for hurts and sadness, breaks down tension, and releases pent-up urges toward self-expression. The activity of play is one of the most important ways in which children learn that their feelings can be safely expressed without reprisal or rejection from others (Cass 1973). Since play is a spontaneous and safe environment, it allows children to express strong emotions and to learn to cope with anxieties and conflicts. During play, children feel free to act out inner feelings of fear, anger, or loss that might otherwise become overwhelming (Segal and Segal 1989). Erikson (1977) believed that through this process of self-expression in play, children resolve conflicts by reconstructing them in symbolic play. Maslow (1968) observed that though children do not plan or set out to grow, growth takes place, and children express outwardly through play what has taken place and is taking place inwardly.

Fostering a Sense of Control

There are many experiences in childhood in which children feel they have little or no control. Play is children's way of working out accompanying feelings of anxiety and fear and reestablishing some sense of balance and control in their lives. A child in the hospital might play out the events of that experience with the use of dolls. In doing so, the child gains a sense of control over the hospital procedures and is freed from thinking that the event is taking place as a punishment. When children have experienced a traumatic event, they will play it out in an effort to gain understanding (Erikson 1963). Curry and Arnaud (1984) described an experience in which a preschool teacher had fainted in front of her class and eventually died from a terminal disease. After a few weeks of disorganized play in the classroom, the children got caught up in hospital play, which continued until their anxiety was alleviated. This self-expression through play is not only freeing to children but allows them to express new parts of themselves.

Play is an environment children can control. It is this sense or feeling of control, rather than actual control, which is essential to emotional development and positive mental health. Children may experience environments at home or school that are overly structured and controlling, interactions in which they experience being controlled by others, but in unstructured free play, the child is the master, the boss, the person in control, the one who decides what to play, how to play, and the outcome. The story, happening, or activity can be what the child wants it to be. In the safety of play, the child can confront monsters, fantasy characters, and frightening experiences with real people and be in charge of the outcome.

Through the process of expressing themselves in play, children can learn perseverance, the pleasure of choosing a project alone, self-direction, self-responsibility, and that they, along with their choices, are accepted. In addition, the opportunities to engage in problem solving are limitless. Children also develop the self-discipline necessary to engage in a sustained effort, and the resulting satisfaction is a tremendous boost in building positive self-esteem.

Through peer interactions involved in play, real social problems are presented to children that they are fully capable of working through and solving (Rogers and Ross 1986). Social development is thus impacted since play facilitates the learning of negotiating, compromising, and the taking of turns (Greenburg 1989). The development of these cooperative skills thus becomes a quality of the child's positive self-expression in play with others.

Basic messages about self are communicated through play when a child shares a toy with another child, voluntarily gives up a sand scoop to assist in a building project, hides in the cupboard, or paints over another child's picture. How a child utilizes finger paints, with cautious tips of the fingers or with vigorous hand smears, communicates the inner dynamics of the child at that moment. Each painting a child produces is unique in choice of color, amount of paint, design, manner of construction, and hand and body movements employed in its production. Children communicate with peers and others through play; thus play is not only a means of self-expression, as can occur in isolated play, but is also a primary vehicle for communication.

Children's Awareness Is Communicated Through Play

Since children's language development lags behind their cognitive development, they communicate their awareness of what is happening in their world through their play. This awareness may be at a conscious level or an unconscious level as is discussed in the following section.

Because children are in the very process of emerging into consciousness, it is difficult to distinguish exactly that play which is conscious and that which is unconscious. Piaget (1962) has suggested that when a child is assimilating one object to another, the child is doing so on a conscious level. However, when the child is involved in playing a game with two dolls of unequal size and the child makes the smaller one go away on a trip, while the larger one stays with mother, it is doubtful the child is conscious that the smaller doll is a symbol for his younger sibling. Piaget proposed that all symbols may be conscious from one point of view and unconscious from another, and that the same may be said for rational verbal expression.

What first appears in a child's play will often be a reproduction of the child's environment, but as a child's comfort level rises in the play atmosphere, he will begin to express unconsciously whatever ambivalent feelings he may have about his environment (Piaget 1962). Therefore, the basic elements of sensorimotor play are important in later areas of the child's exploration and development of self in that sensorimotor play involves exploration and the establishing of comfort for the child. The child's use of a blanket or some other comforting object suggests that sensorimotor play does more than facilitate cognitive growth. The meeting of emotional needs also seems to be present. Engaging in play naturally brings comfort to a child and is therefore a vital element in the child's movement toward self-expression. As the child feels more comfortable, feelings of safety are enhanced, thus freeing the possibility of exploration and self-expression in relation to physical surroundings, self in relation to experiences, self in relation to others, and self in relation to self. The significance of this comfort dimension of play can readily be observed in therapeutic encounters with children in play therapy.

Although children engage in play activities largely for the sake of pure enjoyment and are seldom aware of the functional elements of play, there are times when play is experienced at a conscious level. Initially in play, children often express what they have observed adults doing. They play out familiar roles and scenes depicting home routines and the roles played by adults in those routines. At other times, it is obviously clear a child is quite aware of what he is expressing in play as in the case of 7-year-old Scott, who grabbed Bobo (the bop bag) around the neck in a hammer lock and yelled, "I'm gonna show you what I did to Roger on the playground today!"

Children's emotions are often diffused and undifferentiated and not directly related to reality, since they have lost contact with the people and situations that originally aroused the feelings of frustration, anger, fear, or guilt. Moustakas (1982) has described five stages through which emotionally disturbed children progress in their play as they move toward self-expression and self-awareness in the therapeutic process of play therapy. Initially diffuse negative feelings are expressed everywhere in the child's play as in the case of a child who cannot tolerate any kind of mess and is overly concerned with cleanliness and neatness. Sometimes the reaction may be diffuse hostility expressed toward the room, toys, and therapist. There may also be accompanying high levels of anxiety as in the case of a child who just stands in the middle of the playroom unable to initiate any activity. Following these expressions, in the second stage the child usually expresses ambivalent feelings that are generally anxious or hostile. Moustakas describes a child who picked up the puppets one by one, banged each puppet on the table with exclamations of disgust, threw each puppet on the floor, and said, "I don't like any of them, but I like this one" as she picked up the mouse puppet. She then quickly added, "I don't like this one either," as she squeezed the mouse's head.

The third stage is characterized by more focused direct negative feelings expressed toward parents, siblings, and other persons in the child's life. These feelings or attitudes are often evident in the child's symbolic play as in the case of a child who acted out strong negative reactions toward her parents and new baby by lining up the mother, father, and baby family doll figures, and then announced, "They're robbers, and I'm going to shoot them," which she did, one at a time.

In the fourth stage, ambivalent feelings are expressed again in the child's play. However, in this stage, ambivalence is a mixture of positive and negative feelings and attitudes expressed toward parents, siblings, and other persons in the child's life. Five-year-old Kathy feeds the baby doll as she rocks the doll and sings to it. Then she takes a nail from a can and says, "I'm going to stick this down her throat so she can't cry so much." Six-year-old David hits and kicks the bop bag with great vigor and expenditure of energy, yelling, "I'm gonna beat you up. Nobody likes you!" Later he gets the doctor kit, doctors the bop bag, and says, "I'll bet that makes you feel better now."

The expression of these feelings in a relationship with an adult who is accepting and understanding frees the child to move to the final stage of expression of self through play which is characterized by clear, distinct, separate, usually realistic positive and negative attitudes, with positive attitudes predominating in the child's play. Moustakas concludes that the child's expression of feelings in a clear and distinct way through play reveals that the child has achieved insight and an understanding of reality; thus self is being expressed fully through the facilitative dimensions of play. The stages in this emotional process and the changes in feeling tones evident in the play process are not always distinctly identifiable and do not occur in a step-by-step process. Likewise, the stages in the process often overlap at many points.

Axline (1982) describes a similar process of stages or patterns of self-expression through play by noting that as play therapy sessions progress, many of the children's feelings and attitudes are expressed symbolically, toy to toy, toy to invisible person, child to imaginary person, child about a real person, and child to the object of his feelings. She observed that at the conclusion of play therapy, children take responsibility for their own feelings and express themselves honestly and openly in their play. Thus, through the process of expressing self through play, children bring their feelings to the surface of awareness and either learn to control them or discard them. That children express their self-awareness through play certainly seems to be fully evident in the descriptions of Moustakas and Axline.

In an accepting and safe environment such as that afforded the child in play therapy, each child's complex uniqueness is expressed more freely and thus more completely. As this uniqueness of self is accepted by the play therapist, the child internalizes that acceptance and begins to accept and appreciate his own uniqueness, thus beginning the process of self-knowledge. This self-knowledge is then expressed through the facilitative process of play.

Symbolic Expression in Play

Fantasy play has been described as functioning as an inner resource to help children adapt to environmental demands (Newman and Newman 1978) and as providing children with an opportunity to assimilate novel experiences into familiar schema (Piaget 1962). Symbolic play provides a safe or controlled way for children to express emotions, since the emotion itself or the target of the emotion is disguised through the symbolism. It would seem, then, that symbolic play is a way to integrate solving problems and expressing emotions. According to Bettelheim (1987b), what a child chooses to play is motivated by inner processes even when the child engages in play partly to fill empty moments. When children encounter an insurmountable problem, they play it out in symbolic ways that they may not understand because they are reacting to inner processes whose origin may be buried deep in the unconscious.

By acting out a frightening or traumatic experience or situation symbolically, and by returning to that happening again and again through play and perhaps changing or reversing the outcome in the play activity, the child moves toward an inner resolution and then is better able to cope with or adjust to the problem in what is sometimes referred to as "real life" – that is, those experiences outside play. As Frank (1982) has pointed out, the child learns to face terrifying objects with increasing self-confidence as he plays out relations to the adult world, and in the process "the child accepts the not-me world of actuality, by learning to relate himself to that world through various modes of activity and response which he develops as his idiomatic way of putting order and meaning into the actual world and dealing with those meanings as his way of stabilizing and equalizing the flux of experiences" (p. 27).

Children communicate their unconscious feelings through play and utilize available toys and materials as symbols to express the feelings of which they may not be aware at that time. Children are unaware consciously that they are coming to terms with their feelings about wetting and soiling as they pour and dribble water or squeeze moist clay. They are unaware that during this kind of play process and expression of self, they are working through their anger toward their parents (Cass 1973). Children can unconsciously express their hatred as they tellingly tear apart the doll they are holding (Caplan and Caplan 1973).

The use of symbols by children enables them to transfer interests and fantasies as well as anxieties and guilt to objects other than people (Ginott 1982). Play is their symbolic language of self-expression and allows them to "enjoy forbidden pleasures in acceptable substitute ways" (Ginott 1982, p. 151). Through play, children can distance themselves from traumatic events and experiences with adults by the use of symbolic materials (Mann and McDermott 1983). Play allows children to work through emotions to their conclusion in an environment the children control. Thus children are safe from the intensity of their own emotional expressions. It could be said that in the expression of self through play, children are safe from themselves. They are not overwhelmed by their own actions because the act takes place in fantasy.

That children unconsciously express happenings, experiences, concerns, and problems in their play can readily be seen in the following cases. Six-year-old Brenda had to wear a catheter as a result of complications following surgery. She experienced considerable difficulty in trying to empty the bag appropriately and make the necessary connections to put it back in place. The connections were always leaking and that caused her a great deal of frustration and embarrassment. In her play, she repeatedly played out a story using the doll house and depicting a problem with a leaky sink or some related plumbing problem. With great exasperation, she would call a plumber to come and fix the plumbing. She stopped acting out these scenes when she learned to attach the catheter bag correctly.

Eight-year-old Jacob played out a scene involving the horses, corral, and barn. He pretended to put a bridle on the horse and commented, "It doesn't hurt his mouth." Then he took the horse to the barn and said, "When the horse kicks the stall, a light comes on over here in the house where the man stays who takes care of the horses so he will know the horse needs help." The significance of this play is evident when it is known that Jacob receives electrical stimulation twice a week to strengthen the muscles in his jaws as a part of his speech therapy program. Small electrodes are placed inside his mouth and the procedure is generally painless. However, sometimes the muscles get tense from the stimulation, and Jacob can let the therapist know he is experiencing some discomfort by pressing a button to make a light come on.

Amster (1982) describes a clinical case in which a child who was encopretic played out his problem by using building blocks to build a house without a bathroom and then later constructed an ornate bathroom outside the house.

Klein (1982) describes the case of Peter, a 7-year-old boy who was neurotic. He was unable to play freely, could not tolerate frustration, was timid, sometimes aggressive, overbearing, and ambivalent toward family members. After sleeping with his parents when he was 18 months old, and having observed their sexual intercourse, he became difficult to manage and demonstrated regressive behavior. In play therapy sessions, Peter repeatedly returned to play scenes of bumping the toy horses together and then would put them to sleep. Although Peter experienced emotions of jealousy, aggressiveness, and anxiety, he did not have a conscious knowledge of these feelings and their association with people in his life. He acted out his aggression by pretending the horses were dead and by throwing them about the room.

Therapeutic Value of Play

The therapeutic value of children's self-expression through play is generally accepted by professionals in the field of play therapy and early childhood education. Play gives concrete form and expression to children's inner world and emotionally significant experiences are given meaningful expression through play. The therapist uses play with children because play is the child's symbolic language of self-expression, and for children to "play out" their experiences and feelings is the most natural dynamic and self-healing process in which children can engage. A major function of play is the changing of what may be unmanageable in reality to manageable situations through symbolic representation that provides children with opportunities for learning to cope by engaging in self-directed exploration.

Children's feelings are often inaccessible at a verbal level. Developmentally, they lack the cognitive, verbal facility to express what they feel, and emotionally are not able to focus on the intensity of what is felt in a manner that can be expressed adequately in a verbal exchange. According to Axline (1969), children's free play is an expression of what they want to do, and when they play freely and without direction, they are expressing and releasing the feelings and attitudes that have been pushing to get out into the open. Permitting children to play freely in a setting of security and acceptance enables them to deal satisfactorily and healthfully with their most urgent problems (Hartley et al. 1952).

Play has therapeutic value for all children, not just those experiencing emotional disturbances. All children may at some time in their life encounter what seem like insurmountable problems in living. However, by playing them out, the child moves toward being able to cope with those problems in a step-by-step process (Bettelheim 1987b). All children are able to express themselves through their play in a way that helps them work out their problems. Hartley and colleagues (1952, p. 4) suggest that "play activities are equally significant for the relatively untroubled youngsters and for the many children who have suffered deprivations, frustrations, neglect, bad treatment, or exposure to crisis and disturbance in the family. . . ."

Play is to children what verbalization is to adults. Given the opportunity, children will play out their feelings and needs in a manner or process of expression similar to that for adults. The dynamics of expression and vehicle for communication are different for children, but the expressions (fear, satisfaction, anger, happiness, frustration, contentment) are similar to that of adults. Children may have considerable difficulty in trying to tell what they feel or how they have been affected by what they have experienced, but if permitted, in the presence of a caring, sensitive, and empathic adult, will show what they feel through the toys and material they choose, what they do with and to the materials, and the story acted out (Landreth 1991).

It is through play that children engage in the process of organizing their experiences, their personal world. This attempt to gain control is described by Frank (1982):

The child in his play relates himself to his accumulating past by continually reorienting himself to the present through play. He rehearses his past experiences, assimilating them into new perceptions and patterns of relating. . . . In this way the child is continually discovering himself anew, revising his image of himself as he can and must, with each alteration in his relations with the world. Likewise, in his play the child attempts to resolve his problems and conflicts, manipulating play materials and often adult materials as he tries to work through or play out his perplexities and confusions. [p. 24]

The process described here is one of play facilitating children's self-expression through a continuous and dynamic process of here-and-now focus. Axline (1969) viewed this process as one in which the child plays out feelings, thus bringing them to the surface, getting them out in the open, facing them, and either learning to control them or abandon them. It would seem then that play allows children to express themselves in a way that reduces tension and anxiety and thus allows them to gain control of their lives. Hartup and Smothergill (1967) write, "It has been said in play the child 'reduces tensions,' 'masters anxiety,' 'generalizes responses,' or manifests a polarity of 'pure assimilation' " (p. 96). As children relive their own experiences in imaginative play, they are able to solve problems or overcome specific fears, and ultimately are responsible for easing their own pain (Weissbourd 1986).

The therapeutic benefit of play in facilitating children's self-expression has been summarized by Hartley and colleagues (1952) as giving children an opportunity to: (1) imitate adults, (2) play out real life roles in an intense way, (3) reflect relationships and experiences, (4) express pressing needs, (5) release unacceptable impulses, (6) reverse roles usually taken, (7) mirror growth, (8) work out problems, and (9) experiment with solutions.

How to Read Play Symbols

Since toys are like words to children in their efforts to communicate their experiences and their world, and play is children's natural language of expression, the importance of understanding the possible meanings in children's play seems obvious. Frank (1982) points out that in observing children's play, we must recognize equivalent stimuli. "Learning to live in a symbolic world of meanings and symbols involves the capacity to accept equivalents (surrogates) of widely varying dimensions and divergence from the actual world and cultural norms, but having equivalent meaning for the individual" (p. 26). He suggests that it may be useful to think of play as a figurative language, recognizing that the child's play reveals equivalents of almost all our familiar figures of speech, metaphor, analogy, hyperbole, synecdoche, onomatopoeia and so forth.

Understanding the meaning in children's play is at best a difficult process, and Amster (1982) insists that the play activity of children "must be recognized always as a complex distorted assortment of the child's conscious and unconscious expressions" (p. 42). Equally as important is the observer's knowledge of child development and how children of a given age typically play. Only then can the observer decide if there is some unique meaning in the child's play. In assessing play behavior, the observer, then, is constantly comparing what an individual child is doing, saying, and feeling to what is normal for that child's age, level of development, and environment. These comparisons can then provide some clues to what the unique meaning may be.

According to Adcock and Segal (1979), children's stories are never completely spontaneous inventions. Themes children use in their play are developed through various experiences in their lives. Previous experiences and problems in children's lives are likely to be depicted in their play activities. As children work through their problems or difficulties, they experiment with different solutions through their play, thus expanding the number of options related to the same theme. Frank (1982) hypothesized that a child will work through a theme until he is comfortable with it and ready to move forward. Themes, therefore, are like the child's unconscious working through of anxieties and fears. When the child has mastered the fear or theme, he will be able to move onward with life.

Emotional experiences and happenings that are important or have in some way significantly impacted children will often show up as repeated behavior in their play. A theme is the recurrence of certain events or topics in the child's play, either within a play experience, such as during a play therapy session, or across several play experiences or sessions. A key point here is the recurrence of the play after some lapse of time or an intervening period of play in which the theme is not played out. For example, 4-year-old Shawn's play with a rubber snake for twenty minutes would not be considered a theme even though that is considered to be an unusually long time for a child that age to engage in such play. Although the play may be significant, the expression must occur more than once or twice to be considered a theme.

When Shawn came to the playroom for his second session and again played out the same scene of the rubber snake crawling around the dollhouse, sticking its head into each window and door, and then slowly and deliberately crawling around the top of the dollhouse, the therapist suspected a theme. This suspicion was confirmed when Shawn repeated the same play in the third session. It was at this point that the therapist learned that Shawn's home had been burglarized twice just a few weeks prior to his first play therapy session.

The theme may not always be readily recognizable because what is being played, the activity, or the toys being played with may be different each time, but the theme of the play or the underlying meaning of the play is the same. This was the case with Paul in his play sessions. A theme of reluctance to leave the security of home was evident in the scenes he played out involving an airplane trip in which he announced, "They're going on a trip to New York," loaded the doll family into the airplane, and then promptly announced, "They're back!" without the people ever having flown away from the dollhouse. A second scene involved a family auto trip in which Paul stayed very close to the dollhouse and never went out into the room with the car. A third scene consisted of his announcing, "They're going to move," loading all the dollhouse furniture and fixtures into the truck and then quickly announcing, "They decided to live here again," and unloading and replacing the furniture in the dollhouse. Paul experienced a tremendous fear of abandonment. Such repeated play behaviors can indicate emotional issues the child is playing out. When the theme is no longer observable, that can be an indication the child has been able emotionally to move on to something else (Landreth 1991).

Caplan and Caplan (1983) have concluded that there are some patterns of play that have fairly universal meaning and may indicate the type of problems that underlie a child's disturbance. They suggest that children who tend to be meticulously clean and avoid dirty or messy play, who arrange toys in only neat patterns, and whose drawings often require the use of a ruler may indicate a rigidity that is seriously limiting their personal development. Also, children who either keep up a constant chatter or play silently for long periods of time may be hiding their feelings. Constant regression to earlier levels of maturity and compulsion to use materials such as sand and water, which may have cleansing symbolism, may signify unresolved conflict.

Waelder (1976) states that children repeat in their play everything that has strongly affected them in their daily life. He gives examples of children who have been sexually abused repeatedly "washing" themselves with sand, covering their genital area with sand while playing in the sand box, burying or otherwise hiding objects from view. Allen and Berry (1987) indicate a child will show his or her own emotional turmoil and chaos in chaotic sand play, where the sand and unrelated toys are tossed in a heap. The use of squares, rectangles, and circles may indicate completion and wholeness. Battles and wars, powerful figures like robots and monsters who all end up killed, are indicative of destructive impulses. Symbols are forms that have significance by virtue of the fact that they mean something (Reifel and Greenfield 1982), and children often identify dolls with people in their lives. Therefore, when children make dolls do what they do to one another, children may be showing exactly how they feel toward those people and how they think those people feel toward them and each other (Caplan and Caplan 1973).

Inferring meaning in the use of certain toys or interpreting children's play can be quite easily accomplished depending on the interpreter's theoretical assumptions. However, Anna Freud (1928) cautioned that the therapist has no right to impute a symbolic meaning to every one of a child's actions. This view is reiterated by Vinturella and James (1987) who encourage the therapist to avoid adhering to a fixed interpretation of symbols. They believe a symbol can have several meanings, and its subjective meaning for the child should be respected. For example, a snake could represent danger, wisdom, fascination, or simply the child's latest object of interest. Irwin (1983) proposes that the data obtained by interpreting play should be used in "the same way other projective data are used – as impressions to be verified, refuted, or altered in the course of ongoing work" (p. 161). Moustakas (1973) points out that objects have varied meanings to different children. Blocks, sand, clay, or other unstructured objects may symbolize a multitude of things such as parents, siblings, a painful experience, as well as feelings of hate, love, or hostility in the imagination of a child. According to Klein (1949), many distinct and different associations are brought by a child to the individual parts of his or her play as evidenced by the fact that a doll may represent either the mother or the child.

It seems obvious that caution should be exercised in interpreting symbolism in children's play. As Ginott (1982) points out, banging two blocks together may represent spanking, or intercourse, or may merely be a test of the therapist's tolerance for noise. However, when a father doll is placed on top of a mother doll with accompanying movements, the possibility of misinterpretation is less likely. As can be seen in these examples, the play materials chosen by the child may be equally useful as a means of expression for the child, but the adult's understanding of the child's expression may be limited by the child's choice of play materials. Therefore, proper selection of toys and materials for children's self-expression in any setting is crucial.

Toys for Facilitating Self-Expression

Careful selection of toys and materials is essential in providing children with opportunities for self-expression through their play. The type of toy a child uses can determine the type and extent of play exhibited, and thus the degree of self-expression. Toys with only one use can limit or inhibit self-expression. Unstructured toys can be used by children in many ways to express themselves. Toys and play materials become an extension of the child's self, just as words are an extension of the adult's self. Therefore, words and play behaviors are idiomatic expressions unique to each child.

Neumann (1971) states that ambiguity and diversity of materials tends to foster creative play in which the child can ascribe the identity and function to the object. Ambiguous materials tend to facilitate reflective, transforming responses, whereas realistic and elaborate materials facilitate stereotyped exploration. Rubin and Howe (1985) conclude from their review of the literature on children's toys and the types of play associated with them, that for younger children realistic toys tend to be more conducive to facilitating pretend play than are abstract toys. The opposite reaction was noted with older children.

Toys and materials can determine or structure the kind and degree of expression by the child and his interaction with the adult. Some toys and materials, by the very nature of their construction and design, are prone to elicit certain kinds of behaviors more than others and to some extent structure the behavior of the child. The bop bag is a good example. As it stands there in the middle of the floor, everything about it seems to say, "Hit me" and so children are more likely to push, shove, or hit the bop bag than to pretend it is a sick friend and nurse it back to health. Some materials should be provided that are nondescript and facilitate the child's creative and symbolic expression. Blocks can become cars, trains, airplanes, fences, houses, and so forth.

Toys and materials that facilitate the self-expression of children can be grouped into three broad categories (Landreth 1991).

1. *Real-life Toys.* A doll family, doll house, puppets, and nondescript figures (e.g., Gumby) can represent family members in the child's life and thus provide for the direct expression of feelings. Anger, fear, sibling rivalry, crises, and family conflicts can be directly expressed as the child acts out scenes with the human figures. Puppets and doll family figures allow children to distance themselves from what is expressed. Attributing feelings to such toys is often easier for children than expressing the same feelings directly. A car, truck, boat, and cash register are especially important for the resistive, anxious, shy, or withdrawn child because they can be played with in noncommittal ways without revealing any feelings. When children are ready, they will choose play media that will help them express their feelings more fully and openly. The cash register provides for a quick feeling of control as the child manipulates the keys and calls out numbers. The car or truck gives an excuse for moving about and exploring the room and can also be used to act out real-life happenings.

2. *Acting-out–Aggressive-release Toys.* Children often have intense pent-up emotions for which they do not have verbal labels to describe or express. Structured toys and materials such as the bop bag, toy soldiers, alligator puppet, guns, and rubber knife can be used to express anger, hostility, and frustration. Aggressive children seem to experience the permission to release aggressive feelings in the accepting environment of a playroom as satisfying, and are able to move on to more self-enhancing positive feelings. Driving nails into a soft wood log or pounding on a pegboard releases feelings, and at the same time facilitates the focusing of attention and energy in a manner that increases concentration.

Ginott (1961) suggests including animal toys that depict wild animals because some children find it difficult to express aggressive feelings even against human figure dolls. These children, for example, will not shoot a father doll but will shoot a lion that may represent the father. Some children will express their hostility through the alligator puppet by biting, chewing, and crunching. Clay is an example of a material that fits into two categories, creative and aggressive. It can be pounded, smashed, rolled out with great vigor, and torn apart with intensity. Clay can also be used by the child to create figures for play.

3. *Toys for Creative Expression and Emotional Release.* Sand and water are probably the most popular unstructured play media for children, and are excellent for expressing feelings. Children can use sand to express their aggression by manipulating it and burying dolls and other items in it. Water allows children to act out

those times when they need to regress. Sand, water, and clay are reversible play materials that allow children to change the identity of the object. When the scene being played out becomes too frightening or intense, the child can make the play material turn into something else. Blocks can be houses, they can be thrown, they can be stacked and kicked down allowing the child to explore what it feels like to be constructive and destructive. As with water and sand, the child can experience a feeling of satisfaction, because there is no correct way to play with blocks. Easel paints afford the child an opportunity to be creative, to be messy, to pretend bathroom scenes and smear, to express feelings.

Millar (1968) reports that the kind and number of available toys make a difference in the manner and kind of children's play. When fewer toys are available, children make more social contact with each other, tend to display undesirable behaviors, and increase play with sand and dirt. When many toys are accessible, social contacts are lessened and individual exploration and construction increases.

Case Illustrations: What Play Reveals

The following excerpt is from 7-year-old Brian's fifth play therapy session. A brief family background is described at the end of the excerpt to allow the reader to form his or her own opinion as to the possible meaning of the play. At the beginning of each session, Brian checked the playroom carefully to make sure everything was there.

Brian: (walks over to the shelf and gets the doctor kit). I'll probably play doctor today.

Therapist: You decided that is something you might like to do.

Brian: Yeah. I never did it before, but I'll try.

Therapist: Hmmm. You seem to like to do all these things you didn't do before.

Brian: (sits down on the floor and opens the medical kit). There's a lot of neat stuff in here!

Therapist: You really like all of that.

Brian: Watch this. (takes the syringe out and pretends to give himself an injection very quickly).

Therapist: You did that one real fast.

Brian: I'm always good.

Therapist: You're good at a lot of things.

Brian: I'm good at everything.

Therapist: Uhmmm.

Brian: I'll try to, umm, do something here on your wrist. (goes over to therapist and puts the blood pressure instrument on her wrist). Check you.

Therapist: You want to see how I am.

Brian: Here. Wait. (works the blood pressure instrument). Pretty low.

Therapist: Pretty low, huh? Doesn't sound like it's very good.

Brian: Me, either. (puts the blood pressure toy back in the kit). Just because I'm playing doctor doesn't mean that it's real.

Therapist: Oh, so, even though it seems like it's low, it doesn't mean I'm really sick.

Brian: That's right, because I'm just playing doctor. (gets the stethoscope out of the kit and goes over to the therapist and listens to her heart). Looks like doctors use this thing. Nothin' to it!

Therapist: Nothing to it. Just as easy as can be.

Brian: Yeah . . . kind of. (gets the syringe from the kit again). Here's that thing. A shot! (goes over and gives the therapist an injection). Right here. (shows her the needle). Look at all this! (gives her another injection).

Therapist: So . . . just like that . . . with one hand.

Brian: Yeah, I can do anything with one hand. (puts the syringe back into the kit).

Comments: Brian's family life was chaotic, his father was an alcoholic, he was abused at home, he had few friends, and his academic progress in school was unsatisfactory. Several features of this play excerpt seem to stand out: Brian's reference to being good at everything, his need to point out that what he was playing was not real, and his pretending to doctor the play therapist. Brian seems to be expressing his need to be important and successful. Taking care of the play therapist seems to be an important issue for Brian, and he makes sure she knows he does not intend any ill will. Checking the room at the beginning of each session seems to be an expression of his need for order and predictability in this relationship, unlike the chaos at home and the unpredictability of an alcoholic father. The need to be good at everything is sometimes characteristic of children who grow up in alcoholic families.

Paul is 6 years old. The following excerpt is from his second play therapy session. In the first session, Paul cooked poison, fed it to Batman (bop bag punching toy), and killed him. The reason for referral is described at the end of this excerpt.

Paul: (going to sandbox). He's going to find something he likes someday, ain't he? Do you have another truck? Now stay tuned for Batman (runs over to bop bag, punches bop bag fiercely nine times in face, wrestles him and pushes him down). He's down for a little while. I'm gonna put him on this chair (puts Batman bop bag on a chair). I'm gonna shoot him. I got these many guns. I'm gonna shoot at him (picks up guns and small plastic TV). Ooooo! This can be a different TV.

Therapist: Uh huh.

Paul: (puts TV in the dollhouse) I guess that's Daddy's TV.

Therapist: So he's going to have a special one.

Paul: Yeah (picks up rifle that shoots ping pong balls). Hey where's those round balls? (picks up ping pong ball). I'm gonna shoot him (Batman) for good, ain't I? Ain't I?

Therapist: So you know just what you're going to do. You've got it planned.

Paul: Look! Ready for Batman? Batman's gonna be in big trouble, ain't he? (shoots). I got him down, didn't I?

Therapist: You got him the first shot.

Paul: I'm gonna kill him more (aims, shoots and misses). Hmmm, better try another gun (tries dart pistol). There's another. I got it (shoots to side of bop bag). I missed him, didn't I?

Therapist: It went right past him.

Paul: (shoots again to side of bop bag) It's a hard shot, ain't it?

Therapist: It's hard to hit it from way over there.

Paul: (shoots again and misses) I missed him a bunch, didn't I? (picks up the darts) When I get him, guess what I'm gonna do? I'm gonna tie him up and kill him. I'm gonna cut him up.

Therapist: You're really going to kill him.

Paul: (shoots and misses, then shoots bop bag again) Got him! (runs over, puts bop bag on the floor, head under a chair so that bop bag is horizontal) Supposed to be dead for a little while. You know what I'm gonna do to Batman? Ahhh. (gets rubber knife and cuts the middle of bop bag, then goes to kitchen and looks through the dishes). You know what I'm gonna do?

Therapist: You've got something planned now.

Paul: I'm not gonna poison him. (He cooked poison last session and fed it to Batman.) You know what I am going to do this time. Na. I'm not going to. I'm gonna kill him again. I'm gonna poison him. That's what I was gonna do. Let's see (picks up hand gun, walks over to Batman, aims gun right next to Batman's face and shoots). Ha. Ha. (goes to sandbox, stands in middle and fills bucket with sand) Guess what I'm gonna do?

Therapist: You can tell me what you're going to do.

Paul: Well, I'm gonna put Batman in this (drops bucket, starts sweeping in the sandbox and outside the sandbox). Sweep the blood off. Ha. Ha. Sweep the blood. Batman's gonna be really dead this time 'cuz I'll really kill him.

Therapist: This time you'll make sure you kill him. -

Paul: You're right. This time I'm going to make sure you're gonna get killed.

Therapist: Oh, I'm going to get it too.

Paul: I know. You're Robin.

Therapist: You're going to kill both of us.

Paul: Bet you're right. Hope I don't miss ya (with lilt to voice and big grin).

Therapist: I'm not for shooting (aims way over therapist's head and shoots wall). I know you would like to shoot me. You can shoot Batman (again shoots over therapist's head – it is obvious he does not intend to shoot the therapist).

Paul: Ohhhh. I missed you (shoots again). Ahhhhh, gosh (begins to play with phone). You know who I'm gonna call? Mmm ammm (gets other phone and dials). Yeah, Batman's dead. Hum hum okay (leaves phone and goes across room). Hey, I'm gonna make a little song to wake Batman up, ain't I? (plays xylophone and looks expectantly at Batman). He's almost woke up (walks over to Batman). Chop his neck off, ain't I? (hits Batman) Now he's dead. Now I'm going to play with Dad again, Mr. old Dad (plays in dollhouse and with the scooter truck). Here's his new truck. That's gonna work better. He bought a new television, didn't he?

Therapist: So now they have two televisions.

(later in the session)

Paul: Oh my God, look! They're having a tornado in this area by their home. They better hurry home, right?

Therapist: Tornadoes are dangerous.

Paul: I know. It can blow houses down. One of them's, one of them's in the graveyard. That's the girl (buries doll in sand – therapist can't see doll being buried).

Therapist:	So the girl got left in the graveyard.
Paul:	Uh uh, she's buried.
Therapist:	Oh, she's buried in the graveyard.
Paul:	She does not want . . . she does not want the tornado to get her.
Therapist:	So the tornado can't get her there.
Paul:	The tornado's past. Oooh. Look what happened! (knocks over toys near the dollhouse) God!
Therapist:	The tornado wrecked some things.
Paul:	Yeah, some but it didn't wreck this (points to scooter truck). All the kids have to get in the house fast, lay down and rest.
Therapist:	So they're hoping they'll be safe in the house.
Paul:	And she told her to get in and rest too, while Daddy got the pickup truck over (pulls truck over). Ah, oh. The tornado's out. Guess what. Daddy's gonna be surprised. Guess what. Stay tuned for Batman!
Therapist:	Now it's time for Batman again.
Paul:	(goes over to Batman and attempts to put handcuffs on himself) Uh, oh, they caught me, didn't they?
Therapist:	You got caught by somebody.
Paul:	The police (continues trying to handcuff his hands behind his back).
Therapist:	Oh the police caught you. Hmm.
Paul:	For killing Batman.
Therapist:	So you killed Batman, and then the policeman caught you.
Paul:	Yeah. Batman is alive now. Ouch. No wonder I can't put these on when I have my hands behind my back. Here (brings handcuffs to therapist for aid; therapist fastens them behind his back). Ok, I'm in jail.
Therapist:	So the policeman handcuffed you and took you to jail.
Paul:	I know. First he has to do something. He can't kill nobody. The police surrounded him, and he has to put this (knife) back.
Therapist:	So they fixed him up so he can't kill anyone.
Paul:	Yeah. They have to put the knife back. The Batman's alive. Better get him up (stands Batman up).
Therapist:	So he's okay now.
Paul:	But first wait (moves Batman around). There. Uh oh, I'm out of jail now. Help me (tries to take handcuffs off). Ouch, ouch (handcuffs pinch his wrists).
Therapist:	Sometimes those things pinch.
Paul:	Yeah (takes handcuffs off).
Therapist:	But you got them off.
Paul:	Guess what. I'm the police now. I'm going to get to be a police, didn't I?
Therapist:	So now you're going to be the one with the handcuffs.
Paul:	I'm the police now. I'm Batman and I'll bring you in jail, okay?
Therapist:	You can pretend that someone is doing that and I'll watch.
Paul:	Okay. That. Mr. Policeman is having trouble, ain't he? (trying to hook handcuffs together).
Therapist:	Looks like he's having a hard time getting those on there just right.
Paul:	Oh no, he got it. Now he don't have trouble.
Therapist:	You figured it out.
Paul:	Uh huh, I found the way (hooks handcuffs on pocket).
Therapist:	Hmmm. You found a way to do it.

Comments: Paul's grandfather, to whom he felt very close, died when Paul was 4 years old. Paul missed his grandfather a great deal and grieved over the loss. During the two years following his grandfather's death, Paul focused so much on his grandfather's death that he developed a fear of death, often made references to death, and pretended to talk to his grandfather. At one point, Paul refused to drink water for two months because he overheard a neighbor remark that the water in their town tasted bad. Paul interpreted bad to mean it would kill you. Paul began to act out his anger, and as a first grade student had been sent to the principal's office several times for hitting other children. When Paul started play therapy, he was watching an average of six hours of television per day. During his play therapy sessions, he made frequent references to television. Paul's great ambivalence about death can readily be seen in this episode as he killed Batman and then made a song to wake Batman up. Death is unexpected and so are tornadoes. Paul played out a dramatic scene of a girl being buried in the graveyard but made no references to her being dead. Later Paul gets punished for killing Batman, but then Batman is suddenly alive again and no one can get killed because the weapons are taken away. It seems quite clear that Paul is expressing his fears and trying to come to terms with the permanency of death. That is the essence of the power of play, the opportunity to express even the deepest and most threatening fears or problems within the safety of play, which protects the child from his expressions because he is separated from that which he plays out.

References

Adcock, D., and Segal, M. (1979). *Play and Learning.* Rolling Hills Estates, CA: B. L. Winch.

Allen, J., and Berry, P. (1987). Sand play. *Elementary School Guidance and Counseling* 21:300–306.

Almy, M. A. (1984). Child's right to play. *Childhood Education* 60:350.

Amster, F. (1982). Differential uses of play in treatment of young children. In *Play Therapy: Dynamics of the Process of Counseling with Children,* ed. G. L. Landreth, pp. 33–42. Springfield, IL: Charles C Thomas.

Axline, V. (1969). *Play Therapy.* New York: Ballantine.

_____ (1982). Nondirective play therapy procedures and results. In *Play Therapy: Dynamics of the Process of Counseling with Children,* ed. G. L. Landreth, pp. 120–129. Springfield, IL: Charles C Thomas.

Bergen, D. (1988). *Play as a Medium for Learning and Development.* Portsmouth, NH: Heinemann Educational Books.

Bettelheim, B. (1987a). *A Good Enough Parent.* New York: Vintage.

_____ (1987b). The importance of play. *The Atlantic Monthly* 259:35–46.

Bruner, J. (1986). Play, thought, and language. *Prospects: Quarterly Review of Education* 16:77–83.

Caplan, F., and Caplan, T. (1973). *The Power of Play.* New York: Anchor.

_____ (1983). *The Early Childhood Years.* New York: Grosset & Dunlap.

Cass, J. E. (1973). *Helping Children Grow Through Play.* New York: Schocken.

Coleman, M., and Skeen, P. (1985). Play, games, and sports: their use and misuse. *Childhood Education* 61:192–198.

Comrie, B. (1987). *The World's Major Languages.* New York: Oxford University Press.

Curry, N. E., and Arnaud, S. H. (1984). Play in developmental preschool settings. In *Child's Play: Developmental and Applied,* ed. T. D. Yawkey and A. D. Pellegrini, pp. 273–290. Hillsdale, NJ: Lawrence Erlbaum Associates.

Ellis, M. J. (1984). Play, novelty, and stimulus seeking. In *Child's Play: Developmental and Applied,* ed. T. D. Yawkey and A. D. Pellegrini, pp. 203–218. Hillsdale, NJ: Lawrence Erlbaum.

Erikson, E. H. (1963). *Childhood and Society.* New York: Norton.

———— (1977). *Toys and Reason.* New York: Norton.

Frank, L. (1952). *The Fundamental Needs of the Child.* New York: National Association for Mental Health.

———— (1982). Play in personality development. In *Play Therapy: Dynamics of the Process of Counseling with Children,* ed. G. L. Landreth, pp. 19–31. Springfield, IL: Charles C Thomas.

Freud, A. (1928). *Introduction to the Technic of Child Analysis.* Trans. L. P. Clark. New York: Nervous and Mental Disease Publishing Company, 1927.

Ginott, H. G. (1961). *Group Psychotherapy with Children: The Theory and Practice of Play Therapy.* New York: McGraw-Hill.

———— (1982). A rationale for selecting toys in play therapy. In *Play Therapy: Dynamics of the Process of Counseling with Children,* ed. G. L. Landreth, pp. 145–152. Springfield, IL: Charles C Thomas.

Greenburg, P. (1989). Learning self-esteem and self-discipline through play. *Young Children* 45:28–31.

Guddemi, M. P. (1987). Play/playgrounds/safety. *Dimensions* 16:15–18.

Guerney, L. F. (1984). Play in developmental preschool settings. In *Childs Play: Developmental and Applied,* ed. T. D. Yawkey and A. D. Pellegrini, pp. 273–290. Hillsdale, NJ: Lawrence Erlbaum.

Hartley, H. E., Frank, L. K., and Goldenson, R. M. (1952). *Understanding Children's Play.* New York: Columbia University Press.

Hartup, W. W., and Smothergill, N. L. (1967). *The Young Child.* Washington, DC: The National Association for the Education of Young Children.

Irwin, E. (1983). The diagnostic and therapeutic use of pretend play. In *Handbook of Play Therapy,* ed. C. E. Schaefer and K. J. O'Connor, pp. 148–166. New York: John Wiley & Sons.

Jernberg, A. M. (1983). Therapeutic use of sensory-motor play. In *Handbook of Play Therapy,* ed. C. Schaefer and K. J. O'Connor, pp. 128–147. New York: John Wiley & Sons.

Klein, M. (1949). *The Psycho-Analysis of Children.* 3rd ed. Trans. A. Strachey. London: Hogarth Press, 1931.

———— (1982). The psychoanalytic technique. In *Play Therapy: Dynamics of the Process of Counseling with Children,* ed. G. L. Landreth, pp. 74–91. Springfield, IL: Charles C Thomas.

Landreth, G. L. (1991). *Play Therapy: The Art of the Relationship.* Muncie, IN: Accelerated Development.

Lee, C. (1969). *The Growth and Development of Children.* 2nd ed. New York: Longman Group Limited.

Mann, E., and McDermott, J. F. (1983). Play therapy for victims of child abuse and neglect. In *Handbook of Play Therapy,* ed. C. E. Schaefer and K. J. O'Connor, pp. 283–306. New York: John Wiley & Sons.

Maslow, A. H. (1968). *Toward a Psychology of Being.* New York: D. Van Nostrand.

Millar, S. (1968). *The Psychology of Play*. Baltimore: Penguin Books.

Monighan-Nourot, P., Scales, B., and Van Hoorn, J. (1987). *Looking at Children's Play: A Bridge between Theory and Practice*. New York: Teacher's College Press.

Moustakas, C. (1973). *Children in Play Therapy*. New York: Jason Aronson.

_____ (1981). *Rhythms, Rituals and Relationships*. Detroit, MI: Center for Humanistic Studies.

_____ (1982). Emotional adjustment and the play therapy process. In *Play Therapy: Dynamics of the Process of Counseling with Children*, ed. G. L. Landreth, pp. 217–230. Springfield, IL: Charles C Thomas.

Neumann, E. (1971). *The Elements of Play*. New York: MSS Information Corp.

Newman, B., and Newman, P. (1978). *Infancy and Childhood*. New York: John Wiley & Sons.

Papalia, D., and Olds, S. (1986). *Human Development*. New York: McGraw-Hill.

Piaget, J. (1962). *Play, Dreams and Imitation in Childhood*. New York: Norton.

Reifel, S., and Greenfield, P. M. (1982). Structural development in a symbolic medium: the representational use of block constructions. In *Action and Thought from Sensorimotor Schemes to Symbolic Operations*, ed. G. E. Forman, pp. 203–233. New York: Academic Press.

Rogers, D. L., and Ross, D. D. (1986). Encouraging positive social interaction among young children. *Young Children* 41:12–17.

Rubin, K., Fein, G. G., and Vandenberg, B. (1983). Play. In *Handbook of Child Psychology*, vol. 4, ed. P. H. Mussen, pp. 693–774. New York: John Wiley & Sons.

Rubin, K., and Howe, N. (1985). Toys and play behaviors: an overview. *Topics in Early Childhood Special Education* 5:1–10.

Segal, J., and Segal, Z. (1989). Child's play. *Parents' Magazine* 64:126.

Tegano, D. W., Sawyers, J. K., and Moran, J. D. (1989). Problem finding and solving in play: the teacher's role. *Childhood Education* 66:92–97.

Vinturella, L., and James, R. (1987). Sand play: a therapeutic medium with children. *Elementary School Guidance and Counseling* 21:229–238.

Waelder, R. (1976). Psychoanalytic theory of play. In *The Therapeutic Use of Child's Play*, ed. C. E. Schaefer, pp. 79–93. New York: Jason Aronson.

Weissbourd, B. (1986). The importance of play. *Parents' Magazine* 61:142.

White, R. W. (1960). Competence and the psychosexual stages of development. In *Nebraska Symposium on Motivation*, ed. M. R. Jones, pp. 97–141. Lincoln, NE: University of Nebraska.

4

Play and the Growth of Competence

JoAnn L. Cook and Mary Sinker

Zachary is 4 years old. He and his play therapist are seated side by side at a small table. They are using interlocking blocks to build an elaborately large, very tall tower. As they build, Zachary talks about what he will be when he grows up. He first says that he'd like to be a pediatrician, because then he could give kids shots. As he builds and talks he comments on his building, which is becoming taller and more elaborate. "Look at this! Did you think I'd be able to build something like this? Have you ever seen anything like it? Can you believe that I'm building this?" Continuing to build, and to comment on his tower, he wonders if instead of becoming a doctor, he'd perhaps become an artist, or maybe an architect. Leaning back and observing his construction from a bit of a distance, Zachary makes a final contented comment. "You know, I think I will be an artist-architect. Look at this! This is the best building! You know what I think? I think there are only two people in the whole United States that could make this building: me . . . and God!"

Clearly, Zachary feels a sense of accomplishment, of mastery, and of control through his play as he completes the tallest tower he has ever constructed. According to White (1959), a theme of mastery, power, and "perhaps even a bit of primitive self-assertion" (p. 320) can be viewed in this child's concentration upon those accomplishments that directly result from his own efforts. A capacity to interact effectively with his environment is the motive for sustaining repeated attempts toward mastery in play. White writes, "To the extent that these results are preserved by learning, they build an increased competence in dealing with the environment. The child's play can thus be viewed as serious business, though to him it is merely something that is interesting and fun to do" (p. 321).

Play simultaneously engenders, as well as expresses, the development of competence in interaction with the environment. During the dynamics of play children take in information from the outside world that results in reorganization of information in their frames of reference (Piaget 1962). Thus, play has an important role in the child's cognitive development, with increasing competency in problem solving attained during play and, later, appearing as the adult's ability to suspend reality and deal with hypothetical situations.

Play has been viewed as the main behavior of children, and the role of player is a primary role in childhood (Schaaf and Mulrooney 1989). Through play, children develop social, language, emotional, and motor competencies. When playing with others, the child's play is not only enriched but also enhanced in both the level of play and competency outcomes. Therefore, play has been widely used as a medium to promote growth by various disciplines.

In play there is little distinction between working and playing. In their play, children gain competencies while enjoying the process of learning. Play is best when the challenge and the individual's skill are nearly matched. Csikszentmihalyi's studies (1989, 1990) indicate that playfulness or flow experiences occur in these matched situations. Then, according to Millar (1968), "Perhaps play is best used as an adverb; not as a name of a class of activities, nor as distinguished by the accompanying mood, but to describe how and under what conditions an action is performed" (p. 21). Such behavior is described as playful, rather than play.

Playful children are characterized by spontaneity, creativity, joyfulness, and sense of humor (Lieberman 1965). Further, playful children are noted to be sponta- neous, flexible and adaptive in their responses to their environment. Characteristics of playfulness and adaptability have also been shown to occur with high frequency in children who are behaviorally and emotionally competent and ego resilient (Earls et al. 1987).

Competence through Developmental Play

According to White (1959), children's interactions with the environment are moti- vated by a desire for control and mastery, resulting in competencies in which the child sees himself as the causal agent. It is play that is the intrinsically motivated activity of children, and, indeed, intrinsic motivation is a determining criterion of play (Rubin, Fein, and Vandenberg 1983). Research suggests that evaluation of mastery motivation during infancy is a better predictor of later competence than developmental test scores (Messer et al. 1982, Yarrow et al. 1983).

Play and development of competencies are interrelated. "The idea is that there is a kind of play-competence spiral: learning leads to more sophisticated play, and play provides a kind of mastery that leads to more learning, which leads to more sophisticated play, and so forth" (Kirschenblatt-Gimblett 1979, p. 23). In motor-, object-, social-, socio-dramatic- and language-play, different competencies are evoked.

Motor Play

As children participate in motor play, they develop physical skills that become increasingly refined, offering them confidence and security in the abilities of their own bodies. Infants play with their bodies, initially simply experiencing movement and later learning to control their movements, building the important image of a body self (Zscheye 1976). Motor play progresses from sitting, through crawling, standing, climbing, running, jumping, kicking, throwing, and catching (Sheridan 1977). The hallmark for motor play at all ages is action, and increasing abilities enable the child to participate in age-appropriate games and sports.

Roberts (1980) noted that between the ages of 5 and 12, children are greatly influenced by their peer group. Doing well in sporting activities during this period is particularly important. Pellegrini (1988) found that for popular children, rough and tumble play leads to games with rules, and is positively correlated with measures of social competence. According to Borman and Kurdek (1984), children who engage in playground games of greater complexity tend to see themselves as more socially and physically competent.

Object Play

Object play develops fine motor skills and understanding of the physical properties of the environment. Construction with objects results in increased understanding of spatial relationships. Variation in the stimulus properties of objects such as novelty, complexity, and manipulability increases motivation for the child to interact with them (Johnson et al. 1987). Significant correlations have been demonstrated between task engagement and other mastery behaviors with manipulative toys at the age of 30 months; levels of task engagement were related to developmental test scores (Messer et al. 1987).

Infants use their simple skills to play with one object at a time. As competencies increase, toddlers use many objects in combination. Object play becomes more decentered and more integrated as the child's competencies grow, leading from simple to complex play by the preschool years. Preschoolers gain control of materials and later are able to manipulate as well as predict the outcome of their actions on a material. The development of the ability to control a manipulative material is called "materials mastery" (Zervigon-Hakes 1984, p. 37).

Social Play

Much of the mastery motivation research has focused on motivation to interact with objects. It is a basic assumption that interacting with other persons in an effective manner would also be a strong motivation. The development of the ability to engage in social interactions has been singled out as one of the crucial tasks of infancy and early childhood (Ainsworth et al. 1978, Erikson 1950, Mahler et al. 1975).

Social play in infancy involves play with a significant other. These early interactions have an important role in the formation of the child's self-concept. From the earliest reciprocal games of smiling and cooing, the infant learns the pleasure of social interaction and the responsiveness of the people in his environment.

As the child matures, peers take a larger role in social play. Turn-taking, sharing, and cooperation are social competencies developed through playing with others. Through role playing, children experiment with the roles and rules of society, and begin to appreciate the perspectives of others. Later, games with rules and sports add more structure and a stronger group identity. Social competency and being seen as competent by one's peers and respected adults results in positive self-esteem (Greenberg 1989).

Socio-Dramatic Play and Language Skills

The toddler identifies with others and imitates their actions and routines in his play with representational objects. Toddlers use objects symbolically in play as they begin to represent their experience, and later are able to engage in fantasy and dramatic play in which they create and recreate a world in which they are in control of their experiences. Singer (1973) suggests that by practicing a variety of make-believe selves and roles, the child gradually differentiates himself and sees new options within himself. Symbolic play is also highly correlated with the development of meaningful language (Lowe 1975).

Preschool-age children engage in highly elaborate and extended socio-dramatic play in which they re-create and master difficult life experiences. Such play has been seen as a central process of social-emotional growth; "to play it out" is one of the primary self-healing methods afforded in childhood (Erikson 1950). Language skills are also enhanced through engagement in socio-dramatic play (Garvey 1977). Dansky (1980) has demonstrated that free play promotes development of creative thinking, but this occurs only in children who frequently engage in make-believe play. The ability to fantasize has also been associated with behavioral self-control (Singer 1961).

School-age children distance themselves from frightening or worrying issues by documenting them in staged dramas and stories. Wolfgang (1974) and Pellegrini (1980) have reported a positive relationship between levels of socio-dramatic play and reading and writing ability with story comprehension enhanced through dramatic play activities (Pellegrini and Golda 1982). In a study of active learning, Sylva and colleagues (1980) observed that when playing with another child, the child's play is richer and more sustained.

Mediated Play

In mediated play, the adult serves as a filter between the child and the environment (Yawkey 1982), encouraging, focusing, extending, and reflecting on the child's achievements. This interaction facilitates transmission of emotional and intellectual resources, and enhances the child's social, emotional, and cognitive competencies. Just such interplay is symbolized and occurs between a parent and child during play (Piers and Landau 1980, Pulaski 1970). Sutton-Smith (1974) suggests that parent–infant social play allows passive experience to be transformed to active mastery of social situations. This play provides selection of one element of the content of the child's life for practice with pleasure to mastery, thus avoiding the negative feelings that might be associated with a real-life event. Play, therefore, is an important medium through which parents and other people can actively join a child in his world and contribute to his competence and feeling of self-worth. The most significant factor of adult intervention in play appears to relate to actual adult participation in the play. The adult must be actively involved as a play partner, thus forming an alliance with the child, rather than merely supervising or directing the child's play (Sutton-Smith, 1979).

A performance-competence discrepancy has been theorized (Belsky et al. 1984). Hrncir (1981) describes the difference between children's defined performance and competence, their ideal performance, as attributable to motivational differences. Performance was defined by the most advanced level of spontaneous play, while competence levels were achieved with mediation – verbal and modeled suggestions. Vygotsky (1978) describes a similar construct that he terms "ZPD, the zone of proximal development" (p. 86). The zone of proximal development is defined as the distance between the child's actual independent developmental problem-solving ability and his developmental ability with mediation by adults or more capable peers. This Vygotskian perspective is supported, for example, in the idea that social pretend play (Miller and Garvey 1984) and language skills (Sachs 1980) are derived through social interaction between the child and a play partner. Higher levels of developmental competence have been demonstrated empirically through ZPD research in which the child's development has been facilitated through involvement with more experienced play partners (Ragoff et al. 1984, Wertsch 1979, Wood 1980). Thus, mediated play allows the child to increase skills, resulting in more complex behavior than would have been attained by the child on his own.

Mediated play episodes with a teacher are more complex and twice as long as peer play episodes (Bruner 1980). Adult mediated play yields the most complex levels of play and language as well as sustained involvement (Dunn and Wooding 1977). Persistence in play can lead to the ability to sustain commitment to tasks, which is crucial for success in school. Through mediated play, parents, teachers, and other significant adults can enhance children's development and their ability to perform independently and competently.

The work of Bruner (1983) supports the value of mediated play for assisting child development within a family, social-cultural context. The mediator's role can be performed by parent, teacher, or an older child. According to Bruner, the mediator provides a framework or scaffolding, which includes provision of a stimulating environment, assisting the child in making choices, reflecting on the child's mastery, thus enabling the child to reflect and verbalize his own competence. Through this process, external actions of play become internalized, raising the play from action to symbolic levels, and providing a basis for guiding future actions.

Greenspan and Greenspan (1985) have defined the milestones of emotional development from birth through early childhood, and advocate that children develop emotionally through an "essential partnership" with their parents (1989). They suggest that parents provide consistent child-directed play opportunities, which they term *floor time*. During floor time, adults are directed to reframe problems into challenges that can be mastered through joint parent–child play. These repeated successes together strengthen the parent–child relationship and promote the growth of self-esteem. Through opportunities to express their unique characteristics through play to mastery, children accomplish successively higher emotional developmental markers.

The competencies derived through play mediated by parents and professionals are numerous, and include increased complexity and length of play, cognitive and language growth, social skills and self-esteem. Parent–child mediated play has been shown to maximize interaction with toys when compared to independent toddler or toddler–peer play (Cohen and Tomlinson-Keasey 1968). Children whose mothers provided high levels of elaborative play were more competent on intellectual measures than children whose parents did not provide such play experiences (Fein 1979). Low socioeconomic status children whose teachers mediated their dramatic play increased their socio-dramatic play skills and improved in cognitive performance (Smilansky 1968). In another study of socio-dramatic play, preschool children from a variety of backgrounds participated in three months of "play tutoring" (Levy et al. 1986, p. 133), resulting in enriched socio-dramatic play and increased language competencies. Teachers' facilitation of spontaneous play can encourage development of leadership behaviors (Trawick-Smith 1988). Leadership skills have been linked to children's socio-dramatic play abilities and social competence (Hazen et al. 1984, Smilansky 1968). Five-year-old children provided with imaginative play and self-concept experiences gained in self-concept scores as well as pretend play abilities (Gomez 1983).

Mediation also occurs as children play with peers and siblings, resulting in increased frequency and complexity of play, with social and communication competencies that would not evolve through solitary play. Peers serve as the most common agents in the social play of young children, particularly in the development of social pretense. Factors important to the emergence of social pretend play with peers include familiarity, friendship, and age. Children have been shown to engage in more social pretend play with familiar rather than unfamiliar peers (Doyle et al. 1979). Experiences in child care settings provide opportunities for children to develop stable friendships. Howes (1983) reported that the social play of peer friendship pairs is more complex than the play of dyads who are not friends. Increased clarity of communication and frequency of fantasy play were reported between preschoolers who were friends rather than strangers (Gottman and Parkhurst 1980). A Vygotskian perspective would support that play with an older child would provide a hierarchy of information and strategies to support a younger child's efforts. The literature on sibling interactions suggests that play is facilitated in mixed-age dyads. Dunn and Dale (1984), described sibling pairs composed of toddlers and preschool-age play partners. The dyads were cited as sharing a framework during pretend play involving mediation, negotiation, and joining of efforts through play partnership alliance.

Mediated Play and Children with Disabilities

Children with special needs, perhaps more than any other population, *require* mediation in play. Despite the nature of the disabilities, be they physical, mental, sensory, or emotional, all children with disabilities have in common an impaired ability to fully explore, interact with, and master their environment, depriving them of essential childhood experience (Mogford 1977). The ability to play may itself be impaired (Munoz 1986). While the development of children with special needs is impacted by their specific disability, there is strong evidence that these children's play develops in the same pattern as does the play of normal children (Gallagher 1975, Hill and McCune-Nicholich 1981, Mindes 1982) when corrections for mental age are made (Brooks-Gunn and Lewis 1982). Therefore, assumptions about the growth of competence through play can be confirmed for children with disabilities as well as for those who develop normally.

For the child with disabilities, the mediator serves not only as a play partner, but, in a prescriptive sense, as an enabler. He assists the child's movement; structures the environment to optimize the child's access to sensory, perceptual, and cognitive stimulation; models play; or even leads the child through developmental play sequences and teaches the child *how* to play (Munoz 1986, Newcomer and Morrison 1974, Peck et al. 1978, Yawkey 1982). Parents, professionals, and peers serve as mediators in carrying out prescriptive play with children with disabilities, with a view to improving cognitive, social, and play skills.

Parent–child play interactions are of particular importance to the play and development of children with disabilities (Yawkey 1982), as early social play and later attachment (Blehar et al.1977) are related to developmental attainment (Beckwith et al. 1976, Lewis and Coates 1980). Studies have shown that premature infants receiving compensatory stimulation from parents will catch up to full-term infants more quickly than premature infants who do not receive additional social play (Field et al. 1980). The parents' role during these play sessions is to maintain the arousal level at an optimal level – neither so low as to be boring nor so high as to be overwhelming (Field 1982). (Interestingly, these are the same parameters that define the flow experience as described by Csikszentmihalyi in 1990.) Studies of Down Syndrome infants found that when the infants were able to initiate, maintain, and control the course of parent–child play, they experienced increased positive affect and social competence (Field 1978, Jaffe et al. 1973, MacTurk et al. 1965).

Professionals, including teachers, psychologists, occupational, physical, recreational, and speech therapists, use prescriptive play not only as a way to accomplish developmental goals for children with disabilities (McConkey and Jeffree 1980, Schaaf 1989, Smilansky 1968, Wehman 1977), but also as a way to reflect and measure the growth of competence (Schaaf 1989). Smilansky (1968) demonstrated that play training of socially disadvantaged, at-risk children led to significant improvement in their symbolic play, with links to cognitive and social competencies. Training in pretend play can promote the social competence of mildly handicapped children (Saltz et al. 1977). Roswal (1979) studied the effects of a nine-week developmental play program on exceptional children ages 5–13, and found substantial improvement in the self-concept and motor proficiency of these children. In a study of the leisure abilities and self-concept of preadolescent children with myelomeningocele, Fine (1982) found that subjects who engaged in a six-week therapeutic recreation program showed highly significant improvement in social interactional abilities. Research has supported the view that intervention programs with developmentally delayed children are most beneficial when the children are provided with the opportunity to become effective agents (Brinker and Lewis 1982).

Nonhandicapped peers serve as models and play mediators for children with handicaps, thus enhancing social and play competencies. In a setting where nonhandicapped peers were trained in play intervention methods, significant changes in the play and social behavior of young handicapped children were noted (McHale and Olley 1982). Untrained, nonhandicapped children playing with autistic children were able to elicit increased social responses, and, over the study period, solitary behavior of the autistic children decreased (Lord 1983). Handicapped children, when integrated with nonhandicapped children, engaged in more peer-directed and less teacher-directed behaviors, leading to higher levels of social play (Field et al.1981).

The importance of *playful* mediated play for children with disabilities is stressed by several studies. Li (1983) indicates that in order for acquired play skills to be maintained and generalized, the play experience must be fun and pleasurable. Eyde and Menolascino (1981) urge that prescriptive play should not mean disguising learning tasks and placing still more demands on the handicapped child, but rather should be a joyful, playful experience. Gunn (1975) suggests that imposed constraints and expectations may well turn playtime into worktime. Increased skills and competencies are not the reason for children to play. Rather, they are the result of play (Caldwell 1985).

Mediated Play as Psychotherapy

Play therapy provides opportunity for intervention with children experiencing emotional, social, or behavioral problems through a medium that is child-oriented and pleasurable for the child. The child's natural interest and participation in play provide the therapist a unique process with diagnostic and therapeutic implications. The play experience with the therapist allows the child to express emotions and concerns, to experience mastery and control through play, and to develop coping abilities and insights with which to meet current and future problems and challenges.

Applications of play therapy are many and varied, differing by theoretical orientation. Many play therapists subscribe to an eclectic approach, choosing techniques based on theory, research, and clinical practice with respect to the population and presenting problem being addressed. For example, the goal of mastery through play would be a therapeutic aim for children experiencing a specific anxiety, while use of play experiences to enhance social competency would be targeted for children experiencing problems with social acceptance and self-esteem.

Theory has asserted that young children can learn to improve their ability to cope with feared real-life situations through playing out fear-related mastery themes (Erikson 1950). Mastery-oriented fantasy play has been shown to lead to subsequent reduction in anxiety in a feared situation, during actual contact with a live snake (Parks 1988). Play therapy is frequently provided to enable hospitalized children to increase coping abilities and experience a sense of mastery in an unfamiliar and frightening environment. Such medical play therapy is based on research demonstrating that active mastery of a passively experienced situation through repetition provides opportunity for catharsis and alleviates anxiety and confusion (Clatworthy 1981, Erikson 1958, A. Freud 1952, Letts et al. 1983). Children are introduced to medical equipment and procedures through play, thus alleviating their sense of loss of control, while therapists become sensitized to individual issues and correct misconceptions.

Many school children experience difficulties and setbacks in areas of academic achievement and socialization that negatively affect their self-esteem. Play therapy is used in school settings to assist such children in attaining greater emotional and social competence in the school environment. Play therapy was shown to result in significant gains in self-concept for first grade children retained because of low reading achievement, compared to children in a group who did not receive play therapy (Crow 1989). Group play therapy provides opportunities to gain age appropriate play and social skills and has been shown to increase social acceptance (Marlowe 1978) and self-concept (McDonald 1988). Opportunities to participate in games incorporating developmentally appropriate motor and social skills resulted in attainment of median rank peer acceptance ratings for fifth graders previously rated as social isolates (Marlowe 1978).

Play therapy resulted in enhancement of global self-concept scores of abused children living in a foster care facility, compared to peers not receiving play therapy (McDonald 1988). Participants also exhibited specific self-concept factor score gains in behavior, anxiety, popularity, and happiness. These children, third through eighth graders, had participated in a daily play therapy program involving cooperative and challenge games.

Competence through Playful Work: The Concept of "Flow"

During childhood, the lines between learning, practice, and play are blurred. The acquisition of new skills affecting play further masks the subtle dividing lines. The joy experienced through mastery in play and learning complicates their separation (Zscheye 1976). According to Roeper (1988), the line between play and work with gifted children is almost nonexistent. Furthermore, play, work, and learning are said to serve a single purpose for gifted children, that of mastery.

The concept of mastery motivation proposed by White (1959) influences a range of activities including, but not limited to, play. Csikszentmihalyi's work describes flow experiences, or play at its best, as resulting from situations in which the challenge most nearly matches the individual's level of skill (Chance 1979, Csikszentmihalyi 1975). He defines the degree of playfulness, or flow, as following an inverted U-curve, with low degrees of difficulty resulting in boredom, and high degrees of difficulty resulting in anxiety regarding the person's perceptions of his levels of skills and talents relative to the task being addressed. Thus, play experiences and the pleasure and satisfaction derived from them assist in achieving an optimal level of stimulation and avoidance of boredom, which are individual in relation to developmental skills, abilities and experiences. Flow and play are viewed as freely chosen, enjoyable, and meaningful to the individual (Eyde and Menolascino 1981). Enjoyment of the process predominates, without thought of productivity or extrinsic reward. During these experiences, children "concentrate their attention on a limited stimulus field, forget their personal problems, lose their sense of time and of themselves, feel competent and in control, and have a sense of harmony and union with their surroundings" (Csikszentmihalyi 1975, p. 182).

The qualities of playfulness described by Lieberman (1965) include spontaneity, joyfulness, and sense of humor. Playfulness is significantly related to creativity and divergent thinking (Lieberman 1977). Children who were viewed as less playful during preschool years later described themselves as unadventurous and inactive compared to their more playful preschool peers, who later described themselves as more assertive and independent (Hutt and Bhavnani 1972). Studies of resilient children cite characteristics of increased divergent or creative thinking (Guilford 1950, Wallach and Kogan 1965), with intellectual strengths and sense of humor, which were related to school and social competency (Masten 1982). Earls and colleagues (1987) studied 3-year-olds who exemplified above-average competence, coping skills, and resiliency. Strong correlations in play characteristics were high initiation, intense involvement, and clear thematic content. The children's strong capacity to engage actively in play was compared to an adult's capacity for work.

Advocates of play and child development have proposed the inclusion of play in elementary school educational curricula requirements, following a play-based preschool experience. Greenberg (1990) advocates a play-based curriculum for all preschool children. She stresses that learning through mastery of challenges in play would facilitate meaningful learning experiences and enhance children's self-esteem. Elkind (1987) defends the continuing role of play for children entering elementary school as the primary means of children's development of feelings of industry and competence, and as the major childhood defense against feelings of helplessness. He differentiates the function of play as "child's work" from work in the academic or traditional sense. Kline (1988) and Block (1984) suggest applications of the concepts of flow and mastery learning for making elementary school activities more play-like. Block proposes that traditional academic requirements are perceived as work-like by students and undermine their development of self-social competence and determination. He asserts that the addition of a play-like dimension to classroom activities would allow students a greater sense of control in their academic outcome by providing choices in methods of learning and mastery.

Conclusion: Developmental Play Results in Competence and Mediation Enhances Outcome

Unlike most living organisms who are ready to function in their society soon after birth, humans have a protracted childhood whose purpose is to afford time to develop into competent adults, capable of dealing with the complexities of life. Children arrive at adult levels of competence through childhood developmental experiences exemplified by play. Through play, children develop cognitive, social, emotional, and motor competencies. In play, there is little differentiation between working and playing, and a child fully engrossed in play is a child engaged at an optimal level of arousal, or flow. Children's playful interactions with the environment are intrinsically motivated by a desire to master the task at hand. The product of this mastery-motivated play is competence. Whether this competence is an advanced motor skill, a new level of understanding, a heightened emotional state, or increased social skills, self-esteem is positively affected. The child comes to believe in his own powers and abilities.

There is strong evidence that play with another person—mediated play—yields not only higher-level play but also increased levels of competence. Mediated play serves an important function in the play and development of children with disabilities, in psychotherapy, and in educational settings.

References

Ainsworth, M., Blehar, M., Waters, E., and Wall, S. (1978). *Patterns of Attachment: A Psychological Study of the Strange Situation.* Hillsdale, NJ: Lawrence Erlbaum.
Beckwith, L., Cohen, S., Kopp, C., et al. (1976). Caregiver–infant interaction and early cognitive development in preterm infants. *Child Development* 47:579–587.
Belsky, J., Garduque, L., and Hrncir, E. (1984). Assessing performance, competence, and

executive capacity in infant play: relations to home environment and security of attachment. *Developmental Psychology* 20:406–417.

Blehar, M., Lieberman, A., and Ainsworth, M. (1977). Early face-to-face interaction and its relation to later infant–mother attachment. *Child Development* 48:182–194.

Block, J. (1984). Making school learning activities more playlike: flow and mastery learning. *The Elementary School Journal* 85:65–75.

Block, M., and Pellegrini, A., eds. (1989). *The Ecological Context of Children's Play.* Norwood, NJ: Ablex Publishing.

Borman, K., and Kurdek, L. (1984). *Children's game complexity as a predictor of later perceived self-competence and occupational interest.* Paper presented at the annual meeting of The American Sociological Association, San Antonio, TX.

Brinker, R., and Lewis, M. (1982). Discovering the competent handicapped infant: a process approach to assessment and intervention. *Topics in Early Childhood Special Education* 2:121–151.

Brooks-Gunn, J., and Lewis, M. (1982). Development of play behavior in handicapped and normal infants. *Topics in Early Childhood Special Education* 2:14–27.

Bruner, J. (1980). *Under Five in Britain.* Ypsilanti, MI: High/Scope Press.

⸻ (1983). *Child's Talk.* New York: Norton.

Caldwell, B. (1985). Parent–child play: a playful evaluation. In *Play Interactions,* ed. C. C. Brown and A. W. Gottfried, pp. 167–178. Skillman, NJ: Johnson & Johnson Baby Products Co.

Chance, P. (1979). *Learning Through Play.* New York: Gardner Press.

Clatworthy, S. (1981). Therapeutic play: effects on hospitalized children. *Children's Health Care* 9:108–113.

Cohen, N., and Tomlinson-Keasy, C. (1968). The effects of peers and mothers on toddler's play. *Child Development* 51:921–924.

Crow, J. (1989). Play therapy with low achievers in reading. *Dissertation Abstracts International* 50/09A:2789.

Csikszentmihalyi, M. (1975). *Beyond Boredom and Anxiety.* San Francisco: Jossey–Bass.

⸻ (1989). Optimal experience in work and leisure. *Journal of Personality and Social Psychology* 56:815–822.

⸻ (1990). *Flow: The Psychology of Optimal Experience.* New York: Harper & Row.

Csikszentmihalyi, M., and Csikszentmihalyi, I., eds. (1988). *Optimal Experience: Psychological Studies in the Flow of Consciousness.* New York: Cambridge University Press.

Dansky, J. (1980). Make-believe: a mediator of the relationship between play and creativity. *Child Development* 51:576–579.

Doyle, A., Connolly, J., and Rivest, C. (1979). The effect of playmate familiarity on the social interactions of young children. *Child Development* 51:217–223.

Dunn, J., and Dale, N. (1984). I a daddy: two-year-olds collaboration in joint pretend with sibling and with mother. In *Symbolic Play,* ed. I. Bretherton, pp. 131–158. New York: Academic.

Dunn, J., and Wooding, C. (1977). Play in the home and its implications for learning. In *Biology of Play,* ed. B. Tizard and D. Harvey, pp. 45–58. London: Heinemann.

Earls, F., Beardslee, W., and Garrison, W. (1987). Correlates and predictors of competence in young children. In *The Invulnerable Child,* ed. E. J. Anthony and B. J. Cohler, pp. 70–83. New York: Guilford Press.

Elkind, D. (1987). *Miseducation: Preschoolers at Risk.* New York: Alfred A. Knopf.

Erikson, E. (1950). *Childhood and Society.* New York: Norton.

Erikson, F. (1958). Play interview for four-year-old hospitalized children. *Monograph of the Society for Research in Child Development* 23: Serial No. 69.

Eyde, D., and Menolascino, G. (1981). Prescriptive play as a prelude to maximizing personality growth among severely handicapped. *Viewpoints in Teaching and Learning* 55:74–81.

Fein, G. (1979). In *Learning through Play,* ed. P. Chance. Skillman, NJ: Johnson & Johnson Baby Products Co.

Field, T. (1978). The three R's of infant–adult interactions: rhythms, repertoires and responsivity. *Journal of Pediatric Psychology* 3:131–136.

_____ (1982). Affective and physiological changes during manipulated interactions of high-risk infants. In *Emotion and Early Interaction,* ed. T. Field and A. Fogel. Hillsdale, NJ: Lawrence Erlbaum.

Field, T., Roseman, S., deStefano, L., and Koewler, J. (1981). Play behaviors of handicapped preschool children in the presence and absence of nonhandicapped peers. *Journal of Applied Developmental Psychology* 2:49–58.

Field, T., Widmayer, S., Stringer, S., and Ignatoff, E. (1980). Black mothers and their preterm infants: an intervention and developmental follow-up. *Child Development* 51:426–436.

Fine, A. (1982). A multidimensional therapeutic recreation program and its relationship to leisure abilities and self-concept of preadolescents and adolescents with myelomeningocele. *Dissertation Abstracts International* 43/05–A:1683.

Freud, A. (1952). The role of bodily illness in the mental life of children. *Psychoanalytic Study of the Child* 8:69–81. New York: International Universities Press.

Gallagher, J., ed. (1975). *The Application of Child Development Research to Exceptional Children.* Reston, VA: Council for Exceptional Children.

Garvey, C. (1977). *Play.* Cambridge, MA: Harvard University Press.

Gomez, R. (1983). An investigation of the effects of types of imaginative play and self-concept on pretend play and self-concept enhancement among five-year-old Spanish-speaking children. *Dissertation Abstracts International* 44/01–A:66.

Gottman, J., and Parkhurst, J. (1980). A developmental theory of friendship and acquaintanceship processes. In *Minnesota Symposium on Child Psychology,* ed. A. Collins. Hillside, NJ: Lawrence Erlbaum.

Greenberg, P. (1989). Learning self-esteem and self-discipline through play. *Young Children* 44:28–31.

_____ (1990). Why not academic preschool? *Young Children* 45:70–80.

Greenspan, S., and Greenspan, N. (1985). *First Feelings: Milestones in the Emotional Development of Your Baby and Child.* New York: Viking Press.

_____ (1989). *The Essential Partnership: How Parents and Children Can Meet the Emotional Challenges of Infancy and Childhood.* New York: Viking.

Guilford, J. (1950). Creativity. *American Psychologist* 14:469–479.

Gunn, S. (1975). Play as occupation: implications for the handicapped. *American Journal of Occupational Therapy* 29:222–245.

Hazen, N., Black, B., and Fleming-Johnson, F. (1984). Social acceptance: strategies children use and how teachers can help learn them. *Young Children* 39:26–36.

Hill, P., and McCune-Nicholich, L. (1981). Pretend play and patterns of cognition in Down's Syndrome children. *Child Development* 52:611–617.

Howes, K. (1983). Patterns of friendship. *Child Development* 43:1041–1053.

Hrncir, E. (1981). Assessing performance, competence and motivation in infant play: relations between 12 and 18 months. *Dissertation Abstracts International* 42/10–A:4276.

Hutt, C., and Bhavnani, R. (1972). Predictions from play. In *Play,* ed. J. Bruner, A. Jolly, and K. Sylva. New York: Penguin.

Jaffe, J., Stern, D., and Peery, J. (1973). "Conversational" coupling of gaze behavior in prelinguistic human development. *Journal of Psycholinguistic Research* 2:321–329.

Johnson, J., Christie, J., and Yawkey, T. (1987). *Play and Early Childhood Development.* Glenview, IL: Scott, Foresman & Co.

Kirschenblatt-Gimblett, B. (1979). What is good play? In *Learning Through Play,* ed. P. Chance, pp. 18–24. New York: Gardner Press, Inc.

Kline, P. (1988). *The Everyday Genius: Restoring Children's Natural Joy of Learning–and Yours Too.* Arlington, VA: Great Ocean Publishers.

Letts, M., Stevens, L., Coleman, J., and Kettner, R. (1983). Puppetry and doll play as an adjunct to pediatric orthopedics. *Journal of Pediatric Orthopedics* 3:605–609.

Levy, A., Schaefer, L., and Phelps, P. (1986). Increasing preschool effectiveness: enhancing the language abilities of 3- and 4-year-old children through planned sociodramatic play. *Early Childhood Research Quarterly* 1:133–140.

Lewis, M., and Coates, D. (1980). Mother–infant interaction and cognitive development in twelve-week-old infants. *Infant Behavior and Development* 3:95–106.

Li, A. (1983). Pleasurable aspects of play in enhancing young handicapped children's relationships with parents and peers. *Journal of the Division of Early Childhood* 7:87–92.

Lieberman, J. (1965). Playfulness and divergent thinking: an investigation of their relationship at the kindergarten level. *Journal of Genetic Psychology* 107:219–224.

—— (1977). *Playfulness: Its Relationship to Imagination and Creativity.* New York: Academic Press.

Lord, C. (1983). Peer interaction of autistic children. In *Advances in Applied Developmental Psychology,* ed. F. J. Morrison, C. Lord, and D. P. Keatiny. New York: Academic Press.

Lowe, M. (1975). Trends in the development of representational play in infants from one to three years–an observational study. *Journal of Child Psychology and Psychiatry* 16:33–47.

MacTurk, R., Hunter, F., McCarthy, M., et al. (1965). Social mastery motivation in Down Syndrome and nondelayed infants. *Topics in Early Childhood Special Education* 4:93–109.

Mahler, M., Pine, F., and Bergman, A. (1975). *The Psychological Birth of the Human Infant: Symbiosis and Individuation.* New York: Basic Books.

Marlowe, M. (1978). The games analysis intervention: a procedure to increase the peer acceptance and social adjustment of socially isolated children. *Dissertation Abstracts International* 39/10–A:6068.

Masten, A. (1982). Humor and creative thinking in stress-resistant children. *Dissertation Abstracts International* 42:3737B.

McConkey, R., and Jeffree, D. (1980). Developing children's play. *Special Education: Forward Trends* 7:21–23.

McDonald, R. (1988). The effect of cooperative, noncompetitive, initiative and challenge games as a treatment to enhance the self-concept of abused children. *Dissertation Abstracts International* 49/06–A:1576.

McHale, S., and Olley, J. (1982). Using play to facilitate the social development of handicapped children. *Topics in Early Childhood Special Education* 2:76–86.

Messer, D., Rachford, D., McCarthy, M., and Yarrow, L. (1987). Assessment of mastery behavior at 30 months: analysis of task-directed activities. *Developmental Psychology* 523:771–781.

Messer, D., Yarrow, L., and Vietze, P. (1982). *Mastery in Infancy and Early Childhood*. Paper presented at the 90th annual convention of the American Psychological Association, Washington, DC, August.

Millar, S. (1968). *The Psychology of Play*. Baltimore: Penguin Books.

Miller, P., and Garvey, C. (1984). Mother–baby role play. In *Symbolic Play*, ed. I. Bretherton, pp. 101–130. New York: Academic Press.

Mindes, G. (1982). Social and cognitive aspects of play in young handicapped children. *Topics in Early Childhood Special Education* 2:39–52.

Mogford, K. (1977). The play of handicapped children. In *The Biology of Play*, ed. B. Tizard and D. Harvey, pp. 170–184. London: Heinemann.

Muñoz, J. (1986). The significance of fostering play development in handicapped children. In *Play, A Skill For Life*. An American Occupational Therapy Association Monograph, pp. 1–12. Rockville, MD: American Occupational Therapy Association.

Newcomer, B., and Morrison, T. (1974). Play therapy with institutionalized mentally retarded children. *American Journal of Mental Deficiency* 78:727–733.

Parks, J. (1988). Play and anxiety reduction in fearful preschool children. *Dissertation Abstracts International* 50/10-B:4780.

Peck, C., Cooke, T., Apolloni, T., and Raver, S. (1978). Teaching retarded preschoolers to imitate free play behavior of nonretarded classmates: trained and generalized effects. *Journal of Special Education* 12:195–207.

Pellegrini, A. (1980). The relationship between kindergartners' play and achievement in prereading, language and writing. *Psychology in the Schools* 17:530–555.

_____ (1988). Elementary-school children's rough-and-tumble play and social competence. *Developmental Psychology* 24:802–806.

Pellegrini, A., and Golda, L. (1982). The effects of thematic fantasy play training on the development of children's story comprehension. *American Educational Research Journal* 19:443–452.

Piaget, J. (1952). *Origins of Intelligence in Children*. New York: International Universities Press.

_____ (1962). *Play, Dreams and Imitation in Childhood*. London: Routledge & Kegan Paul, Ltd.

Piers, M., and Landau, G. (1980). *The Gift of Play*. New York: Walker and Company.

Pulaski, M. (1970). Play as a function of toy structure and fantasy predisposition. *Child Development* 41:531–537.

Rogoff, B., Malkin, C., and Gilbride, L. (1984). Interaction with babies as guidance in development. In *Children's Learning in the Zone of Proximal Development*, ed. B. Rogoff and J. Wertsch, pp. 31–44. San Francisco: Jossey-Bass.

Roberts, G. (1980). Children in competition: a theoretical perspective and recommendations for practice. *Motor Skills: Theory Into Practice* 4:37–50.

Roeper, A. (1988). Play and gifted children. In *Play as a Medium for Learning and Development: A Handbook of Theory and Practice*, ed. D. Bergen, pp. 163–165. Portsmouth, NH: Heinemann Educational Books.

Roswal, G. (1979). The effects of a children's developmental play program on the self-concept, risk-taking, and motor proficiency of exceptional children. *Dissertation Abstracts International*, 40/06-A:3189.

Rubin, K., Fein, G., and Vandenberg, B. (1983). Play. In *Handbook of Child Psychology*, vol. 4, ed. P. Mussen, pp. 693–774. 4th Ed. New York: John Wiley & Sons.

Sachs, J. (1980). The role of adult–child play in language development. In *Children's Play*, ed. K. Rubin, pp. 33–48. San Francisco: Jossey-Bass.

Saltz, E., Dixon, D., and Johnson, J. (1977). Training disadvantaged preschoolers on various fantasy activities: effects on cognitive functioning and impulse control. *Child Development* 48:367–380.

Schaaf, R. (1989). Play behavior and occupational therapy. *American Journal of Occupational Therapy* 44:68–77.

Schaaf, R., and Mulrooney, L. (1989). Occupational therapy in early intervention: a family-centered approach. *American Journal of Occupational Therapy* 43:745–754.

Sheridan, M. (1977). *Spontaneous Play in Early Childhood: from Birth to Six Years.* Windsor, England: NFER Publishing Company Ltd.

Singer, J. (1961). Imagination and waiting ability in young children. *Journal of Personality* 29:396–413.

_____ (1973). *The Child's World of Make Believe.* New York: Academic Press.

Smilansky, S. (1968). *The Effects of Sociodramatic Play on Disadvantaged Preschool Children.* New York: John Wiley & Sons.

Sutton-Smith, B. (1974). *How to Play with Your Children (and When Not To).* New York: Hawthorne/Dutton.

_____ (1979). In *Learning Through Play,* ed. P. Chance. Skillman, NJ: Johnson & Johnson Baby Products Co.

Sylva, K., Roy, C., and Painter, M. (1980). *Childwatching at Playgroup and Nursery School.* London: Blackwells.

Trawick-Smith, J. (1988). "Let's say you're the baby, OK?" Play leadership and following behavior of young children. *Young Children,* July, pp. 51–59.

Vygotsky, L. (1978). *Mind in Society: The Development of Higher Mental Processes.* Cambridge, MA: Harvard University Press.

Wallach, M., and Kogan, N. (1965). *Modes of Thinking in Young Children: A Study of the Creativity-Intelligence Distinction.* New York: Holt, Rinehart, & Winston.

Wehman, P. (1977). *Helping the Mentally Retarded Acquire Play Skills.* Springfield, IL: Charles C Thomas.

Wertsch, J. (1979). From social interaction to higher psychological processes. *Human Development* 22:1–22.

White, R. (1959). Motivation reconsidered: the concept of competence. *Psychological Review* 66:297–333.

Wolfgang, C. (1974). An exploration of the relationship between the cognitive area of reading and selected developmental aspects of children's play. *Psychology in the Schools* 11:338–343.

Wood, D. (1980). *Teaching the Young Child: Some Relations Between Social Interaction, Language and Thought.* New York: Norton.

Yarrow, L., McQuiston, S., MacTurk, R., et al. (1983). The assessment of mastery motivation during the first year of life. *Developmental Psychology* 19:159–171.

Yawkey, T. (1982). Effect of parents' play routines on imaginative play in their developmentally delayed preschoolers. *Topics in Early Childhood Special Education* 2:66–75.

Yawkey, T., and Pellegrini, A., eds. (1984). *Child's Play: Developmental and Applied.* Hillsdale, NJ: Lawrence Erlbaum.

Zervigon-Hakes, A. (1984). Materials mastery and symbolic development in construction play: stages in development. *Early Childhood Development and Care* 17:37–48.

Zscheye, R. (1976). The interaction between play and self-concept in young children. (Doctoral dissertation; University of California, Berkeley, 1976). *Dissertation Abstracts International* 77:37/09-B:4767.

5

Creative Problem Solving

Janet K. Sawyers and Diane M. Horm-Wingerd

It has long been assumed that play and creativity are linked, especially in young children. It has also been assumed that both play and creativity have a positive impact on problem solving. During the past 20 years, researchers have worked to understand each construct and the interrelationships between them.

The constructs of play, creativity, and problem solving, as well as their interrelationships, are the topic of this chapter. As with most topics of contemporary research, there are areas of common agreement and areas of inconclusive findings. This chapter reviews the well-documented and inconclusive findings related to play, creativity, and problem solving. One theme that emerges is that while the constructs and their interrelationships seem intuitively obvious and straightforward, research has shown these constructs to be complex and often elusive. While this state of affairs can be frustrating, it calls for creative problem solving by researchers as they attempt to gather new information, and by practitioners as they use the findings to guide their practice with young children.

Play, Problem Solving, and Creativity

As Vandenberg (1980) noted in his article, "Play, Problem-solving and Creativity," play and creativity have been linked both theoretically and empirically. An understanding of the relationship is tied in part to the ways in which both creative problem solving and play have been defined and measured. It is commonly acknowledged that both constructs are difficult to define and measure adequately. The following review of the theoretical positions and related empirical findings focuses on creativity and play in the young child.

Creativity

The difficulty in defining and measuring creativity lies in part in its multidimensionality. Over time it has been conceptualized as a personality trait, a process, and a product. Current models of creativity incorporate all of these perspectives (e.g.,

Amabile 1983) in the recognition that creative thinking is a dynamic process dependent upon both personality and environmental variables.

Knowledge, Expertise, and Talent

The contribution of knowledge or expertise to creative problem solving has received a great deal of attention. Domain-relevant skills, according to Amabile (1983), include factual knowledge, special talents, technical skills that are dependent upon intelligence, and inborn talents that are developed through education and experience. Domain relevant skills are thought to contribute to creative problem solving by (1) mechanizing many of the needed skills/knowledge, (2) decreasing errors, (3) freeing up the individual's attention to deal with aspects of the problem that cannot be routinized, and (4) increasing the likelihood that any given concept will cue memory of related concepts (Flavell 1985). Theoretically, the more domain-relevant skills one has, the greater the number of potential associations and thus the greater the chance of creative problem solving (Amabile 1983). Creative problem solving has also been characterized as a result of "breaking the rules." From this perspective, the contribution of formal education or training would be knowledge of the rules. For example, a "funny face" is humorous to an infant only if he recognizes that the funny face deviates from the typical facial expression.

Qualitative and quantitative differences in the knowledge and expertise of adults and children have led some theorists to conclude that creativity is not possible in childhood. Areas of expertise at the level of creative problem solving, even in adulthood, are thought to be limited. That is, it is highly unlikely that a creative artist would also be a creative scientist, or vice versa.

Although intelligence and talent are necessary components in creative problem solving, domain-relevant skills alone are not sufficient. Sternberg (1985) reports that it is informal or "tacit" knowledge, not formal knowledge learned in school, that is most often mentioned by successful individuals as contributing to their problem-solving skills. Sternberg, among others, has concluded that research evidence indicates such informal knowledge is not significantly related to IQ.

Evidence from retrospective interviews with creative individuals suggests that the role formal knowledge or training plays in the expression of creative thinking may vary with the domain. For example, a child prodigy in dance, music, and art is far more common than a prodigy in mathematics or science (John-Steiner 1985). Regardless of domain however, these same individuals reported their initial exposure to the domain included a period of "informal" exploration before formal instruction was initiated.

Although creativity is a multifaceted concept, the focus of this chapter is on problem solving in which the task is open ended. When trying to understand this process, it is helpful to consider Guilford's (1956) differentiation between convergent and divergent thought. Problems requiring convergent thought have one correct solution. Problems requiring divergent thought call for the generation of many solutions, a few of which may be novel, or of high quality.

Divergent Thinking Skills

Personality traits, dispositions, cognitive and working styles of the creative person as well as the concepts identified as the stages or processes involved in creative problem solving are subsumed in Amabile's (1983) conceptualization of creativity-relevant skills. These skills are not typically included in a formal education.

Of these creativity-relevant skills, ideational fluency has been cited by numerous theorists as the essential component in the process of creative problem solving (Guilford 1956, 1967, Mednick 1962, Wallach and Kogan 1965). These theorists contend that there is a relationship between the quantity of response and its quality, such that the generation of many potential solutions leads to the production of a few highly original solutions (i.e., statistically unusual and of high quality). The original responses, according to Mednick (1962) are more likely to emerge at the end of the response sequence. Research findings generally support the above-mentioned formulation of the creative process.

Most empirical studies of creativity have used measures based on ideational fluency (Barron and Harrington 1981). Ideational fluency measures typically used include pattern meanings, instances, and uses tasks. A pattern meanings task requires that the subject tell all the things a particular pattern might be. Subjects name all the things they can think of that are red, or that are round, and so forth, in the instances task. On the uses task, the subject is asked to tell all the uses for an object (e.g., a box). The construct validity of these ideational fluency measures has been criticized, particularly the practice of focusing on the quantity of responses rather than the quality.

Difficulties encountered in defining and measuring creativity in adults are even more problematic with young children. Quantitative and qualitative differences between adults and children are such that children cannot be expected to produce something original or valuable in an adult sense. Individual and age differences in the expression of creative problem solving make the selection of a criterion measure of creativity extremely difficult.

One approach to the criterion problem has been to attempt to demonstrate that what we can measure as creativity in children is predictive of adult accomplishment. Therefore, some researchers have attempted to move closer to the examination of real-world creativity in children and young adults by using self-report inventories of hobbies and extracurricular activities (Milgram and Milgram 1976), and/or stringent solution standard laboratory tasks as criterion measures for the lenient solution standard predictor measures (Milgram and Arad 1981, Moran et al. 1985). Findings from one study indicate that this procedure is less than satisfactory. Stringent solution tasks were found to be more highly related to IQ than to ideational fluency in both a preschool and a college sample (Sawyers and Moran 1985). Still other researchers have used "real-world" problem tasks rather than pattern meanings, instances, and uses tasks to differentiate creative from noncreative individuals (Crutchfield and Covington 1965).

Kogan (1983) stated that

> where preschool children are the subjects of one's research, for example, it is dubious whether any criterion (e.g., art products, teacher ratings, story construction) represents a "truer" index of creativity than the divergent task performance itself. Beginning with the primary school years, the predictor-criterion framework becomes more viable, whether applied to concurrent relationships or longitudinal data extending from childhood through adolescence and beyond. Nevertheless, such school-age criteria are intermediate, and their validity with respect to ultimate creativity criteria of adulthood remains an open question. Regardless of subject age, however, ideational fluency and other divergent thinking indices represent modes of thought and, hence can legitimately be studied as such within a developmental and construct validation framework. [p. 635]

In regard to the developmental issue, Ward (1974) recommends that we give up the notion of predicting adult accomplishment, and accept what we can measure in young children as creativity. He further recommends that we take a "pluralistic assessment strategy" by identifying characteristics thought to be important in childhood creative thinking (e.g., divergent thinking, playfulness, openness to experience).

Findings from studies with young children (Moran et al. 1983) indicate creativity as measured by ideational fluency tasks can be measured in preschool children as distinct from intelligence. It has also been demonstrated that the Guilford-Mednick conceptualization of original thinking is applicable to preschool as well as to older children and adults. Moore and Sawyers (1987) and Sawyers and Mehrotra (1989) conclude that creative potential as measured by ideational fluency tasks is relatively stable. Children originally tested at age 4 were retested at ages 7 or 8 and again at 10 or 11. Correlations among the scores at the three testings ranged from 0.45 to 0.57.

Building on their research based on the Guilford-Mednick model and the work of others, Sawyers and colleagues (1990) have conceptualized creativity as the interpersonal and intrapersonal process by means of which original, high quality, and genuinely significant products are developed. Within this conceptualization, a developmental progression in creativity-relevant skills is proposed. For young children, the criterion is originality; for older children, the component of quality (based on self-evaluation) is added; and for adults, the criterion also includes significance based on societal evaluation. Similar to Hennessey and Amabile (1987), their developmental model views creativity as dynamic. From this perspective, creativity is viewed as dependent upon both temporary states and enduring traits. Whether the creative potential of the young child will be realized is determined by the interaction of the major factors of expertise and knowledge, creativity-relevant skills, and the environment.

Context for Creativity

A host of physical and social factors thought to facilitate or inhibit the expression of creativity has been proposed and investigated. For example, features of toys and materials thought to facilitate or inhibit creative expression have been investigated. The environments of cultures, schools, and families have been compared in regard to the relative importance placed on creativity and adherence to traditional norms. The third component of Amabile's (1983) model of creativity focuses on aspects of the social environment that impact on an individual's intrinsic motivation to engage in creative problem solving. In a review of the literature on the influence of the environment on creativity, Hennessey and Amabile (1987) conclude that we know a great deal more about what inhibits creativity than what facilitates it.

Play

The difficulties in defining and measuring play parallel those identified for creativity. Play behavior is expressed in many ways due to individual and age differences. Play behavior is also influenced by the environment. A major difference between the study of play and the study of creativity lies in the age groups studied. Most of the research on creativity has been with older children and adults, whereas most of the research on play has been with young children. Longitudinal studies in both areas are sparse. Thus, we can only speculate about how creativity and play observed in early childhood are expressed in adulthood.

An understanding of play has been approached from numerous perspectives, some of which are complementary and some in direct opposition. Rubin and colleagues (1983), in a review of the various approaches to the definition of play, suggested that most of the approaches can be incorporated in the view of play as "a behavioral disposition that occurs in describable and reproducible context and is manifested in a variety of observable behaviors" (p. 698). According to these authors, three dimensions must be kept in mind when defining play: (1) the disposition, feeling, or motivation; (2) the types of behaviors that are involved; and (3) the environment in which play occurs.

Dispositions of Play

Similarities between play and creativity can be seen in the six criteria for defining the dispositional characteristics of play outlined by Rubin and colleagues (1983). According to these authors, play is (1) intrinsically motivated; (2) focused on the means rather than the ends; (3) dominated by the player, not by the play stimulus as in exploration; (4) nonliteral but carried out "as if" it were real; (5) relatively free of externally imposed rules; and (6) active involvement. These features of play are drawn from different theoretical perspectives and serve to clarify the dispositions that define play. However, it is important to note that there is much variability in the extent to which the six dispositions are embraced by play scholars.

Play Behaviors

As suggested above, play is further defined by the types of behaviors involved. Some of the behavioral topologies are developmental in scope. One example is Piaget's (1962) classifications of practice play, symbolic play and games with rules. Another by Parten (1932), classifies play according to the type of social interaction involved: solitary–child plays alone; onlooker–child watches others play; parallel–child plays near another child; associative–common but unorganized activity between children; and cooperative–children cooperate to construct something, produce dramas, or play games. Another framework for categorizing types of children's play is an adaptation of Piaget's practice play category. In this framework, functional play is the lowest level of practice play in which children repeat simple muscular movements or utterances. The repetitive action provides practice and allows for exploration. Constructive play is observed when children use play materials like blocks, art materials, or clay to create something. A problem noted with the use of these classification systems is that some of the behaviors can occur in a nonplayful manner. Therefore, to have a complete understanding of play, one must consider the dispositions along with the behaviors.

However, as Curry and Arnaud (1984) caution, not all play is good play. Similarly, Nahme-Huang and colleagues (1977) have suggested that some types of play training and experience may not be appropriate for all children. For example, the benefits of symbolic play for children with an identified behavior disorder associated with the inability to distinguish reality from fantasy would appear questionable. Currently, we do not know the normative, let alone the optimal level, for different types of play behaviors at different ages. It is noteworthy that of all the types of play behavior, symbolic play has received the most attention of researchers. This type of play occurs frequently in the preschool years. Although engagement in play is often considered indicative of a positive emotional state and healthy development, cognitive theorists and researchers have given surprisingly little attention to the value of play for emotional development.

Play Environment

The impact of various aspects of the environment or context on play has been the focus of many research studies. Rubin and colleagues (1983) summarized the contextual components found to be important. They include:

> (1) an array of familiar peers, toys, or other materials likely to engage children's interest; (2) an agreement between adults and children, expressed in word, gesture, or established by convention, that the children are free to choose from the array whatever they wish to do

within whatever limits are required by the setting or the study; (3) adult behavior that is minimally intrusive or directive; (4) a friendly atmosphere designed to make children feel comfortable and safe; and (5) scheduling that reduces the likelihood of the children being tired, hungry, ill, or experiencing other types of bodily stress. [p. 701]

A sampling of findings highlights the important role of the various aspects of the environment in encouraging differing types of play. Relative to the social environment, research shows that children play more and at higher levels when in the company of a familiar peer than when alone or with an unfamiliar peer (Rubin et al. 1983). Singer (1973) has found that children who come from homes offering privacy are more imaginative in their play than children with little privacy. Paints, crayons, and scissors elicit nonsocial constructive play, while dress-up clothes encourage social or group pretend play (Rubin 1977a, 1977b). Indoor play is typically constructive, whereas outdoor play is most often imaginative (Henninger 1985). It is clear that a variety of physical and social factors in the environment interact in their impact on children's play.

Play and Creativity Link

Play in relation to creativity has been examined as a related or causal factor (Dansky and Silverman, 1973, 1975, Feitelson and Ross 1973, Johnson 1976, Li 1978, Pepler and Ross 1981, Singer 1973, Smith and Dutton 1979, Sutton-Smith 1968); as a trait characteristic of creative individuals (Dansky 1980, Hutt and Bhavnani 1976, Lieberman 1965, 1977, Singer and Rummo 1973); and as a criterion of creative functioning (Moran et al. 1984). Various explanations of the relationship between play and creativity have been proposed. Play has been thought to contribute to creativity by establishing a playful set (Dansky and Silverman 1975); the opportunity to develop a wide repertoire of associations of objects and ideas (Dansky 1980, Sutton-Smith 1968, Vygotsky 1967); or through the recombination of behavioral subassemblies that typically are not learned directly (Piaget 1962, Smith and Dutton 1979).

Play, particularly in early childhood, is the medium that links creativity to other cognitive processes such as imagination and fantasy, as well as to personality traits such as curiosity and locus of control. It is difficult to separate out the motivational processes associated with play and creativity from the cognitive processes. Renninger's (1990) study of children's play interests led her to suggest that

interest is the individual's cognitive and affective engagement with intended objects of interest. It is thought to vary among individuals and to serve as an organizer of individual activity. As such, interest involves perception of possibilities for action, representation of these possibilities to the self, and the setting, resolving, and resetting of challenges with that object. [p. 130]

Locus of Control

The play of children has been described as internally motivated behavior. The child's control over the direction of play and the content of play is generally a criterion used in distinguishing play behaviors from nonplay behaviors. The motives attributed to the creative process are similar. Saltz and colleagues (1977) postulate that the development of internal cognitive modes of control over behavior is facilitated in children by engagement in fantasy play experiences. Cohen and Oden (1974) propose a conceptual framework linking the behavioral characteristics of creative individuals with the construct of locus of control. They argue that internal control is necessary for creative functioning.

Cohen and Oden (1974) found the expected relationship for older children, but failed to find the positive relationship between ideational fluency and internal control in kindergarten children. However, findings from another study (Sawyers and Moran 1984) indicate that when appropriate stimuli are used, high scores on ideational fluency measures are related to internal control in preschoolers as well as in older children. Rewards, which are thought to shift the control to an external source, have been shown to have a detrimental effect on creativity (Amabile 1983, Groves et al. 1987) and constructive play (Lepper et al. 1973).

Exploration/Curiosity, Play and Creativity

Vandenberg (1980) cited the failure to separate exploration from other types of play as a shortcoming in the research on the effects of play on creativity. The issue is further complicated in that what is referred to as exploration in the play literature is related to, if not synonymous with, curiosity in the creativity literature. Fowler (1965) has suggested that exploratory behavior is the overt manifestation of curiosity.

Several theories have been developed for the understanding of children's curiosity. Berlyne (1960), as the major theorist in the area of curiosity, proposed a perceptual theory: that children explore new or complex things in their environment in order to alleviate perceptual conflict. Other theorists (Maw and Maw 1970) perceive curiosity to be a personality trait that can predict other dispositions and behaviors. Still another theory is that children use curiosity as a way of mastering their environment with the satisfaction derived from learning serving as a motivation for continued exploration (White 1959).

Berlyne (1963) distinguished between epistemic and perceptual curiosity as manifested in different modes of exploration. Epistemic curiosity involves knowledge seeking, such as asking questions and finding solutions to problems. Perceptual curiosity, the amount of attention given to objects in the immediate environment, has been examined in children by the length of time they spend staring at asymmetrical rather than symmetrical figures projected on a screen.

In her application of Berlyne's theory to the object play of children, Hutt (1976,

1979) provides descriptions of children's behavior that help to differentiate exploration from play behaviors. According to her framework, a child confronted with a novel, complex, or discrepant object will cautiously investigate the physical properties of the object in an apparent attempt to answer the question, "What can this object do?" She calls these behaviors specific exploration. In play, or diversive exploration in her terminology, the question addressed by the child becomes one of, "What can I do with this object?" In exploration, the child's movements are more stereotyped and less flexible than those displayed in play. In exploration, responsiveness to the object decreases as familiarity increases, whereas play occurs only in a known or familiar environment after the child has completed the exploration process. Play, as compared with specific exploration, is characterized by a gradual relaxation of tension as evidenced in facial expressions and other body movements, a greater variety of activities, a more variable heart rate indicative of a relaxed state, and more susceptibility to distraction. A provocative proposal in Hutt's framework is the notion that learning takes place only during the exploration process. She contends that any learning that occurs during play is incidental, or, in other words, happens by accident. This notion is similar to the theoretical position advanced by Piaget (1962) that rather than causing development, play is a reflection of the child's developmental level.

Nunnally and Lemond (1973), among others, have advanced the view that exploration is intrinsically motivated. These authors developed a temporal model of exploration and play that answers some of the criticisms of the arousal model of exploration. They related exploration to the process of encoding and thus to cognitive development. They described encoding as the process whereby an individual makes a novel stimulus meaningful. Through this intrinsically motivated process, categories are formed of things that are similar in one way or another. When a young child encounters a novel object to be encoded, either the objects must be reinterpreted to fit an existing category (Piaget's assimilation) or a new category must be formed (Piaget's accommodation). They speculate that if the object is too novel and the child is unable to encode at least part of the stimulus in a short amount of time, exploration will stop, and nothing about the object will be encoded. They also propose that the young child cannot perceive incongruity until a congruent encoding of the stimulus has taken place previously. Therefore, the child may be oblivious to numerous characteristics of the object. In their framework, the act of successfully encoding stimuli is inherently satisfying and thus the child is intrinsically motivated to repeat similar actions. According to these authors, exploration precedes play. When children tire of playing with an object they will seek out another novel one to explore or a familiar one to play with. Kogan (1983) suggests that it is the children's imaginative search for other ways to interact with objects that takes them beyond the stereotyped behavior associated with attention focused on an object's dominant quality or function.

Cohen (1974), in his examination of the relationship between creativity and exploratory behavior, established a twofold rationale for the assumption that any such relationship exists. "First, those characteristics that are related to creativity in adults closely approximate dimensions of exploratory behavior associated with children. Second, the development of creativity as an advanced form of cognition appears to be a logical outcome of early learning associated with exploratory behavior" (p. 263).

While there have been numerous studies of curiosity, exploratory behavior, and play, only five known studies (Cohen 1974, Hutt and Bhavnani 1976, Inagaki 1979, Penney and McCann 1964, and Spector 1984) have investigated the relationship between them. Cohen (1974) assessed the exploratory behavior of kindergarten and second-grade children by a paper and pencil hidden figures task. He found that exploratory behavior and ideational fluency as measured by an instances task were significantly related for kindergartners, whereas the positive correlation for the older subjects was significantly lower. Hutt and Bhavnani (1976) reexamined a previously tested sample of children in an attempt to identify developmental stability or change in exploratory behavior. Preschoolers categorized as nonexplorers, explorers, or inventive explorers in an earlier series of studies were administered the Wallach and Kogan creativity test battery four years later. The results indicated that for boys, the nonexploration classification at the preschool age appeared to be related to a later lack of curiosity, based on self-ratings. In addition, nonexplorers scored considerably lower on the creativity tests than explorers. Penney and McCann (1964) assessed curiosity in children in grades four, five, and six, and found that a positive relationship existed between reactive curiosity and originality for the older children. In the Inagaki (1979) study, curiosity was measured separately by teachers' ratings and an object-curiosity task; creativity was assessed by a verbal fluency test and a perceptual fluency measure. Results indicated that those children rated highly curious by their teachers were more fluent and gave more original responses than those rated less curious.

Using Hutt's framework, Spector (1984) examined the process of exploratory learning in young children: its components, sequence, effects, and relationship to creative thinking. Analyses, using high and low scores on original ideational fluency, indicated significant differences for exploratory behavior. Children scoring above the median on originality spent more total time exploring, and also had significantly greater frequencies of exploratory behaviors and more time in specific exploration than the low originality subjects. Furthermore, the high originality group spent much more time and performed more behaviors in diversive rather than specific exploration than did those low on originality. Spector's finding that diversive behaviors emerge later in the sequence of exploration is consistent with the established evidence in the creativity literature that original ideas emerge later in the response sequence.

In addition to being more curious and thus more likely to engage in exploration, creative individuals have been characterized as exhibiting the ability to sense a gap in knowledge or to note the existence of a problem. This problem-finding ability most often measured in the older child and adult appears to be similar to curiosity and exploration as assessed in young children.

Problem Finding

Although problem finding has been suggested to be the first step in the creative process, only a few investigations of problem finding have been reported in the literature. An even smaller number of researchers has explored the relationship between problem finding and creativity (Crutchfield and Covington 1965, Getzels and Csikszentmihalyi 1976, Smilansky 1984, Wakefield 1985). These studies utilized diverse conceptualizations of problem finding.

In the Getzels and Csikszentmihalyi study (1976), problem finding was assessed by noting the number of objects touched and manipulated by subjects as they selected and arranged a still life for painting. These researchers report a strong relationship between problem finding and the quality and originality of the resulting paintings. Arlin (1975) assessed problem finding by asking college-age subjects to generate questions about twelve common objects. The Getzels and Csikszentmihalyi (1976) measure of manipulation of objects would appear to be identical to assessment of manipulative curiosity in studies with young children, and Arlin's (1975) use of the number of questions asked is similar to measures of verbal curiosity in young children.

Selective Attention and Openness to Experience

The constructs, breadth of attention deployment, and attentiveness to detail have been suggested as cognitive strategies related to problem finding and creative problem solving. Kogan (1983) characterizes breadth of attention deployment as the "extensive and adaptive scanning of the external environment and memory storage" (p. 638). Such scanning is thought to be associational rather than logical, and to vary in degree of purpose attached. Kogan notes that the existing evidence indicates that breadth of attention deployment is not a function of intelligence. From a developmental perspective (Flavell 1985), it appears that the ability to purposefully control the deployment of attention increases. Such development aids in the process of disregarding unwanted or irrelevant information and allows for more flexible, adaptive problem finding/solving. That is, with increasing age, the individual has the ability either to narrow or to broaden his scope of attention and thus to decrease or increase the amount of stimulation attended to at any given time. Young children's breadth of attention has been attributed to the tendency to overgeneralize. Some have argued that what is labeled creativity in early childhood is simply overgeneralization. Nelson and Bonvillian (1978) conducted a longitudinal study of concept overgeneralization in children from 2½ to 4½ years of age and found that overgeneralization was related to both divergent thinking and IQ at age 4½.

Schatel's (1959) perceptual theory of creativity proposes that creative individuals are more open to their environment, tending to go beyond the familiar or routine, perceiving the environment in a new way or in more depth with attention to detail. As Sternberg (1985) noted, creative people do not put constraints on problems that are not there. Thus, it appears that although creative individuals are more open to their environment and attend to it in more depth, they are not stimulus bound.

Behaviors reported by many creative individuals, as well as limited experimental evidence, support the involvement of breadth of attention deployment in creative thought. Gardner (1961) identified a scanning strategy factor related to creative thinking. In another study, children self-reported the use of a category exhaustion problem-solving strategy on instance and alternate uses tasks (La Greca 1980). Ward (1969) classified preschoolers as creative or noncreative on the basis of scores on a uses, pattern meanings, and instances task. Subjects, assigned to either a "cue-rich" or "cue-poor" environment, were subsequently administered an instances task. The results indicated that only the children identified as high-creative benefited from the "cue-rich" environment. Ward concludes that scanning the environment for task relevant information is a strategy used by creative young children.

Breadth of attention deployment is related to flexibility in thinking (switching from one category of response to another), as well as to fluency in thinking. Examination of the tasks typically used to assess ideational fluency reveals that the tasks differ in the degree to which they tap breadth of attention. The generation of original solutions on the uses task requires the strategy of forsaking the obvious and typical uses in favor of less common but appropriate uses. Category exhaustion would be a viable strategy on the instances task. On the other hand, pattern meanings stimuli tend to elicit multiple categories of response. As Kogan (1983) notes, it appears that the verbal and figural nature of the divergent thinking tasks require different strategies that indirectly measure breadth of attention deployment and attention to detail.

Metaphor

Metaphor is still another cognitive skill that has been investigated to determine its relationship to both play and creative behavior.

Metaphor comprehension, production, and preference as an aspect of cognitive style have been explored in a number of recent studies and reviews (Billow 1981, Cerbin 1985, Dent 1984, Holyoak et al. 1984, Kogan 1983, Kogan et al. 1980, Malgady 1977, 1981, Ricco and Overton 1985, Sawyers et al. 1991, Silberstein et al. 1982, Verbrugge 1979, Vosniadou and Ortony 1983, Vosniadou et al. 1984, Waggoner et al. 1985, Wagner et al. 1979, and Winner et al. 1979).

Both metaphoric and divergent thinking involve grouping or associating stimuli on the basis of similarity. Metaphoric thinking involves producing or perceiving cross-domain similarities in objects or ideas, whereas divergent thinking tasks assess the breadth of the subject's similarity class(es) (Kogan 1983, Kogan et al. 1980).

Kogan and colleagues (1980) suggest that, "If metaphor sensitivity bears any relation at all to divergent thinking the common link would clearly have to be the meta-phoric character of the ideas generated in divergent thinking tasks" (p. 6). They further note that the strength of the relationship would likely be low between divergent thinking tasks that require production and metaphoric tasks that require comprehension.

Four known studies have investigated the link between divergent thinking and metaphoric comprehension in children (Kogan et al. 1980, Malgady 1977, 1981, Sawyers et al. 1992). Results from the study by Kogan and colleagues (1980) led these researchers to conclude that it is the quality of divergent thinking responses rather than the quantity that is associated with metaphoric comprehension. In contrast, Malgady (1977) found a relationship between the quantity but not the quality responses to a uses task and sensitivity to metaphor. In a later study, Malgady (1981) concludes that appreciation of figurative language at the kinder-garten level is based on nonverbal creativity, whereas at grades three and six it is related to verbal IQ and verbal creativity.

It appears that the link between divergent thinking and metaphoric comprehen-sion may be different for verbal and figural forms. Kogan and colleagues (1980) report more consistent findings for the relationship with figural (pattern meanings) than verbal (alternative uses) measures of divergent thinking.

Another indirect link between divergent and metaphoric thinking has emerged in the literature. Competence on metaphoric tasks is dependent upon the ability to select and attend to relevant stimulus dimensions. Thus it appears that perceptual information may play a role. Kogan and colleagues (1980) suggest that the imagery evoked by figurative language serves a mediating process in metaphoric comprehen-sion. Verbrugge (1979) also suggests that perception and action, sometimes in combination, are the processes that underlie metaphoric thinking. It appears that imagery, particularly in young children, is tied to motion information. In a study by Dent (1984), subjects responded to a series of stationary and moving stimuli presented in a filmed triad format. Metaphoric comprehension was greater for the moving stimuli. Silberstein and colleagues (1982) also found that school-age children based metaphors on sound or movement. It seems noteworthy that fantasy predis-position, which has been linked empirically to divergent thinking, is often measured by movement responses to inkblots.

Successful metaphoric thinking also appears to be dependent upon real-world knowledge or general intelligence (Kogan 1983, Vosniadou and Ortony 1983). Kogan (1983) suggests that this relationship may be due to the way in which metaphoric comprehension is typically measured. Such tasks are based on a conver-gent thinking format, in that there is one correct or best answer. Vosniadou and Ortony (1983) point out the importance of familiarity with the items being compared in relation to children's ability to distinguish between literal and meta-phorical comparisons. Vosniadou and colleagues (1984) note that metaphoric tasks that require a verbal explanation of the metaphoric association add a cognitive component to the assessments. Thus, this verbal component may be another contributing factor in the relationship between IQ and metaphoric comprehension and may also explain the finding (Kogan et al. 1980) that teachers were unable to distinguish the ability to comprehend and use figurative language from intelligence.

Similarities between metaphor and symbolic play have also received attention (Flavell 1985, Kogan 1983, Levine 1984). Metaphoric production has been described as a mapping process that involves the transfer of knowledge from one situation to another (Holyoak et al. 1984, Wagner et al. 1979). One group of researchers (Holyoak et al. 1984) has speculated that mapping processes are involved in social modeling and symbolic play as well as in metaphoric thinking. Billow (1981) observed a high frequency of spontaneous metaphor in the play of children 2 to 6 years of age. The children were interviewed following the play sessions in regard to their awareness and understanding of their use of metaphors. Billow concludes from the interview data that many of the verbal substitutions were appropriate and deliberate. In this study, the substitution of one object for another accompanied by verbalization was scored as a metaphor. For example, one child substituted the experimenter's hair for grass in play with small rubber animals. Individual differences in the propensity to engage in symbolic play defined in part by such object substitutions, have been related to the child's divergent thinking abilities (Dansky 1980, Dansky and Silverman 1973, 1975, Johnson 1976, Li 1978, Moran et al. 1984, Pepler and Ross 1981, Singer and Rummo 1973, Smith and Dutton 1979, Sutton-Smith 1968).

Sawyers and colleagues (1992) report results that indicate metaphoric comprehension in 4-year-olds is more highly related to IQ than to divergent thinking. Although metaphoric comprehension was related to fantasy predisposition, this relationship was not significant when IQ was partialed out. Metaphoric comprehension was related to popular but not to original ideational fluency scores or to imaginative play scores.

To summarize the literature reviewed, it appears that fantasy predisposition, divergent thinking, and symbolic play are related to each other and to some aspects of metaphoric thinking.

Fantasy

Diverse views of fantasy exist in the literature. In one view, according to Winner and Gardner (1979), fantasy or make-believe is the antithesis of cognition. From this perspective, based on Freudian and Piagetian theory, fantasy occurs when reality-based thought is insufficient or overwhelming, is adevelopmental, and is idiosyncratic. In contrast, Winner and Gardner (1979) propose a framework in which fantasy is viewed as a mode of thought that undergoes adevelopmental progression and that is intersubjective, as evidenced in signals to others in regard to interpretation. Fantasy, expressed in preschool children's play, becomes dominated by concerns from realism in the school age years, and reappears in the adolescent who possesses an adultlike understanding of the elements of fantasy.

Fantasy or imaginativeness has been assessed in a variety of ways including interviews, thought sampling, "thinking out loud," case reports, analyses of projective techniques, and observations of children's play. Results from studies of fantasy indicate it is related to numerous other behaviors, including creativity. In contrast to the prevalent view of fantasy as a unidimensional construct, some evidence indicates that fantasy may be a multifaceted construct composed of several styles, and that individuals differ both in the frequency and style of their fantasy behaviors (Rosenfeld et al. 1982).

Symbolic Play and Creativity

Research investigating linkages between play and creativity has been hailed as some of the most promising work on children's creativity in the last decade (Kogan 1983).

New input on the relationship can be found in a recent translation of Vygotsky's writing on imagination and creativity in young children (Vygotsky 1990). In this work, he states:

> One of the most important questions in child psychology and pedagogy is that of creativity in children, its development and its significance for the child's general development. We find that already at an early age children have creative processes, which are expressed in their play . . . the child's play activity is not simply a recollection of past experience, but a creative reworking that combines impressions and constructs from them new realities addressing the needs of the child. [p. 87]

Dansky (1980) notes the similarity between symbolic make-believe play as described by Piaget, and ideational fluency as conceptualized by Wallach (1970, 1971). Both behaviors are thought to involve a nonevaluative association of a wide variety of schemas (thoughts and behaviors). That is, both processes require the capacity to focus on more than a single aspect of an object or situation at a time. Other researchers (Lieberman 1977, Singer 1973, Smilansky 1968) have suggested that fantasy activities, including imaginative play, increase the child's behavioral repertoire and thus stimulate the development of creativity and divergent thinking.

Typically, in studies of the link between play and divergent thinking, children in the play group are given a set of materials, such as pipe cleaners and paper clips, and are told to play with them in any way they wish. Other children are asked to watch an adult perform several tasks with the materials and then to repeat what they saw demonstrated. All the children are then given a task testing ideational fluency (the nonevaluative association of a wide variety of schemas and the capacity to focus on more than a single aspect of the situation). They are asked, for example, to name all the things they could think of that are red. Children in the play groups consistently outperformed children in the other groups. Investigations of the hypothesized relationship between opportunities for play and enhanced creativity as measured by ideational fluency tasks have been supported (Dansky and Silverman 1973, 1975, Feitelson and Ross 1973, Johnson 1976, Li 1978, Sutton-Smith 1968).

Sutton-Smith has been criticized for failing to control for the amount of exposure to the objects, and thus it is unclear whether his results were due to the play experience or the exposure time (Vandenberg 1980). Also, Smith (1977) has argued that since Feitelson and Ross (1973) as well as Dansky and Silverman (1973, 1975) equate play training with play it is not clear whether their results were due to the play or the training effects.

Although the research generally supports the view that play has a significant effect on creativity, the specific way(s) that play contributes to creative problem solving is unclear. It appears that not all play activities are equally effective in enhancing divergent thinking, however. In one study, children who were instructed to make believe with the materials provided more original responses for an unfamiliar object than children in the free play or control groups (Li 1978). In another study, the influences of both convergent and divergent play materials on the problem-solving performance of preschoolers were investigated (Pepler and Ross 1981). Children between 3 and 5 years of age were assigned to one of four treatment conditions: play with convergent materials, play with divergent materials, observation of convergent activities, and observation of divergent activities. A battery of problem-solving tasks involving two divergent and three convergent tasks were interspersed between the treatment condition and the problem-solving tasks to control for a playful set towards the tasks. Results indicated that overall, children given divergent experiences in both play and observed conditions, generated more responses on the fluency measure than those children given convergent experiences.

Pepler and Ross conclude that convergent play experience results in learning that is applicable only to very similar convergent problems. In other words, it is limited to the lesson inherent in the materials. The divergent play experience, on the other hand, appears to be more general, transferring to dissimilar problem-solving tasks.

The finding that both divergent and convergent play groups scored higher than the observation group on the divergent tasks offers partial support for Piaget's notion that in play the child consolidates knowledge rather than acquires it. It also appears that in convergent play the child may learn the solution but not the principle or strategy that generalizes to other experiences.

Children's behavioral styles and personalities may also contribute to their performance on these tasks. Playfulness traits (social and cognitive spontaneity, manifest joy, and a sense of humor) have been significantly correlated with performance on measures of ideational fluency.

Individual Differences in Play Styles

Researchers have generated considerable information concerning individual differences in children's play (Rubin et al. 1983). Sex differences as well as various personality or trait variables have been investigated. The major personality or trait variables that have been investigated are playfulness and play style.

Playfulness has been defined as involving imaginativeness, novelty-seeking behavior, curiosity, and openness (Lieberman 1965, Singer and Rummo 1973). Research has suggested a link between playfulness in young children, as assessed through teacher ratings, and creativity (Lieberman 1977, Singer and Rummo 1973). However, the pattern of relationships has not been conclusive (Rubin et al. 1983).

Dansky (1980), using an observation-based method for determining playfulness, has also reported evidence that playful individuals are more creative. He classifies children as players (those who engage in dramatic play 25% or more of the time) and nonplayers (those who exhibit dramatic play 5% or less of the time). Players, but not nonplayers, in a make-believe play group produced significantly more responses to an ideational fluency task. These findings caused Dansky to revise his earlier thinking that dramatic play's contribution to ideational fluency is in the generalized "as if" attitude. He concluded:

> The relationship between play and fluency cannot simply be attributed to a relative sense of freedom or perceived lack of situational constraints inherent in the unstructured context of a free-play setting. These situational variables interact with specifiable individual differences among children (player/nonplayer) to yield a particular mode of activity (make-believe) which then has implications for the levels of associative fluency displayed. [p. 578]

The Dansky (1980) finding that only players benefited from the play condition is strikingly similar to Ward's (1969) finding that only creative children profited from being tested in an enriched cue environment as well as with Feitelson and Ross's (1973) observation that subjects with low-level play baselines did not show significant increases in thematic play when given the opportunity to engage in play with props designed specifically to elicit such play.

Johnson (1978) found that the proportion of imaginative to nonimaginative behavior for mothers and their 4-year-old children remained the same across a play condition and a story situation. In another study, Johnson and Erschler (1981) rank ordered twenty-six children on play category totals across a fifteen-month time period. The data shows that a child's ranking on dramatic play indices is more stable than functional or constructive play rankings.

Thus, it appears that individuals differ in the amount of playfulness they exhibit as reflected in their sensitivity to the environment and the way in which they use the environment to gain information. The playfulness trait appears to be stable over time and to be related to creative problem solving as measured by ideational fluency tasks.

Imaginative play in young children is typically described as progressing from play behavior that is dependent on the presence of objects or props to elicit pretend activity (object-dependent), to play behavior, which is free of the need for external props (object-independent). Most major theoretical perspectives assume this object-dependent to object-independent progression is age related. However, recent research has provided suggestive evidence that equally sophisticated players demonstrate individual differences or styles relative to the object dependence or independence of their play. Shotwell and colleagues (1979) and Wolf and Grollman (1982) identify two distinct types or styles of preschool players: "patterners" and "dramatists." The play of patterners is described as object dependent while the play of dramatists is described as object independent. These stylistic differences were found to be unrelated to age, developmental level, or sex (Horm-Wingerd and Lin 1988).

Shotwell and colleagues (1979) and Wolf and Grollman (1982) found that patterners, or object-dependent children, directed their attention to the "object world" and did not typically use play materials in a social or communicative manner. A large portion of their play was devoted to exploring the physical properties and uses of play materials. For example, the patterners often interrupted the flow of their symbolic play themes to investigate some object or event that had captured their attention. Additionally, their symbolic play was characterized by respect for and interest in the qualities of objects. For example, once a child had used a crayon as a nail while playing carpenter, she continued to respect this designated categorization by referring to crayons as nails even when moving on to new play activities. Patterners were found to make these types of object substitutions on the basis of physical realism or similarity. Thus, while a crayon could be a nail, a ball with its different physical characteristics could not serve as a suitable substitute for a nail for patterners.

On the other hand, dramatists, or object-independent children, were found to carry out their symbolic play by using materials merely as props in social interaction. Unlike patterners, it was found that dramatists directed their efforts to the maintenance of fantasy themes. Their play was not characterized by frequent breaks or reality-based object substitutions. Rather, dramatists were reluctant to end or leave fantasy themes and were capable of spontaneously forming a series of outlandish substitutions for an object as the plot of the fantasy theme unfolded. As noted by Sutton-Smith (in Shotwell et al. 1979), the behavior of dramatists is very similar in form to that displayed by the "imaginative" players described by Singer, Hutt, and others.

Play style, as described by Shotwell and colleagues (1979) and Wolf and Grollman (1982), is a stable individual difference that is expected to influence behavior in a variety of areas. It has been demonstrated that play style can be reliably assessed in preschool children through teacher ratings and children's self-assessment (Horm-Wingerd and Lin 1988). Such stylistic differences in play have been correlated with children's preference for activities (Emmerich 1964, Wolf and Gardner 1979, Horm-Wingerd and Sawyers 1988). For example, Horm-Wingerd and Sawyers (1988) found that dramatists spent significantly greater time engaging in dramatic play during free play periods than did patterners. Play style has also been found to be related to problem-solving abilities (Jennings 1975) and specific cognitive abilities (Jennings 1975, Horm-Wingerd 1991). Horm-Wingerd (1991) found that while patterners and dramatists did not differ in overall IQ, they did differ in their performance on specific subtests. Based on teacher ratings of play style, dramatists performed significantly better on the vocabulary and comprehension subtests of the WPPSI (Wechsler Preschool and Primary Scale of Intelligence) while patterners performed significantly better on the block design subtest. These differences were predicted, given the descriptions of the play styles found in the literature. Due to the fact that dramatists rely heavily on the use of language in their play, it was hypothesized that they would perform better than patterners on the subtests that measure verbal comprehension, such as vocabulary and comprehension. Patterners, who are described as devoting large portions of their play to the investigation and arrangement of objects, were expected to score higher than dramatists on the subtests that measure perceptual organization or spatial knowledge, such as block design.

Horm-Wingerd (1991) also investigated the relationship between play style and creativity. Few significant relationships emerged between play style and various creativity measures. Those relationships that were significant were inconclusive. It is suggested that future studies examine possible relationships between play style and creativity in a more diverse sample than that used by Horm-Wingerd due to the relatively restricted range of creativity score evidence in that study.

Conclusion: Symbolic Play Facilitates Children's Creative Problem Solving

The evidence reviewed indicates that creativity is multidimensional in nature. It appears that creative expression and problem solving result from various combinations of the complex and sometimes elusive interactions among knowledge and experience, creativity-relevant skills and traits, and physical and social environmental factors. Although quantitative and qualitative differences in creativity have been identified between adults and children, it has been demonstrated that it is possible to measure creativity-relevant skills in young children. It also appears that the level of creative potential as measured by ideational fluency tasks varies among individuals. Limited evidence from longitudinal studies indicates that young children's level of creative potential is relatively stable over time. Despite noted methodological flaws and the difficulty in comparing findings from studies with diverse samples and contexts, the evidence indicates that play enhances performance on divergent thinking tasks. The findings seem to lead to the conclusion that play, particularly symbolic play, is preferable to direct instruction in promoting children's creative problem-solving abilities.

Similarities in the contexts that have been found to support creative thinking and play are numerous. Although questions remain unanswered, it appears that play and creativity are linked through both personality variables and cognitive processes including an internal locus of control, metaphoric thinking, imagery and fantasy, breadth of attention deployment, curiosity/exploration, and symbolic activity. It is through both exploration and play that children gain the knowledge and experience that have been shown to be necessary but not sufficient for creative problem solving.

Anecdotal Evidence of the Link between Play and Creativity

Through observations of children at play, it becomes clear that play activities afford numerous opportunities for children to find and solve problems. When playing, young children openly and spontaneously express themselves because they are in a nonthreatening environment. The creative process – defining the problem, generating ideas and solutions, evaluating solutions, converting solutions into outcomes – is enhanced in an open and psychologically safe environment. In play, the activity doesn't have to be done "right." It is okay to make a mistake. Children are at ease to explore and experiment with a variety of solutions to different problems during play. The problems encountered in play situations represent the real-life problems in the lives of young children and therefore are meaningful to them. A vivid example is 3-year-old Ashleigh's play with an electric keyboard in her classroom.

Ashleigh watched intently as 4-year-old Robert methodically matched colored notes in a song book to the color-coded keyboard to reproduce recognizable tunes. Ashleigh eagerly slid into place at the keyboard when Robert finished. She tried to play the keyboard as she had seen Robert do. However, at age 3, Ashleigh lacked the skills necessary to reproduce the familiar tunes. After several attempts she jumped up from the keyboard. But rather than quit or ask for an adult's help, Ashleigh found paper and markers with which she created her own color-coded song. Her smile, as she played her song, which did not have to sound "right," indicated a self-confident little girl who solved her own problem. She restructured the situation by altering the challenge of the activity to match her developmental level and skills.

In exploration and play, children are given the time to find and solve problems creatively. The research reviewed has shown that when a child is asked to tell all of the things for which paper could be used, for example, the first few responses are common ones, such as "to draw on" or "to make an airplane." When they are allowed time to think past their initial responses, more original ideas are expressed, such as "a blanket to cover my doll" or "to put on the bottoms of my feet like skates." Time in the typical preschool classroom is often provided through repeated exposure to play materials and experiences. Consider another early childhood classroom where the children were embellishing full-size outlines of their bodies. Most children were adding hair, faces, and clothes to their outlines, while Eric was observed making an original internal drawing of his skeleton.

Children become adept and resourceful in problem solving through symbolic play. Just how resourceful is evident in the following "doctor" dramatic play episode. A group of 3- and 4-year-old children had self-selected a "doctor" dramatic play opportunity. The teacher had provided a cot and a doctor kit, among other things to support their play. But one young "doctor," Courtney, needed a heart "prop" to compliment his open heart surgery play. When none was readily available, he dug through the garbage can unobserved. With great delight, he proudly showed his teacher the great heart he had retrieved – a piece of meatloaf that had been served but not eaten for lunch.

As yet, we do not know if and how Ashleigh's, Eric's, and Courtney's creative problem solving will be expressed in adulthood. But as discussed previously, creative adults recall and trace their creative interests to just such opportunities to explore and play in their early childhood.

References

Amabile, T. M. (1983). *The Social Psychology of Creativity.* New York: Springer-Verlag.

Arlin, P. K. (1975). Cognitive development in adulthood: a fifth stage? *Developmental Psychology* 11:602–626.

Barron, F., and Harrington, D. M. (1981). Creativity, intelligence and personality. *Annual Review of Psychology* 32:439–476.

Berlyne, D. E. (1960). *Conflict Arousal and Curiosity.* New York: McGraw-Hill.

_____ (1963). Motivational problems caused by exploratory and epistemic behavior. In *Psychology: A Study of a Science,* ed. S. Koch, pp. 104–128. New York: McGraw-Hill.

Billow, R. M. (1981). Observing spontaneous metaphor in children. *Journal of Experimental Child Psychology* 31:430–445.

Cerbin, W. (1985). *Young children's comprehension of metaphorical language.* Paper presented at the meeting of the Society for Research in Child Development, Toronto, Canada, April 25–28.

Cohen, S. (1974). Exploratory task behavior and creativity in young children. *Home Economics Research Journal* 2:262–267.

Cohen, S., and Oden, S. (1974). An examination of creativity and locus of control in children. *Journal of Genetic Psychology* 124:179–185.

Crutchfield, R. S., and Covington, M. V. (1965). Programmed instruction in creativity. *Program Instruction* 4:1–8.

Curry, N. E., and Arnaud, S. H. (1984). Play in developmental preschool settings. In *Child's Play: Developmental and Applied,* ed. T. D. Yawkey and A. D. Pellegrini, pp. 273–290. Hillsdale, NJ: Lawrence Erlbaum.

Dansky, J. L. (1980). Make-believe: a mediator of the relationship between play and associate fluency. *Child Development* 51:576–579.

Dansky, J. L., and Silverman, I. W. (1973). Effects of play on associate fluency in preschool-aged children. *Developmental Psychology* 9:38–43.

_____ (1975). Play: a general facilitator of associative fluency. *Developmental Psychology* 11:104.

Dent, C. M. (1984). The developmental importance of motion information in perceiving and describing metaphoric similarity. *Child Development* 55:1607–1613.

Emmerich, W. (1964). Continuity and stability in early social development. *Child Development* 35:311–332.

Feitelson, D., and Ross, G. S. (1973). The neglected factor – play. *Human Development* 16:202–223.

Flavell, J. H. (1985). *Cognitive Development*, 2nd ed. Englewood Cliffs, NJ: Prentice-Hall.

Fowler, H. (1965). *Curiosity and Exploratory Behavior.* New York: Macmillan.

Gardner, R. W. (1961). Cognitive controls of attention deployment as determinants of visual illusions. *Journal of Abnormal and Social Psychology* 62:120–127.

Getzels, J. W., and Csikszentmihalyi, M. (1976). *The Creative Vision: A Longitudinal Study of Problem Finding in Art.* New York: John Wiley & Sons.

Groves, M., Sawyers, J. K., and Moran, S. D. (1987). Reward and ideational fluency in preschool children. *Early Childhood Research Quarterly* 2:335–340.

Guilford, J. P. (1956). The structure of intellect. *Psychological Bulletin* 53:267–293.

_____ (1967). *The Nature of Human Intelligence.* New York: McGraw-Hill.

Hennessey, B., and Amabile, T. M. (1987). *Creativity and Learning.* Washington, DC: National Education Association.

Henninger, M. L. (1985). Preschool children's play behaviors in an indoor and outdoor environment. In *When Children Play*, ed. J. L. Frost and S. Sunderlind, pp. 145–150. Wheaton, MD: ACEI.

Holyoak, K. J., Junn, E. N., and Billman, D. O. (1984). Development of analogical problem-solving skill. *Child Development* 55:2042–2055.

Horm-Wingerd, D. M. (1991). Unpublished data. The University of Rhode Island.

Horm-Wingerd, D. M., and Lin, C. Y. (1988). *Play style assessment: a rating scale.* Paper presented at the biennial meeting of the Southwestern Society for Research in Human Development, New Orleans, LA.

Horm-Wingerd, D. M., and Sawyers, J. K. (1988). *Validation of the play style rating scale.* Paper presented at the annual meeting of the American Home Economics Association, Baltimore, MD.

Hutt, C. (1976). Exploration and play in children. In *Play–Its Role in Development and Evolution*, ed. J. S. Bruner, A. Jolly, and K. Sylva, pp. 202–215. New York: Penguin Books Ltd.

_____ (1979). Exploration and play. In *Play and Learning*, ed. B. Sutton-Smith, pp. 175–194. New York: Gardner.

Hutt, C., and Bhavnani, R. (1976). Predictions from play. In *Play–Its Role in Development and Evolution*, ed. J. S. Bruner, A. Jolly, and K. Sylva, pp. 217–219. New York: Penguin Books Ltd.

Inagaki, K. (1979). Relationships of curiosity to perceptual and verbal fluency in young children. *Perceptual and Motor Skills* 48:789–790.

Jennings, K. D. (1975). People versus object orientation, social behavior, and intellectual abilities in preschool children. *Developmental Psychology* 11:511–519.

Johnson, J. E. (1976). Relations of divergent thinking and intelligence test scores with social and nonsocial make-believe play of preschool children. *Child Development* 47:1200–1203.

Johnson, J. E., and Ershler, J. (1981). Developmental trends in preschool play as a function of classroom program and child gender. *Child Development* 52:995–1004.

John-Steiner, V. (1985). *Notebooks of the Mind.* Albuquerque: University of New Mexico.

Kogan, N. (1983). Stylistic variation in childhood and adolescence: creativity, metaphor, and cognitive style. In *Handbook of Child Psychology: Cognitive Development, 3*, ed. J. H. Flavell and E. M. Markman, pp. 630–706. NY: John Wiley & Sons.

Kogan, N., Connor, K., Gross, A., and Fava, D. (1980). Understanding visual metaphor: developmental and individual differences. *Monographs of the Society for Research in Child Development* 45: (1, Serial No. 183).

La Greca, A. M. (1980). Can children remember to be creative? *Child Development* 51:572–575.

Lepper, M. R., Greene, D., and Nisbett, R. E. (1973). Undermining children's intrinsic interest with extrinsic reward: a test of the overjustification hypothesis. *Journal of Personality and Social Psychology* 28:129–137.

Li, A. M. F. (1978). Effects of play on novel responses in kindergarten children. *The Alberta Journal of Educational Research* 24:31–36.

Lieberman, J. N. (1965). Playfulness and divergent thinking: an investigation of their relationship at the kindergarten level. *The Journal of Genetic Psychology* 107:219–224.

_____ (1977). *Playfulness: Its Relationship to Imagination and Creativity*. New York: Academic Press.

Levine, S. (1984). A critique of the Piagetian presuppositions of the role of play in human development and a suggested alternative: metaphoric logic which organizes the play experience is the foundation for rational creativity. *Journal of Creative Behavior* 18:90–108.

Malgady, R. G. (1977). Children's interpretation and appreciation of similes. *Child Development* 48:1734–1738.

_____ (1981). Metric distance models of creativity and children's perception of figurative language. *Journal of Educational Psychology* 73:866–871.

Maw, W. H., and Maw, E. W. (1970). Self-concepts of high and low curiosity boys. *Child Development* 41:123–129.

Mednick, S. A. (1962). The associative basis of the creative process. *Psychological Review* 69:220–232.

Milgram, R. M., and Arad, R. (1981). Ideational fluency as a predictor of original problem-solving. *Journal of Educational Psychology* 73:568–572.

Milgram, R. M., and Milgram, N. A. (1976). Group versus individual administration in the measurement of creative thinking in gifted and nongifted children. *Child Development* 47:563–565.

Moore, L., and Sawyers, J. K. (1987). The stability of original thinking in young children. *Gifted Child Quarterly* 3:126–129.

Moran, J. D., Milgram, R. M., Sawyers, J. K., and Fu, V. R. (1983). Original thinking in preschool children. *Child Development* 54:921–926.

Moran, J. D., Sawyers, J. K., and Fu, V. R. (1985). Original problem-solving in the early years. Unpublished, NIMH Grant, Final Report.

Moran, J. D., Sawyers, J. K., Fu, V. R., and Milgram, R. M. (1984). Predicting imaginative play in preschool children. *Gifted Child Quarterly* 28:92–94.

Nahme-Huang, L., Singer, D. G., Singer J. L., and Wheaton, A. (1977). Imaginative play and perceptual-motor intervention methods with emotionally disturbed hospitalized children: an evaluative study. *Journal of Orthopsychiatry* 47:238–249.

Nelson, K. E., and Bonvillian, J. D. (1978). Early language development: conceptual growth and related processes between 2 and 4½ years of age. In *Children's Language*, vol. I, ed. K. E. Nelson, pp. 467–556. New York: Gardner Press.

Nunnally, J. C., and Lemond, L. C. (1973). Exploratory behavior and human development. In *Advances in Child Development and Behavior*, vol. 8, ed. H. Reese, pp. 60–106. New York: Academic Press.

Parten, M. B. (1932). Social participation among preschool children. *Journal of Abnormal Psychology* 27:243–269.

Penney, R. K., and McCann, B. (1964). The children's reactive curiosity scale. *Psychological Reports* 15:323–324.

Pepler, D. J., and Ross, H. S. (1981). The effects of play on convergent and divergent problem-solving. *Child Development* 52:1202–1210.

Piaget, J. (1962). *Play, Dreams, and Imitation in Childhood.* Trans. C. Gattegno and F. M. Hodgson. New York: Norton, 1951.

Renninger, K. A. (1990). Children's play interests, representation, and activity. In *Knowing and Remembering in Young Children,* Emory Cognition Series, vol. III, ed. R. Fivush and S. Hudson, pp. 126–165. London: Cambridge University Press.

Ricco, R., and Overton, W. F. (1985). *The role of operational thought in the comprehension and production of metaphor.* Paper presented at the meeting of the Society for Research in Child Development, Toronto, Canada, April 25–28.

Rosenfeld, E., Huesmann, R., Eron, L. D., and Torney-Purta, J. V. (1982). Measuring patterns of fantasy behavior in children. *Journal of Personality and Social Psychology* 42:347–366.

Rubin, K. H. (1977a). The play behaviors of young children. *Young Children* 32:16–24.

—— (1977b). The social and cognitive value of preschool toys and activities. *Canadian Journal of Behavioral Sciences* 9:382–385.

Rubin, K. H., Fein, G. G., and Vandenberg, B. (1983). Play. In *Handbook of Child Psychology 4, Socialization, Personality, and Social Development,* ed. M. Hetherington, pp. 693–774. New York: John Wiley & Sons.

Saltz, E., Dixon, D., and Johnson, S. (1977). Training disadvantaged preschoolers on various fantasy activities: effects on cognitive functioning and impulse control. *Child Development* 48:367–380.

Sawyers, J. K., and Mehrotra, J. B. (1989). A longitudinal study of original thinking in young children. *Creative Child and Adult Quarterly* 3–4:130–135, 162.

Sawyers, J. K., and Moran, J. D. (1984). Locus of control and ideational fluency in preschool children. *Perceptual and Motor Skills* 58:857–858.

—— (1985). Hikers task. Unpublished raw data.

Sawyers, J. K., Moran, J. D., Fu, V. R., and Horm-Wingerd, D. (1992). Correlates of metaphoric comprehension in young children. *Creativity Research Journal* 5:27–33.

Sawyers, J. K., Moran, J. D., and Tegano, D. (1990). A theoretical model of creative potential in young children. In *Expanding Awareness of Creative Potentials Worldwide,* ed. C. W. Taylor. Salt Lake City: Brain-Talent-Powers Press.

Schatel, E. G. (1959). *Metamorphosis: On the Development of Affect, Perception, Attention, and Memory.* New York: Basic Books.

Shotwell, J. M., Wolf, D., and Gardner, H. (1979). Exploring early symbolization: styles of achievement. In *Play and Learning,* ed. B. Sutton-Smith. New York: Gardner.

Silberstein, L., Gardner, H., Phelps, E., and Winner, E. (1982). Autumn leaves and old photographs: the development of metaphor preferences. *Journal of Experimental Child Psychology* 34:135–150.

Singer, D. L. (1973). *The Child's World of Make Believe: Experimental Studies of Imaginative Play.* New York: Academic Press.

Singer, D. L., and Rummo, J. R. (1973). Ideational creativity and behavioral style in kindergarten-age children. *Developmental Psychology* 8:154–161.

Smilansky, J. (1984). Problem solving and the quality of invention: an empirical investigation. *Journal of Educational Psychology* 76:377–386.

Smilansky, S. (1968). *The Effects of Sociodramatic Play on Disadvantaged Preschool Children.* New York: John Wiley & Sons.

Smilansky, J., and Shefatya, L. (1990). *Facilitating Play.* Gaithersburg, MD: Psychological & Educational Publications.

Smith, P. K. (1977). Social and fantasy play in young children. In *Biology of Play,* ed. B. Tizard and D. Harvey. Philadelphia: Lippincott.

Smith, P. K., and Dutton, S. (1979). Play and training on direct and innovative problem solving. *Child Development* 50:830–836.

Spector, A. (1984). Exploratory behavior and ideational fluency in the preschool child. Unpublished Masters thesis, Virginia Polytechnic Institute, Blacksburg, VA.

Sternberg, R. J. (1985). Teaching critical thinking, part 1: are we making critical mistakes? *Phi Delta Kappan* 67:194–198.

Sutton-Smith, B. (1968). Novel responses to toys. *Merrill-Palmer Quarterly* 14:151–158.

Vandenberg, B. (1980). Play, problem-solving and creativity. In *New Directions for Child Development – Children's Play,* ed. K. H. Rubin, pp. 49–68. San Francisco: Jossey-Bass.

Verbrugge, R. R. (1979). The primacy of metaphor in development. In *New Directions for Child Development: Fact, Fiction, and Fantasy in Childhood,* ed. E. Winner and H. Gardner, 6:77–84. San Francisco: Jossey-Bass.

Vosniadou, S., and Ortony, A. (1983). The emergence of the literal-metaphorical-anomalous distinction in young children. *Child Development* 54:154–161.

Vosniadou, S., Ortony, A., Reynolds, R. E., and Wilson, P. T. (1984). Sources of difficulty in the young child's understanding of metaphorical language. *Child Development* 55:1588–1606.

Vygotsky, L. S. (1967). Play and its role in the mental development of the child. *Soviet Psychology* 5:6–18.

—— (1990). Imagination and creativity in childhood. *Soviet Psychology* 28:4–96.

Waggoner, J. E., Meese, M. J., and Palermo, D. S. (1985). Grasping the meaning of metaphor: story recall and comprehension. *Child Development* 56:1156–1166.

Wagner, S., Winner, E., Cicchetti, P., and Gardner, H. (1979). "Metaphorical" mapping in human infants. *Child Development* 52:728–731.

Wakefield, J. F. (1985). Toward creativity: problem finding in a divergent thinking exercise. *Child Study Journal* 15:265–270.

Wallach, M. A. (1970). Creativity. In *Carmichael's Manual of Child Psychology,* vol. 3, ed. P. H. Mussen, pp. 1211–1272. New York: John Wiley & Sons.

—— (1971). *The Intelligence Creativity Distinction.* Morristown, NJ: General Learning Press.

Wallach, M. A., and Kogan, N. (1965). *Modes of Thinking in Young Children: A Study of the Creativity-Intelligence Distinction.* New York: Holt, Rinehart, & Winston.

Ward, W. C. (1969). Rate and uniqueness in children's creative responding. *Child Development* 40:869–878.

—— (1974). Creativity in young children. *Journal of Creative Behavior* 8:101–106.

White, R. W. (1959). Motivation reconsidered: the concept of competence. *Psychological Review* 66:297–333.

Winner, E., and Gardner, H. (1979). *Fact, Fiction, and Fantasy in Childhood: New Directions for Child Development.* Vol. 6. San Francisco: Jossey-Bass.

Winner, E., Wapner, W., Cicone, M., and Gardner, H. (1979). Measures of metaphor. In *New Directions for Child Development: Fact, Fiction, and Fantasy in Childhood,* vol. 6, ed. E. Winner and H. Gardner, pp. 67–76. San Francisco: Jossey-Bass.

Wolf, D., and Gardner, H. (1979). Style and sequence in early symbolic play. In *Symbolic Functioning in Childhood,* ed. M. Franklin and N. Smith. Hillsdale, NJ: Lawrence Erlbaum.

Wolf, D., and Grollman, S. H. (1982). Ways of playing: individual differences in imaginative style. In *The Play of Children: Current Theory and Research,* ed. D. J. Pepler and K. H. Rubin. Basil, Switzerland: Karger, AG.

6

Catharsis

Barry G. Ginsberg

The value of catharsis and emotional release has had a questionable place in history. These factors certainly seem relevant in psychotherapy with young children, as most approaches acknowledge the importance of some expression of emotion as part of the therapy. Since play is observed to be a primary means by which children express themselves, some sort of play activity is included in most psychotherapeutic work with children. Additionally, there is broad acceptance for the idea that these play activities should have an element of freedom to allow children an opportunity to find greater, if not full, expression of their feelings. However, there is mixed opinion on the value or usefulness of this greater expression of feeling. There is also insufficient agreement on what play is or its particular value (Ellis 1973). Nevertheless, there is a consensus of opinion that play is important and useful, that a certain amount of freedom of expression is necessary, and that expressing one's emotions is an important part of play and play activities.

Biber (1984) has extrapolated on the view of Erikson that play has positive qualities. He writes that play

> is distinct from other experiences: there are no directions to follow; the child can indulge and act out the course of his own associations – both feelings and ideas – no matter how far from reality they be, without being corrected or censured; he is his own author and stage manager as he selects from the complex, often confusing, reality of his daily living the pieces of action or meaning or feeling that he wants to relive and with what symbolic forms he wants to reproduce it and rehash it. [p. 192]

Hug-Hellmuth, one of Freud's first followers to use play with children, regarded play as a means to communicate with children and to observe and understand them (Miller 1968). Melanie Klein (1948, 1955) believed that the spontaneous play of children represents the free association considered important in adult psychoanalyses by Freud. A. Freud (1946) emphasized the importance of free play to build trust to enlist the child's confidence and affection in order to help "educate" the child (Miller 1968). Axline (1947), an originator of client-centered play therapy, describes play therapy "as an opportunity that is offered to the child to experience growth under the most favorable conditions. Since play is his natural medium for self-expression, the child is given the opportunity to play out his accumulated feelings of tension, frustration, insecurity, aggression, fear, bewilderment, confusion" (p. 16). Taft and Allen, in applying Rank's relationship therapy, began therapy "where the child was at" (Miles 1981,p. 65). Moustakis, in basing his approach to play therapy on relationships and an existential view of man, emphasized acceptance of the child and use of a setting to provide children with a sense of harmony, tranquility and relatedness (Miles 1981, Moustakis 1970).

Greenberg and Safran (1987) have indicated the importance of emotion in therapeutic change. In particular, they raise two importance corollaries to the notion of emotion as potentially adaptive:

1. Psychological problems are often the result of blocking or avoiding potentially adaptive emotional experience, and affective interventions, in many instances, are designed to overcome these resistances to emotion and to *access* underlying affective experience.

2. The complete processing of a specific emotional experience leads to a shift in the nature of the emotional experience. This shift leads to the emergence of new adaptive responses to problem situations. [p. 7]

The importance of emotional expression and release is acknowledged by most psychotherapists as an essential, if not *the* essential, ingredient in psychotherapy. How it operates in psychotherapy varies with the theory. A related and pervasive concept in psychotherapy is that of catharsis. From Freud through the present, theories and perspectives on catharsis can vary from approach to approach.

The term catharsis has been used in varying ways with different meanings. As a result, it is difficult to assess its therapeutic value in play with children. According to Nichols and Zax (1977), catharsis is generally understood as a process in which unexpressed, unconscious, or hidden emotions are released to relieve tension and anxiety. In investigating the meaning of catharsis, Nichols and Zax acknowledge that the derivation of the word from Greek, meaning to clean or purify, suggests the two ideas of purgation or purification. In physiological terms, it refers to the elimination of congestive matter and bodily waste. Aristotle referred to catharsis as the moral or spiritual purification found to occur at dramatic performances. This was purposeful, as the objective was to release powerful emotions for a spiritual renewal or rebirth (Belli 1986). "All that is required to bring about a cathartic response is that an action or image stimulate some deep emotion, often repressed, in the beholder" (Belli 1986, p. 91).

The first Freudian therapy described by Breuer and Freud (1955) was a cathartic therapy. "The patient only gets free from the hysterical symptom by reproducing the pathogenic impressions that caused it and by giving utterance to them with an expression of affect, and thus the therapeutic task consists solely in inducing him to do so" (p. 283). This was given the term "the hydraulic model," since when emotions are not discharged they build up, creating tension. If this build-up of affective tension is not released, it results in destructive action. This has strongly influenced psychotherapy to this day, even though Freud later rejected the value of cathartic discharge, considering the benefit limited, providing only temporary relief (Freud 1956). However, free expression of affect remained important in psychoanalysis (Menninger 1948).

Dollard and colleagues (1939) applied the principle of catharsis to aggressive behavior. They suggested that "any discharge of aggression – even displaced aggression [contrary to Freud] – should lessen pent-up feelings of aggression. Aggression is not presumed to be a basic drive [contrary to Freud] but the necessary result of frustration" (Nichols and Zax 1977, p. 186). Feshbach (1955) raised the notion of "symbolic catharsis," in which symbolic aggression expressed in fantasy can result through catharsis in a reduction of aggressive drive.

Over the years, the "cathartic technique" has emerged in many popular therapies: reevaluation therapy (Jackins 1962), primal therapy (Janov 1970), new identity therapy (Casriel 1972), psychodrama (Moreno 1958), and short-term dynamic psychotherapy (Davanloo 1980, Nichols and Efran 1985, Sifneos 1979). Therefore, the catharsis hypothesis and emotional release have been important aspects of the development of psychotherapy. Freud (1955) observed of the play behavior of children, "It is clear that in their play children repeat everything that has made a great impression on them in real life, and that in doing so they abreact the strength of the impression, and, as one might put it, make themselves master of the situation" (p. 16). Axline (1947) commented, ". . . the child is given the opportunity to play out his accumulated feelings of tension, frustration, insecurity, aggression, fear, bewilderment, confusion. By playing out these feelings he brings them to the surface, gets them out in the open, faces them, learns to control them, or abandons them" (p. 16). The notion of catharsis remains important to play therapy with children.

Theoretical Issues

The concept of catharsis and emotional release has been strongly influenced by Breuer and Freud (1895/1955). The basic premise of this notion is that the failure to express emotions, particularly those tied to a traumatic event, is responsible for maladaptive attitudes and behavior. Releasing the repressed emotions that relate to the traumatic event frees the person from those emotions. As a result, the person experiences improved well-being and has more adaptive functioning. The implication of this is that through release of emotion and cathartic expression, feelings that have been repressed are reduced and change occurs. A further implication is that emotions are withheld until discharged, and when discharged are no longer retained. The research and literature around this are mixed, even though this "hydraulic theory" of emotions has been discarded. The key question is, do catharsis and emotional release produce significant behavioral change?

Biaggio (1987) conducted a survey of the perspectives of psychologists on catharsis. She found that professional psychologists, more than students, questioned the validity of the hostility catharsis hypothesis. She also found that clinical psychologists were more apt to endorse the hostility catharsis hypothesis than were social psychologists. She proposed that clinicians might not be as aware of so-cial–psychological research on the catharsis hypothesis or perhaps have gathered clinical data to support the hypothesis. Nichols (1974a,b), in a study evaluating the impact of catharsis on the outcome of brief psychotherapy, indicated that emotive psychotherapy was effective in producing catharsis. However, the results were equivocal on whether this leads to therapeutic improvement. Nichols and Zax (1977) reviewed the literature and research on catharsis. They found that catharsis was useful as a vehicle of behavior change, but made a distinction between cathartic discharge in therapy and behavior outside therapy. Nichols and Bierenbaum (1978), in a study of cathartic psychotherapy, suggest that the principal value of this therapy is in disrupting "a pattern of emotional suppression and avoidance in those for whom feelings do not come easily" (p. 727).

A good deal of the literature on catharsis deals with aggression and its expression. The work of Dollard and colleagues (1939) proposed that inhibiting aggression is frustrating, and that aggressive behavior is cathartic, reducing the instigation (drive) to aggression. Feshbach (1955), drawing upon Freud's idea that unsatisfied wishes are the driving power behind fantasy, investigated whether fantasy expression of hostility would partially reduce aggression. He found support for this hypothesis. However, a subsequent study (Feshbach 1956) involving children as subjects, did not support this and showed that boys initially low in aggressive behavior increased their overt hostility following permissive free play.

Bandura and Walters (1963) considered the issue of catharsis. They stated that evidence from research with children indicates that "far from producing a cathartic reduction of aggression, direct or vicarious participation in aggressive activities within a permissive setting maintains the behavior at its original level and may actually increase it" (p. 256). They cited the studies of Kenny (1952), Feshbach (1956), Bandura and colleagues (1961, 1963a,b) and others to support this view. Bandura (1969) states that from a social-learning perspective, frustration leads to emotional arousal, which facilitates aggression depending upon the type of frustra-tion previously learned and the reinforcement associated with the different courses of action.

Tavris (1982), in a popular book on anger, refutes the idea that aggression is the instinctive catharsis for anger. She draws on the work of Hokanson (1961, 1962a,b, 1968, 1970) claiming that catharsis can be learned. She also refutes the hypothesis that talking out anger gets rid of it or makes one feel less angry. Berkowitz (1960) considered a reduction through symbolic catharsis as possible. However, his subse-quent investigations (Berkowitz 1965, Berkowitz and Green 1967, Green and

Berkowitz 1967) suggest that stimuli associated with aggression could serve as cues for later aggression. Later (1970) he states, "the catharsis hypothesis blinds us to the important social principle that aggression is all too likely to lead to still more aggression" (p. 1).

Feshbach (1984) considered the validity of the concept of catharsis. He suggests the possibility that if cathartic aggressive responses reduce aggressive impulses, the responses will only be reinforced, increasing the probability of aggression on subsequent exposure to the target aggression. This would be particularly so if the cathartic aggressive behavior is very similar to the target aggression. He proposes three conceptions of catharsis: the dramatic model, drawn from Aristotle, has its cathartic effect through vicarious expression of emotion; the clinical model is mediated by the direct recall of an affect-arousing event; and the experimental model stems from the frustration-aggression hypothesis of Dollard and colleagues (1939, Dollard and Miller 1950). "In this formulation, catharsis applies to the reduction of aggression through any aggressive response, whether that response be direct or displaced, verbal or physical, fantasy or real" (Feshbach 1984, p. 97). Therefore, he views the experimental model as addressing the general problem of reducing aggression through aggressive acts. On the other hand, he views the dramatic and clinical models as more germane, as they focus on affective engagement and change. He proposes that "catharsis obtains in the case of inhibited rather than persistent or unresolved affect" (p. 91).

Bohart (1980), in reviewing four counseling-analogue studies, suggested an alternative model to the "hydraulic model" of emotions. He proposed that "anger expression will lead to anger reduction if and only if it leads to coping with the anger-instigating event. Coping can be either through dealing with the environment or through changing one's self-perceptions and attitudes" (p. 192).

Blatner (1965) proposes some interesting ideas regarding catharsis. He understands catharsis as a psychological shift to a new integrative level and separates it into four interacting categories. The first category is the catharsis of abreaction. Here, the reaction is not simply the experience again of the original trauma, but an awareness that one is in a safe context and has a positive alliance with the therapist. This certainly pertains to the environment of play therapy, which will be discussed later. Blatner further suggests that once this catharsis of abreaction occurs, people must be prepared to integrate their disowned feelings in their lives. The second category is the catharsis of integration. Here, the self is expanded to include feelings and role functions previously excluded. This seems very close to self-acceptance, which certainly is a goal in play therapy with children. The third category is the catharsis of inclusion, "discovering that one 'belongs' in a social network of one's choice" (Blatner 1985, p. 162). Often people (children, too) feel alienated and unacceptable. To be able to be oneself with the acceptance of another may help to achieve a sense of relief and thereby self-acceptance. The fourth category is spiritual catharsis. The important aspect of spiritual catharsis is that one enlarges one's capacity to be more open to the environment and others. One outcome of play therapy with children is to help them achieve an increased capacity for openness to the environment.

Nichols and Efran (1985) believe that there is a link between emotional expressiveness and therapeutic gain. They point to Freud's development of conflict theory in place of the traumatic theory of neurosis. Here, "disowned feelings and impulses must be recognized and integrated into the personality. Feelings were not concrete entities which can be stored up and then drained off, but part of disposition to action, to be recognized and given appropriate expression" (p. 48). They believe this supports the idea that catharsis may be a useful part of the therapeutic process. In considering catharsis, they identify their understanding of the nature of emotion. They emphasize that the structure of our language causes our emotional concepts to express relations, not possessions. They believe that emotion words occur out of a context and refer to a class of passive or partially blocked actions. They state, "To feel is to do something. . . . Emotion terms are always associated with a sense of restraint. . . . Some hindrance is necessary to produce any awareness of self (self-consciousness). . . . So, on the one hand, emotions point to obstacles, but, on the other hand, they are the cutting edge of self definition" (p. 52). From this perspective of emotion and emotional expression, they propose a two-stage adaptive process of events labeled emotional. There is an *activation stage* when the goal is blocked, and a *recovery stage* when the obstacle is overcome or becomes less relevant. They cite the work of Kahn (1966) to support the idea that the activation stage is associated with sympathetic nervous system response, and the recovery stage a shift to parasympathetic activity. They compare these to Piaget's concept of assimilation and accommodation. The activation stage (stage 1) reflects assimilation; the recovery stage (stage 2) reflects accommodation. They give an example in which a child is "overwhelmed (unable to assimilate), gives up and easily shifts into recovery with tears being an outward manifestation of the shift. This alerts the parents to come to the rescue: they embrace and comfort the child, restoring a patterned, assimilable environment" (Nichols and Efran p. 53).

Nichols and Efran believe that catharsis never handles a problem but promotes one or two useful actions: (1) a signal and part of the completion of a previously interrupted sequence of actions; (2) a form of self–assertion (self-action) (p. 54). They raise some interesting ideas for the value of catharsis, which has applicability to play therapy with children: emotional expression in catharsis is a beginning attempt to complete an aspect of one's self in relation to others; therapy is a laboratory where one is free and safe to rehearse aspects of oneself; and linguistic self (the words and language we use) becomes consistent with how we "feel" physically. They then define catharsis to be "understood as a label for completing (some or all of) a previously restrained or interrupted sequence of self-expression" and "the expression is that which would have occurred as a natural reaction to some experience had that expression not been thwarted" (p. 55). This is followed by a stage 2 recovery expression such as tears or shouting. They relate the value this has in psychotherapy: "To say that feelings are actions rather than things avoids divorcing patients from aspects of themselves, and reduces their tendency to disclaim action" (p. 55). Finally, Nichols and Efran (1985) describe four therapeutic goals for the usefulness of catharsis. These goals seem to apply to the benefit of catharsis in play therapy.

The first is to do nothing to interfere with the recovery phase (stage two) of catharsis and its manifestations. Catharsis is feeling expression and is a normal part of the adaptive process. The goal is to take on a permissive accepting stance enabling the emotional expression of recovery. This is consistent with the importance of creating a permissive environment in play therapy.

The second goal that Nichols and Efran suggest is that the therapist help patients not short-circuit their own experience by automatically inhibiting their self-expressions. They suggest simple encouragement and reflection of feelings to help patients move into recovery and complete their experience. Acceptance, so integral in play therapy, helps the child accept himself and thereby is less likely to short-circuit his own experience.

The third goal they propose is to use catharsis as a sign of blocked action, providing help to experiment and rehearse action. It is important here that patients take more *responsibility for their actions* and be able to complete the business at hand. Nichols and Efran (1985) recommend that the therapist help the patient learn how to give suitable expression to these restrained feelings in relevant social context. Limits, in addition to providing security in play therapy contexts, also assist the child in finding suitable expression of his feelings in social contexts. It is common to observe children repeat their actions within a play session and across sessions. It has also been observed (L. Guerney 1976a, Stover and Guerney 1967) that after an initial period of increased aggressiveness, there is a lessening of aggression to a level below that of the initial sessions. Furthermore, the inclusion and application of realistic and appropriate limits in play therapy help children to shift their emotional expressions to socially acceptable behaviors. Once this occurs in play sessions, they can begin to implement this learning and related skills to their everyday lives.

The fourth goal proposed by Nichols and Efran (1985) is to help patients use catharsis to "discover, define and enact their selves in relation to others" (p. 57). Here, they emphasize the importance of experiencing feelings and not repressing affect (blocking action) to discover themselves. This is a preliminary step to taking responsibility for "choosing more congruent actions and appropriate social expressions" (p. 57). The combination of permissiveness, acceptance, structure, and limits of play therapy makes the experiencing of feelings and taking responsibility for oneself more possible. Play therapy, primarily through reflection of feelings and acceptance, promotes the learning of a language of self and self-acceptance. This leads to action more congruent with the self and more appropriate social expression.

Axline (1969) expresses a similar view to that of Nichols and Efran:

When an individual reaches a barrier which makes it more difficult for him to achieve the complete realization of the self, there is set up an area of resistance and friction and tension.

The drive toward self-realization continues and the individual's behavior demonstrates that he is satisfying this inner drive by outwardly fighting to establish his self-concept in the world of reality, or that he is satisfying it vicariously by confining it to his inner world where he can build it up with less struggle. The more it is turned inward, the more dangerous it becomes, and the further he departs from the world of reality, the more difficult it is to help him. [p. 13]

Axline relates this to the difference between well-adjusted behavior and maladjusted behavior. Well-adjusted behavior occurs when the individual can develop sufficient self-confidence to bring his self-concept to the surface and consciously, with purpose, direct his behavior through evaluation and action to achieve greater self-realization. The objective then seems to achieve greater congruence between experience and expression of self for optimal self-realization. Maladjustment, on the other hand, occurs when the individual lacks enough self-confidence to direct his actions openly but instead does this vicariously or does little to channel this drive more constructively. Axline (1969) sees play therapy as an opportunity under the most favorable conditions for the child to play out his feelings, get them to the surface, and learn to control or abandon them. Play therapy provides the permissiveness and the security (through acceptance and a few limits) to accomplish this.

Permissiveness

The typical play session is structured to create an atmosphere of permissiveness that is designed to allow a child freedom of expression (Moustakas 1959). This permissive environment makes emotional relief and catharsis possible. It is this "safe" permissiveness that allows catharsis and emotional release to be constructive.

Dollard and Miller (1950) believe that catharsis can only work under permissive conditions. Solomon (1938) developed an approach called Active Play Therapy, in which children, particularly impulsive, acting-out children, are allowed to express rage and fear, and to play without negative consequences, so as to allow for a cathartic reaction and to help the child cope with his feelings. Levy's (1939) Release Therapy was another approach in which permissiveness was achieved through reducing or eliminating the interpretive function of the therapist and allowing "free play." This approach was based on the assumption that the permissive approach would allow the child to recreate traumatic events through play, repeating the traumatic event or related behavior until he could assimilate these negative thoughts and feelings into his own functioning. Landisberg and Snyder (1946) found that play therapy fosters emotional release, an increase in emotion-laden statements, and a parallel increase in activity. Hambridge (1955) developed an approach called Structured Play Therapy, where he deliberately attempted to re-create the traumatic experience in the play therapy session with the child. He believed that it was important for the child to have free play following structured play, to achieve a maximum of emotional release, reduction of impulse, and ego mastery.

Mallick and McCandless (1966) suggest, in their study of aggressiveness in children, that aggressive play in the presence of a permissive adult may lead to an increase in aggression. Kahn (1966), in a study on the physiology of catharsis, found an increase of aggression under permissive and approving conditions. However, he suggests that allowing full experience and expression of an emotion may facilitate a recovery pattern that enables the person to free himself to deal with the environment. This is certainly the view of client-centered play therapy (Axline 1969, Guerney 1983a).

Bandura and Walters (1963) considered the effects of permissiveness. They define permissiveness as "the willingness of a socializing agent to allow a given form of behavior to occur or to continue once it has commenced" (p. 130). They suggest that effects of parental permissiveness are not independent of the consequences that follow the child's acts. Here they bring up the importance of the adult's response to the child's act, particularly that of punishment. This suggests the contrasting response of the play therapist, who provides acceptance but establishes clear limits. (The issues of acceptance and limits in play therapy as related to catharsis and emotional release will be discussed later in this chapter.) Bandura and Walters (1963) further raised the issue of permissiveness in studies of doll-play aggression. They cite studies (Bach 1945, Hartup and Himeno 1959, Hollenberg and Sperry 1951, Sears 1951) in which aggression increases with a permissive adult present within a session and over two to four consecutive sessions. They cite the work of Yarrow (1948) who "found that nonaggressive, as well as aggressive, responses increased in frequency over two sessions of permissive doll play, a finding that suggests that adult permissiveness has a general reinforcing or disinhibitory influence on children's play activities rather than a specific influence on aggression" (Bandura and Walters 1963, p. 132).

It is also important to note the work of Bernard Guerney and colleagues (1971, 1972) and Louise Guerney (1976a–d). In Filial Therapy, after 49,000 observations occurring in 600 play sessions, aggression toward the mother (who was the play therapist) increased and then declined to a low below the initial session. Also, there was increased game playing, cooperative behavior, and conversation about real life matters. Role playing and emotional expression declined as the children increased the above-mentioned behaviors. "As the children experienced the permissiveness and acceptance of their mothers in the playroom, they worked out their aggressive feelings, cut out affectional displays [which probably were a defense against the aggressive feelings that had previously gone unexpressed] and dealt with their mothers more realistically – shared with them, conversed with them, etc." (Guerney 1976a, p. 83). It is important to note that the program lasted twelve to eighteen months and it appears that the number of play sessions per parent–child dyad was more than ten. It is also interesting to note that the majority of studies investigating catharsis were of a much shorter duration. The work of Guerney and colleagues would therefore support the value of catharsis and emotional release in play therapy. In the client-centered approach that Guerney and Stover (1971) took, acceptance and limit setting, as well as permissiveness, are integral components.

Acceptance

In the study of the effects of Filial Therapy (Guerney and Stover 1971), parents who were play therapists with their own children improved in their ability to provide acceptance to their children during play sessions. In specific, parents were trained to "be sensitive to their children's feelings and emotional needs [empathic understanding]; and communicate their sensitivity and understanding in such a way as to permit the child to feel that his feelings and needs are accepted, and he, therefore, is acceptable and worthwhile as a person in his parents' eyes [empathic in responding]" (Guerney 1976a, p. 70). In this Filial Therapy training, other important objectives included creating a permissive environment, structuring the play sessions for security and safety, and establishing few but appropriate limits to achieve these objectives. It seems that the first two objectives not only raise the importance of acceptance (empathic understanding) but also of acknowledgment (empathic responding) of the child's feeling. In an atmosphere of play, where the adult is accepting and acknowledging, children evidenced initial increases in aggression and then a reduction of aggression to below initial levels, and a concomitant increase in pro-active, constructive, and interpersonal behavior (Guerney and Stover 1971).

Rogers (1951) provides a rationale for the importance of acceptance:

> The therapist perceives the client's self as the client has known it, and accepts it; he perceives the contradictory and accepts those too as being a part of the client; and both of these acceptances have in them the same warmth and respect. Thus it is that the client, experiencing in another an acceptance of both these aspects of himself, can take toward himself the same attitude. [p. 41]

Under these conditions, the child

> . . . retains instead a secure self which can serve to guide his behavior by freely admitting to awareness, inaccurately symbolized form, all the relevant evidence of his experience in terms of its organismic satisfactions, both immediate and longer range. He is thus developing a soundly structured self in which there is neither denial nor distortion of experience. [p. 503]

Axline (1969) expresses this similarly:

> Non-directive therapy grants the individual the permissiveness to be himself; it accepts that self completely, without evaluation or pressure to change; it recognizes and clarifies the expressed emotionalized attitudes by a reflection of what the client has expressed; and

by the very process of non-directive therapy, it offers the individual to be himself, to learn to know himself, to chart his own course openly and aboveboard – to rotate the kaleidoscope, so to speak, so that he may form a more satisfactory design for living. [p. 15]

Several studies support the value of parental acceptance. Cox found parental acceptance was highly related to child self-concept. Miller (1971) found that maternal empathy, genuineness, and positive regard were significantly related to child self-esteem. Rohner and colleagues (1980) found children with increased perception of parental acceptance had significantly increased belief in their control over life's events and actions. Eisman (1981) similarly found a significant and positive relationship between parental acceptance and child self-concept.

The correlation between permissiveness, allowing emotional release with acceptance and acknowledgment of the child's experience, and the ability of the child to use this increased emotional expression suggests that the child is able to utilize this cathartic experience to improve his independence, mastery, and social functioning.

Limits

The improved ability of the child to use this opportunity for emotional release and catharsis for more constructive endeavors also depends on the response of the environment to these emotional expressions. Another of the training objectives in Filial Therapy is as follows: "Recognize 'the realistic circumstances' and age constraints for the child which would appropriately lead to some control over his self-direction; and to translate these to operationally defined and enforceable limits" (L. Guerney 1976a, p. 70).

Limits define the boundaries within which the child is free to operate. Limits convey that this type of permissiveness is provided with the consent of the adult and is the responsibility of the child. Limits enable the therapist to remain accepting and empathic. Limits help build self-control because it is the child's responsibility to respect the limits. Louise Guerney (1983b) has elaborated extensively on limits and their management in play therapy. Parents learning to conduct play therapy sessions with their own children (Filial Therapy) are taught a highly structured three-step method to ensure child responsibility for limits, while maintaining the permissive, accepting, and empathic position of the play therapist (parent). This helps to facilitate greater emotional expression of the child within a secure context. Under these conditions, catharsis is likely to be constructive.

Bixler (1949) published an article entitled "Limits Are Therapy." In it, he emphasizes the value of limits, particularly to help maintain acceptance of the child. He also suggests that limits help a child recognize the difference between the therapeutic experience and other relationships. He further suggests that the use of limits on behavior may be equally as important as acceptance.

Ginott (1959) identifies six statements as a rationale for the use of limits. Four of these are pertinent to the issue of catharsis and emotional release: (1) Limits direct catharsis into symbolic channels. (2) Limits enable the therapist to maintain attitudes of acceptance, empathy, and regard for the child client throughout the therapy contacts. (3) Limits assure the physical safety of the children and the therapist in the playroom. (4) Limits strengthen ego controls.

In the first statement, Ginott suggests that the therapist allow the child the opportunity for gratification while changing the choice of object. The second and third create the safety that allows the acceptance, understanding, and empathy so necessary to the play therapy process. The fourth emphasizes that through the play therapy process and the use of limits, a child can learn to regulate his own behavior.

In play therapy, catharsis and emotional release are important components of therapeutic change. The essential conditions necessary for catharsis and emotional release to be integrated into mastery and improved functioning of the individual are a permissive environment, acknowledgment and acceptance from the adult playing with the child, and a few essential limits that are structured for child responsibility. Under these conditions, children are able to release blocked emotions and thoughts, and express them in constructive activities.

Developmental Perspective

Ellis (1973) suggests that play is stimulus-seeking behavior, but not all stimulus seeking is play. Rather, play is "that part of stimulus-seeking behavior to which we cannot ascribe a prepotent motive" (p. 109). He states further that "play is that behavior that is motivated by the need to elevate the level of arousal towards the optimal" (p. 110). Play is also assumed to be based on some intrinsic motivation (Berlyne 1960, Ellis 1973). Berlyne brings up the idea of what he calls epistemic behavior. Here, he proposes that man, who can manipulate his experience through symbolic means, uses this ability to classify and order his experience into understandable concepts that can help him explain and predict events in his environment. The arousal of human cognitive events is largely a result of the emergence of conflicts of ideas (and knowledge) from lack of experience or past experience. The process of resolving these conflicts is what Berlyne (1960) calls epistemic behavior. Perhaps this concept of play as arousal-seeking behavior dependent on conflict provides a rationale for the importance of emotional release and catharsis. Nichols and Efran (1985) suggest that a restrained or interrupted sequence of self-expression is the first stage of catharsis. The conflict created by the restraint or interruption elicits the "epistemic behavior."

White (1959) raises the question of play behaviors in which the behavior is repeated after the novelty has worn off. He suggests that this behavior is motivated by the need to demonstrate a capacity to control or produce effects in the environment (Ellis 1973, p. 100). White (1959) gives this concept the name *competence*. "As used here, competence will refer to an organism's capacity to interact effectively with its environment" (p. 297). White further suggests that the motivation to achieve competence is the need to feel in control. This need is one of mastery, which is an important objective in play therapy. Murphy (1962) has emphasized the importance of mastery and the development of ego controls. This relates to the concept of self-assertion (self-action) that follows stage one (thwarting of action) of catharsis proposed by Nichols and Efran (1985). Erikson (1972) states that "the themes presented betray some repetitiveness such as we recognize as the 'working through' of a traumatic experience, but they also express a playful renewal. If they seem to be governed by some need to communicate, or even to confess, they also seem to serve the joy of self-expression. If they seem dedicated to the exercise of growing faculties, they also seem to serve the mastery of a complex life situation" (p. 131). It is important to consider that a traumatic event is not the only kind to elicit conflict in one's thinking and experience. Any interrupted sequence of action and experience could elicit conflict in one's experience. Many play therapy approaches try to achieve this kind of freedom of self (and emotional) expression. Play therapy can provide a setting in which catharsis and emotional release can be utilized in the service of self-mastery.

Piaget (1970) has emphasized that the establishment of cognition arises through the development of structures performed inside the individual, progressively constructed by the ongoing interaction between the individual and the outside world. Piaget suggests that this is not a passive process, but requires that the individual must act on objects in the external environment and transform them. This objective knowledge, according to Piaget, has its origin in the interaction between subject and object. This necessitates two kinds of activities, coordination of actions themselves and introduction of the relations between objects. These two activities are interdependent, because it is only through action that these relations originate (Piaget 1970). This idea that only through action can an understanding of relations occur raises the prospect that through the opportunity for cathartic action (expression) and emotional release (expression) can understanding emerge to help one gain mastery. This leads to his concept of "construction" of objective knowledge that is dependent on coordination of action. The living organism is not an exact duplicate of the properties of its environment, but develops a structure step by step in the course of adaptation to its environment. Primitive actions have been transformed into operations, which are internal actions that can be performed physically or mentally and are reversible. Through this process, the organism can be self-regulated (develop a self). Piaget proposes that adaptation requires an equilibrium between assimilation, the integration of external elements into the evolving organism's functioning, and accommodation, modifying this integration to fit the demands of external reality.

Nichols and Efran (1985) applied this concept to the issue of catharsis and emotional release. In essence, in the process of adaptation, the individual assimilates his experience and out of blocked action must accommodate to his environment. Play, in Piaget's conception, is characterized by assimilation of elements in the real world without the balancing constraint of having to accept the limitation of accommodating to them (Ellis 1973). "In play the primary object is to mold reality to the whim of the cognizer, in other words, to assimilate reality to various schemes with little concern for precise accommodation to that reality. Thus, as Piaget put it, in play there is 'primary assimilation over accommodation' " (Flavell 1963, p. 65). Piaget believed that with increased cognitive complexity resulting from development, increased complexity of play would ensue. This increased complexity would take the form of constraints or rules imposed on the activity (Ellis 1973). Piaget (1970) defined three categories of play to indicate the increased cognitive development: (1) Exercise games in which the primary object is having pleasure from the activity itself. This is mostly assimilation. (2) Symbolic games involving structuring new meanings that represent realities from one's present perceptual field. This is based on symbols specific to each child. (3) Rule games involving more than one person in which new meanings are constructed. These rules are determined by means of interpersonal interaction.

As a child moves through the development process, he is able to increase his adaptation through greater equilibrium between assimilation and accommodation. The process of catharsis and emotional release (assimilation) that is accepted in play therapy allows the child openness to form greater adaptation. The application of appropriate and consistent limits improves accommodation, enhancing the equilibrium between assimilation and accommodation and improved interpersonal functioning.

Piaget has not been explicit in his formulations on the importance of affect in the developmental process. He did address this issue in a 1981 publication. In this monograph, he relates affect to the function of intelligence. Here, he proposes that affect acts as "an energizing force emerging from disequilibrium between assimilation and accommodation. Cognition provides the structure for this energy" and "affect serves as a regulator of action" (Cowan in Piaget 1981, p. xi). Here, it appears as a view that could help explain the importance of emotional release – as an energizing force, and regulator of action from the disequilibrium between assimilation and accommodation. The function of catharsis and emotional release may provide the energy helping the child to find a greater equilibrium. This suggests the requirement of an interpersonal context and the opportunity to use language to gain mastery.

Piaget states,

> If assimilation and accommodation have their cognitive side . . . they, like all other characteristics of behavior, have an affective side as well. The affective aspect of assimilation is interest, defined by Dewey as assimilation to the self; the cognitive aspect is understanding. Accommodation in its affective aspect is interest in the object in as much as it is new. In its cognitive aspect, accommodation is the adjustment of schemes of thought to phenomena. . . . Affectivity would play the role of an energy source on which functioning but not the structures of intelligence would depend. [p. 5]

Piaget concludes that "affective structures become the cognitive aspect of relationships with other people" (p. 74). He argues further that behavior cannot be classified as affective or cognitive, but that the distinction should be made between behaviors related to objects and behaviors related to people. Both have structural or cognitive and energetic or affective aspects. In behaviors related to objects, the structural aspects are the various empirical and logicomathematical knowledge structures, while the energetic aspects are the interests, efforts, and intra-individual feelings that regulate behavior. In behaviors related to people, the energetic element is made up of interpersonal feelings. Ordinarily, these are emphasized exclusively. They contain a structural element, however, which comes from taking consciousness of interpersonal relationship and leads, among other things, to the constitution of value structures. [p. 74]

Piaget makes the distinction between the self and personality. "The self is activity centered on the self. The personality . . . develops at the time of entry into social life. Consequently, it presupposes decentration and subordination of the self to the collective ideal" (p. 71). The closer one can come to achieve an equilibrium between self and personality, the greater the experience of self-mastery. The opportunity for catharsis and emotional release provided through play therapy allows the child to regulate his actions to achieve improved equilibrium between assimilation and accommodation and improve his experience of self-mastery.

Bearison (1986) points out that according to Piaget (1977), each perturbation to an equilibrated cognitive system gives rise to a higher form of equilibration. Bearison states that "according to the socio-cognitive conflict model, effective social interactions will generate perturbations (i.e., disequilibrations) in subjects' existing knowledge schemes that can be resolved through operational coordinations (intrapersonal and interpersonal) that yield cognitively more advanced levels of understanding" (p. 138). Selman and Demorest (1986) have identified a related model based on Werner's principle of orthogenesis.

Werner (Werner 1957, Werner and Kaplan 1956) believed that whenever a developmental change occurred, it followed the "orthogenetic" principles of development. Werner (1957a) stated that "it is an orthogenetic principle which states that whenever development occurs it proceeds from a state of relative globality and lack of differentiation to a state of increasing differentiation, articulation and hierarchic integration" (p. 126). Wapner and colleagues (1983) point out that this includes increasing knowledge of being and action in diverse domains of action, which enable the individual to differentiate and integrate his transactions with the environment (socialization).

Selman and Demorest (1986) apply the principle of orthogenesis to interpersonal negotiation strategies. By this they mean "dealing with both self and other to pursue goals in an interpersonal context" (p. 100). They propose two conditions in which an interpersonal negotiation strategy can occur. The first, called the condition of *internal disequilibrium,* occurs in a context in which one person in an interaction "is in an initial state of disequilibrium with respect to a self-perceived goal" (p. 101). The second condition, called the condition of *interpersonal disequilibrium,* is defined as occurring when one or both individuals attempt to return to a state of inner balance with each impacting on the other. This is very close to the two-stage theory of catharsis proposed by Nichols and Efran (1985), and adds the dimension of interpersonal negotiation. In a play therapy context, the behavior of the child considered cathartic impacts on the play therapist to acknowledge the action (and feelings pertaining to it) and/or setting a limit. This fosters increased differentiation of self as the child is now better able to distinguish his inner disequilibrium from awareness of the larger interpersonal context. He is then better able to master these emotions that before may have been experienced as uncontrollable.

Catharsis and emotional release, when viewed in light of the proposed development of interpersonal negotiation strategies of Selman and Demorest, is an important component of the process of undifferentiated knowing and action to increasing differentiation, coordination of actions, and socialization.

Franklin (1983) interprets Werner by noting that this increasing differentiation assists the child in moving from a self-world fusion to increasingly differentiated spheres marked by the emergence of differentiated actions and attitudes toward objects, persons, and events. She also posits that as each sphere becomes differentiated, there is an internal differentiation. Therefore, as one's actions become more differentiated, one becomes more differentiated internally. The process of catharsis and emotional release is action that promotes internal differentiation, self-knowing, and knowing of the world.

Catharsis and emotional release are important components of a person's development, and assist in the process of increasing differentiation. Play and play therapy provide the context in which a child can experiment and mature, increasing differentiation and interpersonal competence safely and securely (within clear limits) with an understanding and accepting adult.

The Client-Centered Play Therapy Approach to Catharsis and Emotional Release

When children are referred to a clinical setting, it is often because they are acting out their conflicts through their behavior at home, in school, with their peers, and/or with others. They are evidencing behaviors that frequently are expressed aggressively or through withdrawal. This elicits concern on the part of some adult in their lives, and the referral is initiated. Other times, when adults are concerned about some trauma or distressing experience that the child has had (i.e., physical or sexual abuse, witnessing some upsetting action, or perhaps a loss in the family), they refer the child to a clinical setting to help intervene in the problem. For children younger than age 12, play – and play therapy in particular – is the intervention of choice. These behaviors that are a cause of concern to adults and others in a child's life are often blocked, interrupted, or redirected so that the child has inadequate opportunities to gain mastery over the conflicts these behaviors may suggest. Involving children in a play format allows them freedom to express these conflicts in an accepting and secure environment. This allows the child to have the opportunity to work at gaining mastery over these conflicts and reducing the inappropriate expression of them in their real lives.

Louise Guerney (1983a) believes that more than any other play therapy approach, client-centered play therapy enables the child to be himself or herself without being judged, evaluated, or pressured to change. Axline (1947) specifically describes the process as an opportunity in which the child can experience growth under the most favorable conditions. She writes that by playing out feelings, the child "brings them to the surface, faces them, learns to control them or abandon them and begins to realize the power within himself to be an individual in his own right, to think for himself, to make his own decisions, to become physically more mature and by doing so realize selfhood" (p. 16). Without saying so specifically, Axline is expressing a clear and strong statement on what could be called catharsis. The two-step process of Nichols and Efran (1985) seems to be closely related to Axline's description.

If catharsis is an expression of previously restrained or interrupted sequence of self-expression, then it seems logical that without this freedom one would be unable to complete this self-expression and achieve mastery.

It is interesting that Nichols and Efran (1985) relate language to catharsis. They believe an important objective of psychotherapy is that the linguistic self and the physical self be consistent with each other. It is important that how we define ourselves is consistent with our real actions and interactions with those around us. This helps the individual acknowledge greater responsibility for his actions, which helps him gain mastery and self-assurance. Children, because of their development, may not have sufficient linguistic skill to express themselves. They need a context that will help them accomplish this. Play, and play therapy in particular, can provide this kind of context. When children have this opportunity, they improve the consistency between self-definition and action. Their linguistic abilities improve, particularly in expressing their feelings (motivation for action) and in making feelings more consistent with action. As a result, they can experience increased mastery.

The therapeutic goals that Nichols and Efran (1985) suggest appear to be important for catharsis in play therapy as well. The first goal is for the therapist to adopt a permissive, accepting position and to avoid any direct interference with the emotional manifestations of what they call stage 2 or the recovery phase. They suggest that it is important for the therapist to be able to accept a wide range of feelings of varying intensities. Some therapists use special procedures and conditions to produce the emotional expression of catharsis. Nichols and Efran (1985) believe that this would be necessary only if catharsis were viewed as purging feelings that were locked inside. However, when catharsis is understood as feeling expression, which is a natural aspect of experiencing, then one does not do anything to block this expression in therapy. Because it is natural, it will emerge in a permissive and accepting environment. They recommend that responses such as questioning and reassurance only divert the patient from this expression or block it, thereby undermining the objective of the therapeutic context.

The second therapeutic goal suggested by Nichols and Efran is to help people overcome their tendencies to short-circuit their own experience. Obviously, the permissive and accepting environment contributes greatly to this objective. In client-centered play therapy, the acknowledgments or reflections of feelings of actions on the part of the therapist help the patient acknowledge and be more open to his own experience and action. The third goal they suggest is to use catharsis to provide assistance with experimentation and rehearsal, first in the therapeutic context and then in real life. In play therapy with young children, the play therapy context with its toys and materials allows a child to practice (repeat) these important self-expressions and actions, and experiment with new and perhaps more effective behaviors. Finally, Nichols and Efran suggest that the importance of using catharsis in psychotherapy is to help patients discover, define, and enact themselves in relation to others. Here, the importance of limits in play therapy is important. Although the play therapy context is permissive and accepting, it also needs to be safe and secure for both the child and the therapist. As a result, a few clearly defined and expressed limits are an important part of the play therapy experience and are related to the usefulness of catharsis. In client-centered play therapy, limits are determined, for the most part, in advance. They are clearly expressed (i.e., "I can't be hit" vs. "I can't be hurt") and an opportunity is provided for the child to be responsible for the limit and to gain control of it through a three-step method of limit setting. He is able to express the feelings that represent blocked action in an effort to gain mastery. When a child has to be responsible for the limits that make him and the therapist secure, he can begin to improve his self-definition, particularly, through his relationship with others.

Given the preceding remarks, catharsis and emotional release are important components of the psychotherapeutic process necessary for change. Client-centered play therapy can be useful to provide the context for catharsis and mastery (Axline 1969, Guerney 1983b). Essentially, the objective in client-centered play therapy is to provide a context in which a child's own resources are utilized to foster change and growth. Under these conditions, attention needs to be directed toward the context of play sessions, the materials used, limits including time, therapist's behavior, and the interaction of these components to provide optimum opportunity for the child to be free to express these feelings and to take more responsibility for them.

The context for play therapy needs to be structured to provide optimum opportunities for freedom of expression and behavior. Therefore, the setting chosen to conduct such play therapies needs to be considered carefully. In essence, one must make the attempt to eliminate, as much as possible, any intrusion into the child's own process of expression. An attempt might be made to remove the possibility of any limit, although in reality some limits must be established for the safety of the child and the therapist. The first step in considering the room or area for the play therapy is to remove any furniture, objects, materials, and so forth, that may create some anxiety on the part of the child or the therapist or may be difficult to make secure. Often it is useful for the therapist, before beginning to use the area for play therapy, to sit in the middle of it and contemplate what it might be like to have the child in that context, looking around to see what may provide difficulty for the freedom and permissiveness so important to this play therapy process. After the therapist has removed all objects, furniture, and materials that would provide difficulty to establish this kind of environment, the therapist needs to consider the area chosen and the physical possibilities and limitations that the setting provides. For example, a room that is very large may not provide sufficient opportunity for intimacy between the therapist and the child. On the other hand, an area that is too small may cause discomfort and anxiety on the part of both the child and therapist because there is insufficient room to establish an appropriate separateness and independence between the two. Typically, a 12 × 12 area can be quite satisfactory for play therapy purposes. When considering the play area, the decor needs to be considered in terms of removal or consideration of appropriate limits to protect these things. When a room is used for other purposes throughout the week and is occasionally modified to accommodate play therapy sessions, great care is needed to establish the area and make it secure for play therapy sessions. It is important to consider finding a room with movable furniture, with few decorative objects, and with sufficient space to delineate a play area separate from the entire room.

The materials that are part of the play therapy context are extremely important components of the play therapy itself and to the objectives of the play therapist. It is important that the materials chosen do not impede the child's freedom to bring to it his own personality, self-expression, and needs. In general, the materials, such as toys, should allow for activity, mastery, and/or fantasy expression. Ginott (1961) suggests that these materials (1) permit reality testing, (2) provide an opportunity for symbolic expression, and (3) allow for catharsis and insight. What is particularly important in client-centered play therapy is that the toys are chosen in a more generic fashion to elicit the interest in expression of most children, not necessarily to direct a child in a particular way.

The behavior (positioning) of the therapist is the most important component of the play therapy process. The position of the therapist in relation to the child is the focal point throughout the play therapy process. It is essential that the play therapist's position be one of response to the child's initiation. Any initiation in the play therapy process on the part of the therapist undermines the child's own responsibility and readiness for expression, and often interrupts or thwarts the child's natural direction and responsibility within the play therapy context. Any judgment or question initiated by the play therapist has the potential of redirecting the child or inhibiting his own opportunity for self-expression. Often this results in increasing the child's dependence upon the therapist, and in the case of catharsis and emotional release, the child may not achieve the sense of mastery and self-control so important to therapeutic change. With the exception of limits to be discussed later, the therapist's responsibility is to provide acceptance (nonjudgment) and acknowledgment (reflections of feelings) of the child's expression and experience in the play session.

Acknowledgment and acceptance of the child's feelings helps the child recognize and develop language for self-description, bringing his physical self and linguistic self more in tune with one another. Through this process, the child gains more security and self-assurance through mastery of his own feelings and experience. For this to happen, it is essential that the therapist consistently maintain a position of trust and acceptance of the child's own ability to master whatever is important in the child's own life. The therapist's position and behavior with the child in being noninitiative, nonjudgmental, accepting, and acknowledging of the child's behavior and feelings are the critical ingredients that create this context for the child. As a result the therapist can accept extreme expressions of emotion, recognizing that these expressions represent stage 2 recovery (Nichols and Efran 1985) from the blocked goal to achieve mastery and rebalancing. With the security of the implementation of appropriate limits, the child can then take charge of his own recovery.

Limits are an essential ingredient of the play therapy process. The necessary permissiveness, nonjudgment, and acceptance are only possible in a secure environment for both child and therapist. A few pertinent and specific limits establish the structure and boundaries in which the nonjudgment and acceptance can occur. Guerney (1983b) has identified the usefulness of limits in client-centered play therapy. (1) Limits help the child to define areas within which he is free to operate. They also communicate to the child that the play therapist is interested and caring by providing the security that the child needs to feel safe. (2) Limits permit the therapist to remain accepting and empathic. If the setting were not secure for the therapist as well, the therapist would feel too insecure and defensive to provide the appropriate environment. (3) Limits help the child build self-control since it is the child's responsibility to stay within definite boundaries.

Guerney further suggests the areas in which limits are set: (1) physical aggression against the therapist or self, (2) destruction of expensive or irreplaceable objects, (3) running in and out of the play room, (4) remaining beyond the play period, and (5) undressing (except jackets and shoes) (p. 41). Guerney also considers the inclusion of a very few personal limits, which are sometimes required for a particular person to feel secure. An example of this might be that one person may accept a child pointing a gun at him while another may not. The therapist needs to take some time to consider how limits will be expressed so that the child can recognize his responsibility for the limit. An example of this might be to say, "One of the rules is that I can't get wet," instead of "You're not supposed to get me wet" or "Don't get me wet."

It is also important to consider that children need an opportunity for trial-and-error learning in order to take responsibility for the limits. All too often, we expect children to follow limits after only one explanation of the limit. If the limit pertains to something the child does not resolve in himself, it may take a number of repetitions to gain mastery and be self-limiting. The approach by Guerney (1983b) suggests a three-step method in which the child is warned of the limit on the first transgression. When this occurs a second time in the same play session, the child is reminded of the limit, and the consequence—that of ending the play session—is identified. The third time the child breaks the limit, the therapist states the rule, acknowledges that the consequence is to end the session, and identifies that the child and therapist can play more at the next play therapy sessions. At that point the session ends. This three-step method is conveyed to the child with acceptance and without judgment of the child's behavior. As a result, the child is confronted by the responsibility for his own behavior. Under those conditions, and with a child learning to trust the consistency of this limit setting, the child begins to take responsibility for his own conflicts. Underlying cathartic-like behavior and emotional release is a relief from some of the underlying anxiety caused by the effect of the thwarted action. If the child can then begin to take charge of his behavior related to the anxiety, a sense of mastery and increased security will ensue. As a result, the child will be less likely to act out these feelings that arise from the sense of thwarted action. With the acceptance and the acknowledgment of the play therapist, the child begins to trust that person and himself more. Out of this process over time, the child experiences more acceptance of himself, increased sense of mastery, and security.

Another important aspect of limits has to do with clearly defined time periods for play therapy. It is useful to schedule a regular play therapy time that the child can count on from week to week. Usually a half-hour is sufficient for these sessions. However, with some children more or less time might need to be considered. It is also important that the child be free to reject, at times, the chance to have these play sessions. Play therapy sessions can be threatening for the child, and if a child is close to expressing some feeling that he may not be secure enough to express, it may create tremendous anxiety. As a result the child may refuse play sessions because of fear that these feelings might surface in the permissive environment of the play session. It is important that the therapist respect this, acknowledge that the child does not wish to play at this time, and that he can play again at the next session.

Parents as Play Therapists

Catharsis and emotional release can be even more useful when parents are play therapists for their own children. Much has been written about this approach called Filial Therapy or Child Relationship Enhancement Therapy (Ginsberg 1976, 1989, B. G. Guerney 1964, L. Guerney 1976a, 1983a,b). Parents are most influential in their child's development. The thwarting of self-action occurs often in the child's relationship with the parent. This occurs out of the parenting function necessary for protection and socialization. Many of the child's conflicts arise from the inconsistency of parents' response to their children, inadequate knowledge of effective parenting methods, and/or the parents' own coping difficulties. These behaviors on the part of the parent thwart children's efforts at mastery. Parents are often uncomfortable with the child's expression of feelings. When a child expresses emotion strongly, parents often inhibit this expression through punishment or reassurance. It is not uncommon that when a child behaves aggressively a parent will either punish the child or threaten punishment. When a child cries, a parent often will go to the child and reassure him. In both of these cases, the emotional release, which in fact may be recovery, is responded to in a way that prevents the child from gaining mastery. It is also important to note, however, that the parent usually is the child's most trusted figure, and play sessions with a parent may provide added security for the child to feel free to express himself emotionally.

Another component that relates to parents having play therapy sessions with their own children is the help it provides them to learn how to convey acceptance in a context of security derived from good structure and clear boundaries. Having play therapy sessions with one's own child helps a parent learn to accept the child's emotional behavior and learn to trust the child's capacity to master these behaviors in more socially acceptable ways. Children who are engaged in play therapy sessions with their own parents are better able to generalize their own behavior change derived from play sessions to their real lives. The increased trust, acceptance, and intimacy in the parent–child relationship generalizes to their daily lives together. As a result, children are more readily able to transfer their increased mastery skills in all areas of their lives.

It is important to recognize the stages in the play therapy process as they pertain to catharsis and emotional release. L. Guerney (1983b) has identified this in three stages (early, mid- and later sessions). In the early sessions, the child explores the dimensions of the play therapy context including the person of the play therapist. Aggressive behavior and the application of limits emerge here. Dependent and fearful children will look for direction and reassurance. It is a period in which the child begins to trust the play session context and the play therapist. As a result, children become less and less self-conscious. In midsession, aggressive behavior levels off and increased expression of regressive behaviors occurs. Guerney (1983b) believes that during these midsessions, the child begins the serious work of personality reorganization and begins to develop a growing sense of self. In the later sessions, play session behavior becomes more reality oriented. Aggressive behaviors drop to a low level and are related to recent events. Frustration tolerance increases as well. Play behavior includes role playing and fantasy, but these are more reality oriented. The description of this three-stage process by Guerney does suggest that the child has gained increased mastery, self-acceptance, and maturation. This result is very dependent on the play therapist and play therapy context to provide a permissive, accepting, and secure environment. Under these conditions, a child is freed for expression of emotional release and catharsis, thereby gaining mastery over himself.

Case Illustrations: Acting Out and Abused Children

"Craig" was referred to a community mental health center because of the difficulty adults were having in managing his aggressive behavior. At the time of referral Craig was 8 years of age. He had grown up in a very chaotic family situation, and at the time he was being seen he was living with his mother and two older sisters. Craig's mother had been in a long-term relationship with his father in which there was never any security or regularity. Craig's father had another family in another location and would vacillate for years between these two families. At the time of the referral he was living in a distant state. Craig's mother was aware of her husband's other relationship and family, but out of her own inadequacy and lack of support system, she remained intimately involved with him even when not living with him. This created a highly emotional, often conflictual, environment for Craig in which to grow up. Craig had emotional and behavioral difficulties from his earliest entry into peer-related and school circumstances. He was regularly aggressive and disruptive and did not respond to adult directives and management. As he got older these behaviors increased significantly, to the point that he became unmanageable both at home and at school. He could not be contained in school for a very long period and would run out of the classroom, climb out of windows, hide behind things in a classroom, visit other classrooms in the school, and so forth. At home he was equally difficult, not listening to his mother, threatening suicide, running across streets, jumping into hay lofts. His mother was overindulgent with him, exacerbating these behavioral and emotional difficulties. In essence, Craig would make every attempt to gain adult involvement with him at all times. It was presumed at that time that this arose from tremendous feelings of anxiety.

At the time Craig was referred to the community mental health center, he was in a private school for special education students because he could not be managed within a regular school situation. Even there he was their most difficult student. When Craig first came to the community mental health center and entered the waiting room it was difficult to relate to him and engage him in some sort of play interaction. However, after he was informed that there were a great many toys in the play room and some of them were described to him, he agreed to go with the therapist to the play room. Craig was very excited by the variety of toys available; however, he was immediately threatened by the closeness and intimacy of the play therapy setting. He picked up the rubber-tipped dart and dart gun, put the dart in the gun and shot the dart directly at the therapist. The therapist had already identified the basic structure of the play session in which he was free to do almost anything he wanted, and that if there was something he couldn't do the therapist would tell him. The therapist acknowledged that Craig enjoyed shooting, but the rule was that the therapist could not be hit. Craig then began a diatribe of foul language directed at the therapist. The therapist acknowledged that Craig was angry, but that the rule was that the therapist could not be hit.

After a period of time, Craig wound down from his aggressive expression and began to shoot the dart at various objects in the play room. One time, Craig shot the dart and it hit the wall, then bounced off and hit the therapist. The therapist again acknowledged the enjoyment Craig was having from shooting the dart gun, but that the rule was that the therapist could not be hit and if it occurred again it would mean the end of the play session. Craig became very resentful and angry and stated that he was not responsible for hitting the therapist, that the dart had bounced off the wall and it wasn't fair. The therapist acknowledged that Craig was upset and angry with the therapist for that, but the rule was that the therapist could not be hit and if it happened again it would end the play session. Again Craig expressed a diatribe of foul language toward the therapist and the therapist acknowledged Craig's anger. Craig then put the dart in the dart gun, aimed and shot the dart directly at the therapist. The therapist again affirmed that the rule was that he could not be hit and that the session would end, but that they could play again next time. Craig said that he was not going to come to any "expletive" play session with the therapist any more, but refused to leave the play room. The therapist picked Craig up and removed him from the play session, carrying him down the hall. This first play session lasted less than ten minutes of a half-hour session.

When Craig came to the second session he was initially reluctant, but agreed to accompany the therapist to the play room. Upon arriving in the play room he immediately went over to the dart gun, put a dart in the dart gun and shot the therapist again. The therapist acknowledged that Craig was enjoying shooting the dart gun, but the rule was that the therapist could not be hit. Craig played for a little bit longer. It seemed difficult for him to sustain the tension that he experienced in this context. He again put a dart in the dart gun and shot the therapist. The therapist again identified that the rule was that he could not be hit and that if it happened again it would end the play session. Craig expressed himself angrily toward the therapist, and hit the therapist again. The therapist identified the rule that the play session would have to end, but that they could return to a play session, as he again actively had to remove Craig from the play room.

Craig came to a third session and repeated the same circumstances as the first two. By the fourth session he still had no more than eight to ten minutes of a play session before being removed from the play room. Craig was aware of the rules, and therefore the first time that the therapist was hit he identified the rule and its consequence. By the seventh session, Craig still had no more than eight to ten minutes of a play session. At no time until the fourteenth session did Craig have more than ten minutes of a play session. At the start of the fourteenth play session, Craig asked the therapist if he would do Craig a favor. Obviously the therapist was suspicious of this request, as Craig had been only negative and aggressive toward the therapist. However, he said that he would try if he could. Craig requested that the therapist let him know when there were thirty seconds left in the play session. This was a surprise to the therapist, and, though still suspicious, the therapist agreed to the request. After entering the play room, Craig again took up the dart and dart gun as he had done in all the previous sessions. However, in this case he took great care to shoot it in areas of the play room far from the play therapist. He continued to play in this fashion throughout the entire play session. Five minutes went by, ten minutes went by, twenty minutes went by, twenty-five minutes went by. At no time during this period did the dart come near the therapist, and Craig seemed to be enjoying his activities. The therapist acknowledged this and there was a positive interaction between Craig and the therapist. After twenty-five minutes, the therapist said that there were five minutes left in the play session, and again Craig reminded the therapist that he had requested that the therapist let him know when there were thirty seconds left. As the play session continued, Craig continued to play with other materials in the play room, using the dart gun at times to continue to shoot at various objects. Finally the therapist acknowledged that there was one minute left, and Craig accepted this limit. The play therapist, as requested, identified that there were thirty seconds left. At that point, Craig turned around, pointed the dart gun at the therapist and shot the dart directly at the therapist. The therapist acknowledged the consequence that the play session would have to end, and Craig left the play room cooperatively with the play therapist, smiling as he returned to the waiting room.

In subsequent play sessions, Craig continued to play for the full half hour. He became very active in these play sessions; he attacked the bop bag, rolled and pounded clay, and repeatedly shot the dart gun. After a few sessions, he began to acknowledge his fear and anger while playing. From then on his mother was included more directly in the process by being taught to conduct these kinds of sessions at home with Craig. There was a dramatic change in Craig's behavior in the outside world. His management in school became increasingly improved as he became more cooperative with his teachers, his parent, and other adults. His school activities became more constructive, and he was beginning to show the benefits of his intelligence in his learning activities. Things stabilized at home significantly as he became more responsive to his mother, and there were fewer conflicts between him and his sisters. Craig began to develop more positive peer relationships.

The dramatic change in Craig following this significant fourteenth play session seems to follow the work of Guerney and other play therapists, who have found that in a permissive, accepting environment that has good structure and good limits, children take approximately that amount of time to gain mastery over interruptions or blocks to their ability to gain a sense of mastery in their environment. In this particular case, the chaotic environment in which Craig had grown up and the overindulgent interaction with his mother created great anxiety in him. He was unable to establish a sense of mastery, and as a result needed the constant and immediate attention of others. Through the permissive and accepting environment of the play session and the consistent application of the limits by the play therapist, Craig was in a position where he had to take responsibility for his own anxiety. Each play session in which the play therapist was hit and the play session had to be ended was an attempt on Craig's part to try to gain mastery. In Nichols and Efran's (1985) formulation of stage 2 catharsis, Craig's recovery from his experience of blocked action was expressed again and again in the play session until he could face the responsibility of this difficulty. Because he was bright, he was able to conceive of a way to gain mastery over this difficulty in a very creative way. By taking charge of his own anxiety and the behavior that pertained to it, his anxiety was relieved significantly through the mastery he experienced from this process of catharsis and emotional release.

It is important to emphasize that Craig had no safe outlets for expression of his emotional confusion. In some ways, his acting out elicited relief from tremendous underlying anxiety. At the same time, the reaction of others to these behaviors only exacerbated the anxiety that was relieved temporarily by such attention. This only created a vicious cycle in which Craig's emotional distress and subsequent behavior only worsened. Craig began to learn through the accepting, secure, and consistent play therapy environment that he could be safe while releasing his feelings. The opportunity that free play and play therapy provide for a child to allow for emotional release and cathartic expression helps the child become more responsible for his own behavior, and thereby gain mastery over interruptions in his own coping and development.

"Jordan" was an adopted child with a younger adopted sister. He had been adopted after he was six months of age, and little was known about his earlier development except that he had been in foster care until then. At the time he joined the family he was difficult to care for, showing many signs of discomfort and rejection of his caretakers. When Jordan entered school he was showing a great deal of difficulty in management, both at home and in school. He, like Craig, would find a great many ways to gain attention from others. At times it was hard to engage him and involve him in the activities that the other students were engaged in. At home—a warm, caring environment—he was difficult to manage and had difficulty allowing others to get close to him. As a result, he was referred to the author for assessment and intervention.

Jordan entered into play therapy, but in this case, his parents were trained to conduct play therapy sessions with him. Because of his behavioral difficulties, play sessions continued in the psychologist's office as well as at home for eleven months. Following that, the parents continued to conduct play therapy sessions with Jordan at home, visiting with the psychologist on a monthly basis with Jordan to follow up on this intervention. Jordan's play sessions were very interesting. Throughout the eleven-month period with the therapist and for another three or four months thereafter at home, Jordan would come in and pull all the toys on the floor. He would then kick at a cardboard box that was provided for each session until it was destroyed. After that he would sit down, take off the top of the doll house, put all the people figures inside the top of the doll house and pour water over it. This behavior occurred after appropriate limits were set regarding the throwing and breaking of toys. The cardboard box was substituted to provide Jordan with an object that could be destroyed, thereby setting no limit on this expression. Jordan repeated this behavior in every play session, taking up the entire time week after week. These behaviors continued as the play session progressed to the time in which parents were conducting the play sessions at home exclusively. In later play sessions at home, Jordan began to reduce the number of toys he would pull onto the floor at the beginning of a session. The destroying of the cardboard box began to dissipate, and eventually was no longer part of his play session behaviors. However, the repetitious activity of taking off the doll house roof, putting figures inside, and pouring water over them continued throughout all his play sessions for several years. As did Craig, Jordan began to show significant signs of change in his behavior at school and at home. He was more manageable, began to show the benefits of his learning at school, and was able to be more open in intimate interactions with his parents. He also tended to relate to his sister more cooperatively and they were able to engage in lengthy periods of play behavior with each other. It seems that Jordan's activity in the play session supports the view of Nichols and Efran (1985) regarding stage 2 catharsis. Perhaps Jordan had an opportunity to practice recovery from some thwarted actions that had occurred in his very earliest development. His play behavior appeared to be some repetition of an event in his life that occurred at a preverbal stage of development and therefore could not be expressed directly through language. It is interesting to note that this particular case occurred more than twenty years ago, and the author has had an opportunity to encounter Jordan and his family recently. The changes that occurred in Jordan at this stage of his development became increasingly progressive, and there never was a return to the earlier difficulties that he was showing. He was in his mid-twenties, had graduated from college, and was working as an engineer. The author was contacted because Jordan was about to be married and he and his family wanted the therapist to know.

"Sally," age 7, was living with her father and separated from her mother. This was because the parents were divorced, and although Sally originally resided with her mother, an indication of abuse toward Sally by her mother's live-in boyfriend caused Sally to be removed from that home to live with her father. At the time this occurred, the local children and youth agency was training caregivers of children who had been physically or sexually abused and/or neglected to conduct home play therapy sessions with these children. In this particular program, both natural parents and foster parents were trained to conduct these sessions.

At the time that Sally and her father entered this program she appeared seriously depressed. She often remained listless and introspective at home and she was hard to motivate in school. From the beginning of the play therapy sessions she came cooperatively and was able to engage in minimal play activities, but the depressive affect was evident. After Sally and her father had been having regular weekly home play sessions for approximately three months, Sally began to show more aggressive behaviors. She began to hit the bop bag tentatively at first and then with increasing aggression until she devoted entire play sessions to this activity. Sally's father, who had been trained in play therapy, was able to accept and acknowledge this emerging affect. This continued for several sessions in which this aggression activity increased significantly. However, in one session, when her father identified that it was time for them to have their play session, Sally became extremely agitated and very upset. She ran from the room stating that she never wanted to play again. Her father reflected all of this expression and finally Sally was able to tell him that she didn't want to play because she couldn't do it with her mother. Her father acknowledged and accepted her anger and unhappiness and no play session was conducted that day. The next week at the appointed time, when Sally's father stated that it was time for the play session, she smiled and came willingly to the play session. During this play session Sally's aggressive behavior was absent, and she was more open with her father, talking greatly about her many feelings at being separated from her mother and not seeing her for all this time. The play sessions that followed this were more open, Sally's depressive affect seemed to have left her, and the interaction between father and daughter became closer and closer. Sally showed concomitant signs of change outside the play sessions. Her teachers remarked on how much her affect had changed. She was now smiling more, interacting with the other children, and being very responsive to her teachers and other adults. Again, this example of the value of play therapy acknowledges that given an accepting and permissive environment, a child can take charge of the undermining of mastery caused by some thwarted action in her development. Because Sally could take responsibility for her own recovery from the impact of this separation from her mother she was able to deal with this situation and engage with her environment and others more constructively. Her depression, which had so inhibited her interaction with others and her learning, no longer prevented her from growing and developing in more normative ways.

Each of these examples demonstrates the value of play and play therapy in providing young children with the opportunity for emotional release and catharsis. Here the objective is not to release tension or constricted emotion, but to allow a process where thwarted action can be allowed to be expressed for recovery and mastery. The return to a balanced mode of functioning enables the child to involve him- or herself with others and to be more open to learning and growing. The necessity of repeated behaviors, accepted and acknowledged in the play therapy sessions, allows children to work on recovering from the imbalance created by the stresses and resultant blocked action in their history so that they can achieve a sense of mastery and greater security.

Catharsis Is Vital

Catharsis and emotional release in play and play therapy remains an important construct in children's development and socialization that has been pervasive throughout the history of psychotherapy. It also has been consistently acknowledged as an important part of play behavior and intervention in a child's life through play therapy. Nevertheless, the importance of catharsis and emotional release has been questioned and challenged. Research findings are mixed but suggest that a permissive environment that allows for catharsis and emotional release will likely increase the possibility of that expression. On the other hand, some of the research in play therapy, particularly that mentioned by Louise Guerney (1983a,b), suggests that this increase in emotional expression following in a permissive environment dissipates and is redirected into greater mastery, self-distinction, and interpersonal functioning.

Nichols and Efran (1985) suggest what they call a new perspective on catharsis in psychotherapy. They first define emotions as actions: "To feel is to do something" (p. 52). They believe this "doing something" represents action in a social context. Furthermore, emotions are connected to a sense of restraint and this sense of restraint elicits self-awareness, so that emotions, on one hand, point to obstacles in our way, yet they also help to define us. Therefore, the release of emotions is an important part of the process of self-definition. They further suggest a two-stage process. The first they call *activation,* when a goal is blocked, and the second, *recovery,* when the obstacle to the goal is overcome or the goal becomes less important and can be given up. Nichols and Efran shift the idea of catharsis and emotional release from one of building up internal tensions that require release to a functional and developmental process of self-definition within a social or interpersonal context. Their two-stage process helps a person achieve a sense of greater mastery over the imbalance created by thwarted action.

The importance of this developmental process of catharsis and emotional release takes on particular relevance in play and play therapy. Harter (1983) believes that play provides a symbolic haven for children to master emotional conflicts and the confusing experiences of their reality. She refers to the work of Inhelder and Piaget (1954) and states, "Thus, in play, one observes the symbolic neutralization of fears, liquidation of conflicts, and corrections of reality" (p. 117). She further notes that the process of therapy involves shifting from indirect and more behavioral expressions of needs and conflicts to more direct verbal expression of these issues. The study of Filial Therapy, mothers conducting play therapy with their own children (Guerney 1976a), reported that aggression and emotional expression increased as the sessions increased but then fell to a level below the initial rate of aggression and emotional expression. As this was occurring there were increased game playing, cooperative behavior, and conversation about life matters. The play therapy context provided the setting for the child to release emotions, to recover from blocked action and increase self-definition with more interpersonal and social functioning.

In essence, the permissive environment so necessary to the play therapy process allows for this kind of expression without the usual typical restrictions found in everyday life. Guerney (1983b) in addressing the issue of permissiveness identified how quickly children recognize the uniqueness of this atmosphere of the play session in relation to real life. However, this permissiveness in and of itself is insufficient because both children and adults playing with them need to feel safe to allow this permissiveness. The introduction of a few specific limits combined with a systematic way of helping children be responsible for them establishes the security of this environment. The importance of the adult acceptance of children in this context helps the children to accept their own feelings and thereby be more readily able to achieve mastery over the interruptions in their efforts to develop themselves within a social and interpersonal context. It is particularly important to recognize that this safe and secure play therapy environment enables children to express and release emotions unacceptable elsewhere in their lives. Testing of limits is a way a child secures the safety of the play therapy context. When it becomes clear to the child that he can freely release his emotions, he looks forward to each play therapy session. As the child learns to trust the structure, he begins to express more of his underlying feelings. The therapist becomes less directly involved in the release of emotion, but more included in the sharing of the experience of this emotional release.

The emotional release occurs in stages. The first stage tends to be global release of affect, which tends to be projected onto others. This is a less mature and more dependent means of affect release. The therapist enables the child to feel safer and take more responsibility for his own affect through the consistent acceptance, structure, and limits of the play therapy format. This facilitates the emergence of the next stage, in which the child escalates the release of negative affect but more toward the objects in the play room than the therapist. A more mature and responsible release of affect begins to emerge here. The next stage occurs when the child begins to include episodes of play behavior expressing positive affect. As the child learns to accept his affect more, he begins to integrate positive and negative affect in releasing his emotions. The next stage occurs when the child brings this emotional expression into his fantasy life and includes it in fantasy and role-playing activities. In the final stage, the child begins to share (rather than project) this emotional release with the play therapist. As the child is able to share his feelings intimately and openly with another, he feels safer and is able to achieve a greater level of mastery. This leads to increased expression of real life issues, and initiation of games with the adult. It is important to acknowledge that all children do not experience all these stages. A lot depends on the age and maturity of the child. Certainly an older child (8 to 10 years of age) will be more likely to evidence all these stages. Often, the play therapy sessions do not continue long enough for this to occur. When it does, it makes the play session experience rich, intimate, and satisfying for both child and adult.

Nichols and Efran (1985) identify four therapeutic goals: first, do nothing to block the recovery stage of catharsis. They believe that when feeling expression is accepted as part of the adaptive process, therapists are better able to be accepting and avoid interfering with the client's emotional expressions of recovery. Their second goal of therapy is to help people overcome their tendency to short-circuit their own experience. In play therapy, this is accomplished through acceptance by the play therapist, which enables the child to accept himself thereby helping to overcome the tendency to inhibit this expression in play therapy. The third goal of therapy has to do with the use of catharsis as a clue to blocked action, and to provide assistance in trying out new behaviors or rehearsing these behaviors, first in therapy and then in real life. Under the conditions of play therapy, children are free to work on gaining mastery of these blocked actions. They are then able to shift the way in which they express these emotions and practice them so that they then can internalize them and implement them in real life. The fourth goal is to help people define and enact themselves in relation to others. In the play therapy context, the interaction with the play therapist is critical to this goal. The play therapist establishes the structure, which includes permissiveness, acceptance, and clear boundaries that enable children engaged in play therapy to take greater responsibility for their behavior in relation to others. Catharsis and emotional release in play and play therapy are critical to helping children have the opportunity to improve their self-definition, increase their mastery, and establish more effective relating to others.

Some mention needs to be made of the value of teaching parents to be play therapists with their own children. This approach, entitled Filial Therapy (L. Guerney 1976a, Ginsberg 1976), improves the opportunity for children to gain this sense of mastery, self-definition, and interpersonal functioning. Parent–child interaction, especially with young children, is the primary context in which children learn about themselves and are socialized. Bringing this interactional system into the play therapy context facilitates a concomitant shift between parent and child, and facilitates greater continuity between the child and the child's context. As a child has opportunities to express emotions clearly with the parent's acceptance, clear structure, and limits, the relationship between the parent and child improves with greater intimacy and trust, thereby enabling this important developmental process to improve even more. Parents who learn to accept their children's emotional reactions and allow them to have catharsis within a safe context, improve their ability to tolerate their children's emotions and accept them better in real life. This, combined with a child's own ability to accept these emotions and direct them in more constructive ways, facilitates growth and change for all involved.

References

Aristotle (1951). *The Art of Poetry*. New York: Odyssey.

Axline, V. (1947). *Play Therapy,* Cambridge, MA: Houghton Mifflin.

_____ (1969). *Play Therapy*. Rev. ed. New York: Ballantine Books.

Bach, G. R. (1945). Young children's play fantasies. *Psychological Monographs* 2:59.

Baldwin, A. L. (1967). *Theories of Child Development*. New York: Wiley.

Bandura, A. (1969). *Principles of Behavior Modification,* New York: Holt, Rinehart & Winston.

Bandura, A., Ross, D., and Ross, S. A. (1961). Transmission of aggression through imitation of agressive models. *Journal of Abnormal and Social Psychology* 63: 575–582.

_____ (1963a). Imitation of film-mediated aggressive models. *Journal of Abnormal and Social Psychology* 66: 3–11(a).

_____ (1963[b]). Vicarious reinforcement and imitation. *Journal of Abnormal and Social Psychology.*

Bandura, A., and Walters, R. H. (1963). *Social Learning and Personality Development*. New York: Holt, Rinehart & Winston.

Bearison, D. J. (1986). Transactional cognition in context: new models of social understanding. In *Thought and Emotion,* ed. D. J. Bearison and H. Zimiles, pp. 129–146. Hillsdale, NJ: Lawrence Erlbaum.

Berkowitz, L. (1960). Some factors affecting the reduction of overt hostility. *Journal of Abnormal and Social Psychology* 60:14–21.

———— (1962). *Aggression: A Social Psychological Analysis.* New York: McGraw-Hill.

———— (1965). Some aspects of observed aggression. *Journal of Personality and Social Psychology.* 2:359–369.

———— (1970). Experimental investigations of hostility catharsis. *Journal of Consulting and Clinical Psychology* 35:1–7.

Berkowitz, L., and Green, R. G. (1967). Stimulus qualities of the target of aggression: a further study. *Journal of Personality and Social Psychology.* 5:364–368.

Berlyne, D. (1960). *Conflict, Arousal and Curiosity.* New York: McGraw-Hill.

Biaggio, M. K. (1987). A survey of psychologists' perspectives on catharsis. *Journal of Psychology* 121:243–248.

Bixler, R. (1949). Limits are therapy. *Journal of Consulting Psychology* 13:1–11.

Belli, A. (1986). The impact of literature upon health: some varieties of cathartic response. *Literature and Medicine* 5:90–108.

Biber, B. (1984). *Early Education and Psychological Development.* New Haven, CT: Yale University Press.

Blatner, A. (1965). The dynamics of catharsis. *Journal of Group Psychotherapy, Psychodrama and Sociometry.* 38:157–166.

Bohart, A. C. (1980). Toward a cognitive theory of catharsis. *Psychotherapy: Theory, Research and Practice.* 17:192–201.

Bollard, J., and Miller, N. E. (1950), *Personality and Psychotherapy.* New York: McGraw-Hill.

Breuer, J., and Freud, S. (1961). *Studies in Hysteria.* Boston: Beacon Press.

Casriel, D. (1972). *A Scream Away from Happiness.* New York: Grosset & Dunlap.

Chein, I. (1972). *The Science of Behavior and the Image of Man.* New York: Basic Books.

Cowan, P. H. (1981). Preface. In *Intelligence and Affectivity,* by J. Piaget pp. ix–xiv. Palo Alto, CA: Annual Reviews.

Cox, W. H. (1970). Intrafamily comparison of loving-reject child rearing practices. *Child Development.* 41:91, 437–448.

Davanloo, H. (1980). A method of short-term dynamic psychotherapy. In *Short-Term Dynamic Psychotherapy,* ed. H. Davanloo, pp. 32–64. New York: Jason Aronson.

Dollard, J., Doob, Z. W., Miller, N. E., et al. (1939). *Frustration and Aggression,* New Haven, CT: Yale University Press.

Dollard, J., and Miller, N. E. (1950). *Personality and Psychotherapy.* New York: McGraw-Hill.

Doob, A. N. (1970). Catharsis and aggression: the effects of hurting one's enemy. *Journal of Experimental Research in Personality* 4:291–296.

Eisman, E. M. (1981). Sex-role characteristics of the parent, parental acceptance of the child and child self concept. (Doctoral Dissertation). California School of Professional Psychology, *Dissertation Abstracts International* 41:2013A.

Ellis, M. J. (1973). *Why People Play.* Englewood Cliffs, NJ: Prentice-Hall.

Erikson, E. H. (1972). Play and actuality. In *Play and Development,* ed. M. Piers, pp. 127–168. New York: Norton.

Esman, A. H. (1983). Psychoanalytic play therapy. In *Handbook of Play Therapy,* ed. C. E. Schaefer and K. J. O'Connor, pp. 11–20. New York: John Wiley & Sons.

Feshbach, S. (1955). The drive-reducing function of fantasy behavior. *Journal of Abnormal Social Psychology* 50:3–11.

_____ (1956). The catharsis hypothesis and some consequences of interaction with aggressive and neutral play objects. *Journal of Personality* 24:449–462.

_____ (1961). The stimulating versus cathartic effects of a vicarious aggressive activity. *Journal of Social Psychology* 50:3–11.

_____ (1984). The catharsis hypothesis, aggressive drive, and the reduction of aggression. *Aggressive Behavior* 10:91–101.

Flavell, J. (1963). *The Developmental Psychology of Jean Piaget*. New York: Van Nostrand.

Franklin, M. B. (1983). Play as the creation of imaginary situations: the role of language. In *Toward a Holistic Development Psychology*, ed. S. Wapner and B. Kaplan, pp. 197–220. Hillsdale, NJ: Lawrence Erlbaum.

Freud, A. (1946). *The Psycho-analytic Treatment of Children*. London: Imago.

Freud, S. (1912). The dynamics of transference. In *Collected Papers*, vol. 2, ed. J. Riviere. New York: Basic Books.

_____ (1924). The dynamics of transference. In *Collected Papers*, vol. I and II, ed. E. Jones. London: Hogarth.

_____ (1950). *Beyond the Pleasure Principle*. New York: Liveright.

_____ (1956). On psychotherapy. *Collected Papers*, vol. 1. pp. 249–263. London: Hogarth Press.

Ginott, H. G. (1959). The theory and practice of therapeutic intervention in child treatment. *Journal of Consulting Psychology* 23:160–166.

_____ (1961). *Group Psychotherapy with Children: The Theory and Practice of Play Therapy*. New York: McGraw-Hill.

_____ (1976). Therapeutic intervention in child treatment. In *The Therapeutic Use of Child's Play*, ed. C. E. Schaefer, pp. 279–290. New York: Jason Aronson.

Ginsberg, B. G. (1976). Parents as therapeutic agents: the usefulness of filial therapy in a community psychiatric clinic. *American Journal of Community Psychology* 4:47–54.

_____ (1989). Training parents as therapeutic agents with foster/adoptive children using the filial approach. In *Handbook of Parent Training: Parents as Co-Therapists for Children's Behavior Problems*, ed. C. E. Schaefer and J. M. Breismeister, pp. 442–478. New York: John Wiley & Sons.

Green, R. G., and Berkowitz, L. (1967). Some conditions facilitating the occurrence of aggression after the observation of violence. *Journal of Personality* 35:666–676.

Green, R. G., and Quanty, M. B. (1977). The catharsis of aggression: an evaluation of hypothesis. In *Advances in Experimental Social Psychology*, vol. 10, ed. L. Berkowitz, pp. 1–37. New York: Academic Press.

Greenberg, L. S., and Safran, J. D. (1987). *Emotion in Psychotherapy*. New York: Guilford.

Grinker, R. R., and Spiegel, J. P. (1945). *Men in Distress*. New York: Glakiston.

Guerney, B. G. (1964). Filial therapy: description and rationale. *Journal of Consulting Psychology* 28:303–310.

Guerney, B. G., Guerney, L., and Stover, L. (1972). Facilitative therapist attitudes in training parents as psychotherapeutic agents. *The Family Coordinator* 21:275–278.

Guerney, B. G., and Stover, L. (1971). Filial therapy: final report to NIMH, Grant 1826401. University Park, PA: The Pennsylvania State University.

Guerney, L. F. (1976a). Filial therapy program. In *Treating Relationships*, ed. D. H. Olson, pp. 67–91. Lake Mille, IA: Graphic Publishing.

_____ (1976b). *Foster parenting training project: Final report*. University Park, PA: Pennsylvania State University.

_____ (1976c). *Foster parenting training project: Final report, Part I: Descriptive information about foster parents associated with public child welfare agencies in the western region of Pennsylvania*. University Park, PA: Pennsylvania State University.

_____ (1976d). *Foster parenting training project: Final report, Part II: Description and evaluation of the foster parent skill-training program for parents and for agency personnel*. University Park, PA: Pennsylvania State University.

_____ (1983a). Introduction to filial therapy. In *Innovations in Clinical Practice: A Source Book*, vol. II, ed. P. Keller and L. Ritt, pp. 26–39. Sarasota, FL: Professional Resource Exchange.

_____ (1983b). Client-centered (nondirective) play therapy. In *Handbook of Play Therapy*, ed. C. E. Schaefer and K. J. O'Connor, pp. 21–64. New York: John Wiley & Sons.

Hambridge, G. (1955). Structured play therapy. *The American Journal of Orthopsychiatry* 25:601-617.

Hartman, D. P. (1969). The influence of symbolically modeled instrumental aggression and pain cues on aggressive behavior. *Journal of Personality and Social Psychology* 11:280-288.

Hartup, W. W., and Himeno, Y. (1959). Social isolation vs. interaction with adults in relation to aggression in preschool children. *Journal of Abnormal and Social Psychology* 59:17-22.

Hokanson, J. E. (1970). Psychophysiological evaluation of the catharsis hypothesis. In *The Dynamics of Aggression*, ed. E. I. Megargee and J. E. Hokanson, pp. 195-223. New York: Harper & Row.

Hokanson, J. E., and Burgess, M. (1962a). The effects of status, type of frustration and aggression on vascular process. *Journal of Abnormal and Social Psychology* 65:232-237.

_____ (1962b). The effects of three types of aggression on vascular processes. *Journal of Abnormal and Social Psychology* 64:446-449.

Hokanson, J. E., and Shelter, S. (1961). The effect of overt aggression on physiological arousal level. *Journal of Abnormal and Social Psychology* 63:446-448.

Hokanson, J. E., Willers, K. R., and Koropsak, E. (1968). The modification of autonomic responses during aggressive interchange. *Journal of Personality* 36:386-404.

Hollenberg, E., and Sperry, M. (1951). Some antecedents of aggression and effects of frustration in doll play. *Personality* 6:32-43.

Jackins, H. (1962). *Elementary Counselor's Manual*, Seattle, WA: Rational Island.

Janov, A. (1970). *The Primal Scream*. New York: Dell.

Kahn, M. (1966). The psychology of catharsis. *Journal of Personality and Social Psychology* 3:278-288.

Kenny, D. T. (1952). *An Experimental Test of the Catharsis Theory of Aggression*. Unpublished doctoral dissertation. University of Washington.

Klein, M. (1948). Person in the play of children. In *Contributions to Psychoanalysis*, pp. 215-226. London: Hogarth Press and the Institute of Psychoanalysis, 1929.

_____ (1955). The psychoanalytic play-technique. *American Journal of Orthopsychiatry* 25:223-237.

Landisberg, S., and Snyder, W. (1946). Nondirective play therapy. *Journal of Clinical Psychology* 2:203-213.

Levy, D. (1938). Release therapy in young children. *Psychiatry* 1:387-389.

_____ (1939). Release therapy. *American Journal of Orthopsychiatry* 9:713-736.

Mallick, S. K., and McCandless, B. R. (1966). A study of catharsis of aggression. *Journal of Personality and Social Psychology*, 4:591-596.

Menninger, W. C. (1948). Recreation and mental health. *Recreation* 42:340–346.

Miller, B. (1974). Catharsis and reinforcement in young children's aggression: a test of the meaning and effects of nondirective statements. *Dissertation Abstracts International* 34:6217–6218.

Miller, S. (1968). *The Psychology of Play.* Hammondsworth, England: Penguin Books.

Miller, T. W. (1971). Communication dimensions of mother–child interactions as they affect the self-esteem of the child. *Proceedings of the 79th Annual Convention of the American Psychological Association,* pp. 241–242. Washington, DC: American Psychological Association.

Miles, M. S. (1981). Play therapy: A review of theories and comparison of some techniques. *Issues in Mental Health Nursing* 3:63–75.

Moreno, J. L. (1958). *Psychodrama.* Vol. II. New York: Beacon House.

Moustakas, C. E. (1959). *Psychotherapy with Children.* New York: Harper & Row.

_____ (1970). *Psychotherapy with Children: The Living Relationship.* New York: Balantine Books.

_____ (1973). *Children in Play Therapy.* Rev. ed. New York: Jason Aronson.

Murphy, L. B. (1962). *The Widening World of Childhood.* New York: Basic Books.

Nichols, M. P. (1974a). *Catharsis in Brief Psychotherapy: An Outcome Study,* vol. 35, p. 520. Ann Arbor, MI: Dissertation Abstracts International.

_____ (1974b). Outcome of brief cathartic psychotherapy. *Journal of Consulting and Clinical Psychology* 42:403–410.

Nichols, M. P., and Bierenbaum, H. (1978). Success of cathartic therapy as a function of patient variables. *Journal of Clinical Psychology* 34:726–728.

Nichols, M. P., and Efran, J. S. (1985). Catharsis in psychotherapy: a new perspective. *Psychotherapy* 22:46–58.

Nichols, M. P., and Zax, M. (1977). *Catharsis in Psychotherapy.* New York: Gardner.

Nickerson, E. T., and O'Laughlin, K. S. (1983). The therapeutic use of games. In *Handbook of Play Therapy,* ed. C. E. Schaffer and K. J. O'Connor, pp. 174–187. New York: Wiley.

Piaget, J. (1951). *Play, Dreams and Initiation in Childhood,* New York: Norton.

_____ (1970). Piaget's theory. In *Carmichael's Manual of Child Psychology,* ed. P. Mussen, pp. 703–732. New York: Wiley.

_____ (1981). *Intelligence and Affectivity.* Palo Alto, CA: Annual Reviews.

_____ (1977). *The Development of Thought: Equilibration of Cognitive Structures.* New York: Viking.

Pierce, R., Nichols, M. P., and DuBrin, J. (1983). *Feeling-Expressive Psychotherapy.* New York: Gardner.

Quanty, M. (1976). Aggression catharsis. In *Perspectives on Aggression,* ed. R. G. Green and E. C. O'Neal, pp. 99–131. New York: Academic.

Rogers, C. (1951). *Client-Centered Therapy.* Boston: Houghton-Mifflin.

Rohner, E. C., Chaille, C., and Rohner, R. H. (1980). Perceived parental acceptance-rejection and the development of children's locus of control. *The Journal of Psychology* 104:83–86.

Rosenbaum, M. E., and DeCharmes, R. (1960). Direct and vicarious reduction of hostility. *Journal of Abnormal and Social Psychology* 60:105–111.

Sears, P. S. (1951). Doll play aggression in normal young children: influence of sex, age, sibling status, father's absence. *Psychological Monographs* 6:65.

Selman, R. L., and Demorest, A. P. (1986). Putting thoughts and feelings into perspective: A developmental view on how children deal with interpersonal disequilibrium. In *Thought and Emotion,* ed. D. J. Bearison and H. Zimiles, pp. 93–128. Hillsdale, NJ: Lawrence Erlbaum.

Sifneos, P. E. (1979). *Short-Term Dynamic Psychotherapy.* New York: Plenum.

Solomon, J. (1938). Active play therapy. *American Journal of Orthopsychiatry* 8:479–498.

Stover, L., and Guerney, B. G., Jr. (1967). The efficacy of training procedures for mothers in filial therapy. *Psychotherapy: Theory, Research and Practice* 4:110–115.

Strachey, J. (1934). The nature of the therapeutic action of psychoanalysis. *International Journal of Psycho-Analysis* 15:117–126.

Tavris, C. (1982). *Anger: Misunderstood Emotion.* New York: Simon and Schuster.

Thibaut, J. W., and Coules, J. (1952). The role of communication in the reduction of interpersonal hostility. *Journal of Abnormal and Social Psychology* 60:105–111.

Waelder, R. T. (1976). Psychoanalytic theory of play. In *Play Therapy,* ed. C. E. Schaefer, pp. 80–93. New York: Jason Aronson.

Wapner, S., Cottone, J. L., Hornstein, G. A., McNeil, U. V., and Pacheco, A. M. (1983). An examination of studies of critical transitions through the life cycle. In *Toward a Holistic Development Psychology,* ed. S. Wapner and B. Kaplan, pp. 111–132. Hillsdale, NJ: Lawrence Erlbaum.

White, R. W. (1959). Motivation reconsidered: the concept of competence. *Psychological Review* 66:175–226.

Werner, H. J. (1948). *Comparative Psychology of Mental Development.* Rev. ed. Chicago: Follett.

_____ (1957a). The concept of development from a comparative and organismic point of view. In *The Concept of Development: An Issue in the Study of Human Behavior,* ed. D. B. Harris, pp. 125–149. Minneapolis: University of Minnesota Press.

_____ (1957b). *Comparative Psychology of Mental Development.* 3rd Ed. New York: International Universities Press.

Werner, H., and Kaplan, B. (1956). The developmental approach to cognition: its relevance to the psychological interpretation of anthropological and ethnolinguistic data. *American Anthropologist* 58:866–880.

_____ (1963). *Symbol Formation.* New York: Wiley.

Werner, H., and Wapner, S. (1952). Toward a general theory of perception. *Psychological Review* 59:324–338.

Yarrow, L. J. (1948). The effects of antecedent frustration on projective play. *Psychological Monographs* 6:62.

Zillman, D., and Johnson, R. C. (1973). Motivated aggressiveness perpetuated by exposure to aggressive films and reduced by exposure to nonaggressive films. *Journal of Experimental Research in Personality* 7:261–276.

7

Abreaction

Evelyn K. Oremland

Sigmund Freud (1926) viewed psychic trauma as a sense of helplessness. At times, the effects of psychological trauma may be relieved via symbolic reexperiencing of the overwhelming events with cognitive association of accompanying emotions. Such a relief process has been termed abreaction, that is, a mental process in which repressed memories are brought to consciousness and relived, with appropriate release of affect. Breuer and Freud advocated abreaction in an early collaboration (1895), emphasizing the substitution of words for actual reexperiencing, and associating the related emotions to reduce "strangulated" affects.

In regard to abreaction in childhood, Freud (1920) states:

> We see that children repeat in their play everything that has made a great impression on them in actual life, that they thereby abreact the strength of the impression and so to speak make themselves masters of the situation. . . . It is also observable that the unpleasing character of the experience does not always prevent its being utilized as a game. . . . In the play of children we seem to arrive at the conclusion that as the child repeats even the unpleasant experiences through his own activity he gains a far more thorough mastery of the strong impression than was possible by mere passive experience. Every fresh repetition seems to strengthen this mastery for which the child strives. [pp. 15–16, 43]

Ekstein (1966) elaborates on abreaction as an active process by which children resolve passively experienced traumatic events of the real world by actively repeating them in the microcosmic play world.

This basic idea as translated into children's play therapy presents theoretical and clinical challenges. For children, play, including use of the "toy stage" (Erikson 1950) to represent trauma, is parallel to adults' verbalization of trauma. As both partici-

The author gratefully acknowledges the help of Susan Marchant, who made possible the participant-observation project and the thoughtful, gracious guidance of Maggie Greenblatt, whose rich body of information on the children and their situations provided essential context for work in the playroom. Additional case information was contributed by Camilla Antoncich, Renee Buonocore, Lisa Cartmell, Sherri Cloward, Tom Collins, Andrea Dezendorf, Gerri Faniel, Lisa Ferczok, Anne Flatley, Mona Halaby, Rosemary Koefler, Carol Mann, Linda Okazaki, Susan Stern, and Janice Yoshikawa, child life specialists, students in child life, and nurses. Always welcome and appreciated was consultation with Jerome Oremland, M.D., and editing advice from Celia Teter.

pants in and observers of play, children possess a type of "double vision" (Scheff 1979, p. 119). They simultaneously may believe and not believe in the enactment, knowing that the play in which distress is recognized and discharged is real and yet not "ordinary" reality. This "distanced reexperiencing" in play coincides with Breuer and Freud's considerations relative to recollections reflected in language with accompanying affect, thus serving mastery (Hartmann 1976).

Few references to abreaction *per se* are indexed in volumes of the *Psychoanalytic Study of the Child* (1945–1990). Yet if the concept were deemed relevant to psychoanalytically oriented work with children, one might expect to find many references in this literature. Nevertheless, many theorists agree that changing traumatic events experienced passively into active mastery, a critical dynamic in abreaction, is integrally bound with play therapy (Erikson 1950, Freud 1920, Schaefer 1976, Terr 1990, Waelder 1932). Wexler (1973) underlines how abreacting a trauma is essentially mastery, by turning passive into active.

Definitional difficulties of the term *abreaction* stem from its original connection to hysteria. Redefinitions of hysteria and the clarification of anxiety and other symptoms of disequilibrium have added to the concept's refinement. Additionally, enlargement of the concept of repression, moving away from simplistic notions of mere release of memories and emotions otherwise strangled from within, has increased understanding of the concept of abreaction. Loewald (1970) emphasized that abreaction in words and "associative absorption" is giving words to feelings to repeat original situations on new levels by which linkages can be made between intrapsychic structure and functioning.

Developmental Perspectives

Assuming a validity to the concept of abreaction, developmental plateaus in childhood, particularly relative to cognitive capacities, present questions regarding when children can make connections between events and feelings or cause–effect relationships (Ginsburg and Opper 1969). The Piagetian view generally proposes that young children seldom express causal relations, therefore rendering problematic the synthesis necessary for understanding the effects of trauma.

Arguments over this cognitive view parallel the debate surrounding the developmental level required to integrate loss, in that mourning as a process has equivalents to abreactive processes.[1] Both mourning and abreaction require recalling the trauma with expression of the integrally related personal meanings.

---

[1]The capacity of children to mourn, thereby incorporating early losses, depends on developmental and temporal dimensions (Furman 1964, Wolfenstein 1966). The long-standing debate centers on development and time as the necessary qualifiers influencing completeness and incompleteness in children's mourning capacities. Furman notes that reality testing requires stable and differentiated self and object representations. He observed that even though some 2-year-olds understand the concept of death and some 5-year-olds cannot, he considers 3½- or 4-year-olds *capable* of mourning in that object constancy is generally reached by that age.

A juggling of Freudian and Piagetian perspectives with comparing concepts is necessary to evaluate when mourning or abreaction is possible. Although Piaget's stage of object permanency occurs by the end of the first year of life, the meaning of the loss or trauma with its potential to be overwhelming leaves vulnerable the child who may not be sufficiently developed to grasp its significance until object constancy, as presented by Furman (1964), is reached.

Extending the idea that emotional work on trauma is critically dependent on children's cognitive readiness, Wolfenstein's view (1966) is that mourning, here regarded as functionally similar to abreaction, takes place piecemeal as a defensive function, and that adolescence constitutes the necessary precondition for mourning. Reconciling these views, it seems possible that children begin resolution of trauma early, but only gradually, as development allows, can they experience eventual completion of the process.

Development-supportive play, as distinctive from abreactive play, may be a necessary antecedent during potentially traumatic times for children to pave the way for abreactive play. Yet abreactive-related play may be observed in children concurrent with traumatic experiences, repeating in play what is consciously experienced and remembered. Whereas Freudian perspectives clarify abreaction as relief from hitherto unconscious trauma, observations of children suggest that the conscious and unconscious are not yet as dichotomized as they are in adults. Therefore, in this discussion, abreactive processes in the context of ongoing development include both conscious and unconscious reliving of traumatic experiences.

Play in Pediatric Care

Before viewing the abreactive-related play of children in pediatric care, it is essential to understand specific situations and contexts as evaluated in numerous accounts (Golden 1983, Thompson 1985, Play in Health Care Settings 1988). Abreactive play, with its characteristic of making active what one has experienced passively (Waelder 1932), is seldom as dramatically presented as in pediatric play rooms (Oremland 1988). Even casual observation shows the predominance of medical play,[2] with doll-patients subjected to "medical" interventions from injections to body casting (Figure 7–1). It is important to know how play therapy proceeds in hospitals to view how abreactive-type play can evolve under these circumstances.

Pediatric play rooms where the "medical" enactments typically occur are accepted as part of the architecture and organization of pediatric hospital care. Pioneered in the 1950s by Emma Plank, Director of Child Life and Education at Cleveland Metropolitan General Hospital, pediatric play programs began for chil-

---

[2]Medical play refers to children's interactions with actual medical equipment or, at times, toy representations of apparatus used in hospitals for patient treatment. It is spontaneous, generally guided play with health care themes.

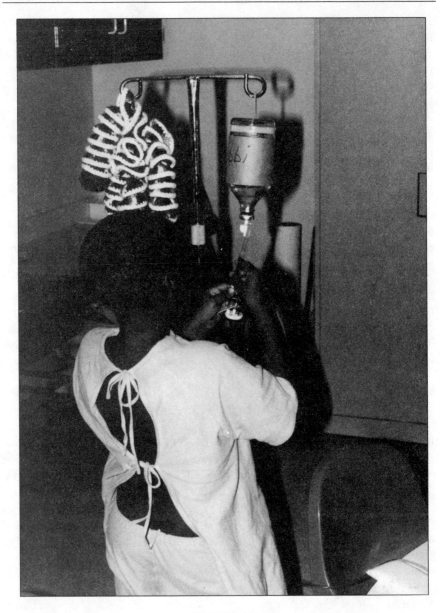

FIGURE 7–1.

dren with poliomyelitis and tuberculosis. Plank's interventions addressed the extraordinary adaptive challenges required of these children (Plank 1971).

Eventually becoming a model for work with all hospitalized children, Plank's interactions from the outset were guided by research that demonstrated the disruption to children's development by separation and other illness-connected traumas.

Pediatric play programs that address these issues have since developed throughout much of the Western world, initially and especially in the United States, Canada, England, and Sweden (Association for the Care of Children's Health 1990).

Although hospitalized children are presented with multiple play partners, their child development coordinators and primary play partners are the designated child life specialists. The specialists' work became professionalized with the establishment of the Child Life Council of the Association for the Care of Children's Health. The Council specifies principles for the practice of these child-development-trained personnel who administer play and related therapeutic interventions in pediatric health care settings (Child Life Council 1989).[3]

The Pediatric Playroom Situation: Clinical Practice

To the untrained eye, a typical play session in a pediatric setting resembles an open classroom or a preschool, albeit with many differences. The ages of children participating in one play room range from infancy to preadolescence. Most of the children are attached to medical apparatus, commonly intravenous tubes carrying fluids from plastic sacks hung on mobile poles. Adults in the room navigate these I.V. poles for children too young or too disabled to understand that their mobility is dependent on such assistance. The mobility of the poles and other medical paraphernalia empowers the children to select where in the room and with what they will play.

In one morning session, five children are attracted to a round table on which a series of doll-patients and supplies of alcohol wipes, syringes, tubing, "butterfly" needles, tape, and I.V. "boards" used as arm supports are arranged. A parent, a professional child life specialist, and volunteers who are familiar with the children seat themselves alongside the children to assist their play.

Two 9-year-old girls, each of whom is being infused from respective intravenous connections, thoughtfully treat dolls with amazing detail, replicating their own medical treatments. Three younger boys individually perform other treatments on their "patients," occasionally looking up to observe the activities of the others.

Concurrently a boy and a girl, each about 2 years old, experiment with pouring cups full of water onto water wheels at the water table. The father of one of the children encourages the activity. A 3-year-old diligently cooks a pretend meal in the child-sized kitchen play area. Next to the windows that view a nearby freeway, a 4-year-old boy whose spastic, neurological disorder renders him unable to walk,

---

[3]Hospital fellowships and college-based child life programs provide education and integrate internships that fulfill the profession's requirements (Education Committee 1991). Certification through the Child Life Certifying Commission attests to and maintains the educational and experiential qualities of individual child life specialists (Child Life Certifying Commission 1991).

The American Academy of Pediatrics and the Accreditation Council for Graduate Medical Education, which oversee the training of pediatricians, specify the critical inclusion of child life and related program interventions as standards required in pediatric care (American Academy of Pediatrics 1990, Accreditation Council for Graduate Medical Education 1990).

delights in pushing miniature cars up a ramp and watching them slide down. A volunteer retrieves them when they go astray.

Meanwhile, a 5-year-old stacks large styrofoam blocks. With wide swinging of the arm that is free of the I.V., he delights in their crashing to the floor. A volunteer, following the child's directions in the building, supports the play.

Nearby, a 9-month-old sits with his mother, intrigued with a "busy box." A volunteer holding another baby shakes a rattle to attract the baby's interest. To the side, two 11-year-old boys and a 10-year-old girl play Monopoly. They discuss the rules of the game and the role of the banker. A newly admitted child comes to the play room to watch familiar play amidst the bewildering sights, sounds, and experiences of the hospital.

An occasional beeping sound emanates from the computerized control boxes on the I.V.s, alerting a child life specialist or volunteer to plug in the cord to charge a low battery or to call a nurse to restart infusions. These simple adjustments can be tended to in the play room, allowing play to continue. At times a pediatric resident or a medical therapist enters the room to talk with a child and escort the child to a treatment room for examination or a medical procedure. A student child life worker who knows a child well may accompany the child to the treatment if the child so chooses. Medical regimens continuously interrupt the play session.

Later the children disperse for lunch. An often-hospitalized 13-year-old boy with cystic fibrosis arrives, pleading, "Isn't there a volunteer who can play Monopoly with me?"

When the afternoon play session begins, some of the same children appear alongside others. Some are acquainted with one another from common experiences in play, their proximity during the current admission, or from previous hospitalizations. The volunteers and several student assistants have changed from the last session, although generally the child life specialist, who coordinates the play and other expressive interventions, remains constant.

This playroom scene demonstrates a variety of play often regarded as "therapeutic" rather than play therapy. These play interactions primarily provide opportunities for the children to engage in development-supportive play – familiar play that enables exploration, fine motor practice, general cognitive advances, and social development. Small children refine motor skills through manipulating play materials. Older children try out social roles with peers and with adults. Support for children's continuing development in the face of critical health care experiences has the potential to minimize disruptions in these vital developmental areas. In fact, these prevention-oriented interactions frequently minimize trauma, modifying abreactive processes.

Therapeutic play interactions also allow the development of supportive relationships through which the children are helped to make sense out of their medical-physical crises and that assist the children in mastering associated anxieties. The key therapeutic dimension is the abreactively related approach that encourages the children to play actively when they are, in fact, passive participants in traumatic experiences. The developmentally supportive play does not necessarily reveal connections to the children's traumatic or potentially traumatic experiences. The child life specialist seeks to recognize trauma enactments in the children's play, and abreactive elements are pursued, albeit complicated by the multiple play partner environment.

Over time, chronically ill children come to know a series of child life specialists, nurses, students, volunteers, and other hospital personnel. Each day or even half-day, children's parents and other family members come and leave, with a rotating staff and volunteers available for play and related interactions. Nevertheless, the primary play relationship is the fulcrum that enables development-supportive and therapeutically engaging play.

Excerpts from pediatric play case histories illustrate many facets in these interactions. Easily discerned are countless expressions of abreactive-type and development-supportive interactions with multiple play partners, presenting challenges for coordination to enable meaningful therapeutic relationships.

Pediatric Play Histories

The data presented were gathered during 60 hours of participant observation in a pediatric playroom, with follow-up interviews of current and former child life specialists, child life students, and other hospital staff.

Abreactive-Enactment Play

Charlotte

Six-year-old Charlotte, scheduled for open heart surgery, was visited by the child life specialist and a student nurse in the child's room, with both parents present. To help the child prepare for the procedure and its aftermath, the child life specialist introduced Charlotte to a large doll presented in play as requiring the same open heart surgery. Charlotte was invited to name the doll. Having recently attended a wedding, Charlotte named the doll "Flower Girl." Accordingly, "Flower Girl" was written on the doll's wrist band.

Oxygen masks, tape, chest tubes, and other medical paraphernalia were collected and brought to Charlotte's bed. Discussion began with why Flower Girl was in the hospital. Although the major focus of the preparation play was on what Charlotte (Flower Girl) would see and feel when she awakened from surgery, the play also encouraged Charlotte to try out the various apparatus on Flower Girl. In the 90-minute play, Charlotte was also given the opportunity to remove the tubes from the doll to emphasize recovery.

The student nurse, attentive to the play process, was encouraged by the child life specialist to spend time during the evening with Charlotte and her parents. She continued to play according to the child's interests, and she supported the parents' involvement in the play, repeating what was worrisome to Charlotte.

The parents continued the play with Charlotte on the morning prior to surgery, recognizing that Flower Girl was "scared." Cued to the play by the child life specialist, the nurse on duty helped Charlotte place Flower Girl on the gurney for the trip to the surgical suite.

When the oxygen mask was introduced by the anesthesiologist, Charlotte promptly ordered, "Flower Girl first," according to her previous play. The nurse indicated to the anesthesiologist the importance of the play, and the anesthesiologist complied with Charlotte's requests. Flower Girl preceded Charlotte for all the procedures prior to the anesthetization.

Following surgery, Charlotte spoke of Flower Girl's discomfort and hurting. She indicated what Flower Girl needed to feel better, from ice chips for sucking to a hand to hold. These cues to her own situation were then pursued.[4] The Flower Girl theme, stimulated and coordinated by the child life specialist, continued with the support of the parents' uninterrupted presence and at different times by a large cast of adult play partners.

Charlotte's play focused on her anxieties over the experience of preparation for and anticipation of surgery and the post-surgical period. Several elements were key to her continuing play along the themes introduced by the child life specialist. The play, molded by the child, was supported by the pivotal role of her parents, who were the ongoing, coordinating persons for the child and her play. In a secondary but substantive role were the hospital staff members, each in turn following the child's interests and lead, as modeled and coordinated by the child life specialist. Cooperative guidance helped Charlotte master the hospital events.

In Charlotte's situation, the delimiting time for the spontaneous, yet guided play became the context within which multiple play interventions merged, contributing to her parents' ongoing work with her. For Charlotte, the preparation play was almost a reversal of abreactive enactment, and yet it was reflective of anxieties raised through the preparation itself. It was preventive of overwhelming trauma, reducing the intensity of the issues, and foreshadowing the abreactive play that followed.

Edgar

Edgar, an 8-year-old truck accident victim, lay in traction for three weeks with a fractured femur. Prior to discharge from the hospital, Edgar would be cast from his ribs to the toes of one leg, partially encasing the other leg, with a positioning bar separating his legs. Almost daily, Edgar agreed to have his bed, complete with traction apparatus, moved into the play room. He shyly responded to various invitations to play offered by the succession of volunteer play partners over the period of hospitalization.

At the outset, Edgar was not an initiator in play, waiting to be approached. Sometimes, nearly inaudibly, Edgar requested Tinkertoys, other play building materials, and math games. He seldom interacted in play with the children around him, although he quietly related to his 5-year-old roommate who was hospitalized for similar reasons.

---

[4]This sequence follows the model developed by the Child Life Research Project at Children's Hospital in Phoenix, Arizona. In that project, each child admitted to the hospital was presented with a muslin doll that the child named and otherwise personalized. Rehearsals for procedures were played out on the doll, as was postprocedural play (Gaynard et al. 1990). The model specifies a strategy for helping children prepare for procedures, and it acknowledges that children need to know in advance what will occur. Most frequently, the interventions are called "preparation."

After playing with a particular set of materials, Edgar characteristically asked his adult play partner for another activity. From one child life student, he requested assistance in finding some adhesive to connect the joints of a car, his Tinkertoy creation. The car's shape was made solid by Edgar's use of surgical tape, and it included a driver with arms to manipulate a moveable steering wheel. Proud of his accomplishment, Edgar aggressively tore and cut the tape, dismembering the car with interest equal to that of its creation.

Seemingly a condensation of Edgar's perception of the accident and the subsequent treatment, this abreactive enactment promoted discussion of his feelings about these experiences. However, Edgar's major interest was the "scary" casting process looming on his horizon. The principal child life specialist guided him in repeated play on a doll-patient, simulating the casting that was to take place prior to discharge from the hospital. Edgar showed remarkable interest in the play casting in spite of reiterating his fright at the prospect of being put into a cast. He asked few questions.

As Edgar became familiar with other adult play partners, he often mentioned the casting, but grew more quiet with discussion about recovery. Emotionally composed most of the time, Edgar's quietness covered anxiety that he eventually confided to the child life specialist, particularly his anxiety about the injection that would precede the removal of the pin from his leg. He expressed hope that his mother would be present when this and the casting procedure took place. He added that should she not be able to be present, he wanted to be accompanied by the familiar child life specialist or one of the child life students with whom he had become acquainted.

Edgar's mother did not come to the casting, but the child life student, witness and partner during many play sessions, was at his side. Her presence and validation of his fears, often anticipated during the play interactions they shared, perhaps enabled Edgar's uncharacteristic outcry during the procedure. Edgar tightly grasped both hands of the child life student as he sobbed, "I want my mother."

The principal child life specialist, not at work the day of Edgar's discharge from the hospital, left him a good-luck message, noting the telephone number of the play room office. He called her the following week with a friendly report, reverting to his quiet, shy style.

Edgar's integration of the accident experience suggested by his Tinkertoy play was intermixed with play interactions centered around the casting procedure, about which Edgar's anxiety was the most pronounced. These two themes were predominant in Edgar's hospital play and were coordinated through the work of the child life specialist.

Edgar's play gave clues related to anxieties over his accident that required hospitalization and orthopedic treatment. Themes suggested by the child life specialist centered on procedures yet to happen and about which Edgar felt particularly anxious. It was assumed that the repeated casting preparation play allowed Edgar the opportunity successfully to anticipate this procedure. However, his anxieties about the procedure, specifically his ideas about the removal of the pin, were probably insufficiently attended. The trauma he was experiencing as a result of his fantasies about this removal could have been central to an abreactive process that did not occur at this time due to Edgar's imminent discharge from the hospital.

Communication among his play partners, coordinated by the child life specialist with the parents, was necessary for continuing interaction to help Edgar understand and integrate the themes within his play.

Andre

Rapidly tapping the doll's hand three times to "expose veins," 7-year-old Andre mimicked the doctor's professional style in preparation for a transfusion. Having been diagnosed with a chronic blood disorder at 17 months, Andre explained that he had had fifty of these treatments. He went through the steps of the procedure on the doll-patient, allowing the child life specialist to cut tape so he could fasten the wrist board to secure the intravenous connection on the doll.

The child life specialist had been involved with Andre in related abreactive enactments for over a year, whenever he was hospitalized or otherwise admitted for his infusion. As a demonstration of his knowledge, Andre spoke of the circulatory system with its arteries and veins as a "two-way highway," repeating a description often offered to him.

This day, under the child life specialist's thoughtful guidance, Andre compared the doll's treatment with his own, speaking of the easy and the difficult aspects of what he endured. "Getting stuck" was easy, the pinch of the tourniquet, difficult. He also made reference to specific moments of a prior medical encounter, an intensive care experience during which he had diminished opportunities for participation through play.

Moments later, when the nurse technician began the procedure on Andre's hand, Andre checked the accuracy of the way he had treated the doll, noting that he had neglected to dry the doll's hand in his play. The nurse, who knew Andre, sensitively listened as he made suggestions as to which of his veins to use.

He tolerated the procedure without wincing, but admitting the hurt. He was eager to continue his play in the play room. Once in the play room, Andre chose not to treat the doll further. Rather, he elected to draw a rainbowlike design with crayons, selecting his favorite color, turquoise, to sign his name on the page. A similar sequence of play interactions and procedures was repeated the following week. The child life specialist recalled that following individually oriented medical play, Andre (and other chronically ill school-age children) frequently chose art or other expressive-type activities rather than games with specific rules, which were selected at other times.

At age 11, Andre continued to be a "regular" in the hospital, familiar to a new cadre of hospital employees. At each admission he was examined by three or four pediatricians and physicians from the subspecialties. Rotating shifts of nurses brought him in contact with additional personnel.

In the play room, seemingly comfortable playing a game of Monopoly with two other patients, ages 10 and 11, Andre maintained a mature decorum as banker, tolerating the antics of one of his fellow players. His group play in structured games was in contrast to his medical play – his aggressive management of the doll-patient that he subjected to constant "pokes," at times infusing the doll with red-colored water that spread "everywhere." The latter abreactive enactment was complicated by fantasies or other anxieties, differing from his earlier medical play.

Responding to questions about the doll-patient's need for treatment, Andre occasionally said he did not know why the doll needed care, although at times he reported that the patient was in a car accident and required leg amputation. This play occurred in the play room in the presence of other children, rather than in one-to-one interaction with the child life specialist. The play recurred during several hospitalizations. Whenever group participation events took place in the play room such as singing with a guitarist, Andre preferred to be a bystander, anxiously fingering or poking at small toys.

The current child life specialist had known Andre for the last three-and-a-half years. She noted that he tested limits to a degree not seen before. Whereas generally Andre was a "model" patient, on one occasion he challenged a nurse as he rolled by on a wheelchair, tipping it on its back wheels to do "wheelies."

During this period, Andre remained stoic about his physical condition, especially when he did not want to miss summer camp because of pain. He once needed to be hospitalized from camp because of severe pain. He later masked his pain, tolerating great discomfort so that he could be discharged early to see his mother before she left on a business trip. Evidence of Andre's pain was recorded on the computerized device by which he regulated his pain medication to the degree permitted by the medical prescription. He "treated" pain by pressing the button, which released the analgesic, simultaneously indicating discomfort, which he didn't report to the nurse.

Generally when experiencing pain in his knees or hips, Andre played a video game, perhaps as a distraction. Sometimes he and a hospital roommate played cooperatively with the game.

Preparatory to adolescence and supporting Andre's mature qualities, he was introduced to the adolescent program and the "teens" child life specialist. She noted that when Andre felt physically better he came to the teen lounge to use play equipment such as the pool table that was not available in other parts of the hospital. Being familiar with this hospital, Andre would come to the teen lounge without needing an invitation. At these times, he interacted with other patients, his age and older.

Andre's play progressed from specific, often structured art projects, to increased interests in complex games with peers. However, his interest in imaginatively treating doll-patients did not wane. The child life specialist who had known Andre the longest continued to watch for opportunities to help him develop this abreactive enactment and interpret the related anxieties.

Andre's play history in health care continued over an extensive period of time. Although earlier records were not reported here, the recent interactions in and observations of his play revealed anxieties in the context of his greater understanding of the abstractions involved in his condition and treatment. His development and behaviors approached a newer level of independence.

The child life specialist found sufficient clues to indicate Andre's concern about losing control over the management of his disorder, as represented in the doll play, characterized by the red-colored water spreading across the doll's limbs. Whereas it was essential that developmental issues, particularly regarding peer relationships, were addressed in the play interactions, there were suggestions that the major therapeutic play partner engage Andre in play therapy to discover fantasies he may have had regarding his vulnerability.

Carolyn

Carolyn, age 11, was well-known to staff members of all the disciplines in the hospital for at least three years. She had had many years of complex medical treatments for her metabolic disorder, genetic glycogen storage disease. She endured rectal abscesses, naso-gastric tubes, and intensive care experiences with various monitors and multiple intubations. Her perception of her illness was complicated by an older sister's having the same genetic disorder. Due to insufficient early treatment, the sibling was severely disabled, requiring constant nursing care.

Because dozens of hospitalizations had interrupted her schooling, Carolyn was late in beginning to read; yet she was articulate and clever. She frequently played with dolls, often pushing a stroller of dolls through the hospital corridors and insisting that these were not dolls but "babies." She liked to surround herself with the dolls and much related child care paraphernalia in her hospital room.

Carolyn was generally nurturant and caring in her play with dolls, feeding them and gently covering them with blankets. However, provocative moments were noted by hospital staff members. She asked one nurse to restrain her by tying her to the bed. Also in contrast to nurturant interactions, Carolyn tied arms and legs of dolls together, using adhesive strips to cover genital areas of cloth dolls and the genitals of gender-explicit dolls.

Her medical play with dolls, her further abreactive enactment, reflected a wide range of medical interventions, some benign, others intrusive. Each doll was often subject to many intravenous connections. In one session, Carolyn sewed a Broviac device[5] onto a doll, reflecting with the child life student's help her fear that her own Broviac apparatus would be pulled loose. Interspersed in the play were Carolyn's comments about fears that her mother would think she was ugly with all these medical attachments. At times Carolyn explained that the dolls required treatment because of car accidents.

Psychiatric care for Carolyn was intermittent, often interrupted because of her mother's feeling of alienation from the psychiatric clinic. Carolyn's interactions showed clear enjoyment of the nurturance of staff members, as well as her difficulties in play relationships with other children over issues of taking turns and accepting loss in games. Led and coordinated by the child life staff, play partners attempted integration with the psychiatric services where abreactive play was more central. The child life staff members were primarily the ones to answer Carolyn's many questions about medical procedures and her illness, and to give her the kind of nurturance and acceptance she sought.

Tim

Tim, age 13, was a quiet, bright boy who seldom played expressively. Obviously self-conscious about the attached "bile" bag he needed for collecting fluids as part of the treatment for his nonmalignant pancreatic tumor, Tim generally avoided the play room. He spent much of his hospitalization reading and playing solitaire in his room.

While Tim was hospitalized, a magician visited the play room, showing the children a series of tricks. Since Tim did not come to the play room for the performance, the magician went to see him. Stimulated by this encounter, Tim made his only play room visit later that afternoon.

His production in the playroom was a single drawing (Figure 7-2). The castlelike structure on the horizon of the ominous world of graves and more nebulous structures, signed by the artist whose name dripped blood, prompted an untrained adult play partner to ask if Tim could locate himself in the picture. He said he was in the castle, presumably protected, even if temporarily, from the awesome and menacing future outside.

Abreactive enactment was initiated when, during the same session, Tim also briefly played with dolls. He rendered a doll helpless by tying it up in "bondage." His play continued to suggest the potential for abreaction, which might well have reflected Tim's feeling of

---

[5]A Broviac device is a surgically placed catheter, usually in the chest area, through which chemotherapy, blood drawing, and other treatments can take place without injecting veins.

FIGURE 7–2.

helplessness. Later, Tim accepted involvement with the hospital's adolescent program when he became interested in participating in an art project. His drawing and coloring for the resulting mural were meticulous, although he generally avoided interaction with the other adolescents.

Tim's pediatric play history was complicated by the multiplicity of intervenors and interventions. His feelings of helplessness reflected in his play required further attention within a play relationship. The fact that pointed but disparate attention to these concerns caused Tim to lose interest in the process suggested that a continuing helping relationship beyond the hospitalization period was needed. Timely mental health-oriented consultation conceivably might have enabled a smoother progression in a focused systematic play relationship.

If Tim's hospitalization had been longer, perhaps the child life specialist for adolescents could have spent further individual time with him, separate from the teen lounge, concentrating on his interest and ability in art. The potential for developing a helping relationship, beginning with the more public, nonpersonal art in which Tim easily engaged, might have led him to work on "private" art to consider issues an abreactive process would address, particularly those implied in his veiled expressions. Clarification of Tim's fears with realistically possible reassurance might have supported his dealing with his physical situation.

Links Between Abreactive-Enactment and Development-Supportive Play

The preceding examples of abreactive enactment play, some preprocedural or pretraumatic, contrast with play that does not suggest particulars of actual experience, but is more like the play of children under normal circumstances and may prefigure abreactive play. Development-supportive play, as the name implies, emphasizes efforts toward supporting developmental progressions, not to suggest that the abreactive enactment examples do not incorporate developmental issues. Identifying and ameliorating traumatic experiences such as separation, restraints, and immobilities support ongoing development, rendering traumas less potent as disruptive or "strangling" phenomena (Goldberger and Wolfer 1991).

Development-supportive play and abreactive-enactment play can be parallel events in a group setting, as illustrated by the responses of children to a hospital-related event that was confronted in a school setting. The meanings particular experiences have for specific children underlie the directions they spontaneously pursue in sensitive environments.

Arden

Arden, the child most closely connected with the trauma to be described, was a 6-year-old first grader who was taken home from school by friends on a Friday because her mother had to rush Arden's father to the hospital for emergency surgery. The following Monday morning, Arden returned to school, not yet having seen her father since the operation. The teachers, ready to respond to this child's anxieties, had set up a hospital play area including an examination table, syringes, tubings (there had been some explanation to Arden about her father's need for "tubes" in the immediate aftermath of surgery), surgical gloves, masks, bandages, and blood pressure cuff. A sign on the wall read "Doctor's Office." An adjoining space reserved for waiting was stocked with books and a teddy bear.

Almost all of the class members, even though essentially untouched by the trauma, quickly embarked on the doctor play, pretending medical examinations as suggested by the arrangement described. Arden remained far from this play, selecting to "write." The teacher suggested several writing choices including a get-well card for her father. Arden chose to write and illustrate a book for him, focusing on what in their relationship she missed.

With a teacher at her side, Arden worked intensively on her project over several days. Writing with her own invented spelling, she noted how she missed playing with her father in the swimming pool. To accompany the text, Arden drew herself jumping into the pool toward her father, with his outstretched arms ready to catch her. She drew their special somersault game, her father holding her hands as she turned through a hoop made of their arms. In another scene, Arden drew herself riding on her father's back. Arden captioned each drawing with a description of the play and how much she loved her father. She illustrated the loss she was enduring, her understanding that her father could not play with her, and her fear that their relationship was gone forever.

In her first visit to her father at the hospital, Arden came away shocked by the sight of her father with a tube in his mouth and unable to talk. The next day, with the tube removed, he could talk, and they were able to have dinner together. The following day they walked down the hospital corridor together.

At school, the children's medical play evolved into a maternity ward scenario created primarily by the girls. They carried dolls under their sweaters and dramatically appeared for delivery. Medically related themes continued to emerge in the play of the majority of the children, eventually focusing on the dispensing of medications. With Arden's book-writing activity completed, she might possibly have entered the more generic medical examination play had it not evolved beyond the original doctor's office scenario.

The contrast here is between the child experiencing trauma and children whose personal lives were untouched by the event. Elaborations in the play of the latter could follow imaginative courses, supportive of explorations in social and cognitive realms; the play of the former had a specific prescription. Nonetheless, both the human and physical environment were developmentally supportive. When Arden's abreactive enactments had reached resolution (as her trauma was being resolved in reality), she was ready to engage in the more expansive play.

Similarly, a child in another classroom pursued story writing that focused on her mother's giving birth to a new baby under traumatic circumstances. The child's resulting essay covered her own mixed responses of joy and fear, while simultaneously, her classmates wrote of dinosaurs and mythical characters (Kroll 1990).

Development–Supportive Play

Neil

Neil, a somewhat developmentally delayed 2-year-old child of a southeast Asian family, was hospitalized for several weeks for treatment for his cancer. Separation was the critical issue. Neil's parents lived quite a distance from the hospital and worked full time. Although they were attentive and Neil remained positively responsive to them, they were absent a great deal of the time. When either or both were present, they brought Neil to the play room, which delighted him. Neil expressed intense distress when any family member was out of sight, even if for a few minutes.

Due to the parents' external constraints, they assigned visiting responsibilities to their 16-year-old daughter, a high school dropout. She resented being required to stay with her sick little brother, and he was miserable with his depressed, generally abrupt sister at his side. She never encouraged his coming to the play room. Instead, she often got into bed with Neil. This may have reflected the family practice of sleeping together.

During a change of medical dressings, when Neil's sister was absent, a volunteer play partner attempted to soothe Neil's distress by offering him toys in his bed. He cried "No–no!" although he accepted a small toy car and tightly clutched it as the nurse completed the medical procedure.

Neil's negative responses reflected his parents' ambivalence toward the hospital and its care. Western medicine was foreign to this family, and their fears influenced their initial refusal of aspects of medical care for Neil. In fact, on two occasions, the hospital had to seek court orders to proceed with treatments.

The hospital staff paid special attention to Neil's family relationships and the family's anxiety regarding the hospital. Although the counseling offered the 16-year-old sibling was rejected, she occasionally attended the adolescent session in the hospital's teen lounge. The staff hoped to provide the sister with some social activities directed to satisfying her own needs so that her presence would be less negative for Neil.

The nurse who most often tended Neil presented the child with positive play interventions. Even when assigned to administrative work, she came to see Neil. She sang children's songs to him, eventually encouraging him to mimic her finger motions for the trail of the "eensy, weensy spider." She noted that his capacities for play were diminished when he had a fever or when he felt ill from his chemotherapy.

Although Neil showed no interest in medical or hospital experience-related play under these circumstances, there was the potential for these to occur when he would develop a capacity for symbolic play and abreactive enactment and when he would be less overwhelmed.

Belinda

Belinda, initially a non-English-speaking 3-year-old patient with leukemia complicated by neurological involvement, was at first unable to come to the play room because of a physical condition likened to a wakeful coma. Because her physical therapy appointments at times conflicted with play room sessions, Belinda was frequently visited at her bedside by the child life specialist. During the period when Belinda's neurological status was unclear, the child life worker presented her with a "busy box" and guided Belinda's hands to touch it. Eventually Belinda reached for the busy box, and finally, with purpose, opened and closed its "doors."

When Belinda first came to the play room she was placed on a mat for play. After a number of weeks, she played at the water table and on the rocking horse, both of which she enjoyed. At these times, she wore a mask due to her high susceptibility to infection whenever she was with others.

Her mother was generally present after the beginning period of the hospitalization, and brought ethnic food from home for her sick child. Belinda's greatest distress was registered when her mother needed to leave. When Belinda was upset, as when her mother left or when bone marrow aspirations were performed, only her primary nurse could calm her. In addition to nursing care, this nurse spent time in play with Belinda, identifying in English words important people and things for her.

Initially, it was difficult to determine if Belinda's reticence and lack of expression in play were illness-related or integrally associated with her feeling that her parents had abandoned her, leaving her with strange persons in an environment unreflective of the child's ethnic language and world. After about two months of hospitalization, Belinda became more expressive, beginning to use new words in English and in her native language.

Play interactions with familiar caregivers supported Belinda's ability to manage her hospital experiences. She achieved some mastery over separation through developing relationships with her nurse and several volunteer play partners. Although her play did not display connections to her illness and hospitalization, through play she made developmental progressions, particularly in language. She showed growing enjoyment in play, which continued along development-supportive lines while she was encouraged to pursue symbolic play as an antecedent to abreactive enactment.

Sam

A staff child life specialist recalled that as an infant, Sam, his twin sister, and his mother came together to the hospital's developmentally oriented preschool. Sam had been diagnosed with failure to thrive. From about age 9 months to 1 year, Sam was noted to be lethargic and uninterested in his environment. The staff members often had to feed him, as his mother was more interested in the twin sister. The counselors were unable to help the mother improve her interactions with Sam at this critical time.

Although Sam, now age 6, had been familiar with the outpatient Child Development Clinic for several years, his first hospitalization occurred recently. This admission was to rule out physiological bases for his failure to thrive.

Sam was a wiry, thin, exceedingly active boy who quickly became known to a number of play partners, a child life specialist, child life students, and volunteers. Each in turn grew fatigued attempting to follow Sam's play and protect him from getting hurt through his flitting from one thing to another. Other children had to be protected from Sam's fast-moving paths and the toys he threw.

Sam's family was fraught with problems—a schizophrenic father, two brothers with complex behavioral difficulties, a favored twin sister, and an ineffectual mother. A major deficit in Sam's development was his difficult-to-understand speech. His attempts to name what he was seeing or doing were not hampered by the unsuccessful efforts of his play partners to understand Sam's communication.

In the play room, Sam initially needed the protection of a play partner to reserve a space for his play. For brief periods he could build with blocks and other objects as long as other children did not intrude. When other children played in Sam's vicinity, he grabbed their toys.

After realizing that the play room was overly stimulating, play partners encouraged Sam's play activity elsewhere. Sam collected large play items from the play room to take to his own room. His interest in electric plugs became evident as he would rush to plug in unconnected cords from children's I.V. devices. He also showed intense interest in the waxer and buffing machine as they were alternately maneuvered by a custodian down the corridor each morning.

As the days passed, the play staff noticed that Sam, becoming more familiar with individuals, was more receptive to their warmth. He grew more communicative as certain play partners were able to understand his words, beginning with "vacuum," "plug," and "unplug," the words he was most excited to convey. Prior to discharge to a foster home, Sam could play at a particular activity for as long as forty minutes.

The hospitalization period allowed the medical tests and important observation of Sam's behaviors not possible in the outpatient setting. Especially important and developmentally supportive were the play relationships. As Sam became sufficiently trusting, he could focus and communicate with more purpose and greater success.

Thomas

Thomas, age 13, who had cystic fibrosis, came to the hospital frequently. His admission was termed a "tune up" for his respiratory system, which was compromised by his chronic disease.

Thomas was small for his age. Although he enjoyed play activities alongside the younger children and showed particular interest in visibly impaired children, he sometimes "terrorized" or insulted the children. Thomas quickly pushed limits in organized play, requiring that an adult play partner curtail his aggressiveness. For example, in making play dough, Thomas pounded a mound of the clay with extra handfuls of flour, thoroughly dusting himself and all the others in his immediate area.

The nurses' complaints about Thomas led to his transfer to a unit of the hospital for older children. He missed the more familiar pediatric play area and the play partners he came to know. Thus he was particularly receptive to the company of a young male volunteer with whom he shared many games.

Gradually, Thomas became acquainted with the child life specialist of the teen unit. She introduced him to several cystic fibrosis patients older than he. Although less regressed in his play, through the development-supportive interactions, Thomas's concerns—including the arrival of a new sibling in the family—were addressed in play and in the social interactions of the environment.

Multiple Play Partners: Complications for Abreaction

Hospital Sociology

A critical component of the abreactive process is the helping relationship through which a therapist comes to know a child's traumatic experiences and recognizes their meanings to the child. Suggested in this is continuity of the therapeutic dyad so that effective association of traumas with emotional responses can be systematically accomplished.

The hospital setting is characterized by a multiplicity of significant interactions and play partners. In sociological terms, the interactions are circumscribed by and dynamically interrelated with a particular institution, more specifically, a medical one with its own history, traditions, and reasons for being. Traditions of the medical professions and their various interrelations, although influenced by politics and economics, reinforce the superseding development and institutionalization of specializations. Profoundly affected by the introduction and continuing refinement of science and technology, the resulting social environment largely accounts for the nearly countless interactions that characterize patient experiences in the hospital.

The complexity of society's newer movements, according greater voice to individuals and their rights, has enabled the introduction of ideas that support and give credence to patients' perspectives and their psychological and social needs. Whereas medicine has been at the forefront in enabling and extending life in ways not heretofore imaginable, it is in the related fields including the nursing profession that, for a variety of social and political reasons, the emphasis has centered on individuals and quality of life. In particular, this latter orientation has placed attention on understanding chronic illness and the patient's and the family's treatment of disease aside from, yet required by, medical regimens (Strauss and Glaser 1975). These considerations do not discount sensitivity to individual patients' medical needs.

Although pediatric departments have recently incorporated child life specialists and other educational and mental health professionals, there remains the recognition that these nonmedical services provide secondary, although important, roles. Children are not admitted to the hospital to engage in play programs, for example. Hospital and pediatric departments' acceptance of play programs is, however, seen as enhancing patient care and helping children and families in addition to medical treatment.

Because of the general social context, in spite of emphases on individuals as persons, the potential for fragmentation in medical care is high at any one time or in a trajectory of events over time. Mental health and child life specialists view their approaches as a corrective to such fragmentation, enabling children and their families to integrate their experiences into meaningful and effective ongoing development. Nevertheless, given the complex situations in hospitals, it is important to question whether play relationships and related interactions are counterfragmenting or if they merely replicate the fragmentation characteristic of the institutions in which these nonmedical services are embedded. Further, it is important to evaluate whether the disparate therapeutic play relationships characteristic of the hospital add confusion rather than the integration and consolidation of experiences for children that are the articulated goals of therapeutic play.

Therapeutic Play

For the child life specialist, dilemmas are inherent in delimiting the focus of play programs, only partially reflected in the generally short-term nature of any hospitalization period. Whereas "normal" children's activities available during hospitalization are thought to minimize potential disruptions to development, it is easily observed how complicated are these children's lives, medically, socially, and psychologically. All issues arise in play, yet the chief focus in pediatric hospitalizations is on normal development and enabling children to respond effectively to their health care experiences. The time-limited constraints of a hospitalization period generally preclude work that allows broader interpretation of circumstances relative to outside problems. Yet the integrally related nature of the issues challenges separations that could result in care that is incomplete and without full understanding.

In that therapeutic work in pediatric play relationships, unlike play therapy as usually defined, does not have as its primary goal basic personality change, "therapeutic play" as a modality is akin to crisis intervention. Play therapy, with its strong emphasis on abreactive enactment, addresses basic and persistent difficulties in a patient's interactions in his or her world and generally occurs in the context of a continuity figure. In a less structured way, therapeutic play focuses on spontaneous phenomena as the child engages in play to master developmental challenges and critical events. Therapeutic play encompasses play expressions that are developmentally related and developmentally supportive as well as the abreactive enactment of illness and hospitalization issues. Therapeutic play and play therapy are thus more alike than dissimilar, as mastery toward adaptation predominates in both.

In therapeutic play, educated guesses at meanings are necessary. More important, given its goals, therapeutic play supports the ongoing nature of play, enabling children to maintain interactions expressively in play with their feelings reenforced and validated. The cases described demonstrate that even with multiplicity of play partners, the therapeutic processes in abreactive-enactment and development-supportive play continue. It is assumed that this quality reflects the self-healing nature of play (Erikson 1950). As an internal locus of control in the child is facilitated through the supportive play relationships, the potentials for mastery are enhanced (Bolig et al. 1986).

It has been recognized how avidly children grasp the chance to play, organizing the activities according to their perceptions of their experiences (Erikson 1950). Often a condensation of the confluence of their experiences, children's play provides extraordinary opportunities for mastery of anxieties. It behooves the adult sponsors of the play environment, as well as those whose interactions are integral for the children's care and medical treatment, to understand and respond accordingly, so that abreactive-enactment play occurs.

Most of the pediatric play histories presented demonstrate abreactive-enactment *and* development-supportive play in multiple therapeutic play relationships. That the hospital and all its personnel become part of the ongoing lives of chronically ill children is obvious; the support for the children's development is thus a mandate for all of the staff. Under these circumstances, limiting attention in play relationships to only those issues related to illness and hospitalization is artificial. At times, interpretive interventions of the complex themes in play, associating intertwining traumas with emotional responses, can be approached.

Influenced by their illnesses and the attention bestowed on them, the children's development is integrally related to the interactions with the host of caregivers over time. Particular opportunities to observe children in their daily lives, albeit in the hospital, aside from specific therapeutic sessions, yield direct information about the nature of the traumas so that abreaction can be more immediately used in the intervening play. With coordination of play relationships, other complex issues including familial ones, often observable in the hospital, arise in play, providing the potential and challenges for play therapy and abreactive enactment.

Facets of the Play Relationship

Each of the play histories presented reveals multiple issues that relate to the individual child's composite life and health experiences. Children of various developmental levels were described, with several play histories illustrating complicated nonmedical issues where coordination was particularly important, given the multiple issues and persons involved with each.

In some situations, the children's play described as abreactive enactment was enabled by supporting developmental progressions. The play categorized as developmentally supportive suggests potential for abreactive enactments. Although the children's expressions are not so easily interpreted as being reflective of trauma, support for development through enabling key attachments and children's capacities for attachment with familiar persons responsive to each child's distress, allows and encourages children's continuing to play – a precondition for abreaction-related play. The development-supportive play, especially for the young child, enables abreaction as each is developmentally ready to incorporate the related issues. Minimizing disruptions to a child's integration of critical experiences is also a major facet of the therapeutic interventions supporting development.

Therapeutic play with doll-patients confronted issues the children projected onto dolls. Abreactive enactments were observed as the children repetitively expressed through play the anxieties that otherwise were potentially disruptive to their development whether during one-time or multiple hospitalizations.

Play coordination through a continuous play relationship was especially critical for the youngest children who were less able to relate to multiple persons, but whose interactions with parents and selected key staff members enabled the play, conceivably prefiguring abreactive enactments. For those children whose play presented issues that were potentially readable, particularly expressive of medical and illness issues, the continuity figure was also the most likely figure in whom each child's trust supported exploration and potential abreaction.

The development-supportive play relationship requires somewhat different but complementary orientations to abreactive-type play. The same is true for therapeutic play and play therapy. Flexibility allows different relationships with different children. The approach depends on the goals set for each child, determined by evaluation of the child's needs. The orientations presented require a primary coordinating player who is as continuously available as possible.

Greater attention to coordination of the concomitant and sequential roles of play partners should ameliorate the confusion in multiple play relationships, and should enable abreactive-enactment as well as development-supportive play. Although the hospital environment's organization is sociologically determined and influenced, reflecting the multifaceted interactions of the various specialties, coordination of approaches is possible (Wojtasik et al. 1985). Sharing of information with a developing consensus among the social actors, both medical and nonmedical, regarding a unified and integrated series of goals and methods is an ideal to be achieved.

Children generally experience multiple caregivers and potential play partners throughout their formative years. Day care and schools are prime examples of institutions whose dimensions are similar, relative to integration with children (Chehrazi 1990, Murphy and Callaghan 1989). It is suggested that the ideas presented here, applicable beyond the health care world of children, serve as cautionary notes to minimize fragmentation and create conditions enabling development-supportive play and abreactive play in multiadult helping relationships. Considerations of preparatory play, based on abreactive-type interactions, are additionally viewed as preventive mental health measures, laying the foundation for minimizing current and future trauma.

References

Accreditation Council for Graduate Medical Education (1990). *Residency Review for Pediatrics.*
American Academy of Pediatrics (1990). *Accreditation Manual for Hospitals, Child and Adolescent Services.* Chicago, IL: American Academy of Pediatrics.
Association for the Care of Children's Health (1990). *North American Directory of Child Life Programs.* Bethesda, MD.
Bolig, R., Fernie, D., and Klein, E. (1986). Unstructured play in hospital settings: an internal locus of control rationale. *Children's Health Care* 15:101–107.
Breuer, J., and Freud, S. (1893–1895). *Studies on Hysteria.* New York: Basic Books, 1957.
Chehrazi, S., ed. (1990). *Psychosocial Issues in Day Care.* Washington, DC: American Psychiatric Press.
Child Life Certifying Commission (1991). Bethesda, MD.
Child Life Council (1989). *Standards for Clinical Practice.* Bethesda, MD: Child Life Council.
Education Committee (1991). Child Life Council documents. Bethesda, MD: Child Life Council.
Ekstein, R. (1966). *Children of Time and Space, of Action and Impulse.* New York: Appleton-Century-Crofts.
Erikson, E. (1950). *Childhood and Society.* New York: Norton.
Freud, S. (1920). Beyond the pleasure principle. *Standard Edition* 20:7–64.
——— (1926). Inhibitions, symptoms, and anxiety. *Standard Edition* 18:77–175.
Furman, R. (1964). Death and the young child. *Psychoanalytic Study of the Child* 19:321–333. New York: International Universities Press.

Gaynard, L., Wolfer, J., Goldberger, J., et al. (1990). *Psychosocial Care of Children in Hospitals: A Clinical Practice Manual from the ACCH Child Life Research Project.* Bethesda, MD: Association for the Care of Children's Health.

Ginsburg, H., and Opper, S. (1969). *Piaget's Theory of Intellectual Development.* Englewood Cliffs, NJ: Prentice-Hall.

Goldberger, J., and Wolfer, J. (1991). An approach for identifying potential threats to development in hospitalized toddlers. *Infants and Young Children* 3:74–83.

Golden, D. (1983). Play therapy for hospitalized children. In *Handbook of Play Therapy,* ed. C. Schaefer and K. O'Connor, pp. 213–233. New York: John Wiley & Sons.

Hartmann, H. (1976). Psychoanalytic theory of play. In *Psychoanalysis,* ed. S. A. Guttman, pp. 84–100. New York: International Universities Press.

Kroll, L. (1990). *Making meaning in writing: a longitudinal study of young children's writing.* Presentation for meetings of the American Education Research Association, Boston, April.

Loewald, H. (1970). Analytic theory and the analytic process. *Psychoanalytic Study of the Child* 25:62–63. New York: International Universities Press.

Murphy, J., and Callaghan, K. (1989). Therapeutic versus traditional foster care: theoretical and practical distinctions. *Adolescence* 24:96.

Oremland, E. (1988). Mastering developmental and critical experiences through play and other expressive behaviors in childhood. *Children's Health Care* 16:150–156.

Plank, E. (1971). *Working with Children in Hospitals.* Cleveland: Case Western Reserve.

Play in Health Care Settings (1988). Theme issue: Play in Health Care Settings. *Children's Health Care* 16:132–237.

Schaefer, C., ed. (1976). *Therapeutic Use of Child's Play.* New York: Jason Aronson.

Schaefer, C., and O'Connor, K., eds. (1983). *Handbook of Play Therapy.* New York: John Wiley & Sons.

Scheff, T. J. (1979). *Catharsis in Healing, Ritual, and Drama.* Berkeley, CA: University of California Press.

Strauss, A., and Glaser, B. (1975). *Chronic Illness and the Quality of Life.* St. Louis, MO: C. V. Mosby.

Terr, L. (1990). *Too Scared to Cry.* New York: Harper & Row.

Thompson, R. (1985). *Psychosocial Research on Pediatric Hospitalization and Health Care.* Springfield, IL: Charles C Thomas.

Waelder, R. (1932). The psychoanalytic theory of play. *Psychoanalytic Quarterly* 2:208–224.

Wexler, H. (1973). The life master. *Psychoanalytic Study of the Child* 27:591. New Haven: Yale University Press.

Wojtasik, S., Mattsson, A., Longman, C., and Lewis, N. (1985). *An interdisciplinary model to extend the child life role in the care of families in crisis.* Presentation for meetings of the Association for the Care of Children's Health, Boston.

Wolfenstein, M. (1966). How is mourning possible? *Psychoanalytic Study of the Child* 21:93–123. New York: International Universities Press.

8

Role Play

Eleanor C. Irwin and Nancy E. Curry

Most troubled children are unable to tell their therapist what they think or how they feel, either because they do not know or cannot say. To bridge this communication gap and start a dialogue, clinicians look for ways to help the child begin to talk about ideas and feelings. A pleasurable and psychically safe way for many children to begin a dialogue is through symbolic play activities. Diagnostically and therapeutically, role play is especially useful in this process of helping children via play. Because most children engage in spontaneous dramatic play during their early years, this mode of expression is natural and comfortable for most, providing the safety of disguise along with the pleasure of play.

But what, actually, is role play? In this chapter, the term is meant to apply to the play patterns and behaviors that the child develops over time, under the influence of significant people in his world. Roles that are enacted can be *implicit* or *explicit*. The latter term refers to those roles that are consciously undertaken and exposed to the observation of others. This is generally the meaning that one implies when "role play" exercises are used in a learning situation, to sharpen skills, try on new behaviors, or increase sensitivity to another's point of view. This use of role play will be illustrated in the final part of this chapter with examples of a child's rehearsing a feared event, and another's practice in being more assertive.

Roles are more often *implicit*, when patterns of behavior are out of awareness, and/or unconsciously determined. Implicit roles express personality attributes that originate in early internalizations and identifications, enduring psychological patterns that are the outgrowth of countless interactions between the growing child and his caretakers. These early relationships with people, especially mother, become an integral part of the internal self (as ego, id, superego), and the external, social self in the wider world with others. Expressed in object relations terms, then, the child's implicit portrayal of roles demonstrates how he has internalized aspects and functions of external objects. Through scenes that are dramatized and roles that are adopted or rejected, children tell us a great deal about their identifications, preoccupations, and defenses. This chapter will explore this topic, presenting a theoretical and clinical basis for the use and meaning of role play in child therapy.

Historical Foundations

Because the child's spontaneous play has historically been seen as analogous to the adult's free association, play has been especially valued in child therapy. Hermine Hug-Hellmuth (1921), child analyst and pioneer in play therapy, was one of the first to propose the use of play in treating troubled children. About that same time, Anna Freud (1930), with combined training as a teacher and analyst, began to analyze children and train others to do the same. In connection with the Vienna Institute of Psychoanalysis, Freud established a child guidance center that was apparently similar to those in the United States (Francis 1978). Cases presented in seminars and study groups emphasized the centrality of play – especially dramatic play – in understanding the child's core conflicts and defenses.

Berta Bornstein (1949), a member of the study group, wrote about the three-year analysis of Frankie, a phobic child of 5½. The youngster's fear of abandonment, his jealousy and sadistic rage, especially after his brother's birth, are documented in her case study presentation. Bornstein's report clearly attests to the importance of Frankie's dramatic play in his analysis. Just as in current practice, Frankie sometimes directed Bornstein to play certain roles under his direction (Irwin 1985); other times he played all the roles himself. Bornstein tells us how helpful the role play was. She writes: "His dramatic play during his first session led straight into his conflicts, just as in adult analysis the first dream often leads into the core of the patient's neurosis. His play revealed at once the experiences that had led to his phobia and thus betrayed the meaning of his symptom" (p. 184).

In his first session, Frankie built a hospital with sections for ladies, babies, and men. "In the lobby, a lonely boy of 4 was seated all by himself, on a chair placed in an elevated position" (p. 185). Later, taking the roles of doctor and nurse, the child was very loving toward the babies. Caught up in the play, however, Frankie's ambivalence emerged; he pretended that a fire broke out and killed all the babies. Frankie, playing the role of the lonely child, wanted to run home but remembered that no one would be there. Taking the role of a fireman, he tried to save the babies, but alas, the women (whom Frankie called "mommy"), most of the men, *and* the babies burned to death. In this range of roles, therefore, we see Frankie's inner drama, which expressed fear of abandonment and marked ambivalence toward his parents and brother. In this detailed case study, Bornstein makes it clear that the on-going dramas provided pleasure and in-depth understanding; but these "games" were also helpful in tying past to present and fantasy to reality, eventually freeing Frankie from his phobia.

The state of the art in psychodynamic child therapy has not changed much from Hug-Hellmuth's day. In current practice, fantasy and enactments continue to constitute a major mode of communication between child and therapist. Although dramatizations are often used with preschoolers, they are just as common with children in latency, for whom fantasy serves as the *sine qua non* as an avenue of discharge. Sarnoff (1976), who has written extensively about latency children, disagrees with Freud's notion that the sexual drives "go underground" (i.e., are repressed) in latency (Freud 1925). To illustrate, Sarnoff (1976) presents several cases. In one, an 8-year-old boy, enraged with his abusive father, left the play room and began an enactment in Sarnoff's office. Saying that the desk was a castle, the boy enacted the story of poor peasants who were being mistreated by a king. The boy assumed the role of the leader, Marshall (his middle name), and then had the "multitude" storm the castle, ready to kill the king. At that precise moment, the child interrupted the play and went to the bathroom. Upon returning, the boy had no recollection of the (interrupted) fantasy of killing the king.

Just as in Bornstein's example, cited above, it is clear that the child takes advantage of the drama to play roles that carry powerful feelings and contain symbolic meanings. The enactment of these inner scripts is not without its hazards, however. For some, the play may bypass defenses, allowing the forbidden wish to be expressed. For others, the drama may upset the psychic equilibrium, bringing into motion the interplay of conflict and defense. The expression of powerful conflicted wishes stimulates anxiety, which, in turn, mobilizes defenses. If the child's characteristic defenses are not strong enough to contain the anxiety, then play disruption may result (Erikson 1950).

For example, Frankie was unaware that *he* was the lonely boy in the hospital lobby, since he didn't *feel* lonely, nor did he realize that while part of him felt loving toward the babies, part of him also wanted the babies to burn to death. With strong defenses of denial, repression, and reaction-formation, Frankie expressed these conflicted wishes under the protection of the "pretend" umbrella. Marshall, on the other hand, was unable to continue his play. After initiating the pretend uprising to kill the king, he went to the bathroom, and then the play stopped. We surmise that even this disguised, pretend killing stimulated guilt. Both boys, therefore, played out dramas in which murderous aggression was expressed. But because superego defenses came to the fore, Marshall "forgot" what he was doing. Later he poignantly explained, "I get angry. I run away and think of killing them and saying to myself, I hate them. I hate them. But then I forget it and before you know it, I'm making up these stories to take out my feelings" (Sarnoff 1976, p. 25).

In this kind of play, therapists can see the child's identifications or internalizations (i.e., self and other representations) in the roles that are chosen or rejected, the intrapsychic defenses that may be aroused in reaction to these enactments, and the compromise solutions the child uses to solve his problems. Before presenting further clinical examples from our work, we will discuss the theoretical rationale, and illustrate how an understanding of object relations theory can provide a conceptual scaffolding for analyzing the child's role play.

Object Relations Theory

Melanie Klein (1932, 1961), one of the originators of play therapy and an innovative analyst, is often credited with developing theories of object relations. Working with and trying to understand the behavior of psychotic and borderline children, Klein began to attach much importance to early fantasy life. Her work foreshadows that of Fairbairn (1952), Jacobson (1964), Kernberg (1966, 1980), Kohut (1971, 1977), Mahler (1952), Mahler and Furer (1965), Mahler and colleagues (1975), Spitz (1965), Winnicott (1965, 1971), and others.

In psychoanalytic jargon, *object* is a term that refers to someone other than the self. The object is a mental image, one that is colored with feelings. The residues of these early object relationships endure over time and can account for a wide range of normal, adaptive behaviors as well as neurotic, maladaptive ones. Object relations theory posits that life begins with the merger of self and other. Over time, especially during the first three years of life, these merged images separate into self and object representations (Kernberg 1966, 1980).

Winnicott (1965) has called attention to the importance of the "holding" that a "good enough mother" provides, which can allow the child to move from a state of fusion and merger into stages of separateness. In suggesting these concepts, Winnicott emphasizes that maturational processes are dependent on having parents who will adapt to the infant's needs, and having a sufficiently stable and nurturing environment that will stimulate growth and development.

Kernberg (1980) describes the process of internalization:

> Object relations theory considers the psychic apparatus as originating in the earliest stage of a sequence of internalization of object relations. The stages of development of internalized object relations – that is, the stages of infantile autism, symbiosis, separation-individuation and of object constancy – reflect the earliest structures of the psychic apparatus. Discrete units of self-representation, object representation and an affect disposition linking them are the basic substructures of these early developmental stages, and will gradually evolve into more complex substructures, such as real-self and ideal-self, and real-object and ideal-object representations. [p. 17]

Perceptions of the self and others grow out of complex daily experiences that begin with birth or before. Stern (1985) refers to these experiences as RIGs, that is, *Representations of Interactions that have become Generalized.* Bowlby (1982) and his followers call them *internal working models.* These experiences, whether comforting and soothing, or painful and ungratifying, build up over time, contributing to a sense of self.

Margaret Mahler (1952) and Mahler and colleagues (1965, 1975), were also major contributors to clinical research in child development in the area of object relations. Mahler held that there are three major phases of early development: *autistic, symbiotic,* and *separation-individuation.* The last is believed to consist of four subphases: *differentiation, practicing, rapprochement,* and *on-the-way-to-object constancy.* Recent research indicates that babies are much more alert and knowledgeable than had been hitherto supposed (Brazelton and Als 1979, Stern 1985) and this has led to dispute about whether infants actually have an autistic phase. Nevertheless, Mahler has added greatly to an understanding of object relations theory, pointing out that the child is not a blank slate and that the mutuality of the mother–infant dyad is a crucial factor in development. The child's ability to be a separate, distinct person will either be promoted or limited, depending on the child's environment and the nature of the mother–child interaction. Spitz (1965) proposed the concept of *organizers,* which indicate the emergence of the self and the beginning of social relations on the human level. These include the *smile,* indicating that the human face has become a "whole" precept; *stranger anxiety reaction,* which suggests that the child has cathected (that is, recognized or attached to) a specific other; and *speech and language,* which indicate a higher level of organization and integration. Object relations, therefore, emerges out of human interaction with a specific other, and, as Kernberg (1980) has said, carries with it an image of the self, an image of the other, and an affective charge.

As the child becomes increasingly able to venture into the wider world, it is crucial that he feel safely attached to the caretaker. Sometimes caretakers relish the gusto with which the child explores the world. Eager for "grown-up" behavior, they encourage the child's pseudo-mature actions but fail to empathically support and comfort the child when all does not go well (Speers 1975). Some mothers stimulate an avoidant attachment, while others, in their failure to set limits and affirm boundaries, unwittingly encourage the child's grandiosity and narcissism. This is thought to stimulate an anxious attachment (Ainsworth 1972). If, however, the environment is "good enough" (Winnicott 1965), the child will be able to merge the split images of the good and bad mother, that is, the mother who is both gratifying and depriving. In being able to hold on to the image of the "good enough" mother, in tolerating the ambivalence that is part of the human condition, the child signals readiness to separate and differentiate, and is on the way to object constancy. This "whole" mother is not destroyed or rejected when the child is angry or disappointed, and the child can therefore safely separate without undue anxiety.

Current psychoanalytic theory has expanded and deepened to include the self psychology of Kohut (1971, 1977) and his followers. Like other theorists, Kohut stresses the importance of the parents' role in the child's formation of a cohesive self. Kohut's contributions are many, including his insights on the treatment of narcissistic individuals who develop idealizing, mirror, and twinship transferences. The crucial impact of early experiences on the development of the self has been buttressed by child development researchers who have investigated the first three years of life (e.g., Mahler and colleagues 1975, Sander 1975, and Stern 1985). These authors and others representing the field of social psychology (e.g., Lewis and Brooks-Gun 1979), note the child's gradual awareness of the sense of self as evidenced by recognition on videotapes and in mirrors.

Play is another mode that can be used to evaluate the child's burgeoning sense of self. The developmental task of establishing a solid, comfortable sense of self has landmarks that are observable and can be manifest in play from early infancy. Curry (1986) and Curry and Bergen (1987) list play behaviors that are characteristic of each of the subphases proposed by Mahler and colleagues (1975). If enough characteristics of a subphase are absent, one can peg where the child may have experienced an arrest or fixation. Mahler and colleagues (1975) give specific behavioral descriptions at each subphase of the separation-individuation process. Play indicators (see Table 8-1) are described for each of these subphases to enable therapists to determine where the child may be blocked, and to plan therapeutic strategies utilizing role play to help the child resume a normal developmental progression.

Autistic and Symbiotic Phases

The *autistic phase* is characterized by a relatively high stimulus barrier, which becomes broached by and replaced through the caregiver's careful reading of the child's signals and temperament. While many argue that there is no true autistic phase (i.e., Stern 1985), Mahler uses the term to describe the infant's inward-directedness and seeming preoccupation with visceral sensations with only fleeting awareness of what goes on outside. As the bonding process takes place, through the need-fulfilling ministrations of the caregiver, the infant and caregiver become engaged in a mutually gratifying closeness to which each contributes. Thus, Mahler labels this period as the *symbiotic phase.*

Separation-Individuation Subphases

While Mahler was a pioneer in studying severe psychopathology of early child-hood, her research about distorted development of severely disturbed children led her to delineate the normal phases of autism, symbiosis, and separation-individuation. Mahler learned that each parent–child dyad has a period of normal symbiosis from which the child begins to "hatch" at about four months. The period when the child begins to distinguish himself from the human and nonhuman environment is called the *differentiation subphase.* There is a new look of alertness on the baby's face, a turning away from being snuggled into the breast, and a preference for sitting in a way so that the child can see the world. As motor development permits, the child slides down from the mother's lap, sits at her feet, and explores the environment, using newly developed eye-hand-mouth coordination. Thus the child begins intense exploration of his own body and that of the caregiver, of toys and items of the everyday world.

Games of naming and touching of body parts begin, as do the traditional lap and knee games. These activities assist the child in differentiating himself from others, and the child finds out how others fit in the world and relate to each other. Caring adults keep up a running commentary, label their experiences and feelings, and play separation games like peek-a-boo and catch me. A clear symbol of differentiation is the creation of the transitional object (Winnicott 1965), a representation of both child and mother that aids the separation process.

With the advent of crawling and walking, at about nine months, the child enters the *practicing subphase.* The child can now initiate separations and determine the distance between himself and others. Mahler speaks of the elated investment in locomotion and the heady excitement of being the one who goes away and comes back. While elation is the primary mood, children become "low-keyed" when separated either physically or psychologically from their caregivers, a forerunner of depressive affect.

Play during this period is characterized by the practice of all kinds of physical capacities. Furthermore, the child begins to imitate the actions of beloved others – cuddling a baby doll and patting it tenderly, making noises while pushing an object on the floor, trying on daddy's hat. These tendrils of beginning role play indicate that the child is aware of others as separate from self, and this includes awareness of the *functions* of others.

A deviation of the separation-individuation process is the run-and-chase (Speers 1965), which has its roots in this period. Speers adds that if the child cannot be sure of having a secure base to return to, the child must force the mother to come to him. The youngster does this by getting into dangerous situations through darting-away behaviors. Similarly, if the mother is too smothering, unable to allow the child to engage in the exploratory forays typical of this time, the child may need to run away from the feelings of engulfment such a mother stimulates. When seen in therapy, such youngsters may run out of the play room, climb precariously on shelves and window sills, and force the therapist to keep an eye on them at all times. Psychologically, this run-and-chase behavior may be seen in attempts to draw the therapist close, only to push her away. Since such behaviors can arouse strong countertransference feelings, the therapist who has a developmental point of view may be better able to understand, tolerate, and interpret such behaviors.

Object relations theorists have alerted us to the importance of the preoedipal period, which in earlier Freudian theory was given short shrift in favor of the oedipal period, from which neuroses supposedly emerge. Mahler and her colleagues have helped us to see that the period of *rapprochement*, with its coalescing of a number of physical and cognitive achievements, can produce pathological deviations on a par with oedipal conflicts. With intellectual understanding of the realities of separation and the bursting of the omnipotent bubble, the child must confront the ambivalent wish to be autonomous (Erikson 1950), and yet still be the cuddled baby he once was. This wish/fear for dependence/independence is a lifelong struggle for most of us, but is rarely played out more vividly than in the temper tantrums ("do it myself!"), assertions, stubborn stances, and clingyness of the older toddler. Hence the label, the "terrible twos." Coming to terms with feelings of goodness and badness is the task of this age, with youngsters splitting and acting out their self and other-representations of good/bad, powerful/powerless. This good/bad play continues throughout the preschool years and even until latency, which speaks to the power of this dilemma for all human beings.

Fortunately, youngsters have two major tools available to them for work on this major developmental task of coming to terms with these split images of good/bad self and good/bad other. At this age, the cognitive capacity for both symbolic play

Table 8–1. Play Indicators and Remedial Play Activities

Ages	Mahler's Separation-Individuation Subphases	Play Indicators	Remedial Play Activities
1–4 months	Birth to 6 weeks – autism	Parent play around caretaking activities.	Creating a predictable physical and emotional environment.
	6 weeks to 4 months – symbiosis	Parent and child play with objects.	Buffering environmental encounters. Evoking and responding to baby's cues. Play around caregiving functions.
4–9 months	First subphase – differentiation	Specific smile. "Pleasure in being the cause." Manual, tactile, and visual exploration of mother's body, one's own body, and toys. Passive peek-a-boo. Pushing away from mother's body Sliding off mother's lap. Play at mother's feet. Comparative scanning of other-than-mother ("Customs Inspection"). Reciprocal play around caretaking functions. Intentionality and directedness in environmental exploration.	Mutual body part naming and touching. Mirror play. Peek-a-boo. The introduction of objects with a variety of sensory modalities – touch, taste, odor, sound. Physical play (lifting, swinging, pushing, pulling, jumping) with the caregiver's body as home base. Commenting on the baby's activities ("You are shaking the rattle").
9–18 months	Second subphase – practicing	Transitional objects. Elated investment in locomotion. "Love affair with the world." Establishing familiarity with wider world ("into everything"). Mother used for "emotional refueling" as home base after play sorties. Active peek-a-boo. Beginning imitative play. Intense practice of body functions. Running and being scooped up.	Adaptive physical equipment, if necessary. Labeling to bring focus to everyday experiences and feeding ("You like the red ball"). Continued peek-a-boo and mirror plays. Encouraging exploratory play with blocks, pegs, simple puzzles, sand, water, crayons, dolls, stuffed toys. Run and chase games. Games to encourage discrimination of sound, sights, and objects.

Table 8-1. *(continued)*

Ages	Mahler's Separation-Individuation Subphases	Play Indicators	Remedial Play Activities
18–24 months	Third subphase – rapprochement	Discrimination play. Disappearance–reappearance play. Imitation-identification, play with nurturing dolls and soft toys. Social interaction – ball play. "Watch me" – "Look at me." Showing possessions to parent. Beginning play with families. Temper tantrums. Mother sometimes used as extension of self. Clinging and pushing away. Stranger reaction. Beginning of symbolic play. Mastery play – toys and materials. Collecting/gathering, emptying/filling.	Sorting toys or objects. Toys that allow for disappearance/reappearance. Balls – nerf and ping-pong (sight and sound). Introduction of peers. Presentation of desirable choices to reduce indecisiveness. Toys that elicit representation and imitation – dress-up clothes, dolls, soft toys. Containers and objects to put in and out of such containers. Caregiver's use of self as playmate and as an appreciative audience.
24–36 months	Consolidation of individuality and the beginning of emotional object constancy	Purposeful constructive play. Beginning of fantasy, role play, and pretend.	Modeling the role of playful person. Engaging in pretend play, facilitating symbolic play with props, etc.

and language is developing, and children can be helped to use these symbol systems to express, guide, and understand their strong emotionality, which until this point would have flooded them with feelings of helplessness and rage. With increased fears around separation, children in this period begin to bring toys and play products to their caregivers. Their catch words become "watch me!" and "show me!" This clinging behavior is startling to parents who had been used to the earlier, more independent practicing junior toddler. The clinging, of course, is accompanied by an equally forceful pushing away. An empathic stance is needed to deal calmly and consistently with these bewildering ambivalent manifestations, which, in therapy, can easily become the root of countertransference problems.

Children use dramatic play to help ease their good/bad, powerful/powerless feelings, as well as to manage separation issues. A higher level of discrimination play also occurs, with toddlers often seeming to be obsessive-compulsives-in-the-making, as they sort through every imaginable medium, from blocks, to colors, to containers, to people. Big/little, boy/girl, inside/outside, mommy/daddy – all these perplexities are a source of fascination to toddlers. Gender identity (Galenson and Roiphe 1977) becomes established at this period, and toilet-training surfaces as an issue. Children are fascinated with protrusions of any kind, and engage in the mastery play of emptying and filling and putting things in and out of holes.

Dramatic play during this age period includes imitation/identification play, mostly around parents and family members. The 3-year-old begins to imitate monsters and scary animals; this merges with emphasis on biting mouths and scary sounds. Children who are less well-nurtured cannot engage in such play and continue the sensory-motor explorations of infancy.

One of the deviations of the rapprochement period is the pseudomature child (Speers 1965), who seems to individuate, but not separate. Such a child is given the message that he "cannot go home again," as most children can, when confronted with the cognitive realization that he is truly a separate person. Pseudomature youngsters are often well endowed physically and intellectually; they are often seen by their parents as narcissistic extensions of themselves (Miller 1981). Often told how big or brave they are, they are shamed into behaving in "grown-up" ways – for instance, "What is a big boy like you doing sucking your thumb?" The affect of shame is strong in such children and they hide their strong dependency longings behind a facade of super-competence and independence. Pathological narcissism haunts these children into adulthood; they often wilt suddenly and feel the affects of rage and helplessness when their pseudomature facade is breached.

On-the-Way-to-Object Constancy

The task of achieving self and object constancy is referred to as *on-the-way-to-space-object constancy*. In the preschool years, children are developing enduring feelings about themselves and meaningful others, and come to see that they and others remain the same, in spite of fluctuating feeling states. Now the self and other representations are available for scrutiny in the roles that children play. At this age, dramatic play reaches its zenith (Fein 1981, 1984), and we have ample opportunities to view children's self and other representations. Gould (1972) has given us a useful model to diagnose the child's "core me" image through play. Her position is that children who have been well nurtured and valued develop a primary identification with the nurturant provider. Youngsters who have not been so fortunate, however, develop a primary identification with the aggressor or victim. These identifications are observable through role play – the good mommy, the bad witch, the mean dinosaur, the eating-up monster, or the friendly puppy.

Further, Gould (1972) believes that the style and approach to play can be analyzed along the nurturer/aggressor/victim line. That is, a child with a predominant identification with the nurturer can distinguish between real and imaginary; can maintain a steady period of pretend play; has a sense of entitlement; behaves out of love for the other rather than out of fear; and can play a variety of roles, both aggressive and nurturant. Such youngsters can, for example, play super-heroes, but super-heroes can be good guys or bad guys; they can rescue as well as attack.

On the other hand, the child who has had poor nurturing and identifies with the victim or aggressor, cannot distinguish between real and pretend. Gould calls this *fluctuating certainty* and suggests that the child may then *become* the role, rather than *pretend to be* the role. Such children also behave only to avoid punishment, and may play aggressor or victim roles compulsively and without variation. While young children (under 3 years) have difficulty distinguishing between real and pretend, by the age of 4 or 5, this should no longer be an issue.

Clinicians, like parents, promote development by helping the child be aware of what comes from inside, what from outside, and through play episodes and verbalizations, they quicken pleasurable interaction. Also like the caregiver, the therapist may need to help the child be aware of inner and outer worlds, and may need to stimulate, facilitate, or redirect play, as well as to understand and make sense of it. The development of a sense of self is linked to and mirrored in the symbol system of play and language. An examination of the child's play, especially role play, can give greater understanding of the way the child views himself, and the way he views others.

Role Play in the Autistic, Symbiotic, and Separation-Individuation Subphases

Clinical examples are presented to illustrate aspects of object relations as articulated by Mahler in her autistic, symbiotic, and separation-individuation stages of development. Treatment begins with diagnosis and with the attempt to understand where development may have been faulty. The following case histories will highlight some aspects of child play to indicate how far the child has traveled along the path toward object constancy, and how the child seems to see others in his representational world.

Autism: Tommy and His Chaotic Search

Sometimes children cannot play. Because of neurological or biological impairment, some youngsters are unable to grasp the symbol systems that make play possible, and they turn away from the interpersonal encounters that are necessary to separate and individuate. Tommy was a 7½-year-old child who was congenitally deaf but was able to use a few signs to communicate. When he came into the therapist's office for the first time, he went straight for the play cupboard. Pulling things off the shelf in a random fashion, he searched furtively, making plaintive cries, seeming to be unaware of the chaotic mess he was creating. He did not respond to the therapist's efforts to engage him in signing and ignored her attempts to redirect his forays, continuing his agitated search of the room. Finally his attention focused on the portable heater; he happily turned the dial up and down, delighting in the action. Clearly Tommy was interested in *things* – things that go up and down, in and out, mechanical things like heaters and electric pencil sharpeners. Tommy was not interested in people, and that included the therapist.

Such a youngster would be labeled as being in the autistic stage by Mahler. Others (e.g., Bowlby 1982 or Stern 1985) have different names for this stage, but there would likely be agreement that for this child, even beginning play has no meaning. There was no awareness of the therapist as a person, nor did Tommy use transitional objects, which are generally the child's first symbols. While there was interest in mechanical objects that made noises, and pleasure in up/down and in/out motions, this could not be expanded to an interest in filling/emptying, which some have called early ego play. Tommy's profound deficits limited him to a joyless, quiet world, devoid of a sense of self and other.

Symbiosis: Liza and Her "Fuzzy"

With a scared, mile-wide smile, 5-year-old Liza was a puzzle to the hospital treatment team, who could not come to a consensus on her diagnosis. Sometimes she seemed to be a high-functioning autistic child; other times she seemed to be unable to relate to others in even a marginal way. She was referred for twice-weekly psychotherapy, with the hope that this interaction might stimulate her play, speech, and language skills. Like Tommy, Liza initially avoided speech and personal contact, seeming to be more interested in things than in the therapist. Unlike Tommy, however, she was more goal-directed in her search, as though driven to make physical contact with toys, even though she did not pick them up or play with them. As she journeyed around the room, she made soft sounds, occasionally glancing at the therapist, vaguely indicating awareness of her presence. In her fourth session, Liza focused on "Fuzzy," a soft yellow puppet that eventually became her transitional object. This encouraging sign seemed to indicate that Liza was making some attempt to differentiate. When Liza's session was almost over, the therapist suggested that Fuzzy be put to bed in a shoebox, covered with a tissue blanket; he could be wakened for the next session. Liza clapped her hands, excited about this idea.

Fuzzy was central in therapy for three or four months. Liza often soothed herself with the puppet, rubbing its fur on her cheek or lips, seeming to be out of touch with reality. At such times the therapist would sit nearby, occasionally commenting on how comforting it was to have such a pretend friend. After six months or so, Liza showed further personalization of Fuzzy. She asked it questions ("What doin' 'day?" or, "You want play?") and, on one occasion, she had the puppet speak for her ("Liza play"). Over time, as the differentiation process continued in therapy, the child relied less on Fuzzy, more on the therapist. She maintained eye contact for longer periods of time, showed slow gains in speech and language, tolerated some physical closeness without stereotypic hand gestures, and was better able to wait and delay gratification.

After nine months of twice-weekly treatment, Liza talked of a monster, finally letting the therapist know this was a dream. The monster had come in her window, she said, and was going to eat her. The therapist suggested they play out the story, first with a doll and puppet, then by taking the roles themselves. Liza agreed, but after selecting the toys, could not take the role of either the monster or the sleeping girl. The therapist then asked Liza to narrate the dream while the therapist enacted it with the toys; then both worked together to dramatize the dream. Liza became very animated with the "eating-up" part of the drama and clapped her hands gleefully. Seeming not to be frightened or anxious, she exclaimed, "*He* eating her; *we* eating her!"

Suggesting that they enact the story themselves, the therapist asked if Liza would like to be the monster or the sleeping girl. Liza looked confused and could not make a choice. A narrative drama was then proposed: they would both play, and they would play both roles. Together they set up the room – bed here, window there, and so forth. Both pretended to be asleep until Liza gave the play signal that a monster was coming in the room. Jumping to her feet, Liza stood immobile, then frightened, hugged the therapist and cried, "MONSTER!" Recognizing that Liza was experiencing confusion about real/not real (what Gould [1972] calls *fluctuating certainty*), the therapist talked about dreams, explaining the play was not for real, although the *feelings* were real. Liza was then encouraged to make a series of pictures of the dream – the girl sleeping, the monster coming in the window, the girl waking and calling for help. While the pictures were rudimentary marks on paper, they seemed to help integrate idea and affect, clarifying the sequence of the drama with a beginning, middle, and end. Liza became calmer, seeming to gain psychic distance and see this as play – pleasurable play.

Since Liza continued to talk about her fear of monsters in the night, the therapist initiated role play. She suggested that they both pretend to be the monster; could Liza show how he looked, walked, growled? Then, having "rehearsed" the roles, both played at being monster and the sleeping/wakened girl. When, after several sessions of such imitative, mirrored play, the therapist suggested they each take a role, Liza initially agreed. In this play, however, Liza was unable to "hold" a role by herself. Once the therapist assumed a different role, Liza immediately left her assumed role and joined the therapist; that is, if Liza was the sleeping girl, and the therapist the monster, then Liza would immediately jump up and become a monster, too.

These play sequences, therefore, seemed to suggest that the child was capable of beginning symbol play with the transitional object (Winnicott 1965). There was scant symbolic play as such, but Liza was developing the capacity for some language and play. Emotionally, the child seemed to be between the autistic-symbiotic and the differentiation play phase, but cognitively she seemed to have moved to the symbolic play phase. The transitional object (in this case, Fuzzy) is the first symbol used by the child, generally in the second half of the first year. Liza's imitative play, characterized by fusion with the therapist, made possible some tentative role play. In this case, the content of the play (i.e., the role) is not as significant as the form and process of the play. The process suggested that the child needed to "twin" with the therapist, indicating symbiotic fusion and the lack of separation between self and other. Psychic tension could not be maintained as a separate self, however briefly, without the help of the other.

Differentiation Subphase: Jeffrey and the Wild Things

Jeffrey was a 6½-year-old youngster diagnosed with pervasive developmental disorder. A verbal child, he jabbered in snatches of television segments, songs, and commercials. He made no eye contact, nor did he want the therapist to be physically near him. If that happened, the vocal inflection, pitch, and force of his gibberish would signify his distress, and his stereotypic movements would increase.

The therapist soon found that the most feasible way of relating to Jeffrey was to sit in the corner of the room and narrate what was going on. Early on, Jeffrey accepted this as the *modus operandi* and settled down to work in the sandbox. He found a box of traffic signs and began to set them up in a seemingly random fashion. Soon, however, he developed a ritual. He would select three "Stop – children crossing" signs, and put them outside the office at the beginning of the session; he retrieved them when the session was over. The rest of the signs were set up in the sandbox where he played, his back to the therapist.

After three months or so, Jeffrey began to investigate the felt-tip markers. One day, he scribbled on the therapist's desk with a black marker. She commented that it looked as though he wanted to make marks; she would get him some paper. Doing so, she held the paper down for him while he made a few wild black marks; then he scurried off. With his penchant for ritual, Jeffrey repeated this activity in his next session, adding more marks to the paper. Over the months, as the child's comfort increased, the art work became more pleasurable and he experimented with the use of other colors. Eventually he made many pictures, covering each paper with beautiful variations of blue, red, and black.

About this time the therapist added a ritual of her own. She began to use a tape recorder at the end of the session, reviewing the hour and what Jeffrey had done. Invited to make comments, he refused at first, but then he spoke nonsense words. Later, as he became more comfortable, his speech became more appropriate – often a song from television about colors, cars, or signs. Following this minimal communicative attempt, Jeffrey began to experiment with dramatic play. Eventually, wild fantasies emerged – fantasies of destruction wherein the contents of the room were burned, destroyed, and eaten up, including (or perhaps one should say, especially) the therapist. The play was reminiscent of Sendak's *Where the Wild Things Are* (1963), where "Max wore his wolf suit and made mischief of one kind and another" (pp. 1–3). Jeffrey was definitely one of "the wild things." He came alive as he pretended to tear, devour, destroy. These wild episodes were recounted on the tape recorder by the therapist at the end of the session. Jeffrey now faced her, looking animated and excited, occasionally adding something that had been forgotten.

As Jeffrey symbolically enacted the destruction and resurrection of the room and the therapist, his teachers began to notice behavioral changes. The gibberish toned down and was often absent, except in times of stress; Jeffrey made eye contact and no longer assiduously avoided physical contact. One day he began to read *The Lion, The Witch, and The Wardrobe* by C. S. Lewis. This amazed his teachers, none of whom had any idea he could read, let alone a book of such complexity.

According to Mahler's play indicators, Jeffrey's play developed symbolically from transitional object play (stop signs in the room, stop signs outside the room), to symbolic play of fantasies. The path from one to the other was facilitated by the therapist joining his world as a symbiotic partner. This seemed to lead to his realization that he could trust the therapist not to engulf him, eat him up, or destroy him. Instead, he could count on her to be reliably present, to help him to fill in the blank spaces in his emotional life, finding meaning and color. Gibberish was given up in favor of words that had meaning to both of them. In Mahler's terminology, meaningful language helped Jeffrey to "hatch." Language was used to label, signal, frighten, soothe, capture, and recall experiences – in short, to communicate. Thus, the child was able to move out of the land where the wild (id) things are, to paraphrase Sendak, and find his way home. Why? Perhaps because, like Sendak's Max, he began to feel lonely and long "for someone who loved him best." In Sendak's story, Max's aggression is tamed with mother's help – she sets boundaries on his wildness and he internalizes his rage via fantasy when she sends him to his room. There his aggression is satisfied in glorious daydreams of omnipotent control where he is the *king* of all the wild things! Jeffrey, with the therapist's occasional narration, acted out similar fantasies of omnipotence and primitive power, certain that these impulses would not destroy or devour self or other. Then he, like Max, returned to "mother." Winnicott (1971) wrote of this process that the child needs to "destroy" the mother (and see that she is not destroyed by him) in order to become separate and create a true self.

Rapprochement: Jennie and the Game of BOO! (Hoo . . .)

There is hardly a child therapist who has not had experience with the peek-a-boo game. While children of all ages enjoy the game, for some it is a repetition compulsion. Youngsters who have not worked through the rapprochement stage of separation-individuation often seem compelled to find, lose, seek, and refind the mother. Eight-year-old Jennie was such a child. Jennie's mother was depressed when Jennie was born, and problems were compounded two years later when a brother was born. Jennie's teachers, who suggested the referral, were concerned about her sadness and poor academic performance, in spite of her high intelligence.

After a few months of therapy, Jennie lightened up and began to play lost and found stories over and over. Sometimes she was the lost and abandoned dog, and the therapist was the worried mistress, hunting for him; later she was a witch, looking for the bad girl to imprison or to eat. Significant psychic change was signaled by a change in roles when Jennie began to take the role of a veterinarian, caring for sick and stray puppies. In her role play choices, she gradually shifted from what Gould (1972) calls identification with the victim, to identification with the aggressor, and then to identification with the nurturer.

On-The-Way-To Object Constancy: Mad, Sad Carrie

Carrie, age 5, was referred by her parents for an evaluation because of her aggressive outbursts, from biting in preschool to hitting in kindergarten. Her parents feared that these outbursts would result in a bad reputation in her prestigious private school.

In her first session, Carrie curtly told her mother to leave: "I don't need you!" She then proceeded to touch most of the toys in a frantic way, but stopped herself, saying she wanted to draw. She produced a lot of little designs, then scribbled on them and tore them up, saying, "I hate these! They are baby stuff." The therapist said that this was a place where it was okay to show baby feelings. Carrie then began to talk "baby talk." She drew a stereotyped rainbow, but because she seemed so sad, the therapist wondered if that was, indeed, how she might be feeling. Carrie was startled, denied she had such feelings, but began to wail softly like a baby. The therapist added that sometimes kids were sad and mad at the same time. With that, Carrie carefully and stiffly walked away; then with great restraint she hit all the cushions on the chairs and table.

Spying the puppets, Carrie commented on the "ugly people." She surrounded herself with the large snake, dragon, bee (with a huge stinger), witch, and alligator puppets, saying that she loved them. She looked at the therapist provocatively from her nest of nasty puppets and asked coyly if the therapist didn't agree that they were the nicest puppets ever.

This vignette is used to illustrate how a child may, in the initial contact, reveal her view of herself as babyish, unacceptable, and unlovable. A much-wanted child with a 16-months-younger sibling, Carrie had inconsistent caregiving from birth. The nanny who adored her left when Carrie was 2; she was "Daddy's girl" until her younger sister walked and took part in sports, much to the father's delight. Other caregivers came and went, most of them preferring her younger sister. Although her parents loved and treasured her, Carrie spent most of her time in the care of people who did not value her. Her sense of self-worth faltered and she became increasingly aggressive, behavior that made her even less likable. Although there was emphasis on the "core bad me" (Gould 1972), Carrie was on-the-way-to object constancy.

On-The-Way-To Object Constancy: Daniel–Tough Guy or Wimp?

Daniel, an appealing 8-year-old, frequently played out stories in which he was the victim. A fearful child, he often imagined that monsters or Frankenstein characters were coming to get him. His troubling dreams, enacted in therapy, centered around themes of robbers who came into the house and killed him; of being in the woods attacked and eaten by wild animals, and so forth. In his role play, Daniel took one role only–that of the victim. These repetitive dreams of being attacked by bad guys or animals always took place at night. The therapist noted this and asked about associations to his fear of the dark, to "things that go bump in the night." Daniel was reminded of his parents' fights, which usually happened after he went to bed. He was angry with his "wimpy" father as well as his "mean" mom.

Asked to demonstrate how he *wished* his father would react, Daniel tried, but his drama lacked zip. He felt "funny," he said, playing his dad. Well, the therapist wondered, what might be easier? Daniel then thought of playing the cop in one of his recent stories, the part where the cop was telling off the witch. The story was played (or, more accurately, replayed, as Daniel had been very timid in earlier confrontations with the witch); this time, the cop successfully encountered the witch and even put her in jail! The fantasy element of this story allowed the play to be enacted with a minimum of guilt. Reality, as often happens, was too close to home.

In time, Daniel played other stories, taking both active and passive roles, being both dominant and submissive. More important, he began to *think* psychologically, seeing that all these roles were part of himself. In some ways *he* was a wimp, allowing other kids to push him around; in some ways, he was an aggressor, especially when he attacked himself for his supposed failures, or attacked other kids because of their "meanness."

Change for Daniel took place first in therapy as he became aware of and talked about these parts of himself; then change took place in sports, where he was able to be more assertive and not let kids push him around; and then at home, when he was able to speak up to both his parents. Daniel was able to change in these ways because he had sufficiently mastered rapprochement and was on-the-way-to object constancy. Unfortunately, like Carrie, there was an emphasis on the "core bad me" sense of self as victim.

Carrie and Daniel were emotionally blocked in certain ways, their cognitive abilities outstripping their emotional capacities. With help, they were able to use their abilities to symbolize and psychologically understand their difficulties, working through their conflicts, moving toward greater growth. The cognitive capacities of these two youngsters enabled them to use their superior play skills to work on long-standing, deeply rooted concerns.

Role Play as a Tool for Developing Empathy

The research literature often emphasizes the use of role play to foster altruism or to facilitate empathy with another's point of view. Empathy, sometimes called "trial identification," is generally understood to mean the ability to recognize and identify with the feelings of another. One need not necessarily experience the same situation as another to identify with his experience. It is hypothesized that one may have similar feelings, even if the external situation is different. In this regard, role play has been used to help children develop empathy for one another (e.g., Dorta 1983, Feshbach 1975, Hummel 1974), as well toward those who have different life experiences, such as handicapped peers (e.g., Cerreto 1977, and Harte 1981). Research outcomes on such work have been variable, reflecting, in part, the difficulty of changing deep-seated patterns and ways of thinking that often operate out of awareness.

Therapists, however, attempt to do just that. They work for change, as in the foregoing examples, facilitating play by providing appropriate play materials; entering into the role play under the child's direction; modeling playfulness and experimentation; and confronting, clarifying, and interpreting the child's communications. Just as Gardner (1971) does in his *therapeutic communication with children* technique, the therapist may change the story line to help the child see that there are other ways to view the situation. In so doing, the clinician gradually focuses on the disowned or warded-off aspects of the self that are repressed or projected onto another. It is, after all, the child's fear of his *own* denied feelings that prevents empathic identification with another. In helping youngsters examine and accept these "forbidden" impulses – whether they are aggressive, loving, rivalrous, jealous, deprived, or whatever – the therapist promotes empathy. From an object relations point of view, the clinician attempts to help the child examine and alter these emotionally loaded self and other representations.

An example of work with a child that focused on fostering empathy is the case of Jerry, referred for therapy at the age of 9. As a preschooler, he had been especially traumatized by harsh treatment from a grandmother-caretaker who had little tolerance for his separation fears. Angered by Jerry's cries for his mother, his grandmother disciplined him by locking him in a small room, where, understandably, he became even more terrified. When his grandmother died suddenly, Jerry became more anxious and told everyone that he loved grandmother and wished that she had not died. His encopresis, always a problem, became even more troublesome and served to alienate him even more from others.

Jerry's intelligence and quick wit served him well for a number of years, but when his anxiety and depression became more marked, he was referred for treatment. He quickly began a repetitive game of hide-and-seek that seemed to reflect the search for the lost mother and his panic about being closed up in the small room. When that play waned, Jerry began an intense game of good and bad guys. He always played the bad (omnipotent) characters, while the therapist was assigned the role of the good guys. The bad men *always* won, inasmuch as they were omnipotent and ever so much smarter than the therapist's men. As his identification with the bad guys escalated, Jerry assigned himself the role of the Devil and then of "Hitler H. Hitler," the most evil man in the world.

As the good/bad play was perseverative and failed to alleviate anxiety, the therapist decided to stop her participation as the defender of the good guys. She told Jerry that her guys were no longer going to fight but were going to take on a new assignment, that of protecting the baby. The therapist told Jerry that there was a baby who was scared of the bad guys; this baby missed his mommy, felt unprotected, and was afraid someone might get hurt. This invented piece of play, of course, was rooted in Jerry's early history. The therapist was symbolically re-creating the boy's inconsistent mothering and early trauma at the hands of the harsh grandmother. The therapist, frustrated because she could not get Jerry to play any role other than the omnipotent, powerful self, decided to play the role of the helpless, scared baby.

Jerry was nonplussed at first by the therapist's deviation from her assigned role, but he was intrigued to see the good guys surround and protect the tiny baby. While Jerry clearly wanted to continue the good/bad fight, he did not attempt to hurt or kidnap the baby. Instead, he offered to have his bad guys take the baby on rides in their military transports. Later, the boy assigned parents to the baby and planned pleasant adventures for them all. The intense absorption with the good/bad guys theme lessened. Jerry's encopresis, in turn, waned and then stopped. He showed improvement in home and school in demonstrating greater control, and in the sessions was even amenable to talking about the past and the scared baby he once was.

When the baby play was introduced, however, Jerry was oblivious to verbal interpretation about his own little boy feelings. His narcissism would not allow him to acknowledge any suggestion that he himself might ever feel scared by such powerful attacks. The baby play softened his sadistic forays in battle, while allowing him to become more protective of the baby. In this way, past history was reshaped and he was able to give the baby the protection that he had not had. The therapist led the way by talking directly to the small, helpless child. This intense role play thus helped Jerry to modify his perception of himself as either omnipotent and sadistic, or as weak and helpless.

Role Play as a Tool for Learning New Skills

The research literature on role play often emphasizes the use of this activity in developing assertiveness (e.g., Michaelson et al. 1982), rehearsing new behaviors, and thinking through solutions to problems. This explicit use of role play presents consciously enacted scenes in an effort to teach new skills. Therapists often use role play in this way to help a child with a particular problem. Several examples of such situations follow.

Sam

Sam was a 6-year-old who was caught in an ongoing war between his parents. Although long divorced, Sam's folks continued to battle about matters large and small. When the father became angry at the mother, he would withdraw and cut off communication. This, unfortunately, meant that he would not talk to Sam either, for the boy lived with his mother. When a battle erupted, the father would be "out of town" for the weekend, or "on the road" and thus unable to see the boy or take phone calls. Similarly, when the mother was angry at the father, she would find ways to retaliate. If especially angry, she would recount all the sins committed by the father, all within the boy's hearing. Sam was understandably angry when he heard his parents demean one another. He cared for and needed both of his parents, even though he was also enraged at them. He felt, he said, like a tennis ball, being bounced back and forth between them.

Once he understood more about why he was so angry, Sam learned that it was easier to talk out feelings than act them out. While it was relatively easy to learn to tell his mother that he hated to hear her "talk bad" about his dad, it was *not* easy to talk to his father about his disappointment and anger about the missed visits. Loving his dad as he did, Sam was afraid that any confrontation would anger his father and drive him further away. To help the boy with this dilemma, the therapist suggested that they write a letter to his dad and he could say what he really felt. Naturally the letter would not be sent – the purpose was to help Sam put feelings into words. So Sam dictated, and the therapist wrote, then typed, the letter. That done, Sam and the therapist talked on the play phones with Sam being his father and the therapist being Sam. The call was replayed several times with different themes: father was angry and hung up; he denied he ever missed a time with Sam; he was sure that the boy was mistaken, and so forth. After a number of rehearsals, Sam played himself, and the therapist, his father. Although it was hard for Sam to confront his father, even in pretend play, it was made somewhat easier because he had the previous conversations to model. Geared up from the practice, Sam was prepared to confront his dad that week, but lost his nerve at the last minute. It took several more rejections from his father, and another practice session, for Sam to gather courage to talk with his dad. Although the phone call went better than he thought, the father's behavior changed only minimally. Nevertheless, facing such a tough task was helpful to Sam. He learned to state his feelings with more directness, and gradually accepted his father as he really is, warts and all.

Maria

Nine-year-old Maria was intimidated by tough classmates who teased her about her ethnic name and her clothing. In addition, Maria was also teased because she was a timid victim who never fought back, let alone tell the teacher. To help her feel more comfortable with aggressiveness, the therapist used puppets. The theme of aggressor–victim was played out, but with "tough" and "scared" puppets. Maria selected the spider puppet as the tough one, and the little dog puppet as the victim. In this play, Maria took the role of the aggressor and devoured, maimed, or frightened off most of the puppet characters. Relishing the aggressive role, Maria began to feel more comfortable with the pretend expression of anger. In time, people puppets were substituted for the animal ones. Again Maria played the aggressive role first. In these activities, the child gradually became much less anxious and more assertive in her play. Although it took some time, Maria was eventually able to transfer her new-found toughness to the school situation, where, as was predicted, her classmates found it was no longer so much fun to tease her.

This chapter presents a psychoanalytic, object relations view of development as a way of understanding children and helping them progress in treatment. Clinical material has been presented using Margaret Mahler's framework of the developmental stages of the first three years of life. The therapeutic protocols, the children's role play, and their behaviors are used to highlight self and other representations, which are then examined for diagnostic and clinical data. It is understood that often children's cognitive capacities outstrip their emotional abilities, leaving them with unresolved emotional issues as residue from the early years of life. An object relations point of view can help the therapist make sense of the child's play and give direction to therapeutic efforts.

References

Ainsworth, M. D. (1972). Attachment and dependency: a comparison. In *Attachment and Dependency*, ed. J. L. Gerwitz, pp. 97–137. Washington, DC: Winston.

Bornstein, B. (1949). The analysis of a phobic child. Some problems of theory and technique in child analysis. *Psychoanalytic Study of the Child* 3–4:181–226. New York: International Universities Press.

Bowlby, J. (1982). *Attachment and Loss.* Vol. 1: *Attachment,* 2nd ed. New York: Basic Books.

Brazelton, T. B., and Als, H. (1979). Four early stages in the development of mother–infant interaction. *The Psychoanalytic Study of the Child* 34:349–370. New Haven: Yale University Press.

Cerreto, M. C. (1977). The effects of empathy training on children's attitudes and behaviors toward handicapped peers. *Dissertation Abstracts International* 38:1394–1395.

Curry, N. E. (1986). Where have all the players gone? In *The Feeling Child: Affect Development Reconsidered,* pp. 93–111. New York: Haworth.

Curry, N. E., and Bergen, D. (1987). The relationship of play to emotional, social and gender/sex role development. In *Play as a Medium for Learning and Development,* ed. D. Bergen, pp. 107–132. Portsmouth, NH: Heinemann.

Dorta, C. V. (1983). Modeling influences on the acquisition of empathy skills in children. *Dissertation Abstracts International* 44:1956.

Erikson, E. (1950). *Childhood and Society.* New York: Norton.

Fairbairn, W. (1952). *An Object Relations Theory of Personality.* New York: Basic Books.

Fein, G. G. (1981). Pretend play: an integrative review. *Child Development* 52:1095–1118.

———— (1984). The self-building potential of pretend play or "I got a fish, all by myself." In *Child's Play: Developmental and Applied,* ed. T. D. Yawkey and A. D. Pellegeini, pp. 125–142. Hillsdale, NJ: Lawrence Erlbaum.

Francis, J. J. (1978). The teaching of child psychoanalysis in the United States. In *Child Analysis and Therapy,* ed. J. Glenn, pp. 709–742. New York: Jason Aronson.

Feshbach, N. D. (1975). Empathy in children: some theoretical and empirical considerations. *Counseling Psychologist* 5:25–30.

Freud, A. (1930). *Psychoanalysis for Teachers and Parents.* New York: Emerson.

Freud, S. (1925). An autobiographical study. *Standard Edition* 20:7–70.

Galenson, E., and Roiphe, H. (1977). Some suggested revisions concerning early female development. In *Female Psychology,* ed. H. P. Blum, pp. 27–57. New York: International Universities Press.

Gardner, R. A. (1971). *Therapeutic Communication with Children: The Mutual Storytelling Technique.* New York: Science House.

Gould, R. (1972). *Child Studies through Fantasy.* New York: Quadrangle.

Harte, T. F. (1981). The relationship between self-concept, empathy training, and attitudes toward the physically handicapped in ten- to eleven-year-old boys and girls. *Dissertation Abstracts International* 41:4741.

Hug-Hullmuth, H. (1921). On the technique of child analysis. *International Journal of Psycho-Analysis* 2:286–305.

Hummel, R. A. (1974). Empathy, social problem-solving and the social behavior of preschoolers. *Dissertation Abstracts International* 44:3198.

Irwin, E. C. (1985). Puppets in therapy: an assessment procedure. *American Journal of Psychotherapy* 39:389–400.

Jacobson, E. (1964). *The Self and the Object World.* New York: International Universities Press.

Kernberg, O. F. (1966). Structural derivates of object relationships. *International Journal of Psycho-Analysis* 47:236–253.

———— (1980). *Internal World and External Reality.* New York: Jason Aronson.

Klein, M. (1932). *The Psycho-analysis of Children.* New York: Norton.

———— (1961). *Narrative of a Child Analysis.* New York: Basic Books.

Kohut, H. (1971). *The Analysis of the Self.* New York: International Universities Press.

———— (1977). *The Restoration of the Self.* New York: International Universities Press.

Mahler, M. S. (1952). On child psychosis and schizophrenia: autistic and symbiotic infantile psychoses. *The Psychoanalytic Study of the Child* 18:286–305. New York: International Universities Press.

Mahler, M. S., and Furer, E. (1965). *On Human Symbiosis and the Vicissitudes of Individuation.* New York: International Universities Press.

Mahler, M. S., Pine, F., and Bergman, A. (1975). *The Psychological Birth of the Infant.* New York: Basic Books.

Michaelson, L., DiLorenzo, T. H., Calpin, J. P., and Ollendick, T. H. (1982). Situational determinants of the behavioral assertiveness role-play test for children. *Behavior Therapy* 13:724–734.

Miller, A. (1981). *Prisoners of Childhood.* New York: Basic Books.

Sander, L. W. (1975). Infant and caretaking environment. In *Explorations in Child Psychiatry,* ed. E. J. Anthony, pp. 129–166. New York: Plenum.

Sarnoff, C. (1976). *Latency.* New York: Jason Aronson.

Sendak, M. (1963). *Where the Wild Things Are.* New York: Harper & Row.

Speers, R. (1965). Variations in separation individuation and implications for play ability and learning. In *The Infant at Risk,* ed. D. Bergma, pp. 77–100. New York: Intercontinental Medical Book Corporation.

Spitz, R. (1965). *The First Year of Life: A Psychoanalytic Study of Normal and Deviant Development of Object Relations.* New York: International Universities Press.

Stern, D. (1985). *The Interpersonal World of the Infant.* New York: Basic Books.

Winnicott, D. W. (1965). *The Maturational Processes and the Caretaking Environment.* New York: International Universities Press.

———— (1971). *Playing and Reality.* New York: Basic Books.

9

Fantasy and Visualization

Dorothy G. Singer

Definitions of Imagery

... symbolic language is the one foreign language that each of us must learn. Its understanding brings us in touch with one of the most significant sources of wisdom, that of the myth, and it brings us in touch with the deeper layers of our own personalities . . . it helps us to understand a level of experience that is specifically human because it is that level which is common to all humanity, in content as well as in style.

—Erich Fromm
— *The Forgotten Language,* p. 10

Imagery-laden thought and its symbolic language is indeed one of the human being's greatest gifts. But just as our thoughts can offer us solace and joy, they can also cause us pain and grief and become a curse. One task of the psychotherapist is to try to understand the hidden meanings that weave their way through a client's private thoughts and experiences. Sometimes, this jumble of images, perceptions, fantasies, and memories, when tapped and brought to the surface through various techniques, can be fruitful in helping a patient make connections between imagination and reality. Although many such techniques utilizing imagery approaches have been attempted with adults, there has been increasing interest in their application to young children. Those of us who engage in standard methods of play therapy realize that much of what we do is interpretation of the symbolic play of our clients who rely on imagery in their make-believe play. We see and hear these images come to life as children utilize materials and "dress-up," changing their voices and adopting the mannerisms or movements of the characters they play. A major component, then, of pretend play is the capacity of young children actually to experience symbolic or imagery-laden thought. This capacity to use imagery or fantasy as a coping skill can be developed and encouraged by the therapist. Fantasy can help a child explore repressed ideas, feelings, and memories. It can help reduce pent-up distress, resolve disturbing conflicts, and effect cognitive change. Children who learn this skill are able to gain insight concerning their troubles and can begin to deal with their anxieties. Feelings such as loneliness, boredom, and fear can be worked through in image formation. Not only is fantasy useful in dealing with the negative aspects of our personalities, but it can be a source of pleasure and even lead to creativity. As Hellendoorn (1988) remarks: "In imagery interaction the therapist actively helps the child (a) to fully develop his or her own play themes, and (b) to work through those play themes, differentiating and shading them, and gradually influencing them in more desirable directions" (p. 45).

This chapter will enumerate a variety of imagery approaches and, where possible, present the related research. The chapter is divided into six sections: Types of Imagery, Developmental Differences in Imagery, Measurement of Images and Fantasy Production, Applications of Imagery Techniques in Psychotherapy with Children, Case Illustrations, and Applications of Imagery Techniques in Educational Settings.

Types of Imagery

What do we mean by imagery? Images appear to be associated with the right hemisphere of the brain and its functions, which include visual and auditory imagery, spatial representation, pure melodic thought, fantasy, and emotional components of ongoing thought (Singer and Pope 1978). Farah (1984) suggests that different components of mental imagery ability might have different neuroanatomic loci. She was able to identify a number of case reports of adult patients who lacked the ability to visualize a mental image from stored, long-term, visual memory information. These patients evidenced damage in the left quadrant of the brain close to the posterior language centers of the left hemisphere. Many of these patients with this particular lesion were unable to communicate their loss of imagery. Image generation per se, according to Farah, appears to be a left hemisphere function, while spatial ability and higher visual processing may be a right hemisphere function.

Our earliest forms of cognition are images, and words come later as a means of expression of internal symbols. Bruner (1964), and later Horowitz (1978), conceptualized three modes of representation of images: the enactive mode, which reflects events through motor responses (the baby waves "bye bye" without the words); the iconic mode, which selectively organizes individual perceptions and images (games such as "let's make believe I'm a cowboy"); and finally, the symbolic mode, which transforms experience into abstract and complex methods of representation (the words used to describe an image without its physical representation).

Various researchers have developed definitions and theories of imagery (Korn and Johnson 1983, Kosslyn 1983, 1990, Marks 1990, Morris and Hampson 1983, Norman 1976, Singer 1988, and Singer and Kolligian 1987). Images have been described as evolving from "top-down" processes, where the system generates hypotheses about external events and then tests these assumptions through movements from the lexical mode down to image generations to see if the hypotheses are correct. Finke (1989) has identified five major principles of imagery: implicity encoding, perceptual equivalence, spatial equivalence, transformational equivalence, and the principle of structural equivalence. His excellent book, *Principles of Mental Imagery*, expands upon these concepts and presents research and examples to convey his theory.

It is useful to differentiate *images, imaging* and *imagination. Images,* according to Sherrod and Singer (1984), are internal representations of sensory data in the absence of actual stimulation. Thus we may re-create a picture of a child or of a room in our mind's eye. *Imaging* is the manipulation of these images. The child may be seen riding a hobby horse, or we may picture the room upside down. *Imagination* not only requires skill in forming clear images and manipulating these images, but involves an entire complex process that may generate hypotheses about a set of events, and then through search and scanning, develop a script or story. It is this capacity for imagination that is likely to be evidenced in play therapy. The child who approaches the doll house, chooses the miniature baby doll and hides it under the toy bed may be acting out the desire to be rid of the new baby in the family. The girl who dresses up as a fairy princess and builds a castle out of blocks enacts the image in her mind of a story she has heard about a fairy kingdom, perhaps more beautiful than her own environment may be at this moment in time. The therapist listens to the child's narrative as it unfolds and interprets the meanings latent in each story.

Memory and *imagination images* are slightly different. *Memory images* represent a reconstruction rather than an accurate report of a scene, object, or person. *Imagination images* draw on memory information and may be an altered or new construction of the original percept. When we search for a memory image, we tend to suppress competing processes that interfere with the display. Imagination images may include the selection and integration of several memory images (Morris and Hampson 1983).

After-images occur when we gaze at a colored shape for at least thirty seconds and then transfer our gaze to a blank wall. We may then see a positive after-image that may gradually fade or turn into a negative image or the complementary color of the original image. *Hypnagogic* and *hypnopompic* images take place during the stages between waking and sleep. *Hypnagogic imagery* occurs just prior to falling asleep; *hypnopompic imagery* occurs in the state just immediately after awakening. These states are associated with extremely vivid imagery, but generally are short-lived as the individual falls asleep or awakens.

Hallucinations are the most vivid and real-appearing forms of imagery. Individuals may experience hallucinations in any or all of the five senses (Vernon 1963). Although we generally associate hallucinations with psychoses, there are conditions that lead to hallucinations in normal people, such as severe illness with high fevers, use of various drugs, hypnosis, crystal gazing, and sensory deprivation.

Eidetic images, related to photographic memory, are usually under voluntary control of the imager. They are as vivid as a perception, can be scanned (they do not require a fixed gaze), may be spontaneous or produced, are externally localized, and may persist for weeks or even years. These vivid images are most frequently found in children and tend to decrease as they grow older (Haber 1979). Developmental psychologists, including Piaget and Bruner, recognize that imagery is an important part of a child's early cognitive growth. Whether all children have eidetic imagery is still unclear, but most of the reviews of the literature indicate about ten to fifteen percent of children are true eidetics (Morris and Hampson 1983). There is some belief that children's imaginary companions are a result of their capacity for eidetic imagery; a child invents a friend or animal who becomes a constant companion, usually in the absence of other persons. One of the characteristics of these children who report imaginary playmates is that they enjoy imaginative play with more positive outcomes, such as more smiling, creativity, and ability to concentrate for longer periods of time (Singer and Singer 1981, Singer and Singer 1990, Somers and Yawkey 1984).

Dreams are another form of imagery, but perhaps the most elusive in terms of empirical study. In the dream state, there is less control and less direct processing of material than in the waking hours. The dream appears to be a "succession of constructs activated in the memory by related information, or by the needs and general state of the individual" (Morris and Hampson 1983, pp. 77–78). Much work, mainly with adults, has been carried out examining the physiological activity during dream states and the role of REMS, rapid eye movements (Dement and Kleitman 1957, Reyher and Morishige 1969, Roffwag et al. 1966, Tilley 1981). Studies of REMS indicate that people generally produce more dream recall during REM sleep and that more visual imagery and greater autonomic nervous system activity also take place during REM sleep.

The latest research on dreams indicates that nightdreams, although more vivid and seemingly more real than daydreams, are generally "found to be continuous with the waking thought styles and daydream content of normal persons" (Singer and Bonanno 1990, p. 437). It appears that physiological conditions in dream states are similar to those during the waking thoughts in daydreams. Indeed, waking fantasies scored by "blind" raters were considered to be more dreamlike than actual REM dream reports.

Daydreams and *fantasies* have been studied systematically in terms of the kinds of daydreams reported and their frequency with such variables as age, gender, and race taken into account. Most of the research has been carried out with adults (Giambra 1974, Klinger 1980, Segal, Huba, and Singer 1980, Segal and Singer 1976, Singer 1974, 1988, and Starker 1982), and has explored daydreams and fantasies in relation to self-concept, drugs, television, and achievement. Some studies have examined daydreams and fantasies with children and adolescents (Csikszentmihalyi 1984, McIlwraith and Schallow 1982–1983, Rosenfeld et al. 1982). Daydreaming is a form of information processing of material related to self, current concerns, and problem solving. Daydreams are constructed in the *process of daydreaming* instead of being stored as memories.

Singer (1978) and Klinger (1971, 1990) have examined the various themes found in daydreams and discuss the affect related to daydreams in terms of both positive and negative emotions. Using the Imaginal Process Inventory scales, they find that daydreams fall into four categories: positive-vivid daydreaming, guilty and negatively emotionally-toned daydreaming, anxious distractability, and controlled thoughtfulness and objectivity, which at times overlaps the positive-vivid daydreaming pattern (Singer 1978, 1988).

Developmental Differences in Imagery

Does the very young child think in forms of images? At what stage in life do images actually occur? It is difficult to test Freud's assumption that the baby begins to image the mother's face or breast. According to Freudian theory, this recognition leads to the infant's ability to delay gratification and move from primary process id functioning to secondary process ego functioning. Surely, the contours of the caregiver's face must leave an impression on the infant quite early in life, manifested by the infant's smile at about 6 weeks. It is true that mother's odor, touch, and voice all can evoke the smile of the infant, but think how much more effective is the animated face of the adult in stimulating this smile and its accompanying global movement response. Piaget believed that images begin to form in the later part of the sensory-motor period of life, ages 18–24 months, at about the time that object permanency develops. The baby now can search for objects he drops, or be upset if mother leaves the room, because no longer is "out of sight, out of mind" a truism. During this stage of life, and perhaps earlier, as Meltzoff and Moore (1983) suggest, the infant also is able to imitate movements of others without seeing the movement on his own body. For example, infants can imitate opening and closing of eyes or mouth. They can defer imitation as well, suggesting that the external object is visualized.

As the infant attempts to adjust to the world through the process of accommodation and assimilation – the two fundamental processes by which a child organizes his experiences – he attempts to use his available cognitive and motor apparatus in order to make sense out of the confusing environment that surrounds him. First using perceptual skills (eyes tracking a mobile or the rattle or bottle), he later grasps these objects and attempts, if he can reach them, to put them into his mouth. As the infant matures, he learns to differentiate more facets of the environment both physically and perceptually. Material gets organized into complex structures and hierarchies. If all basic needs are met, the infant explores his world, and the control of material leads to interest and positive affect. Because of the complex stimuli in the physical and social environment, the child, with his limited vocabulary and schema, may actually interpret material in ways that we see as cute or quaint, but from his perspective are correct and logical. Thus, the imaginative play of children reproduces what a child has lived through by means of symbolic representation. This reproduction is "primarily self-assertion for the pleasure of exercising his powers and recapturing fleeting experience" (Piaget 1962, p. 131).

During the early preoperational stage, ages 2–3, some make-believe play develops, reaching its peak at ages 4–6 when symbolic play (the substitution of objects for real objects or persons) occurs with greater frequency. Now, the child's mental images are active and internalized imitation, with a close relationship existing among mental image, imitative gesture, and graphic image (Piaget and Inhelder 1971). In addition to language, children now can represent their internal images through drawing or even movement, such as imitating various animals or gestures of people.

In the stage of concrete operations, ages 7–12, children gradually move away from make-believe play to more games with rules, but they can also manipulate images more easily, and can use images for anticipatory ends. Language skills increase, and for some children graphic expression is a favored mode. From age 12 on (the stage of formal operations), children can "think about thoughts" with daydreaming playing an increasingly important role, especially during adolescence (Singer and Singer 1990). The images adolescents use revolve around future plans and the exploration of different roles in society. In this last stage, as in adulthood, individuals are processing external information into their private streams of thought.

Most researchers accept the notion that children use imagery in their thinking more than adults do, and there have been enough empirical studies to support this (Kosslyn 1980, Leuner et al. 1983, Lusebrink 1990) and qualitative reports by keen observers (Gould 1972, Paley 1988, 1990, Pitcher and Prelinger 1963). Because Kosslyn believes that imagery consists of a collection of distinct subabilities, a person can be good or bad at imagery formation depending upon which of the subabilities are developed. Kosslyn and colleagues (1990) tested image generation, image maintenance, image scanning, and image rotation by comparing the performance of 5-year-olds, 8-year-olds, 14-year-olds, and adults on four imagery tasks utilizing these processes that are commonly used in visual thinking. Results suggest that there are clear differences based on age for image generation. Older subjects were able to scan and rotate images better than younger subjects (the data of the youngest were dropped because of a ceiling effect), and older subjects were better at generating images. No differences were found over age in image maintenance. Females were generally superior in generating and maintaining images, but within the 8-year-old group the males were faster than females in an image maintenance test. The researchers found no evidence to suggest that younger children have fewer processing components, but that the very youngest are relatively poor at scanning, rotating, and generating objects, yet relatively good at maintaining images. This finding seems to support the eidetic imagery capability of children who can keep these images over time.

Certainly, the work of Mischel and colleagues (1972) is important when we think of image-producing capacity in children. In studying preschoolers, researchers found that delay of gratification was dramatically facilitated when the children were able to "think fun," thereby using pleasant cognitive distractions to postpone the receiving of a reward. However, when children thought sad thoughts or thought about the rewards themselves, delay time was shortened. This seems to be in contrast to the notion that when the baby "hallucinates" or internalizes the image of the mother, delay of gratification begins. If we accept Mischel's data, it would appear that thinking about the mother would *increase* tension and shorten the ability to delay gratification, rather than the opposite Freudian notion of delay developing as a result of primary process images. An additional step must be taken before effective delay is established: the ego must be able to divert energy away from the "mother" image to other images of a pleasant nature or to some instrumental activity (playing with a mobile or rattle) while awaiting the reward (the milk).

One particular aspect of imagery formation in children is the fear or frightening aspect that is associated with presleep or nighttime. There are many events that occur during the day in a young child's life, including the numerous television images viewed. Given the limitation of young children's cognitive processes and their difficulty in assimilating all the various information to which they are exposed, the night noises and shadows on the wall take on strange properties that during the day seem more benign or may not even be noticed. Indeed, even if we accept the psychoanalytic interpretation that nighttime fears may be related to fears of separation, rejection, or loss of the external object in the shutting of eyes and preparation for sleep, these fears may be only one part of an assimilation process that children must experience at night. There is reduced sensory input at this time and as a result, the child experiences a greater awareness of the processing material of the brain and of the images and partially assimilated materials that are the prominent part of what Freud termed the *day residue,* or what Klinger (1971) has called the *current concerns.* Although adults may be able to recognize the sounds and sights and control the strange fantasies that intrude at sleep onset, children need to learn how to master this material so that they can fall asleep. It takes years of growth before a child can truly assimilate the myths, teasing, threats, fairy tales, supernatural materials, religious ideas, and television content that are part of our daily exposure. The nighttime presleep fantasies and dreams of children may get woven into the complex symbolic combinations that emerge later in adult dreams or the imaginary trips that are part of particular forms of psychotherapy.

In summary, the imagery and fantasy processes of adults are extensions of specific imagery into chained sequences that originally developed "out of the accommodation-assimilation cycle in which the child attempts to process information" (Singer 1986, p. 119). The process continues throughout childhood and well on into adult life, where we must constantly sort out the enormous input of information and integrate it into our existing schemas. Information that does not fit may disturb us and erupt in our fantasies or nocturnal dreams. The exploration of these images through various psychotherapeutic techniques or through self-awareness or introspection leads to a clearer understanding of these images, their symbolism, and relationship to our everyday lives.

Measurement of Images and Fantasy Production

How do we know if an individual is capable of producing images and the nature of such images? With regard to children, Piaget and Inhelder (1967, 1971) describe four methods for obtaining such information: (1) verbal descriptions, (2) drawings produced by the child, (3) asking the child to select a drawing from prepared drawings (an assortment of correct and incorrect solutions to a problem such as how a cube would look if opened and flat), and (4) reproduction by gesture. Expanding on Piaget and Inhelder's measurement approach, there are six techniques I wish to describe in this section: (1) performance tests of visual-spatial ability requiring only mental elaboration; (2) visual-motor tasks requiring encoding procedures; (3) observation of children and recording their fantasy games and conversations; (4) self-report measures such as questionnaires, diaries, stories, interviews, or reports elicited by the experimenter at random time periods; (5) projective techniques; and (6) physiological measures.

Tests of Visual-Spatial Ability

Tests of *visual-spatial ability* are those similar to Finke's exercises discussed in *Creative Imagery* (1990). For example, imagine a letter B; turn it on its side so that the vertical line is now horizontal; remove the line and report the name of the letter, which now is W. Barell (1980), Finke (1990), and Kosslyn and colleagues (1990) are interested in how individuals generate visual images, scan them for parts, rotate or transform images, and sustain them. Finke's work has been carried out mainly with undergraduates, but both Barell and Kosslyn have examined children's capacities for visual-spatial imagery. Earlier work by Wertheimer (1945) demonstrated that a 5½-year-old girl was able to change a parallelogram into a rectangle by regrouping or reorganizing the components of the original figure. The child actually had to cut the figure, removing the left-hand portion and placing it on the right side to form the rectangle. We are not sure if she was engaging in what Piaget and Inhelder (1971) call *geometrical intuition*. These researchers suggest that children are able to reproduce perceived images at the preoperational level of thought, but that anticipatory images appear during the concrete stage. Thus, they believed that children could manipulate objects internally only from the age of 8. The child who transformed the parallelogram – if we accept Piaget and Inhelder's thesis – needed to actually perform the transformation rather than image it and describe what must be done to change the form. Through a series of experiments, Piaget and Inhelder deduced that the representation of a perceived object did not become a cognition or image until the child thoroughly understood the transformations necessary to account for the image.

Visual-Motor Tasks

It may be useful to measure a child's capacity to see an abstract form and then copy this form as a means of assessing the child's perceptual ability in terms of remedial procedures. If a deficit is suspected because of reading or short-term memory problems, tests such as the Bender-Gestalt Visual Motor Test or the Benton Test of

Visual Memory (Benton 1963) are useful. The child copies a form after a brief exposure. Thus, not only are recognition and encoding skills tapped, but the ability to transform information from the visual modality to the motor one is measured. Similarly, picture recognition or word recognition tasks may be used to assess memory for details as well as expressive abilities (Marks 1973, Paivio 1970). One test battery used with children, Thinking Creatively with Sounds and Words (Khatena and Torrance 1973, Torrance et al. 1973), has been used to assess children's abilities to produce original responses. Those children who do so score higher on a test of visual imagery (Khatena 1978).

Observations

A technique we have been using over the years in our studies of children's play and imagination is the direct observation of participants in our studies as they engage in free play in nursery schools or day care centers (Singer and Singer 1981, 1990). This approach is particularly useful when attempting to get data on preschool children's fantasy productions (Piaget 1962). Generally, research assistants are trained over a period of time in order to get reliable agreements in fantasy productions. Verbatim records are kept by two raters who observe a target child for ten minutes on different occasions over a time period ranging from one month to a year, depending on the particular study. The researchers then independently rate the child on a five-point scale after each observation period of ten minutes, with a 5 given to a child who, for example, evidences transformations (a stick becomes a doll or toy soldier); vocalizations, using changes of voice to become other people; and elaboration of a script so that a narrative unfolds. The children who are rated with higher scores are those who also score higher on other measures of imagination and fantasy such as a simple questionnaire, the Imaginative Play Predisposition Interview, or Barron inkblots (both described below).

Self Report Measures

Questionnaires, journals or diaries, interviews, story-telling, and naturalistic reports yield information about the *types* or *styles* of fantasy or imagery production. Few questionnaires, however, have been used with children, although the literature dealing with this form of measurement of imagery offers a wide variety for use with adults (Ahsen 1972, Gordon 1950, Marks 1973, Paivio 1971, Sheehan 1967, Shorr 1974, Singer and Antrobus 1972). In general, these tests yield information concerning not only types of fantasies, but the degree of vividness in imagery production.

Rosenfeld and colleagues (1982) developed and refined a fantasy measure (the only one that seems to have a large sample and good validity), testing 748 first- and third-grade children. The instrument consists of forty-five items that yielded nine empirically derived nonorthogonal scales. Three fantasy styles emerged from a factor analysis: active-intellectual, dysphoric-aggressive, and fanciful-intense. Basically the children's styles of daydreaming closely paralleled adult styles, but with some unique aspects. The *fanciful fantasy* scale measured behavior that involved ghosts, fairy tales, and bizarre fantasies that do not seem to have the same negative connotations as they do for adults. Boys scored higher on active-heroic fantasies than did girls, while girls scored higher on the fanciful fantasy scale. The authors suggest that girls appeared to be more willing to admit to both positive and negative affects in their fantasy activity.

Using a modified version of the Rosenfeld measure, McIlwraith and Schallow (1982–1983) tested eighty-two first grade children to assess ongoing patterns of television viewing and imaginal activity. They found a positive correlation between heavy television viewing and dysphoric, hostile, ruminative fantasies. The authors did not find, however, that television substitutes or replaces self-produced fantasy.

Interviews with children about their imaginative life were a major source of data for Piaget's important book *Play, Dreams and Imitation in Childhood* (1962). Influenced by Piaget, an Imaginative Play Predisposition (IPP) interview was developed by Singer (1973). It consists of four questions scored on a five-point scale: "What's your favorite game?" "What do you do when alone?" "Do you have an imaginary playmate?" "Do you ever see pictures in your head?" This simple measure has proved to be effective in assessing children's imaginative predisposition, and correlates significantly positively with children's scores for imaginative play and with their ability to produce the movement (M) response on an inkblot task (Singer and Singer 1981).

The use of journals or diaries with older children and adolescents is another fruitful technique for assessing the types of imagery and fantasy produced, as well as the vividness of imagery. A more systematic approach has been developed by Applebee 1978, Gould 1972, and Pitcher and Prelinger 1963. Gould not only relied on stories that nursery school children aged 3 through 5 years produced, but on songs, dream accounts, observations, and verbatim recordings of children's dramatic play in groups and in monologues. About 100 records were analyzed for fantasy expression. Pitcher and Prelinger's approach was a bit more directed. The only instruction given to the children (137 children of nursery school and kindergarten age) was "tell me a story." Several dimensions were used to analyze approximately 360 stories, such as use of physical and fantasy space in the stories; clarity with which main characters were differentiated, and in what ways they reflected boundaries of the self and of animate objects; the inner complexity of characters; the activity and passivity of characters in relation to mastery of the world and its inhabitants; the degree of realism in the stories; and the degree to which descriptions of thought and of emotional processes appeared in the stories (pp. 19–20).

Applebee's work with children aged 2 to 17 focused on the language children use in story telling. He not only used stories collected by Pitcher and Prelinger, but used new samples from older children, ages 6, 9, 13, and 17. In terms of fantasy, he found that the younger children had difficulty separating fact and fantasy and that the "world of stories is part of the world in which they live; its events are as important and meaningful to them as anything else that happens" (Applebee 1978, p. 132). Boys tended to venture farther afield in their stories, while girls remained closer to home. A study of children's stories told to abstract films further supported these results, with middle childhood boys telling more adventure stories (Gottlieb 1973). These story-telling techniques are easily reproducible with even one child in psychotherapy. Therapists are constantly interpreting the play of children, and work by the above researchers suggests a more systematic way of making sense out of children's play scripts and narratives.

Interviews with young children can be structured, such as the IPP, or can be open-ended. Direct questioning in a sensitive manner can often help children uncover and reveal images and fantasies that they tend to keep to themselves because of shame, guilt, embarrassment, or even fear of revealing such images. Sometimes the interview will serve to release these fantasies later through play or story-telling.

Another self-report technique is one requiring the subject to wear a paging device or beeper, and to write down internal images, thoughts, and feelings when it is activated. The time intervals may be preselected or randomly assigned (Csikszent-mihalyi 1984, Singer and Kolligian 1987). This technique has been used with adolescents, but not with very young children.

Projective Techniques

Of special importance in the clinical setting are those instruments that tap a child's ability to produce images associated with presented stimuli. These images or percepts may reveal unconscious thoughts and fantasies related to conflict or motives that are hidden during play therapy or interviews, or that cannot be elicited by self reports.

The use of word association tests, sentence completion tests, and projectives such as the Blacky Test, Children's Apperception Test, Thematic Apperception Test and the Rorschach have proved to be valuable instruments in uncovering themes, fantasies, or images that concern clients. The use of movement or the (M) response on the Rorschach is one method of measuring individuals' ability to be reflective, fanciful, or purposeful and creative in their thought processes (Rorschach 1942). The Barron movement threshold inkblots, a set of twenty-six blots that show increasing tendency to evoke (M) responses, have been used with children, and also correlate positively with imaginativeness (Singer and Singer 1981).

Using the Rorschach, a divergent thinking measure, and an Affect in Play Scale with sixty first and second grade children, Russ and Grossman-McKee (1990) found, for example, that primary process expression on the Rorschach was significantly, positively related to the amount of affective expression, intensity of affect, and general comfort in the play situation. Primary process expression was also significantly related to divergent thinking. The authors suggest that it is access to "dangerous taboo-laden primary process thinking, around which the individual has experienced conflict, that is facilitative of divergent thinking" (p. 769).

We can also uncover children's fantasies or thoughts through the use of tests such as House-Tree-Person (Hammer 1980) or the Kinetic Family Drawing test, where a child draws members of the family and self engaged in an activity. After the drawings are completed on either test, questions are posed concerning the figures in order to uncover conflicts, affect, basic needs and drives, self-concept, and attitudes toward the environment. Hammer has developed a scoring system and has gathered numerous samples of House-Tree-Person drawings over the years. As far as imagery and fantasy are concerned, the stories about the pictures can be revealing of a child's capacity to elaborate or move beyond the stimulus. Similarly, when using the Children's Apperception Test or the Thematic Apperception Test, a score can be given for general imaginative tendencies, not just motivational themes. For example, in response to the card where a child is shown on a bridge, one person may attend to the visible details in the picture, "a girl or boy is standing on a bridge," while another person may describe the child's thoughts, feelings, friends, house, or parents, thus *transcending* what is actually portrayed in the scene. Using this transcendence score, psychologists can obtain some estimate of a client's ability to image. Transcendence scores correlate with other measures of imagination, especially the human movement response on the Rorschach.

Physiological Measures

The use of physiological measures of imagery with children has been carried out mainly in laboratory settings, especially in connection with REMS during dreaming. Measurements can be made of breathing, while awake and imaging; muscle tension, particularly facial muscles; eye movements; and brain waves. Most of the work using physiological measures has been with adults (see Tower and Singer 1981 for a review, and Tower 1979). As clinicians working with children, we can use direct observation to note changes in facial expression, breathing, muscle tone, and eye movements when clients engage in fantasy, especially when methods are employed to help relax the child before and during some techniques that will be discussed in the following section.

The area of physiological measurement of imagery in children needs to be more thoroughly studied and could be fruitful in determining which techniques or methods of imagery are useful in the psychotherapeutic setting. In addition, this information could be used to help children and adolescents become aware of changes in their physiological state, so that a cognitive label may be attached to such changes leading to a lowering of blood pressure or heart rate, and relaxation of muscle tension.

Applications of Imagery Techniques in Psychotherapy with Children

Material that may be unavailable to children through the lexical system may emerge through images or through the enactive systems (see above for definitions). One major function of imagery techniques in psychotherapy is that they permit communication between child and therapist that may be blocked through verbal descriptions without this prior imagery release. Reyher (1963) believes that verbalizations are freer from defensiveness during imagery-association than during other forms of therapy, and that physiological measures of arousal during such imagery productions suggest that the client is more involved. Aylwin's (1990) research indicates that affect or emotion is most frequent in enactive imagery, that is, imagery using both temporal and affective aspects of a stimulus. Actions are expressed in transitive verbs, space is relative, there is no static environment, and spatial relationships are direct through actions linked by the client. There is more dynamic representation in enactive imagery than expressed in visual imagery. Possibilities in enactive imagery are included for the future, and clients refer more frequently to feelings and emotions.

This notion of affect related to enactive imagery is important in such methods as Guided Affective Imagery (to be discussed below), which relies on movement across space and time in its application. In a review of the research concerning affect and memory, Singer and Salovey (1988) report on several studies where self-generated imagery experiments with children found happy, but not sad, mood-dependent recall in both free and cued recall tasks. Certainly, if experiments report the relationship between enactive imagery and affect, this portends for the value of imagery use in our attempts to help our clients deal with the emotional aspects that such images evoke.

Before turning to the different techniques that utilize imagery, some cautions must be considered. Rosenstiel and Scott (1977) outline four major points: (1) Imagery scenes must be geared to the cognitive abilities of the child. Children aged 6 to 8 can use complex images, while younger children may follow more simple directions such as thinking "fun" or sad thoughts. (2) The therapist should include children's naturally occurring imagery as a basis for therapy. The child will be more interested if scenes are familiar. Hypnosis and emotive imagery, for example, are especially adaptable to children's fantasies. Using familiar characters, superheroes, fairy tale characters and so forth, enables a child to image himself in settings with these "friends." (3) Attention to nonverbal cues such as flushing of the skin, increased body movements, muscular tension, breathing patterns, and changes in facial expressions will enable the therapist to identify anxiety-provoking images and when anxiety diminishes. (4) Attention should be paid to the descriptions and emotions aroused by an imaged scene or event. Questions should be asked about each segment of an image in order to assess the degree of comfort or discomfort.

The question of the ability of young children to use imagery effectively in treatment is still open to research. Studies indicate that 5 and 6-year-olds do not use mental imagery in recall as well as 7 and 8-year-olds (Purkel and Bornstein 1980). Lazarus and Abramovitz (1962) support the Rosenstiel and Scott argument that if children imagine themselves in the company of a favorite hero while encountering a difficult event, the visualization process is more meaningful. Imagery interaction in play therapy where both the adult and child are involved, sharing images and play, seems to be a productive method (Hellendoorn 1988).

Finally, the notion of narrative enters into the child's ability to translate the image into a story or script. The narrative account reflects the child's experience of historical truth that is colored by highly personal meanings. When images are produced and then reported to the therapist, the distortions, omissions, elaborations, or fragmentations are influenced by unconscious motives and feelings. Logical sequence may disappear as themes and fantasies of conflict and defense are visualized and verbalized. Primary process material will appear in imagery as it does in spontaneous play, and the therapist must be able to make "the critical transition from assessment to treatment . . . in creating and maintaining the necessary therapeutic environment to enhance and cultivate the unfolding of the child's narrative account" (Brandell 1988, pp. 248–249).

Jerome Bruner (1990) would agree that a narrative is composed of a unique sequence of events, mental states, and happenings involving human beings as characters or actors, but that the interpreter – in this case, the therapist – must grasp the "narrative's configuring plot in order to make sense of its constituents, which he must relate to that plot" (p. 43). Indeed, this is the task of the therapist while listening to the reports of a client who is experiencing an image. Depending upon the imagery technique employed, the therapist may either just listen and interpret later or may interpret as he listens to the image unfold.

Let us now examine the various types of imagery techniques that are more systematic in approach. Eight methods utilizing imagery in psychotherapy with children will be discussed: relaxation therapy, systematic desensitization, cognitive therapy, eidetic imagery therapy, guided affective imagery, mind play, art therapy, and movement and drama therapy.

Relaxation Therapy

The therapist asks the client to relax his muscles, close his eyes and image a quiet, pleasant, peaceful scene. Deep breathing is encouraged; the child may be seated or lying down. Hypnotic induction procedures and relaxation therapy share similarities. There are changes in autonomic function such as decreased heart rate, respiratory rate, and blood pressure. A relaxation response generally precedes a hypnotic state. If suggestions are given to a client to experience some sort of cognitive change such as perceptual distortions, age regression, posthypnotic suggestions and amnesia, relaxation therapy moves into the realm of hypnosis. In other words, in hypnosis the client is asked to use imagery to focus on specific goals other than relaxation. The interaction between client and therapist plays an important role in the transition from relaxation therapy to hypnosis. The major characteristics of hypnosis that may separate it from relaxation therapy are the fading of a general reality orientation, the total absorption in the experience, the receptive, expansive, free-floating attention that allows the mind to wander freely and admit whatever floats into awareness, and fluctuations in trance depth (Fromm 1982, p. 210).

In a study of both relaxation training and hypnosis with children and adolescents suffering from problems in attention, anorexia nervosa, poor peer relationships, impulse control problems, and authority issues, experimenters found that after a three-phase program of training, participants improved their self-concepts, displayed an increased readiness to learn, and gained control of serious behavior problems (Ebrahim et al. 1982).

Working with more normal children aged 10 to 18 years of age, Setterlind (1982) found that relaxation training in conjunction with a physical education program in the schools was successful. Children listened to tapes over an 8-week period for 8 to 12 minutes, 3 times a week. Physiological and psychological measures were administered before and after training. Results indicated increases in positive self-insight, self-control, and self-influence.

Graziano and Kean (1971) have used relaxation therapy with autistic children who had no behavioral referent for the concept "relax," but who could be trained with highly structured, brief, concrete behavior-level sessions. Much verbal reinforcement was necessary. The researchers found that not only were they able to train these autistic children to relax, but that there was a marked decrement of the generalized excitement response throughout the same day of each session. In addition, these children spontaneously practiced relaxation training at other times than the scheduled sessions, and even did so at home.

Systematic Desensitization

A procedure that evolved from classical conditioning is *systematic desensitization* (Wolpe 1958). This method assumes that the imagined stimulus matches the real stimulus to such an extent that equivalent anxiety is induced. The belief underlying this form of treatment is that certain cues in the child's environment trigger anxiety or fear reactions. The fear can be reduced by conditioning an alternative response to stimuli or cues that are incompatible with fear responses. Relaxation and anxiety are considered to be incompatible states; therefore, relaxation should inhibit the anxiety aroused by exposure to the cue or stimulus. Fear-eliciting stimuli are placed in an ascending order on the hierarchical list on the basis of their ability to arouse anxiety. They are paired with a relaxation response. First the child relaxes and is asked to imagine a scene with only some mildly anxiety-provoking stimuli. Deep breathing is encouraged, and as a result this should inhibit the mildly arousing anxiety. Step by step, other stimuli on the list are introduced and paired with relaxation. The goal is to eventually eliminate the capacity of the stimuli to evoke anxiety. The child can now imagine an anxiety-provoking scene with relative calm. It is hoped that this relaxation and anxiety reduction will carry over into a real situation.

Systematic desensitization theory contends that the imaging of a stimulus is as powerful as real life situations. Harris and Ferrari (1983), however, warn against its use in treating children's fears. The literature they reviewed consisted mainly of case reports with only a few of sufficient rigor to "permit any sort of cause and effect outcomes" (p. 62). In general, research data seem to support the notion that real life exposure, although more stressful, may be more useful with clients who do not easily generate images in therapy. Nevertheless, it is important to determine the feasibility of such exposure where it may be impractical or even dangerous. It is also important to note that imagery ability alone may not predict how well a child can respond to *systematic* desensitization techniques (Martin and Williams 1990).

Covert sensitization is a variation of desensitization and is used primarily in aversive conditioning. A client imagines himself engaged in an undesirable behavior such as overeating. Thus, an aversive consequence such as nausea can be associated through imagery with the overeating. This builds up an aversion to the stimulus, food, which previously was desirable. This technique, utilizing the child's imagery, actually is a substitute for engagement in the undesirable behavior.

Another variation of systematic desensitization is called bibliotherapy desensitization. In a case analysis of a child, Tom, with intense fears of flying objects such as insects and birds, and a fear of spiders and crawling bugs, a fear hierarchy was established with flying planes being the least feared and flying insects the most feared (Edwards 1978). In addition to this standard desensitization technique and parental consultation, *emotive imagery stories* were told to Tom by his mother. These stories emphasized the courage of the hero, Tom, who was able to handle difficult, fearful situations. Later, bibliotherapy was used again over a period of three weeks wherein Tom was the hero and was able to make friends and help others. A follow-up report after two years indicated that Tom was still free of his phobia and had made a good adjustment to school.

Cognitive Therapy

There are two strategies that are effective in producing cognitive changes for self-control and for reducing anxiety: imagery-based and self-instruction techniques.

Imagery-based procedures relying on the client's production of thoughts and images have been outlined by Beck and colleagues and summarized by Martin and Williams (1990, p. 279) as follows:

1. *Turn-off technique* – the client is trained to "turn off" autonomous images or fantasies by increasing sensory input such as clapping hands or blowing a whistle.
2. *Repetition* – by forcing repetitions of an image, the content becomes more realistic and anxiety may be reduced.
3. *Time projection* – if the client can image a scene in the future when the troublesome event is past, he may be able to distance the self from current anxieties about the event.
4. *Symbolic images* – symbols may be modified or changed. If, for example, a client images someone attacking, a shield can be added to the image to afford protection.

5. *Facilitating change in induced images* – an anxious fantasy may be changed into a neutral or positive image by having clients imagine themselves painting an image of their choice.

6. *Substituting a positive image* – the client images a comforting scene in a potentially anxiety-inducing situation and focuses on all sensory modalities involved in this image.

7. *Exaggeration* – the client images a consequence worse than his own fears so as to put them in perspective.

8. *Coping models* – the client images someone whom he considers capable of coping with the feared situation and then models the behavior. A child can choose an older sibling, friend, parent, or teacher.

9. *Imagery to reduce threat* – the feared stimulus is made less threatening through imagery (for example, imagining the doctor in a clown's suit).

10. *Goal rehearsal* – the client images a new, frightening situation and then images ways to cope with it (useful for children starting a new school, or for a child afraid of the dark).

The value of this therapy depends on the ability of the client to change the thought and image content while working on false appraisals of danger. The researchers suggest that the imagery and automatic thoughts are warning signals, and that removing them would not diminish the fear of the situation. The client in cognitive therapy, however, learns that the warning system is overactive and distorted and that he must gain mastery over it, which then provides him with confidence for "appraising more realistically the feared situation" and for coping with it (p. 279).

The use of covert modeling developed by Cautela is a form of imagery-based cognitive therapy. Basically, the client need not perform an act, but through the imaging of a model, the client is able to visualize himself performing various acts or holding conversations in specific scenes presented by the therapist or on tape. Treatment consists of utilizing several scenes that relate to aspects of behavior targeted for change or that the client wishes to develop (Cautela and McCullough 1978).

The second grouping of cognitive therapy procedures, *self-instruction techniques,* is described by Meichenbaum and Goodman (1971). It involves teaching an individual to make statements that reflect appropriate competence and problem-solving strategies for a targeted response. First, children are instructed to make these self-statements out loud and then to gradually learn to shift over to covert or silent self-verbalization. Spivack and Shure (1982) have developed a program for problem-solving skills training that focuses on a child's perceptions, self-statements, attributions, expectations, and problem-solving skills. The primary focus is on the *thought* processes rather than on specific outcomes or acts. The child moves from thought to self-instructions to structured tasks involving games, academic activities and stories, to real-life situations. The therapist is a role model and an active partner in treatment by making verbal self-statements, applying sequences of statements to problems, cueing the child to prompt use of specific skills, and giving feedback and praise continually (Kazdin 1988).

Eidetic Imagery

The most active exponent of so-called eidetic imagery techniques is Achter Ahsen (1984). He believes that this imagery is formed and retained because it has emotional and significant meanings for the individual. It may be an image or recurrent fantasy that is impressed upon the individual and related to formative events in life. Thus they are "developmentally determined, affect laden, vivid, repeatable, and almost universally present images that pertain to key memories and fantasies associated with basic growth and conflict situations and are arranged in a predetermined sequence" (Sheikh 1978, p. 202). There are three components involved: the visual, the somatic or bodily feelings, and the experiential or cognitive meaning. Ahsen has developed the Eidetic Parents Test (EPT) designed to uncover images related to a client's interactions with parents and the client's perceptions of polarities that existed in the parent–child relationship. This instrument might be useful in working with adolescents, but to my knowledge, research in this area seems nonexistent. A description of the test and the technique is expanded upon in Ahsen's book *Eidetic Parents Test and Analysis* (1972) and in the paper cited above.

Guided Affective Imagery

This is a psychoanalytically oriented technique that is used with adults and children as young as 6 years of age. This method, utilizing imagery, differs from cognitive therapy in that the topics or *motifs* that are offered to the client are not directly related to the presenting disorder. Leuner and colleagues (1983) describe the procedure of Guided Affective Imagery (GAI) and offer numerous clinical examples in their book. Basically, GAI is a projective procedure; the client closes his eyes and projects images generated by the motifs suggested by the therapist. The child may lie on a couch or be seated in a comfortable chair and encouraged to relax with eyes closed. Observation of a child's facial expression, muscle tension, and breathing can be indicators of the degree of relaxation. If there is difficulty in generating images, Leuner suggests offering some images of a meadow where one can rest after a long summer's walk, or other such peaceful scenes.

When the therapist is assured that the child is completely relaxed, a choice from eight standard motifs is offered: the meadow, the ascent of a mountain, the pursuit of the course of a brook, visiting a house, an encounter with relatives, the observation of the edge of the woods from the meadow, a boat, and a cave. The meadow is usually introduced first.

Treatment consists of a 15- to 30-minute duration period preceded by and following the therapist–client conversation. Steps consist of the relaxation, the starting point where the first motif is suggested (generally one or two motifs are used per session), the unfolding of the client's imagery or "waking dream," encouragement by the therapist with restatements or reflections, questions about the imagined scene, and occasionally suggestions by the therapist as to what the client may do during the imagery.

Leuner suggests that adults write down their impressions after a session, but with children it is appropriate to ask them to draw their images. I find that this generally leads to even further discussion and associations about the images. Children often use body movements during GAI, waving hands, moving feet up and down, nodding the head. Klessman (1983), describing special features in working with children, suggests that a sitting position be used. She also interprets children's body movements as their way of reducing anxieties about being at the therapist's mercy. GAI is particularly useful with children because they are extremely suggestible. But the therapist must also be cautious. Children may become so immersed in their images that it is important for the therapist to recognize if the child is made anxious by the vividness of the image. Klessman gives an example of a 9-year-old patient who was so deeply into her image, that upon opening her eyes, she was confused and startled, not quite knowing where she was. For this reason one must be quite expert in using GAI. GAI has been used successfully with cases of childhood phobias, compulsions, enuresis, stuttering, drug abuse, and psychosomatic illness (Leuner et al. 1983).

Bott and Klinger (1985–1986) have synthesized a variety of rating methods to develop an instrument for assessing GAI protocols with adults. This method could be adapted for children's protocols as well, and could be useful for quantifying and categorizing the stream of images reported by clients over time. Such features as vividness of imagery, formal transformations of objects, and details such as fading or brightening of images, theme content of scenes and features of scenes, thematic transformations, and affect variables relating to the client's sensations during imagery can be considered in a scoring procedure. From their preliminary work, Bott and Klinger conclude that increases in detail during imagery require experimenter intervention. This suggests that inquiries during GAI may encourage a *deeper experience* of the imagery, and this differentiates the guided dream from spontaneous waking dreams or daydreams. The interruptions, however, do not seem to interfere with image transformations.

The GAI technique wherein parent motifs are suggested may not be suitable for clients who have experienced difficulty with early caregivers, especially the mother. According to the psychoanalyst Peter Neubauer (1987), the "object representational world and inner psychic life are not synonymous and . . . our understanding of the establishment of a representational world in the first three years of life is primarily based on inferences" (p. 335). As evidence for this statement, he presents three cases of patients who experienced abnormalities of visual representation of faces, but could remember objects or places. This difficulty in remembering faces, prosopagnosia, may be congenital or acquired. What is interesting about Neubauer's work with his clients is that the inability to visualize faces was a part of their lives since early childhood, and that none of his patients spontaneously revealed their inability. They would tell him only when asked. Since one of the main aspects of GAI is the therapist's persistent encouragement to take an active stand toward threatening images, it may be that more conventional explorations of the child–mother relationship are indicated with children or adolescents who block when attempting to image such motifs.

Other problems raised in using GAI are noted by Schoettle (1980). Young children have difficulty separating reality from fantasy; they find it difficult to maintain the relaxed, eyes-closed posture for more than several minutes and need to open their eyes to talk about reality-based issues. Some children tend to recount episodes from television or movies, or favorite stories rather than their own private images, and some children may fear that if they described a vivid scene, it might really happen. Finally, Schoettle mentions the possibility that religious convictions may be interwoven with fears of fantasy materialization. Thus, it might be difficult for these children to "progress past the stage that an evil thought constitutes an evil deed for which they will be punished" (p. 226).

Mind Play

A technique using mind play wherein directed imagery is the main focus can prove to be a fruitful play therapy technique. Exercises or games such as described in *Put Your Mother on the Ceiling* (de Mille 1973), can help children gain control over their fantasies and encourage a belief in their own effectiveness, self-assertion, and more positive self-esteem. In addition, these games are useful in facilitating a child's ability to use imagination as a controlled source of pleasure and gratification. Through these images, tension may be discharged. Johnson and colleagues (1987), for example, carried out an experiment using the de Mille exercises with chronically ill children aged 5 through 9. Mothers were trained in the procedure and worked with their children for approximately fifteen minutes a day over a two-week period. The control group played games of skill and chance. Results demonstrated that the experimental group showed reduced anxiety on a standardized test and displayed an increased use of fantasy in their play compared to the controls. The authors suggest that the results provided encouraging evidence that the imaginative capacities of children can be an excellent resource that may be utilized to help chronic patients cope with the stress that accompanies such illness.

Some of the exercises in the de Mille book deal with images about mother, father, school, manners, food, and pain. For example, a child in the exercise dealing with parents is stimulated by such images of father and mother growing smaller, turning various colors, standing on a roof, going deep into a mine, having a dragon breathe fire on them, having a steamroller flatten them, and having the parents upset the steamroller. The game ends by having the parents "wink" at the child and ask, "What would you like to do with them now?" Discussion following the exercises focuses on the images that were generated and encourages children to bring up fears or difficulties that are bothering them.

In my use of the de Mille games with Daniel, a 6-year-old aggressive child, I found that the games relaxed him considerably. He was especially fond of playing the parents exercise where he displayed much positive affect when he used his imaging to shrink his parents and have a shark open his mouth to eat the parents. With much glee after the exercises, Daniel drew pictures of his tiny parents again sitting in a shark's mouth. Daniel's parents were two busy restaurant owners who spent very little time with him. He was resentful of this and angry, and acted whiny and babyish in order to get their attention. This seemed to have an opposite effect on his parents, who appeared to reject him even more. Through fantasy, Daniel was able to control his parents, and through discussion after each exercise, he began to learn how to become more independent and less angry. Once he understood that the demands of his parents' work kept them busy, he was able to tolerate their unusual working hours. At the same time, Daniel's parents tried to arrange for more time to be with him. Daniel also learned that fantasy is pleasurable, and could use his images to play out games with his miniature toys.

Poetry can also be used to stretch a child's imagination and to give practice in imagery production (Koch 1970). In a short poem, feelings can be expressed on a variety of topics. A stimulus word or phrase such as "wish," "dream," "baby," "the things I hear," "I seem to be/but really am," or "strange things" can probe into a child's unconscious and help reveal feelings and conflicts. Similarly, pantomiming images that pertain to emotions may help a child express fears or even joy and perhaps remove some blocks. *The Magic If* (Kelly 1973) offers many suggestions and exercises that tap into a child's awareness and foster imagination. Imitating a person's walk or movements and facial expressions forces a child to concentrate and generate images pertaining to the stimuli. Children are encouraged to think about adaptation to another person's mood by imaging how the other person might look and act if a request were made. These exercises are useful when helping a child understand how to improve interpersonal relationships with peers, siblings, parents, and even teachers.

Words or phrases may also be used to stimulate drawings that express a child's feelings, or a drawing or color may be used to stimulate an image (Goodnow 1977, Wood 1986). Finally, the Mutual Storytelling Technique (Gardner 1983) is a method that encourages the child to tell a self-created story, and permits the therapist to examine the psychodynamic meanings, and create a responding story. The story can be taped and listened to by client and therapist. Generally, the therapist warms up the child by telling him he will be on TV or on the radio, asking him brief questions about age, address, school, grade, and teacher, and then telling him to tell the story. After the child tells the story, or even while presenting it, the therapist tries to determine themes, symbols of the child's personality, and who the significant people are in the child's life. The therapist may question the child in order to clarify the symbols. When the child has completed his story, the therapist creates his or her own story using the same setting and characters used by the child, but with more appropriate methods of resolving conflicts. After this, the child is questioned to see if he understood the lesson in the therapist's story. Discussion after the story enables the child to gain insight into his difficulties and gives the therapist an opportunity to clarify symbols and meanings for the child.

Art Therapy

There are two main approaches to art therapy: first, the use of visual media with emphasis on the artistic aspects of the product itself, with verbalization about the product as secondary and mainly about the use of media and socialization and second, the actual rendition of the product, but with verbal free association to the images created, and insight concerning these associations. The first approach is applied usually as an adjunct to other forms of therapy. Here the therapist may simply want the child to find an outlet for expression, or to draw because the child is blocked in verbal expression.

The second approach, which may be called *art psychotherapy*, relies on the rendered product as the sole approach utilized in therapy. The therapist must be circumspect, however, in utilizing either approach with respect to severely disturbed or brain-damaged children, because there is an inherent freedom in creative art that might be upsetting and could lead to disruptive or uncontrolled behavior. Uhlin and DeChiara (1984) do suggest the cautious use of art therapy with neurologically handicapped children.

Kramer (1971, 1979), one of the leaders in *art therapy* with children, believes the creative process itself is therapeutic, but that the therapist can nurture and support this process through comments, interpretations, and even with technical advice. The underlying premise of art therapy with children is that through the manipulation of art materials, children not only impose structure and form on the materials selected, but are able to organize and control their emotions through the artistic expression. There may be wishes or fantasies children may experience, but when they actually draw an object, kinesthetic, emotional, and intellectual functions come into play. When a child views the finished work, there may be both confrontation with bizarre ideas and even with pathology, but Kramer believes there is some narcissistic gratification in viewing this work. She conceives of art therapy as a means of supporting a child's ego, fostering a sense of identity, and as a step towards maturation in general (Kramer 1971).

Rubin (1987) uses art psychotherapy in her approach. According to her, art can help a child uncover unconscious imagery, communicate, and express feelings. It is also useful in diagnosis as described previously in this chapter under the section *Measurement of Imagery*. Art psychotherapy can be used, according to Rubin, in helping the child deal with defenses. The therapist asks open-ended questions, observes the child's nonverbal behavior during the art session, and encodes the child's symbolic expressions.

A child I worked with in play therapy often made drawings, clay models, and even *papier maché* volcano renditions over a period of months while he dealt with strong aggressive impulses and anger toward his parents, who not only were drug abusers, but had frequent violent arguments and fights. Through his art forms, play, and my interpretations, he began to understand his rage and inability to control his parents' behavior. The repetition of his volcano images helped him release tension and work through unacceptable feelings. He also was able to recognize and deal with his sense of helplessness that had been manifested through the opposite emotion of anger. When children tell stories about their renditions, they reveal some of the intrapsychic difficulties that were deeply hidden but now emerge stimulated by the art form.

An interesting use of art therapy with children aged 6 and 13 with learning disabilities and limited impulse control is described by Fino (1979). The children had been in individual therapy in a psychiatric outpatient department of a hospital. The group met twice weekly in 3-hour sessions for a twelve-week period. After the eighth week, when children had been successful in drawing self-portraits, drawings of each other, joint pictures (by pairs of children), and a picture drawn in parts, a new task was introduced. Children were told to image themselves as astronauts traveling to the moon in a rocket. The instruction was to move bodies, not mouths, to "speak," and this "speaking" could be by drawing imaginary lines in space and pastel lines on paper. Warm-up exercises enabled the children to experience becoming small, large, tall, short, and so forth. Then they slowly "drew" these movements in the space around them. Other imaginary exercises were carried out; the children, in their imaginations, went to the moon, explored the surface, and returned to earth. Finally, the children were instructed to work as a group and draw with pastels everything they could remember on a 3-by-10-foot sheet of paper spread on the floor. They were permitted to write comments on the paper as well. Fino claimed that the guided imagery exercises led to a more enjoyable experience for the children as evidenced by laughter and giggles as the children produced their group picture. Their drawings were less stereotyped than previous efforts, and in general there was a more relaxed mood among the children.

The author cautioned that in attempting a fantasy game of swimming under water to explore the ocean depths, the children lost control and became overstimulated by the contact of bodies on the floor. Carefully selected step-by-step movements and slow pacing seem necessary. In addition, slowly drawing imaginary lines in space paved the way for observations of each other, as did a game of "statues." This preparation led to the success of the group drawing and to the fruitful discussion that followed at the end of the completed project.

Movement and Drama Therapy

The American Dance Therapy Association (1972) defines dance therapy as "the psychotherapeutic use of movement as a process which furthers the emotional and physical integration of the individual." (p. 1). This form of therapy originated as an adjunctive approach in the treatment of psychiatric patients. Although adults were the first patients to receive this therapy, it is now also used with children both in institutional settings and in private practice. Deaf children have been helped through dance therapy and through music, which promotes the use of their residual hearing.

The aspect of movement or dance therapy that is of concern in this chapter is that of imagery and the unconscious processes and their relationship to movement. Movement is believed to facilitate the issuance of fantasies, unconscious memories, and even primitive ways of coping with traumatic experiences. Based on Piagetian theory, it is presumed that the prerepresentational level of concrete action schemas exist in the sensory-motor period of life, during the first eighteen months of infancy. Piaget suggests that long before the child's mental images form, the body movements, grasping, touching, feeling, crawling, and the affective reactions such as smiling help the child make sense of the world, and these motor activities imply the attribution of memory. Later, different behaviors of an individual such as posture, gait, voice, and even handwriting are manifestations of personality and convey much to the skilled movement specialist. The basic premise of these specialists is that changes in personality can occur if the body structure and its functional mobility can be modified. Body movement exercises, physical manipulation of the skeletal musculature, and deep breathing may be part of movement therapy. Dance therapy is even broader in scope. As Geller (1978) states:

> In dance therapy, patients are given the opportunity to move freely in space, to discover or rediscover what it means to play, to discover what it feels like to have sensations in different body parts, to risk abandoning themselves to compelling musical rhythms, to become a member of a cohesive group, to participate in rituals, to spontaneously express or dramatize emotions, to shout or attach concrete images and metaphors to their actions, to touch and be touched by others. [p. 349]

Dance therapists, like art therapists, are trained in special programs and are then registered or certified by their national associations, which set criteria. In some states, they are licensed as professional counselors. Dunne (1988), a registered drama therapist, has an approach based on the philosophy of Carl Rogers and Abraham Maslow. The environment must be safe, relaxed, creative, and trusting. Dunne uses guided imagery techniques as well as pantomime and creative movement relaxation (the therapist plays music with a strong beat and asks the client to mirror it and perform it first with the therapist and then initiate his own movements). Dramatic enactment is improvisational. The subject chosen for enactment can be either a true experience or an imagined one. First, an opening scene is selected; the client chooses roles for himself and for the therapist (the client or therapist may be in primary or secondary roles depending on the comfort of the client). The drama may last from 5 to 30 minutes. After the drama, the therapist asks questions based on issues raised and helps the client reflect on what has transpired. In addition, the therapist asks about areas of unresolved or continuing conflicts. Clients may also draw pictures of an important moment, concern, or conflict, and act these out in pantomime or improvisational scenes based on these pictures. Dunne has used drama therapy with disturbed children and adolescents in one-to-one therapy and believes that her technique, because it is a projective one, helps the client to distance himself from the hypothetical material and feel safe and less exposed. It is different from psychodrama where more direct, confrontational approaches are used and the chosen scenes are actually drawn from the client's life.

Case Illustrations: Adjusting to Divorce and Overcoming Phobia

I have chosen two cases from my practice to illustrate applications of Guided Affective Imagery (GAI) and systematic desensitization. In both instances, these techniques were used along with more traditional play therapy.

GAI was used with Jean, a 7-year-old child whose parents were recently divorced. The father has remarried and has a child with his new wife. Jean's mother works as a secretary and is a sensitive, caring person who expressed concern about Jean's depression, anger toward her, and Jean's desire to live with her father.

Jean is a pretty, dark-haired child with large brown eyes, but she is thin and pale. During the first weeks of therapy, her expression was usually sad and worried-looking. It was easy to establish rapport with Jean, however, and she entered into house and doll play quite readily. She told me that she wants to live with her father and "argues with Mommy all the time" but didn't seem to know why she was so angry. Jean told me she would say "I hate you" to her mother, but "I don't really hate her, it's just that I don't know why I say that." Jean did bring a book about divorce to our second session and read it to me, but did not seem convinced by the gist of the story – that parents can still love you even if they are divorced.

Since Jean seemed to enjoy puppet play and doll house play, evidencing much imagination, I decided after a month of therapy to try GAI in order to help her uncover some deeper feelings and also to accept the finality of the divorce. I also planned to use GAI for only a small part of each session, allowing her time to draw after the GAI and then to choose whatever game or activity she wished to play during the last part of the session. It was relatively easy for Jean to relax. She quickly got into the spirit of GAI and often, while seated in a comfortable chair, did move her hands and legs to help express her images. I started with the meadow motif and we stayed with that for two sessions when I then introduced animals into the meadow, as Leuner suggests. Jean made the cow (the mother symbol) a frightened animal who would run away whenever an elephant (Jean's own animal interjection) appeared. The elephant was "strong and big like my Dad – if you jump on my Dad with shoes on, it doesn't even hurt him." This elephant played an important role in subsequent GAI sessions, where it chased the cow frequently, but as we progressed through the doll play that followed each GAI session, the cow and elephant became friends.

The cave motif was introduced and became a place where Jean could "hide," and where her "Daddy, king of the cavemen, could stop all the other cavemen from fighting." Drawings after the addition of the cave motif were generally of the elephant, the favorite drawing since it was first introduced by Jean. I followed Leuner's use of the eight motifs, and presented them in the order he outlines. The use of imagery uncovered feelings about Jean's mother that were more tender than the way she was portrayed in doll play. Gradually, some of the cow's gentleness was transferred to a doll who earlier had been portrayed as the "mother-boss" who "got a divorce and chased the father" out of the house. As imagery sessions progressed, each time Jean drew an image she liked, the doll play began to reflect direct changes. The father doll who was the "strong caveman" in the GAI became a more "polite Daddy" figure. Both mother and father dolls learned to become "friends" just as the cow and elephant learned how to "drink from the same pond" and play together. We had sixteen GAI sessions, carried out twice a week over a two-month period. During this time, Jean's relationship with her mother improved. Jean was able to accept the finality of the divorce and no longer needed to see her parents as battling. She was able to "come out of the cave" and face the "nice animals in the meadow," such as the "deer and birds" and even the "mean ones who chase you." She could accept her mother as capable of protecting her and loving her, while the "king" no longer needed to assert his power.

The second case involved 6-year-old Meggin, who was phobic and was treated with systematic desensitization. Her parents both worked, spent relatively little time with her, and left her in the care of a loving, but psychologically naive, housekeeper. Meggin was particularly afraid of ceiling fans, which were used instead of air conditioning to cool the house. Meggin's problems were not confined to phobias. She was extremely shy, withdrawn, overweight, and to add to her difficulties, enuretic. Again, as in Jean's case, my main course of treatment was play therapy, but to deal with the enuresis, a behavior modification plan including an apparatus – the liquid sensitive pad and alarm similar to that proposed by Mowrer and Mowrer (1938) – was used at night.

Systematic desensitization involved first teaching Meggin to relax and image a mildly anxiety-provoking cue that was paired with the relaxation. A hierarchy was then defined, using the noise of Meggin's mother's electric mixer as least feared and the ceiling fan as most feared. In addition, I asked Meggin to rate herself on a scale from 1 to 10 to describe her degree of fear as each item on the hierarchy was offered. This training continued for ten sessions with noticeable reduction of anxiety as we approached the fan item on the list. Meggin was also encouraged to free-associate about the fan. She began to image "flying witches who whirred through the air," and told me about a "scary story" she heard in school before Halloween and at about the time her phobia began. Meggin had such vivid images and dreams about this flying witch that she had found it hard to separate the noise of the fan, which was on at night when her parents were up late sitting in the kitchen, from her images and dreams. Somehow the fan and the flying witch became one for Meggin and her fears began. Through systematic de-sensitization, drawing pictures, and later her willingness to talk about her associations to the fan, Meggin was able to control her fears. If she entered the kitchen, Meggin used her deep breathing and image of a less threatening item on the list (such as a vacuum cleaner, or her father's car starting up) to cope with the fan's noise. Once this phobia was eliminated, Meggin was able to deal with some of her other issues in a more receptive way.

Applications of Imagery Techniques in Educational Settings

The thrust of this chapter has been mainly on clinical uses of imagery. There is some pioneering work, however, utilizing imagery techniques with more normal populations in school settings. Briefly, imagery and fantasy techniques have been successfully used with disadvantaged preschoolers (Saltz and Johnson 1974). The researchers found that fantasy play was significantly related to a higher incidence of spontaneous sociodramatic play, to higher scores on certain subtests of IQ measures, to superior performance on a test of interpersonal perception, and to better story-memory and story-telling skills on specifically constructed tasks. Saltz and Dixon (1982) examined the usefulness of motoric imagery in memory for sentences and words. Subjects in their experiments ranged from ages 5 to 9. Results indicate that motoric imagery – that is, repeating a word such as "monkey" and demonstrating what a monkey can do, such as climbing – facilitated memory under conditions where visual memory with no enactment had no effect. A sizeable component of the meaning of stories can be mediated by motoric actions, and may be useful in helping children comprehend and remember these stories.

In a clever experiment dealing with memory, Tomasulo (1982–1983) assessed children's ability to recall normal, low bizarre, and high bizarre line-drawn interactive objects as pairs. Older children (55 months) were able to do well in all three conditions, while younger children (42 months) found bizarre matchings difficult to recall. An example of a bizarre image would be a fish smoking a pipe. The author suggests that the effect of bizarre imagery on memory is a function of cognitive maturity. The rich imagery that some isolated or shy children produce in their natural play situations in preschool settings could be used by the sensitive teacher to help children gain control over some of their impulses or help them learn how to develop better interpersonal skills (Paley 1988, 1990, Singer 1986).

Older children as well can profit from imagery training in the schools. Creative drama is used in some classrooms to help children develop socialization skills, ability to think on one's feet, and develop "as if" behavior (McCaslin 1984, Rosenberg 1987, Rosenberg and Pinciotte 1983–1984). The essential phases are imaging, enacting, and reflecting. Materials using imaging exercises such as those used in play therapy, which were described earlier, have been effectively utilized in elementary school classrooms. Music can also be used to help children explore their inner feelings (Bonny and Savary 1973). Relaxation training with large groups of children aged 10 to 18 has been already described in this chapter (Setterlind 1982). Guided Affective Imagery (GAI) has been used in elementary and secondary schools (Galyean 1982–1983). Mind games to help high school children perform more effectively in mathematics and science are offered in a provocative book by Barell (1980), and Finke (1989) advocates the use of mental practice for athletes preparing themselves for a sporting event. This ideomotor effect refers to a subtle tendency for movements to be initiated automatically whenever such movements are imaged. These movements are especially useful in helping the athlete coordinate hand and foot movements. Finke believes that mental imagery can also be useful for prospective inventors, and for experts such as physicists, architects, engineers, designers, and even business people. Finally, Tower (1982–1983) has developed an imagery training model that could easily be adapted for students. She points out the relationships among imagery, imagination, and creativity, and suggests that imagery training should include all sensory modalities.

Looking to the Future

I have attempted to trace definitions of imagery and theory to the practical applications of imagery in clinical and educational settings. There are numerous definitions, types of imagery, and various methods utilizing imagery techniques with children. Much of the research has been with college students and other adults, but the studies that were cited demonstrate considerable success with children when intrapsychic conflicts can be tapped through images and symbols.

The recent reawakening in the study of imagery and the development of new techniques and approaches to facilitate fantasy production suggests a vast potential for the benefits of these methods. Some psychotherapists, as noted, have used imagery with their clients to reduce anxiety, transform attitudes, effect cognitive and behavioral changes, release repressed memories, express painful emotions, and gain relief from boredom and fears. The use of fantasy as a coping skill is only one aspect of this human capacity. Fantasy can afford us pleasure, stimulate creativity, and lead to a more positive outlook.

What is needed, it seems, is more systematic, rigorous investigation of imagery methods with children. In addition, psychotherapists who use play therapy might try to venture into this realm of imagination and pay more attention to the fantasy productions of their clients. The therapist is the facilitator, teacher, and guide who uses a variety of techniques to help the child relax, attend to mental images and later, relate these images to current concerns. In Jean's fantasy, cited earlier, mother was tender, but in her play, mother was portrayed as bossy and mean—the everyday, realistic, child's view of a harassed single parent. The images uncovered Jean's true feelings toward her mother, feelings she was afraid to show. In the playgrounds of our minds we may find some answers that will make life more tolerable and perhaps more of an adventure into the possible.

References

Ahsen, A. (1972). *Eidetic Parents Test and Analysis.* New York: Brandon House.
_____ (1984). Imagery, drama and transformation. *Journal of Mental Imagery* 8:53–78.
American Dance Therapy Association (1972). *What is dance therapy really?* Combined proceedings for the 5th and 7th annual conferences, 1970 and 1972. Columbia, MD: American Dance Therapy Association.
Applebee, A. N. (1978). *The Child's Concept of Story.* Chicago: University of Chicago Press.
Aylwin, S. (1990). Imagery and affect: big questions, little answers. In *Imagery: Current Developments,* ed. P. J. Hampson, D. E. Marks, and J. T. E. Richardson, pp. 247–267. London: Routledge.

Barell, J. (1980). *Playgrounds of Our Minds.* New York: Teachers College Press.

Benton, A. L. (1963). *Revised Visual Retention Test: Manual.* New York: Psychological Corporation.

Bonny, H., and Savary, L. (1973). *Music and Your Mind.* New York: Harper & Row.

Bott, J., and Klinger, E. (1985-1986). Assessment of guided affective imagery: methods for extracting quantitative and categorical variables from imagery sequences. *Imagination, Cognition and Personality* 5:279-293.

Brandell, J. R. (1988). Narrative and historical truth in child psychotherapy. *Psychoanalytical Psychology* 5:241-257.

Bruner, J. S. (1964). The course of cognitive growth. *American Psychologist* 19:1-15.

_____ (1990). *Acts of Meaning.* Cambridge, MA: Harvard University Press.

Cautela, J. R., and McCullough, L. (1978). Covert conditioning: a learning theory perspective on imagery. In *The Power of Human Imagination: New Methods in Psychotherapy,* ed. J. L. Singer and K. S. Pope, pp. 227-254. New York: Plenum.

Csikszentmihalyi, M. (1984). *Being Adolescent: Conflict and Growth in the Teenage Years.* New York: Basic Books.

Dement, W., and Kleitman, N. (1957). The relationship of eye movements during sleep to dream activity: an objective method for the study of dreaming. *Journal of Experimental Psychology* 53:339-346.

de Mille, R. (1973). *Put Your Mother on the Ceiling.* New York: Viking.

Dunne, P. B. (1988). Drama therapy techniques in one-to-one treatment with disturbed children and adolescents. *Arts in Psychotherapy* 15:139-149.

Ebrahim, D., Elliott, J. E., and Summers, J. K. (1982). The use of hypnosis with children and adolescents. *International Journal of Clinical and Experimental Hypnosis* 30:189-234.

Edwards, S. S. (1978). Multimodal therapy with children: a case analysis of insect phobia. *Elementary School Guidance and Counseling* 13:23-29.

Farah, M. J. (1984). The neurological basis of mental imagery: a componential analysis. *Cognition* 18:245-272.

Finke, R. A. (1989). *Principles of Mental Imagery.* Cambridge, MA: MIT Press.

_____ (1990). *Creative Imagery: Discoveries and Inventions in Visualization.* Hillsdale, NJ: Lawrence Erlbaum.

Fino, J. K. (1979). Guided imagery and movement as a means to help disturbed children draw together. *American Journal of Art Therapy* 18:61-62.

Fromm, E. (1951). *The Forgotten Language.* New York: Rinehart & Co.

_____ (1982). The essential aspects of self-hypnosis. *International Journal of Clinical and Experimental Hypnosis* 30:189-234.

Galyean, B. C. (1982-1983). The use of guided imagery in elementary school. *Imagination, Cognition and Personality* 2:145-151.

Gardner, R. A. (1983). Treating oedipal problems with the mutual storytelling technique. In *Handbook of Play Therapy,* ed. C. E. Schaefer and K. J. O'Connor, pp. 355-368. New York: John Wiley & Sons.

Geller, J. D. (1978). The body, expressive movement, and physical contact in psychotherapy. In *The Power of the Human Imagination: New Methods in Psychotherapy,* ed. J. L. Singer and K. S. Pope, pp. 347-378. New York: Plenum.

Giambra, L. M. (1974). Daydreaming across the life span: late adolescent to senior citizens. *International Journal of Aging and Human Development* 5:115-140.

Goodnow, J. (1977). *Children Drawing.* Cambridge, MA: Harvard University Press.

Gordon, R. (1950). An experiment correlating the nature of imagery with performance on a test of reversal of perspective. *British Journal of Psychology* 41:63–67.

Gottlieb, S. (1973). Modeling effects upon fantasy. In *The Child's World of Make Believe*, ed. J. L. Singer, pp. 155–182. New York: Academic.

Gould, R. (1972). *Child Studies through Fantasy*. New York: Quadrangle Books.

Graziano, A. M., and Kean, J. E. (1971). Programmed relaxation and reciprocal inhibition with psychotic children. In *Behavior Therapy with Children*, ed. A. M. Graziano, pp. 215–219. New York: Aldine Atherton.

Haber, R. N. (1979). Twenty years of haunting eidetic imagery: where's the ghost? *Behavioral and Brain Sciences* 2:583–629.

Hammer, E. (1980). *The Clinical Application of Projective Drawings*. Springfield, IL: Charles C Thomas.

Hampson, P. J., and Morris, P. E. (1990). Imagery, consciousness and cognitive control: the boss model reviewed. In *Imagery: Current Developments*, ed. P. J. Hampson, D. E. Marks, and J. T. E. Richardson, pp. 78–102. London: Routledge.

Harris, S. L., and Ferrari, M. (1983). Developmental factors in child behavior therapy. *Behavior Therapy* 14:54–72.

Hellendoorn, J. (1988). Imaginative play technique in psychotherapy with children. In *Innovative Interventions in Child and Adolescent Therapy*, ed. C. E. Schaefer, pp. 43–67. New York: John Wiley & Sons.

Horowitz, M. J. (1978). *Image Formation and Cognition*. 2nd ed. New York: Appleton-Century-Crofts.

Johnson, M. R., Whitt, J. K., and Martin, B. (1987). The effect of fantasy facilitation of anxiety in chronically ill and healthy children. *Journal of Pediatric Psychology* 12:273–282.

Kazdin, A. E. (1988). *Child Psychotherapy: Developing and Identifying Effective Treatments*. New York: Pergamon.

Kelly, E. (1973). *The Magic If*. New York: Drama Book Specialists.

Khatena, J. (1978). Frontiers of creative imagination imagery. *Journal of Mental Imagery* 2:33–46.

Khatena, J., and Torrance, E. P. (1973). *Thinking Creatively with Sounds and Words: Norms Technical Manual*. Rev. ed. Lexington, MA: Personnel.

Klessman, E. (1983). Special features of working with Guided Affective Imagery in the treatment of children and adolescents. In *Guided Affective Imagery with Children and Adolescents*, ed. H. Leuner, G. Horn, and E. Klessman, pp. 41–58. New York: Plenum.

Klinger, E. (1971). *Structure and Function of Fantasy*. New York: John Wiley & Sons.

———— (1980). Therapy and the flow of thought. In *Imagery: Its Many Dimensions and Applications*, ed. J. E. Shorr, G. E. Sobel, P. Robin, and J. A. Connelia, pp. 1–20. New York: Plenum.

———— (1990). *Daydreaming*. Los Angeles: Jeremy P. Tarcher.

Koch, K. (1970). *Wishes, Lies and Dreams: Teaching Children to Write Poetry*. New York: Vintage Books.

Korn, E. R., and Johnson, K. (1983). *Visualization: The Uses of Imagery in the Health Profession*. Homewood, IL: Dow Jones–Irwin.

Kosslyn, S. M. (1980). *Image and Mind*. Cambridge, MA: Harvard University Press.

———— (1983). *Ghosts in the Mind's Machine*. New York: Norton.

Kosslyn, S. M., Margolis, J. A., Barrett, A. M., et al. (1990). Age differences in imagery abilities. *Child Development* 61:995–1010.

Kosslyn, S. M., Van Kleeck, M. H., and Kirby, K. M. (1990). A neurologically plausible model of individual differences in visual mental imagery. In *Imagery: Current Developments*, ed. P. J. Hampson, D. F. Marks, and J. T. E. Richardson, pp. 39–77. London: Routledge.

Kramer, E. (1971). *Art as Therapy with Children*. New York: Schocken.

_____ (1979). *Children and Art Therapy*. New York: Schocken.

Lazarus, A. A., and Abramovitz, A. (1962). The use of "emotive imagery" in the treatment of children's phobias. *Journal of Mental Science* 108:191–195.

Leuner, H., Horn, G., and Klessman, E. (1983). *Guided Affective Imagery with Children and Adolescents*. New York: Plenum.

Lusebrink, V. B. (1990). *Imagery and Visual Expression in Therapy*. New York: Plenum.

Marks, D. F. (1973). Visual imagery differences in the recall of pictures. *British Journal of Psychology* 64:17–24.

_____ (1990). On the relationship between imagery, body and mind. In *Imagery: Current Developments*, ed. P. J. Hampson, D. F. Marks, and J. T. E. Richardson, pp. 1–38. London: Routledge.

Martin, M., and Williams, R. (1990). Imagery and emotion: clinical and experimental approaches. In *Imagery: Current Developments*, ed. P. J. Hampson, D. F. Marks, and J. T. E. Richardson, pp. 268–306. London: Routledge.

McCaslin, N. (1984). *Creative Drama in the Classroom*. New York: Longman.

McIlwraith, R. D., and Schallow, J. R. (1982–1983). Television viewing and styles of children's fantasy. *Imagination, Cognition and Personality* 2:323–331.

Meichenbaum, D. H., and Goodman, J. (1971). Training impulsive children to talk to themselves: a means of developing self-control. *Journal of Abnormal Psychology* 77:115–126.

Meltzoff, A., and Moore, M. K. (1983). Newborn infants imitate adult facial gestures. *Child Development* 54:702–709.

Mischel, W., Ebbeson, E. B., and Zeiss, A. R. (1972). Cognitive and attentional mechanisms in delay of gratification. *Journal of Personality and Social Psychology*, 21:204–218.

Morris, P. E., and Hampson, P. J. (1983). *Imagery and Consciousness*. New York: Academic.

Mowrer, O. H., and Mowrer, W. A. (1938). Enuresis: a method for its study and treatment. *American Journal of Orthopsychiatry* 8:436–447.

Neubauer, P. B. (1987). Disturbances in object representation. In *Psychoanalytic Study of the Child*, ed. P. B. Neubauer and A. J. Solnit, 42:335–351. New York: Quadrangle.

Norman, D. A. (1976). *Memory and Attention*. 2nd ed. New York: John Wiley & Sons.

Paivio, A. (1970). On the functional significance of imagery. *Psychological Bulletin* 73:415–421.

_____ (1971). *Imagery and Verbal Processes*. New York: Holt, Rinehart & Winston.

Paley, V. G. (1988). *Bad Guys Don't Have Birthdays*. Chicago, IL: University of Chicago Press.

_____ (1990). *The Boy Who Would be a Helicopter*. Cambridge, MA: Harvard University Press.

Piaget, J. (1962). *Play, Dreams and Imitation in Childhood*. New York: Norton.

Piaget, J., and Inhelder, B. (1967). *The Child's Conception of Space*. New York: Norton.

_____ (1971). *Mental Imagery in the Child*. New York: Basic Books.

Pitcher, E. G., and Prelinger, E. (1963). *Children Tell Stories*. New York: International Universities Press.

Purkel, W., and Bornstein, M. H. (1980). Pictures and imagery both enhance children's short-term memory and long-term recall. *Developmental Psychology* 16:153–154.

Reyher, J. (1963). Free imagery: an uncovering procedure. *Journal of Clinical Psychology* 19:454–459.

Reyher, J., and Morishige, H. (1969). Electroencephalogram with rapid eye movements during free imagery and dream recall. *Journal of Abnormal Psychology* 74:576–582.

Roffwag, H. P., Muzio, J., and Dement, W. C. (1966). The ontogenetical development of the human sleep dream cycle. *Science* 152:604–618.

Rorschach, H. (1942). *Psychodiagnostics.* New York: Grune & Stratton.

Rosenberg, H. S. (1987). *Creative Drama and Imagination.* New York: Holt, Rinehart & Winston.

Rosenberg, H. S., and Pinciotte, P. (1983–1984). Imagery in creative drama. *Imagination, Cognition and Personality* 3:69–76.

Rosenfeld, E., Huesmann, L. R., Eron, L., and Torney-Purta, J. V. (1982). Measuring patterns of fantasy behavior in children. *Journal of Personality and Social Psychology* 42:347–366.

Rosenstiel, A. K., and Scott, D. S. (1977). Four considerations in using imagery techniques with children. *Journal of Behavior Therapy and Experimental Psychiatry* 8:287–290.

Rubin, J. A. (1987). Freudian psychoanalytic theory: emphasis on uncovering and insight. In *Approaches to Art Therapy: Theory and Technique,* ed. J. A. Rubin, pp. 7–25. New York: Brunner/Mazel.

Russ, S. W., and Grossman-McKee, A. (1990). Affective expression in children's fantasy play, primary process thinking on the Rorschach, and divergent thinking. *Journal of Personality Assessment* 54:756–771.

Saltz, E., and Dixon, D. (1982). Let's pretend: the role of motoric imagery in memory for sentences and words. *Journal of Experimental Child Psychology* 34:77–92.

Saltz, E., and Johnson, J. (1974). Training for thematic-fantasy play in culturally disadvantaged children. *Journal of Educational Psychology* 66:623–630.

Schoettle, U. C. (1980). Guided imagery: a tool in psychotherapy. *American Journal of Psychotherapy* 34:220–227.

Segal, B., Huba, G. J., and Singer, J. L. (1980). *Drugs, Daydreaming and Personality: A Study of College Youth.* Hillsdale, NJ: Lawrence Erlbaum.

Segal, B., and Singer, J. L. (1976). Daydreaming, drug, and alcohol use in college students: a factor analytic study. *Addictive Behavior* 1:227–235.

Setterlind, S. (1982). Teaching children to relax. *International Journal of Clinical and Experimental Hypnosis* 30:189–234.

Sheehan, P. W. (1967). Visual imagery and the organizational properties of perceived stimuli. *British Journal of Psychology* 58:247–252.

Sheikh, A. A. (1978). Eidetic psychotherapy. In *The Power of Human Imagination: New Methods in Psychotherapy,* ed. J. L. Singer and K. S. Pope, pp. 197–224. New York: Plenum.

Sherrod, L. R., and Singer, J. L. (1984). The development of make-believe play. In *Sports, Games and Play,* ed. J. H. Goldstein, pp. 1–38. Hillsdale, NJ: Lawrence Erlbaum.

Shorr, J. E. (1974). *Shorr Imagery Test.* Los Angeles: Institute for Psycho-Imagination Therapy.

Singer, D. G. (1986). Encouraging children's imaginative play: suggestions for parents and teachers. In *Play-Play Therapy-Play Research,* ed. R. van der Kooij and J. Hellendoorn, pp. 89–99. The Netherlands: Swets & Zeitlinger.

Singer, D. G., and Singer, J. L. (1990). *The House of Make Believe: Play and the Developing Imagination.* Cambridge, MA: Harvard University Press.

Singer, J. A., and Salovey, P. (1988). Mood and memory: evaluating the network theory of affect. *Clinical Psychology Review* 8:211–251.

Singer, J. L. (1973). *The Child's World of Make-Believe.* New York: Academic Press.

_____ (1974). *Imagery and Daydream Methods in Psychotherapy and Behavior Modification.* New York: Academic.

_____ (1978). Experimental studies of daydreaming and the stream of thought. In *The Stream of Consciousness,* ed. K. S. Pope and J. L. Singer, pp. 187–223. New York: Plenum.

_____ (1986). The development of imagination in early childhood: foundations of play therapy. In *Play-Play Therapy-Play Research,* ed. R. van der Kooij and J. Hellendoorn, pp. 105–131. The Netherlands: Swets & Zeitlinger.

_____ (1988). The conscious and unconscious stream of thought. In *Energy Synthesis in Science,* ed. D. Pines, pp. 142–180. New York: John Wiley & Sons.

Singer, J. L., and Antrobus, J. S. (1972). Daydreaming, imaginal processes and personality: a normative study. In *The Function and Nature of Imagery,* ed. P. W. Sheehan, pp. 175–202. New York: Academic.

Singer, J. L., and Bonanno, G. A. (1990). Personality and private experience: individual variations in consciousness and in attention to subjective phenomena. In *Handbook of Personality: Theory and Research,* ed. L. Pervin, pp. 419–444. New York: Guilford.

Singer, J. L., and Kolligian, J., Jr. (1987). Personality developments in the study of private experience. *Annual Review of Psychology* 38:553–574.

Singer, J. L., and Pope, K. S., eds. (1978). *The Power of Human Imagination: New Methods in Psychotherapy.* New York: Plenum.

Singer, J. L., and Singer, D. G. (1981). *Television, Imagination and Aggression: A Study of Preschoolers.* Hillsdale, NJ: Lawrence Erlbaum.

Somers, J. U., and Yawkey, T. D. (1984). Imaginary play companions: contributions of creative and intellectual abilities of young children. *Journal of Creative Behavior* 18:77–89.

Spivack, G., and Shure, M. B. (1982). The cognition of social adjustment: interpersonal cognitive problem solving thinking. In *Advances in Clinical Child Psychology,* ed. B. B. Lakey and A. E. Kazdin, vol. 5, pp. 323–372. New York: Plenum.

Starker, S. (1982). *Fantastic Thoughts: All about Dreams, Daydreams, Hallucinations and Hypnosis.* Englewood Cliffs, NJ: Prentice-Hall.

Tilley, A. J. (1981). Retention over a period of REM or non-REM sleep. *British Journal of Psychology* 72:241–248.

Tomasulo, D. J. (1982–1983). Effects of bizarre imagery on children's memory. *Imagination, Cognition and Personality* 2:134–144.

Torrance, E. P., Khatena, J., and Cunnigton, B. F. (1973). *Thinking Creatively with Sounds and Words.* Lexington, MA: Personnel.

Tower, R. B. (1979). *The physiological measurement of visual imagery.* Unpublished manuscript, Yale University.

_____ (1982–1983). Imagery training: a workshop model. *Imagination, Cognition and Personality* 2:153–162.

Tower, R. B., and Singer, J. L. (1981). The measurement of imagery: how can it be clinically useful? In *Cognitive-Behavioral Interventions: Assessment Methods,* ed. P. C. Kendall and S. Holland, pp. 119–159. New York: Academic.

Uhlin, D. M., and DeChiara, E. (1984). *Art for Exceptional Children.* 3rd ed. Dubuque, IA: Wm. C. Brown.

Vernon, J. A. (1963). *Inside the Black Room.* New York: Clarkson Potter.

Wertheimer, M. (1945). *Productive Thinking.* New York: Harper & Brothers.

Wolpe, J. (1958). *Psychotherapy by Reciprocal Inhibition.* Stanford, CA: Stanford University Press.

Wood, M. (1986). The circular floor painting game. In *Play-Play Therapy-Play Research,* ed. R. van der Kooij and J. Hellendoorn, pp. 145–151. The Netherlands: Swets & Zeitlinger.

10

Learning by Metaphor

Diane E. Frey

A father once brought home a rabbit, intending it to be a family pet. As he was discussing the rabbit with his family, he was called to an emergency phone call. When he returned, his wife had cooked the rabbit. The father was very upset and told his wife that the rabbit spoke five languages! His wife said, "Why didn't he say something then?" [Frey 1984, p. 29]

Such a metaphor has relevance to children and adults. While metaphors can be interpreted in many different ways, a common message of this metaphor is that it is important to use one's abilities. This metaphor could be used in a variety of ways with children, but has particular relevance for underachieving children.

The significant difference between the use of metaphors in therapy and the use of metaphors in other settings is in the goal(s). Metaphors outside of the therapeutic setting, such as stories told by grandparents, or fairy tales, aim to teach specific messages and make definite points. The goal(s) of therapeutic metaphors is to offer new choices, show different ways of perceiving a situation, and tap a variety of dormant beliefs, attitudes, and values of the child. The therapist creates individualized metaphors for the child, based on psychodynamic qualities.

Metaphors can have many different forms. They can be allegories, analogies, similes, proverbs, anecdotes, stories, parables, art, objects (for example, puppets, toy animals, toy trucks), cartoons, poetry, music, and games. According to Mills and Crowley (1986), metaphor has been used for centuries as a method of teaching in many fields. Lakoff and Turner (1989) write that metaphor lets us understand ourselves and our world in unique ways, and that we automatically acquire a mastery of metaphor when we are children.

An example of analogy as a metaphor could be when a child says he feels like a toy top sometimes – dizzy and confused. Children in play therapy often say they feel like a certain toy or stuffed animal. Analogies and similes can also be effectively used by the therapist to help children learn about feelings.

Anecdotes, Proverbs, and Parables

It is not unusual for children to hear proverbs such as "The grass is always greener on the other side of the fence," or "People in glass houses shouldn't throw stones."

Proverbs can be a less threatening way of communicating with them than telling the message directly. However, proverbs are sometimes overused or become clichés. As such, this use needs to be limited.

The following is an example of an anecdote as a metaphor (Frey 1984):

> Once there was a woman who was walking through a park. She saw a man and a dog playing together on a nearby park bench. When she got closer to them she asked the man what the dog's name was. The man replied that the dog's name was Rover. The woman said, "Does your dog bite?" to which the man replied, "No." The woman then proceeded to pet the dog whereupon the dog viciously tore into the woman's hand and arm. The woman, profusely bleeding and very upset with the man, said, "I thought you said your dog didn't bite!" The man responded, "That's not my dog. *My* dog doesn't bite." [p. 29]

Many meanings can be derived from such an anecdote. For example, a situation might not always be the way it seems upon first viewing it; or, a person does not necessarily know everything about everything; or, be cautious about initially trusting others. There can be many interpretations of this anecdote for children.

A story often used with children in play therapy to help them understand another person's point of view is *The Maligned Wolf* by Leaf Fern, which can be acted out using costumes or puppets (Palomares 1984):

> The forest was my home. I lived there and I cared about it. I tried to keep it neat and clean. Then one sunny day, while I was cleaning up some garbage a camper had left behind, I heard footsteps. I leaped behind a tree and saw a rather plain little girl coming down the trail carrying a basket. I was suspicious of this little girl right away because she was dressed funny – all in red, and her head covered up so it seemed like she didn't want people to know who she was, where she was going, where she had come from, and all that. Naturally, I stopped to check her out. I asked who she was, where she was going, where she had come from, and all that. She gave me a song and dance about going to her grandmother's house with a basket of lunch. She appeared to be a basically honest person, but she was in my forest and she certainly looked suspicious with that strange getup of hers. So I decided to teach her just how serious it is to prance through the forest unannounced and dressed funny.

> I let her go on her way, but I ran ahead to her grandmother's house. When I saw that nice old woman, I explained my problem and she agreed that her granddaughter needed to learn a lesson, all right. The old woman agreed to stay out of sight until I called her. Actually, she hid under the bed.

> When the girl arrived, I invited her into the bedroom where I was in the bed, dressed like the grandmother. The girl came in all rosy-cheeked and said something nasty about my big ears. I've been insulted before so I made the best of it by suggesting that my big ears would help me to hear better. Now, what I meant was that I liked her and wanted to pay close attention to what she was saying. But she makes another insulting crack about my bulging eyes. Now you can see how I was beginning to feel about this girl who put on such a nice front, but was apparently a very nasty person. Still, I've made it a policy to turn

the other cheek, so I told her that my big eyes helped me to see her better.

Her next insult really got to me. I've got this problem with having big teeth. And that little girl made an insulting crack about them. I know that I should have better control, but I leaped up from that bed and growled that my teeth would help me to eat her better.

Now let's face it—no wolf could ever eat a little girl, everyone knows that—but that crazy girl started running around the house screaming—me chasing her to calm her down. I'd taken off the grandmother's clothes, but that seemed to make it worse. And all of a sudden the door came crashing open and a big lumberjack is standing there with his axe. I looked at him and all of a sudden it became clear that I was in trouble. There was an open window behind me and out I went.

I'd like to say that was the end of it. But that Grandmother character never did tell my side of the story. Before long the word got around that I was a mean, nasty guy. Everybody started avoiding me. I don't know about that little girl with the funny red outfit, but I didn't live happily ever after. In fact, now us wolves are practically extinct! And I'm sure that little girl's story has a lot to do with it! [pp. 118–119]

Parable use, like proverb use, is best when it is not cliched. Parables such as *The Sun and The Wind* (Eberle and Hall 1975) seem to be effective for children in play therapy:

One day the Sun and the Wind were arguing about their power, each claiming to be the more powerful. Suddenly, the Sun spied a man walking along the beach. "Aha," said the Sun. "The man walking along the beach can settle this argument for us. The one who causes the man to take off his coat is the more powerful." The Wind demanded first chance, and the Sun slipped behind a cloud to watch. At first the Wind blew gently and the man walked a little more briskly. Then the wind blew cool and a little harder and the man scowled, walked faster and drew his coat together. The Wind became angry and blew as hard as he could, and the man frowned, buttoned his coat and jogged along the beach. The Sun took his turn and smiled gently as he sent a few warming rays toward the man. The man slowed to a walk, returned the smile, and removed his coat. [p. 81]

Children who believe aggressive and confrontational styles of conflict management are the only or best method of solving problems could benefit from this parable metaphor.

Use of Art Forms in Play Therapy

Figure 10–1, completed by a child in play therapy, was described by the child as follows: "Here is a flower, here is a flower dying, here is a flower which is dead." He was a victim of physical and verbal abuse, and the flower represented himself. As such, this is a good example of the use of art as a metaphysical communication in play therapy.

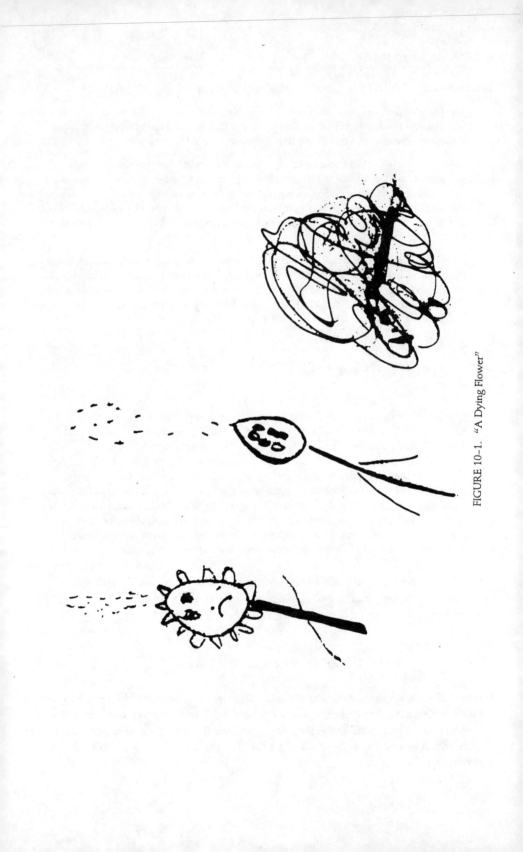

FIGURE 10-1. "A Dying Flower"

Mills and Crowley (1986) discuss the use of the "Pain Getting Better Book" with children in therapy. In this approach, the child is asked to draw how his pain is right now, how the pain would look when it is "all better," and what will help the first picture change into the second picture. This approach for helping children in pain is another example of the use of drawings as metaphors. Many other art forms can be used to create metaphors, including clay and paints.

Objects as metaphors are used often in play therapy. Puppets can often communicate to others information that cannot be said directly. For example, a child client during a puppet play suddenly stopped the interaction among the puppets and indicated that the hero puppet of the play just couldn't go on with the story. The puppet flopped over the stage. When asked what was wrong with the puppet, the child informed the therapist that he needed much more love, hugs, and kisses. The child came from a physically abusive home and was in foster care. He was beginning to recognize that his need for affection was not being met but could only communicate this through puppeting. Likewise, through puppeting, the therapist used metaphors to teach the child how to ask for affection.

Toy tricks, guns, animals, typewriters, and telephones, to name only a few, can also serve as metaphorical objects. These objects symbolically represent other people or things to the child in therapy, and help the child learn to express his feelings. Metaphorical objects can also be given to the child to take home from therapy. A creation out of clay might represent the self in the process of becoming and, as such, be helpful to have at home as a concrete reminder of therapy goals. Children often give therapists gifts of their metaphorical objects.

Cartoons also have metaphorical uses in play therapy since they can be symbolic of the child's experiences. Children frequently bring cartoons to therapy, draw cartoons in therapy, and respond to cartoons presented to them in therapy. It is not uncommon for children to be very interested in the "cartoon-for-the-day" type of calendar that can be found on many professionals' desks. Children, of course, are most responsive to those cartoons that have relevance to them. Child clients of low self-esteem often relate to Ziggy cartoons and the Charlie Brown character in Peanuts. Mills and Crowley (1986) suggest asking children to select a cartoon character who could help them cope with problems. The child is then asked to draw such a character and then tell a story about it.

Children often communicate using metaphors in poetry. Poetry is naturally metaphorical and can also be used by the play therapist quite effectively.

Many forms of music use metaphors. Musical approaches in play therapy can also be very therapeutic. One child, who could change her behavior but could not maintain the change, listened to the play therapist sing "The Itsy Bitsy Spider." The discussion that followed focused on the value of perseverance in attaining and maintaining a new behavior. Later, the play therapist and the child created, with clay, an itsy bitsy spider that became a metaphorical object for the child.

Games can also be used metaphorically with children in play therapy. Card games, checkers, and board games often utilize metaphors. While playing a brief game of ping pong, a child client once expressed his feeling of being much like the ball, tossed back and forth between two parents involved in a custody battle for him. Playing on a see-saw can be a metaphor for the client–therapist relationship and its give-and-take quality – a cooperative venture that involves some risk.

Current events can be woven into metaphorical stories for children. An event such as the opening of a new store presents the opportunity for the play therapist to discuss with the child the concept of new beginnings, and the excitement and hopefulness of such an event with all its promise. This type of metaphor might be especially helpful for a child who is school phobic, mostly due to fear of new beginnings or the unknown.

Universal and Prescriptive Metaphors

Many play therapists choose to use both universal and prescriptive metaphors with the same client. Some situations call for the use of only universal or prescriptive metaphors. Each clinical situation needs to be evaluated individually.

Universal metaphors focus on issues that are common to human existence. Such metaphors might have themes of anger, embarrassment, irrational thoughts, or procrastination, for example (Frey 1984). Prescriptive metaphors focus on specific, unique issues of each child in therapy. Gordon (1978) recommends the following guidelines for developing individualized metaphors:

1. They should be well formed, involving changes over which the child has some control. It would be pointless to use a metaphor in which the child just magically wishes a bad situation to disappear.
2. They should be isomorphic, involving the same environment and situation as the child's. If the child lives in a family with one brother and sister and two parents, the metaphor should have the identical number of people as characters (i.e., a bear family with two parents and a baby bear who has a brother and sister).
3. They should be logically constructed to contain a facilitative message, indirect advice, modeled success, and acceptable problem resolution.
4. They should be deliberately vague, using unspecified verbs and referential indexes. In this way children can fill in the details themselves and, thus, personalize the message.
5. They should be concise and efficient, using the fewest words possible to convey the most powerful image.

Advantages of Metaphor Use for Children

Most children prefer hearing or experiencing metaphors to being talked at by adults. Since children frequently use fantasy as a way of communicating and processing information, metaphors in play therapy are quite easily used. Play therapy often involves the use of fantasy as children, for example, dress up as witches, knights, kings or queens.

Children often speak quite naturally in metaphorical ways. For example, a child once told his father on the way to a therapy session that he knew there was a log in the load of wood in the back of their truck that did not want to come in their house for use in the fireplace. When the father questioned the child about that log, the child said that log just needed to stay outside for awhile. He just wasn't ready to come in yet. The child wanted to know if the log could stay in the garage for awhile; the father consented. This child had been a victim of sexual abuse and had just recently been adopted into this family. His discussion of the log, of course, represented himself.

Children usually like to use concrete ways of communicating. Since play therapy is experiential, it lends itself well to the use of metaphorical objects, stories, music, art, games, and poetry. A child in play therapy once wanted to play the same game of hide and seek every session. He indeed felt as if he was in a real life game of hide and seek, as his divorced parents frequently tried to hide the child and/or kidnap the child from each other. The play in the session became a metaphorical way of describing how he felt.

Much of play therapy involves symbolic interaction. Often a game of checkers is a life metaphor for how children relate to others. Many play therapists report children changing checker rules to their favor when they are losing. Often such children feel that this is how rules have been for them in their life. Other children play checkers by cheating or "accidentally" knocking over the board. Perhaps this is a metaphor of their life experience.

Since children most often feel comfortable with play, play therapy becomes an effective way of building rapport with them. Since metaphor use is a natural part of this interaction, it can be enhanced even more by a knowledgeable play therapist.

Barker (1985) indicates several advantages of using metaphors. First, the use of metaphors is usually more interesting than direct communication. Second, clients interpret their own meanings from metaphors. In this way metaphors are much like projective testing. Third, metaphors are often less threatening and confronting than direct communications. Therefore, they are a good approach to use when children are resistant. If a direct message to the child would be too personal or difficult to deal with, a metaphor can frequently reduce the threat of the communication.

A fourth advantage of metaphors lies in their ability to affect the unconscious mind. A child may experience a metaphor literally on the conscious level and experience the metaphor's symbolic meaning at the unconscious level. Thus, new meaning on many different levels is experienced by the child.

A fifth advantage of metaphors is their ability to communicate in a very direct way to the child through the use of quotations. The power of a metaphor is in its ability to reach the aspects of personality too strongly defended to be reached in other ways. Consequently, a fox in a metaphorical story could say, "That was not a smart decision." The child most likely would not be threatened by such a comment because it was said by a fox.

Metaphors also are an excellent method to establish rapport with children. Children are familiar with metaphors and view this process as fun.

Developmental Issues and Metaphor Use

While there are many advantages to metaphor use with children, there are developmental issues to consider when using them. Gardner and Winner (1982) report that even very young children use metaphors frequently. These metaphors are usually based on physical properties and are usually found in the form of analogies from one physical form to another. For example, a child might liken a potato chip to a frisbee or a yellow balloon to the moon.

By age 3 and 4, metaphor making evolves from action or symbolic play. Since, according to Piaget (1954), children of this age are very concrete and action oriented, a child may twist a pipe cleaner around his finger and pretend to be wearing a ring. Siegelman (1990) states that the rule, therefore, for use of metaphors with preschoolers is that comparisons across domains be based on perceptual resemblance, similarity in action, or both. Santostefano (1988) found that as children progress in therapy, they are more likely to use verbal metaphors than enact nonverbal metaphors.

Gardner and Winner (1982) found that as children enter elementary school, metaphor making diminishes. Children of this age tend to use metaphors that are less vivid, less individualistic, and less imaginative. Elementary school age children do not stop using metaphors; their metaphors are, however, more conventional. By adolescence, the use of metaphors increases again. At this age, students begin to understand the connection between physical and emotional states. Adolescents use metaphors to link the abstract and the concrete. A teenager, for example, might say her love is like a rose.

Theoretical Aspects of Metaphors

Erickson and Rossi (1979) postulate that the brain's right hemisphere is engaged when processing metaphors. And since the right hemisphere is more involved in mediating emotional and imaginative processes, it is most likely where metaphorical language originates. Because symptoms are expressed in the right hemisphere's language, using metaphors may be a direct means of communication with that hemisphere in its own language. More traditional approaches to therapy translate the right hemisphere's language to the left hemisphere, which must then translate back to the right hemisphere in order to change the symptom. Metaphors, by contrast, communicate directly with the right hemisphere.

Clinical Uses of Metaphors

There are many clinical situations with children where metaphors can be very useful. Barker (1985) and Zeig (1980) list the following uses of metaphors in therapy:

Metaphors can be used to illustrate a point. For example, the strong metaphor of the *Wizard of Oz* could be used to illustrate the point that we all have within ourselves those qualities we often seek outside ourselves.

Metaphors can be used to suggest solutions to children; through telling a child a story about how someone managed anger, the therapist can communicate anger management solutions to the child. Direct expressions of these solutions might not be as readily accepted by the child.

Children frequently recognize aspects of themselves by being told through metaphors about other people in similar situations. Children may not accept direct descriptions of themselves from the therapist, but may more readily accept descriptions through metaphors. For example, a child may not recognize himself as having temper tantrums but would accept a description of another child in a similar situation having temper tantrums.

Therapists can often transmit ideas and increase motivation in children through metaphor use. By telling children stories about how other people have overcome similar problems, therapists can increase hopefulness and motivation in child clients. If a therapist tells a client an anecdote about a bear who was very shy but learned to overcome this shyness through various methods, the shy child client gains motivation to pursue behavior change.

Zeig (1980) also stated that metaphors can be used to reframe or redefine a client problem in such a way that the problem is viewed in a different context with a different meaning. For example, a child may learn through metaphors that having a problematic teacher is a stressful situation, but is also an opportunity to learn how to deal with difficult people.

Metaphors can also be used to increase self-esteem. For example, while a child may not accept positive feedback directly, the same child may accept such feedback through metaphors in the form of stories, anecdotes, analogies, or artistic forms.

Children can enhance their communication through the use of metaphors by their therapists. As such, metaphors represent a model for children for more effective communication. It is not unusual for children's metaphor use to increase as the therapist increases their use. Metaphors can also serve to remind children of their own inner resources that they can use to resolve their difficulties. Children are taught, through metaphors, about many coping strategies they have already learned but perhaps have forgotten. Further, children can become desensitized to fear through the use of metaphors. By dealing with the fear indirectly through metaphors, the child is more able to face fear and develop coping strategies.

Mills and Crowley (1986) list a wide variety of applications of metaphors with children in therapy. Their review of the research literature includes such clinical applications as bedwetting, oedipal problems, school phobias, sleep disorders, self-concept enhancement, and thumbsucking. In all these cases, metaphors were successfully used to effect therapeutic change.

Appropriateness of Metaphor Use

Barker (1985) lists four criteria for the use of metaphors in therapy – type of therapy, the clinical situation, the responsiveness of the client, and the preferences and experience level of the therapist.

Certain types of therapy lend themselves more to metaphor use than others. It appears that strategic and systemic therapies, hypnotherapy, and relationship therapies offer more opportunities to use metaphors than do psychoanalytic or behavioral therapy, where metaphor use is more limited. Since therapist activity is focused on asking questions and making comments in psychoanalysis, and on developing a contingency plan in behavioral approaches, the opportunity for metaphor use is more limited. In psychoanalysis and behavior therapy, metaphors may be more useful in the initial stages of therapy and at certain critical points (Barker 1985).

Metaphors are also more appropriate in certain clinical situations than others. Barker indicates that metaphors are especially helpful for pessimistic and resistant clients. Metaphors are also helpful when the direct expression of an idea would upset a client or damage the therapeutic relationship. Metaphors can communicate the idea in a more gentle manner. Children can be enlivened through the use of metaphors when they are becoming bored, restless, or their concentration is dwindling.

Some children accept direct communication very well and, therefore, more indirect methods such as metaphors are less utilized in therapy. Other children who communicate more indirectly through the use of similes, analogies, poetry and/or art are often more effectively treated through therapist metaphors. Children who accept direct communication but intellectualize it are good candidates for metaphor use. By communicating with these children indirectly, less intellectualization occurs and more therapeutic gains are made.

Some child therapists are more at ease with metaphorical communication than others. The effective use of metaphors requires confidence and a feeling of ease with story-telling. If therapists do not initially have these qualities, practice in story-telling outside the therapy session can aid in increasing this skill.

The Processing of Metaphors

Regardless of the type of metaphors being used, the process in this technique includes three phases: identification, projection, and insight and integration (Frey 1984). Through these phases, the child client comes to benefit from metaphor use.

In the identification phase, children align themselves with the significant character of the metaphor. This reaction leads to an emotional investment by the child.

In the projection phase, the child interprets the motives of the character with which he identified, and analyzes the relationships between and among characters. The child develops metaphorical meaning and a moral or lesson is usually learned.

In the insight and integration phase, the child develops a recognition of self and/or significant other in the symbols or characters used in the metaphor. The moral or lesson is integrated into the child's life, often with the assistance of the therapist. This lesson may provide a helpful solution for the child in dealing with difficult problems. In order for metaphors to be used effectively in therapy, all three of these phases need to be processed.

Delivering Metaphors that Are Stories or Anecdotes

Metaphors that are similes or analogies are frequently interspersed in communication with children. When considering the use of a metaphor or anecdote with children in therapy, it is very important to deliver the metaphorical story in a certain manner. First, child therapists who intend to use therapeutic metaphors should make story-telling the norm in their approach to the child from the very first sessions of therapy. According to Barker (1985), the correct context for delivering metaphors is one in which stories are told and tasks are given from the beginning. This sets the expectation for the child to understand that stories are commonly told in therapy sessions. To introduce metaphors out of the blue renders them ineffective.

When story-telling is established as the norm in therapy, certain key phrases can be helpful. These include, "You might be interested in . . ." or "I wonder what you will make of this. . . ." When assigning a therapeutic task to a child through metaphor, the therapist might begin by saying, "An experiment that might be fun for you is . . ." (Barker 1985).

When actually delivering the metaphorical story, Barker suggests the following guidelines:

1. Be prepared with the story before beginning.
2. Vary the pace and style of delivery. Take your time.
3. Give special attention to what needs to be emphasized, such as key phrases, by slowing the delivery or altering tone or pitch.
4. Tell the story in such a way as to make it interesting.
5. Note the response of the client and modify the delivery accordingly.

It is important to be succinct. While the therapist will not want to sacrifice content, the more succinct the story the better the child's concentration will be.

Nonverbal messages offered during the story-telling are also very important. Use gestures, facial expressions, laughter, and variations of voice. The impact of the metaphor on the right hemisphere of the brain may depend more on the nonverbal message than on the verbal message (Watzlawick et al. 1967).

The timing of metaphor use is also important. Similes and analogies are usually interspersed in conversation. Metaphorical stories are best told at or near the end of a session, often presented as a time-filler, especially for resistant clients (Barker 1985). Metaphorical objects such as dolls, toy animals, cars, trucks, ships, ambulances, fire trucks, toy guns, tanks, planes, and/or dollhouses can be introduced into therapy with effectiveness at any time. Due to the symbolic significance of such objects in play therapy, their role as metaphorical objects is invaluable.

Pitfalls in the Use of Metaphors

Siegelman (1990) summarized the major pitfalls of metaphor use in therapy. The first danger seems to be in over-reliance on metaphors. Certainly, metaphors need to be used in conjunction with other therapeutic approaches for children.

The other major pitfall in metaphor use is failure of the therapist to recognize the subtle or implicit metaphors that clients use to communicate to the therapist. Many children use a variety of metaphors; if they go unnoticed by the therapist, a valuable aspect of communication is lost. An example of a subtle metaphorical object used by a child in therapy occurred when a child brought a plastic hibiscus flower in a plastic cap to his therapist, who was known to work and vacation in Hawaii. The child presented the gift as a trick; he wanted to see if the therapist could tell the flower was not real. On a subsequent visit, the child shared with the therapist a small package of macadamia nuts given to him by neighbors who had just returned from a Hawaiian vacation. Although the child said he had brought the nuts as a snack to be shared, clearly any nuts or food could have served this purpose. The symbolic value of the object being Hawaiian unmistakably indicated the child's metaphorical method of trying to establish a relationship and rapport with his therapist. Had the therapist not noticed the metaphorical nature of this communication, a valuable aspect of the therapeutic interaction would have been lost.

In summary, the overuse of metaphors by the therapist and the lack of recognition of metaphors directed to the therapist by children and adults are important potential pitfalls for a therapist to recognize.

Specific Clinical Applications

Of particular interest to the use of metaphors with children is the Resource Board Game developed by Mills and Crowley (1986). This game is created by the child client, and each time the game is played it is created anew. Information from the child is changed into metaphors that represent the child's program and goals, conscious and unconscious blocks, and inner resources. After the child creates the board game, the therapist and child play the game until the child reaches the desired goal.

The game is created by asking the child to draw something he wants to have in his life, something important to him, on the upper corner of a long piece of paper. On the opposite corner of the paper the child is asked to draw a favorite character or object that could help the child attain the goal. Then the child is asked to imagine a map that would lead the character or object to the goal. The child is then asked to draw the map.

Then the child is asked to draw three obstacles that could impede the character from attaining the goal. The instruction to the child might be, for example, "Now draw three things that might get in the way of Leonardo getting the treasure." Next, the child is asked to draw a resource for each obstacle. Each resource is drawn on a separate paper approximately 3″ × 5″. These resource cards represent the child's view of his inner resource to deal with these obstacles. After this, the child is asked to make as many connecting spaces as desired along the way, thus creating the spaces to be used in the game.

Next, the child creates the markers used to move along the spaces. These can be made of clay or any other materials available in the playroom. Last, the therapist or child draws a circle about six inches in diameter and divides it into equal, pie-shaped pieces. The child draws each of the pictures from the resource cards on each of the pie-shaped pieces and numbers each piece with a number from one to six. These numbers represent the die used in the game.

The game begins with the child and the therapist placing their markers on their favorite characters and throwing the die. If the player lands on an obstacle, he or she throws the die until attaining the number necessary to match the resource on the larger resource card. The player is then handed the corresponding 3″ × 5″ resource card, which is the ticket to proceed forward, according to the number on the die thrown. The game proceeds with each player taking a turn until the child reaches the goal. If the therapist reaches the goal first, play continues until the child reaches the goal.

The Resource Board Game affords children the opportunity of seeing the problem from their point of view, rather than others' viewpoints. The game also allows children to become more aware of their goals in overcoming the problem and their resources for accomplishing the goals. Much of this is accomplished through metaphors. In addition, the game is three-dimensional, making it an evocative sensory experience for the child in therapy.

Card tricks in play therapy can also be metaphorical. While it is generally accepted that play therapists should have a repertoire of card or magic tricks to use with children, some tricks are more metaphorical than others. Of particular value to children are age-appropriate tricks that can be learned and understood easily by the child. Children usually think they cannot do the trick; it seems indeed magical.

When taught by the therapist how to do the trick, the child develops an "I can" concept. Later, the child can show others how he can do the trick. It is easy to understand the symbolism of this as applied to the therapeutic process–children thinking at first they cannot make therapeutic changes, then realizing they can, then demonstrating this for others, all the while guided by the play therapist.

Materials for Metaphor Use in Play Therapy

Some play therapy materials lend themselves more effectively to metaphor use than others. Of specific value are such board games as the Ungame, Reunion, the Storytelling Land Game, Our Game, and Ups and Downs With Feelings (Zakich 1975). In the Ungame, when the therapist lands on a "Do Your Own Thing," he or she can tell a metaphor. In Reunion (Zakich 1979), the Relate cards themselves are metaphors for feeling exploration, and the Imagine cards often result in metaphor development. The Storytelling Card Game (Gardner 1988) focuses on the telling of metaphors using different characters with varying settings. Our Game (Vlosky 1986), a game especially appropriate for preschoolers, focuses on metaphor development by the child and the play therapist. In Ups and Downs With Feelings (Gesme 1987), therapists can use metaphors when responding to children's feelings. The Mutual Storytelling Technique, Board of Objects Game, Boy of Toys Game, Boy of Things Game, Boy of Words Game, Scrabble for Juniors, and the Alphabet Soup Game (Gardner 1975) all lend themselves very well to the effective use of metaphors. In addition, of course, therapists can develop their own board game for using metaphors. In this way the game may be individualized for the child more effectively.

Card games, such as the Ungame Card Game/Kids' Version, also afford ample opportunity for the play therapist to use metaphors when drawing a Question or Comment card. Therapists can develop their own card games, using blank cards available from many play therapy suppliers, to individualize their metaphor approach with children.

The Anti-Coloring Books (Striker 1982) represent an opportunity to utilize metaphors through art. In addition, the child will frequently tell a story about the drawing, thus assisting in the communication process.

It has been said that Milton Erickson told a metaphor much like this one to his therapist in training:

> You might be interested in knowing that there once was a horse that ran away from his home. A boy, not knowing where the horse was from, mounted the horse and allowed the horse to lead him, being careful, however, not to allow the horse to go into a ditch or a barbed-wire fence. Eventually the horse turned up a lane to a farm. The owners came running from their house, very surprised and happy to see their horse. They asked the boy

how he ever discovered where the horse belonged. The boy said he just let the horse lead, while he gently guided him away from excessive danger. [Frey 1984, p. 29]

This metaphor represents, among other things, the effective process of metaphor use with children.

Case Illustration: Childhood Grief Reaction

A 5-year-old girl was referred for therapy due to the substantial number of losses she had experienced in her life in one year. During this time, she lost her mother, two aunts, and a grandmother to death. Also during that year, her father was incarcerated in a prison quite a distance from the home. The child's remaining grandmother experienced a psychiatric hospitalization due to these circumstances. Consequently, the child was referred for play therapy because of the trauma of these events, extensive daydreaming, and underachievement.

The grieving process was so great for this young child that she could not talk about the experiences directly. She did speak to the therapist about other topics, frequently using analogies or metaphors. She seemed a very appropriate client for the use of metaphors in play therapy.

Art as a metaphor was used as a way of establishing rapport with this client as she enjoyed drawing. The client's drawings had very little shape or form. The drawings represented a catharsis for the child inasmuch as she verbalized a great deal about her feelings as she drew, and her pictures comprised many long strokes of red and black crayon.

As therapy progressed, the child chose to develop a board and a game with a medieval theme to play in the sessions. On the board, the client drew a king, queen, prince, princess, and flying horse, among other things. The client produced many metaphorical stories using this game board. Most of them had a theme of the princess on a quest on the flying horse to find the mother, aunts, and grandmother in heaven. It was an arduous quest inasmuch as the princess had a difficult time finding them. When she found them, they assured her that they were doing well and were fine. She informed them that she wanted to join them. When she took her turn, she told a story about a princess wanting to join her deceased relatives, but the relatives told her she could not do that, that it was not in her control or their control. The client persisted in wanting to find a way to join the relatives for about two sessions. In the third session, the client took the play therapist with her on the flying horse to heaven, and a discussion ensued about how one gets into heaven.

At the end of the rather prolonged discussion, which was primarily carried out by the client, the client informed the play therapist that they couldn't go there and they had to return to earth. The client decided you could go there to visit but you could not go there to join the relatives. Of course, it is obvious how parallel the metaphorical story is to the real life situation of the client.

This child then switched her play therapy medium and decided to play with a large Lego castle. A similar theme began, and another theme was added. The princess was put in the dungeon because she was bad and had caused others pain. The therapeutic theme of this metaphor, of course, was the child blaming herself for the relatives' deaths. As the interaction of the child and the play therapist continued for the next two sessions, the princess finally was allowed to leave the dungeon.

The princess then began to act out and kick others and yell at them. (This behavior was one of the most troublesome symptoms the grandmother experienced with the child–a lack of anger management skills.) The client was vacillating between the denial and anger stages of grieving, and, being so young, was lacking in appropriate management skills to deal with the tremendous anger she had. Through the Lego play, the princess was taught anger management strategies, which the client began using at home.

Music metaphors were also used with this child in therapy. The child was very fond of the song, "He's Got the Whole World in His Hands." The therapist and client made a recording of the song and the client drew a picture of what the song meant to her. The pictures became an object metaphor, which she took home.

As therapy continued, the child was introduced to the metaphorical story, "The Fall of Freddie the Leaf" by Leo Bus. The therapist and child discussed Freddie the Leaf, and the child eventually began talking about the deaths directly.

Traditional therapy followed, with a discussion of the client's pain and feelings. Play therapy using metaphor then became an auxiliary aspect of the therapy. The client was successful in working through the stages of grieving and discontinued daydreaming at school. Her grades became commensurate with her ability.

It is believed that metaphors in play therapy were crucial in the success of therapy for this child. They provided a vehicle for rapport and effective communication about feelings that were too difficult to discuss directly.

References

Barker, P. (1985). *Using Metaphors in Psychotherapy*. New York: Brunner/Mazel.

Eberle, B., and Hall, R. (1975). *Affective Education Guidebook*. Buffalo, NY: D. O. K.

Erickson, M., and Rossi, E. (1979). *Hypnotherapy: An Exploratory Casebook*. New York: Irvington.

Frey, D. (1984). The use of metaphors with gifted children. *Gifted/Creative/Talented* 34:28–29.

Gardner, H., and Winner, E. (1982). The child as father to the metaphor. In *Art, Mind and Brain: A Cognitive Approach to Creativity,* ed. H. Gardner, pp. 158–167. New York: Basic Books.

Gardner, R. (1975). *Psychotherapeutic Approaches to the Resistant Child*. New York: Jason Aronson.

_____ (1988). *The Storytelling Card Game*. Cresskill, NJ: Creative Therapeutics.

Gesme, C. (1987). *Ups and Downs With Feelings*. Minnetonka, MN: Carole Gesme.

Gordon, D. (1978). *Therapeutic Metaphors*. Cupertino, CA: Meta.

Lakoff, G., and Turner, M. (1989). *More Than Cool Reason: A Field Guide to Poetic Metaphor*. Chicago: University of Chicago Press.

Mills, J., and Crowley, R. (1983). Positive effects of cartoon images. Telemedia 1:11–16.

_____ (1986). *Therapeutic Metaphors for Children*. New York: Brunner/Mazel.

Palomares, U. and Logan, B. (1984). The maligned wolf. In *A Curriculum on Conflict Management,* pp. 118–119. San Clemente, CA: Magic Circle Publishing Company.

Piaget, J. (1954). *The Construction of Reality in the Child*. New York: Basic Books.

Santostefano, S. (1988). Process and change in child therapy and development: the concept of metaphor. In *Organizing Early Experience: Imagination and Cognition in Childhood,* ed. D. C. Morrison, pp. 139–172. Amityville, NY: Baywood.

Siegelman, E. (1990). *Metaphor and Meaning in Psychotherapy.* New York: Guilford.

Striker, S. (1982). *The Anti-Coloring Book.* New York: Holt, Rinehart & Winston.

Vlosky, M. (1986). *Our Game:* Broomfield, CO: Transitional Dynamics.

Watzlawick, P., Beavin, J., and Jackson, D. (1967). *Pragmatics of Human Communication.* New York: Norton.

Zakich, R. (1975). *The Ungame.* Anaheim, CA: The Ungame Company.

_____ (1979). *Reunion.* Anaheim, CA: The Ungame Company.

_____ (1983). *The Pocket Size Ungame.* Anaheim, CA: The Ungame Company.

Zeig, J. (1980). Appendix. In *A Teaching Seminar with Milton Erickson,* pp. 295–354. New York: Brunner/Mazel.

11

Attachment Formation

Ann M. Jernberg

Attachment as a developmental necessity has come to be taken for granted. Viewed as a given, attachment has been found to exist between mother and child (Cicchetti 1985, Emde and Sameroff 1982, 1989) and between child and father (Pedersen and Robson 1969). Adult–child play activity has likewise received considerable attention. Interactive play with the mother has been found to facilitate growth and therefore health. Interactive play, furthermore, enhances the child's intellectual and social-emotional development, the degree to which he finds joy in learning (Levenstein 1985), becomes socially responsive (Brown and Gottfried 1985), and develops group relationships (Winnicott 1990). Stern (1974) writes, "The more games with which a mother can interest and delight an infant, the more practice he will have in experiencing affectively positive arousal in different interactive situations involving more sense modalities in more patterns, i.e., in a greater number of human situations" (p. 416).

The specific relationship between attachment and play has been questioned. Sameroff and Emde (1989) for example, maintain that play and attachment differ. Differences pertain to differing underlying motives, to the display of quite different qualities or to the serving of quite different functions. Beckwith (1985) contrasts the reassuring, consoling, comfort-providing, stress-and-anxiety-reducing attachment behaviors with the emphasis on interest and delight, the heightened affective level, and the mutual pleasure and shared codes of conduct that characterize social play. Yet for Beckwith (1985) "infants who have had more fun with their mothers tend to become more securely attached" (p. 156). For Stern (1974) play and attachment are causally related in that one purpose of play is the enhancing of attachment.

Assessing Parent–Infant Interaction

Let us begin our own discussion of play as an enhancer of attachment by inviting you, the reader, to participate in a field trip. We are going to take you to visit a happy

Author's note: Before I undertook to write this chapter, I had invited my colleague, Phyllis Booth, to be my co-author. She chose instead to act as editor and consultant. I wish to give her my special thanks. Also, many thanks to Jean Mendoza for assistance researching the literature and to Sandra Lindaman for additional editorial help.

family in its home. For this particular trip we will focus on the nursery and on one parent in interaction with one baby. The baby is approximately 5 months old. The parent can be either Father or Mother; the baby can be whichever gender you choose. The primary conditions are as follows: (1) The parent is engaged with the child; (2) The parent is so finely attuned to the child's every internal experience, including his internal response to an external stimulus, that the parent can replicate this – even going so far as to do so in a modality different from the one the child has used;[1] (3) The two partners are having great fun together; (4) The two are alert, awake, and active; (5) The activity is so memorable to both that, as each is falling asleep that night, each will remember quite clearly what happened, and what the other sounded, felt, smelled, and looked like.[2] The child plays with confidence that "the person who loves and who is therefore reliable is available and continues to be available when remembered. . . ." This person furthermore, "is felt to reflect back what happens in the playing" (Winnicott 1990, pp. 47–48). Additionally, (6) The infant will have gained some small increment of emotional growth from just this one experience; and, finally, (7) The adult's impact on the infant, although perhaps hardly discernible, will have altered their meaning to one another in some positive way.

We begin now with a list of the parent–child activities we might observe as we peek in through the nursery window:

Parent plays peek-a-boo with baby's hands
Parent plays peek-a-boo with baby's feet
Parent uses diaper or pillow to play peek-a-boo
Parent uses own hands to play peek-a-boo
Parent blows noisily on baby's tummy
Parent blows gently on baby's eyelids
Parent "walks" finger tips up baby's tummy, chest, chin, nose, and forehead singing "Itsy bitsy spider"*[3]
Parent plays "This little piggy" with baby's toes
Parent "nibbles" on baby's ears
Parent gently bunts foreheads with baby**[4]
Parent "walks" baby's feet up parent's chest

---

[1]"Attunement can be made with the inner quality of feelings of how an infant reaches for a toy, holds a block, kicks a foot, or listens to a sound. . . . This is exactly our experience of feeling connectedness, of being in attunement with another. It feels like an unbroken line. It seeks out the activation contour that is momentarily going on in any and every behavior and uses that contour to keep the thread unbroken" (Stern 1985, p. 157).

[2]Citing Nachman (1982) and Nachman and Stern (1982), Stern discusses "continuity of affective experiences" (Stern 1985, p. 93) that is, infants recall pleasurable experiences such as play episodes.

[3]Asterisked items have a quality ensuring the eliciting of maximum attention. " 'Baby talk' and 'baby faces' are among the caregiver social behaviors that are pretty much invariant; these have characteristics which tend to assure maximum attention by the infant" (Stern 1985, p. 73). Tronick and Adamson's (1980) "still-faced" mothers, in contrast, generate the opposite response.

[4]**Marschak 1980, p. 268.

Parent sings to baby

Parent makes "prrrrr" and other sounds to baby

Parent winks at baby*

Parent smiles at baby

Parent giggles with baby

Parent feeds baby

Parent zooms face in toward baby's*

Parent makes funny faces*

Parent's face approaches baby's from a variety of surprising angles*

Parent looks at baby upside down

Parent wiggles tongue at baby*

Parent extends two index fingers for baby to grab (by which to lift self up)

Parent "walks" baby

Parent very gently tickles soles of baby's feet

Parent chatters to baby

Parent "baby talks" to baby*

Parent stands baby and "dances" with him

Parent "throws" baby over parent's shoulder, "hangs" baby upside down alongside parent's back. Parent slowly lowers child until child's head peeks out from between parent's legs. Parent lowers own head until they face each other making good eye contact. Parent exclaims "Well *there* you are! I been a-lookin' *all over* for you!"

Parent plays "I'm gonna getcha!"

Parent lies on back, knees bent, and helps baby "slide down" from parent's knees to parent's thighs

Parent, still lying on floor, places child on soles of parent's feet and slowly extends straightened legs, holding tightly to child's hands

Parent lowers child, enabling child to slide down entire length of parent's extended legs

Parent plays "Row row row your boat" with parent and child in sitting position facing each other

Parent rocks child in parent's lap. Child is horizontal. They are making good eye contact

Parent is sitting in chair. Child stands on parent's lap. Parent waves child's arms, "conducting" the music parent sings or hums

Parent is sitting in chair, child on lap facing parent. Parent makes "horsey galloping" sounds raising and lowering knees so child is bouncing on them. Parent has secure hold of child's hands and lower arms. Unexpectedly, parent's knees part and child "falls into the ditch"

Parent is sitting in chair. Child sits bouncing on parent's ankles and feet as parent jiggles them.

The above list is a small sample of the many hundreds of pleasurable, interpersonal activities that would go on in the course of any normal, happy day between a parent and small child. In addition to being physical, frivolous, fun-filled and personally engaging, what are some of the dimensions that characterize what we have seen? Generally, we have found that the dimensions of nursery play tend to fall into four categories: *structuring, challenging, intruding,* and *nurturing* (SCIN), with *playfulness* underlying and broadly defining the quality of many of the interactions.

In the activities we define as *structured,* there are implied rules. There is a beginning, a middle, and an end. Time is sequenced, planned, and finite. There is a rhythm. The rider on horseback stops his ride at the point where he "lands in the ditch," "Row row row your boat" stops with "life is but a dream," "This little piggy" stops at "all the way home." "Patty cake" stops with "and put it in the oven for baby and me." Some games have a predictable prelude, for instance, "1-2-3." Of course, the timing rule includes that the play stops if the child appears to be at all uncomfortable. Space is also ordered. The parent's "How tall is the baby? THIS tall!" sets clearly defined boundaries. Peek-a-boo is played within the baby's range of vision. Some play is done on the changing table, some in the high chair, and other kinds of play take place in the bath tub. There are also safety rules. Some places and some times are appropriate; others carry a risk of injury and are to be avoided. It is safe to play piggy back outdoors or in a good-sized room. It is not safe to play it in a crowded kitchen or workshop. It is better to do some of the more lively activities before dinner than it is to do them on a full stomach afterwards. Beckwith (1985) discussing Bruner writes, "The parent provides the scaffold for the infant's emerging skills, in what is done, when it is done, and the affect with which it is done" (p. 154).

Some of the activities are more *challenging* than others. It is challenging when the parent's index finger is extended for the baby to grab. Peek-a-boo is challenging, and so is standing the baby on the parent's lap. It is challenging when a parent lifts the baby high to touch the ceiling or low to "wheelbarrow" on the floor. It is challenging when one parent tosses the baby into the arms of another or when a parent, lying on the floor, flips the baby to do a somersault in the air. It can be a challenge to the baby to discover the parent's face hiding behind a diaper, or to change a parent's mouth with his fingers from a frowning position into a smile. It can also be a challenge for the baby to touch the parent's nose so that it goes "beep." Bretherton (1985) says, "The infant has to distinguish between somebody frightening and Daddy doing something that seems to be frightening but isn't really" (p. 77). To quote Beckwith (1985), "In a game of 'peek-a-boo' the parent does not really separate, and the infant does not show separation distress. Such games help the child master tension-arousing experiences and understand the boundary between real and make believe" (p. 154).

Some activities are intrusive, unexpected, delightful, and stimulating. Variation is the hallmark of *intrusion.* High-pitched baby talk, mock surprise, facial expression, and head cocking, are some behaviors that Stern (1985) characterizes as infant-stimulated variations of normal social behavior. "All variations," he writes (1974), "serve to engage the baby and maintain his/her interest" (pp. 408–409). The game of the rider at the point where he falls in the ditch offers one such variation; surprise blowing on a baby's tummy is another. The parent's fingers making variations in the way the "itsy bitsy spider" unexpectedly crawls up the baby's tummy, neck, chin, and mouth (landing at last at the tip of the baby's nose or the top of his head or the lobe of one ear) is yet another intrusive form of play. "I'm gonna getcha!" is, of course, intrusive, as is the adult's falling over backwards every time the baby squeaks or blows or grunts. Parental funny faces, unexpected winks, and surprise kisses on the eyelids are intrusive as well. "The infant can be with an other such that the two join their activities to make something happen that could not happen without the commingling of behaviors from each," writes Stern (1985). "For example, during a 'peek-a-boo' or 'I'm going to getcha' game, the mutual interaction generates in the infant a self-experience of very high excitation, full of joy and suspense and perhaps tinged with a touch of fear" (p. 102).

Some activities are *nurturing,* as when the parent sings to the child, rocks, feeds, cuddles, lotions, powders, strokes, or coos. Nurturing activities comprise what we generally think of when we consider soothing, calming, quieting or reassuring an infant. Nurturing activities make the world feel safe, predictable, warm, and secure. Nurturing activities lend credence to notions of comfort and stability.

There are many activities in the nursery where the dimensions are not clear cut, that is, where one dimension overlaps with another–for example, intrusion with challenge or challenge with structure. Some activities have a challenging dimension even though challenge may not be their primary intent. Peek-a-boo, for example, shares intrusion and challenge.

The nurturing dimension, on the other hand, tends to be just that–pure nurturing. Parents who choose to feed their child using distractions like "Here comes the airplane heading for the hangar" demonstrate an exception to this purity. Some babies find this game not always a pleasurable experience (indeed, perhaps this is because challenge has intruded into the nurturing dimension).

There are many other dimensions characterizing the scenes we have witnessed, to be sure. The selected dimensions spell out SCIN, which itself is significant, for it is *skin* contact (together with eye contact) that is the hallmark of much of what goes on in a playful, happy interaction between an infant and its parent. "It seems that touch is instrumental in the development and maintenance of attachment" observes Reite (1984, p. 64), and goes on to suggest that "perhaps on some symbolic level touch invokes mechanisms associated with attachment that ultimately can lead to optimal physiological functioning" (p. 65). While we have been saying that touch, eye contact, and so forth are important for normal babies, pre-term, low birth weight and especially "cocaine babies" need some modulation. "Cocaine babies," it should be noted, react to these contacts as though they were painfully over–stimulating. The fragile organ systems of many preterm and low birth weight babies require that any stimulation be done with extreme care so as not to overtax them and provoke crisis. T. B. Brazelton in Greenough 1984, and Rose 1984 puts it this way:

> For a pre-term or Small-for-Gestational-Age (SGA) baby who has not developed the capacity to modulate appropriately, a stimulus that a full-term neonate can accept may be too much. If you say "How are you doing?" to a full-term [baby] she'll probably search for your face and find it. But a preemie might avert, go into an arched state and perhaps spit up, have a BM, and become cyanotic. [Greenough p. 37] I think it's a very big job for

pre-term infants to get their systems working together–to establish basic rhythms of attention and withdrawal . . . homeostatic systems. [Rose p. 99] We have found essentially the same thing in our study of the face-to-face rhythms that mothers and normal babies develop when the babies are between 3 and 5 months old. [Greenough p. 37]

The Infant's Self-Image

As we return now to watching the happy nursery scene described above, and assuming that our infant could use language to express himself, how would we answer these questions: What would this infant say to himself about himself? What would he say to himself about the peopled world he lives in? That is, how would he complete a sentence beginning, "I am . . ."? And how would he end a sentence beginning, "The world is . . ."?

If he were allowed a list of adjectives to define the kind of person he sees himself as being might he not say the following?

> I am beautiful
> I am special
> I am powerful
> I am nifty
> I am important
> I am talented
> I am fun to be with
> I am extraordinary
> I am lovely
> I am capable
> I am fun-loving
> I am coordinated
> I am courageous
> I am curious–and last, and perhaps most important,
> I am lovable

Flint (1959) summarizes these conclusions as follows:

While changing, dressing, feeding and bathing him, [his mother] will tickle, talk to, coo at, cuddle, pat, scold, and rock her child. This, in turn, elicits a response of chuckles, gurgle, kicking, hand-waving, and general delight from the baby, as he slowly grasps the thought that he is a person of value to his mother. This gradually becomes established in his mind as a feeling of self-worth. [p. 18]

And might he not complete the sentence beginning "The world is. . . ." with one of the following?

A place that is safe
A place that is joyous
A place that is predictable
A place that is fun
A place that is exciting
A place that is varied
A place that is interested
A place that is focused on me
A place that is trustworthy
A place that is delightful
A place that is secure
A place that is colorful
A place that is happy and, of course,
A place that is loving

Were we to ask the parent to complete the sentence beginning, "I am . . . ," we would expect the parent in this example to tell us:

Caring
Trustworthy
Fun
Interesting
Warm
Appealing
Lovely
Strong
Competent
Responsive
Talented
Wanted
Needed
Resourceful
Engaged
Focused
Pleasure-providing
Attuned
Empathic – and, above all else,
Loving

One early intervention program (Rauh et al. 1986), which included instructional sessions on mutual enjoyment through play "[resulted in] more favorable mother-infant transactions [and] the boosting of maternal morale" (p. 155). Stern (1974) puts it this way: "The infant, of course, provides for the mother an array of infant acts consisting of smiles, head movements, coos, etc. These are immensely important in reinforcing the mother's behaviors and in providing feedback for the mother's modifications of her behavior" (p. 409).

> Increasingly, we have come to appreciate the back-and-forth nature of the developmental process involving infants and parents. Rewards result from sequences of interaction, and are reciprocal. For example, the infant who has been given to, who has experienced rewards, is more likely to be rewarding for caregivers. Correspondingly, parents who have been rewarded by their infant are more likely to feel better about themselves and continue caregiving in a rewarding manner. [Emde and Sorce 1983, p. 20]

The scene we have described above is the scene of attachment-in-the-making. Each tiny interchange contributes to the infant's internal organization and to his view of his caretaker as someone he can trust and with whom it is safe and pleasurable to enjoy a lifelong engagement. From quite early on – from as early as his prenatal life (DeCasper and Spence 1982, Jackson and Todd 1950, Jernberg 1985, 1988) – the infant has been aware of his mother's characteristic voice, pace, and so forth. As early as the first few days of life, he is able to imitate this adult (e.g., sticking out his tongue) and, a little later, wishes to identify with him or her (Marschak 1967). Throughout, he feels certain that the primary focus when he is with this other person is himself and himself alone. The focus is not what he might be made to become or what he is not supposed to be at the moment. The agenda is himself together with all that that entails – sweet or sour, noisy or quiet, self-centered or altruistic, beautiful or ugly, bright or dull, calm or restless, coordinated or clumsy; and just looking like himself, not looking like Mom or Dad or Aunt Kate or Grandfather (Fraiberg et al. 1975). It is out of this attachment to a playfully attuned other that he will develop into a curious, spontaneous, optimistic (Seligman 1991), joyful, confident, courageous, and loving toddler, school child, adolescent, and adult.

For purposes of better understanding the point made above, as well as for better understanding what remediation we might offer in the event of a quite different kind of outcome, let us now look at a contrasting scene. The scene is still a nursery and there is still one parent and one infant in it. But what happens between them lacks the sparkle, the luster, the zest, and the playfulness of the earlier scene. It is, in fact, in every qualitative way, the opposite of what we have just viewed. What is happening in this second nursery?

The baby may be physically clean, well-fed and well-cared-for. However, as Burlingham and Freud (1943) have observed, "It is certain that the care and attention given by the mother, i.e., in a special atmosphere of affection which only the mother can supply, is more satisfactory to the baby than more indifferent and mechanical ministrations to its needs" (p. 46). So what about his life beyond that, especially as that life relates to the interactions with the adult in the room? In place of the joyous engagement and happy in-synchrony that we witnessed in Nursery I, we may see, in this second nursery, the following:

> Parent sits in a chair, infant lies silent in his crib staring straight ahead
> Parent sits in a chair, infant is screaming
> Parent sits gazing vacantly into space
> Parent sits reading
> Parent sits looking down
> Parent sits crying
> Parent sits polishing her nails
> Infant reaches out to parent, parent pushes his arms down and places him on his back in crib
> Parent frowns
> Parent hits baby
> Parent speaks harshly to infant
> Parent yanks infant's limb
> Parent scrubs infant's face brusquely
> Parent speaks demeaningly to infant
> Infant coughs, parent snaps, "shut up"
> Parent vigorously tickles infant, infant begins to cry or
> Infant sobs, parent tickles him, laughing
> Infant is resting quietly, parent flicks the soles of his feet talking boisterously and laughing
> Infant feeds, parent abruptly interrupts or
> Parent forces feeding upon reluctant infant

What we have seen in these vignettes is no interaction at all, interaction that is functional only, or interaction that is abusive. What we have seen is bleak, cacophonous, or empty. It is anything but playful. Even if there had been the opportunity for play, the parent's failure to engage expressively would have negated its attachment potential. According to a study by Main and Weston (1982), "Maternal inexpressiveness in a play setting has been found associated with infant avoidance in the strange situation" (p. 47). When we ask the question "How does this infant come to see himself?," the answers might go like this:

> I am unattractive
> I am hopeless
> I am not pleasing
> I am not valuable
> I am impoverished
> I am dull
> I am ugly
> I am incompetent

I am clumsy
I am undesirable
I am a nobody
I am a turn-off
I am weak
I am helpless
I am hard to please
I am bewildering
I am noxious
I am nothing
I am unworthy
I am frustrating
I am invalidated
I am evil – and, of course,
I am unlovable

Regarding the presumed loss of hope and the often-implied distance we observed in the nursery above, Winnicott (1987) states that even a normal baby at a normal separation feels: I am "going to pieces, falling forever, dying and dying and dying, losing all vestige of hope of the renewal of contacts" (p. 86). Having experienced so much distance and so much loss of hope in Nursery II, what would our baby feel about his world? He might say to himself:

The world is painful
The world is rejecting
The world is distant
The world is unempathic
The world is dull
The world is cold
The world is hostile
The world is preoccupied
The world is cruel
The world is overstimulating
The world is selfish
The world does not validate
The world is conditional
The world is punitive
The world is uncaring
The world is dangerous
The world is unpredictable
The world is untrustworthy
The world is chaotic
The world is noisy

The world is not in tune with me, and finally,
The world is an unloving place

Citing Egeland and Farber, Levenstein (1985) writes that the data "indicate that the supportive parent–child network formed through mother's play interactions . . . can be torn apart by a mother's insisting on the child's learning until it becomes too boring and no longer play. . . ." (p. 165). Infants with mothers who are tense and irritable during early interactions are more likely to become anxiously attached or avoidant. Unlike the parent of the infant first described, a parent caught up in a relationship like this one may well say to him- or herself, "I am:

Inadequate
Unappealing
Incompetent
Ungiving
Misunderstood
Alone
Guilty
Helpless
Inferior
Worthless
Lacking
Empty
Cold

We can predict that the resulting parental behaviors will have an effect upon the infant's behavior. Biggar (1984) writes, "There is a significant relationship between mother's aversion to physical contact with the infant and [later] infant conflict behavior" (p. 69). What behavior would we see if we were to observe through the window of his first grade classroom a child who has viewed himself and the world in the ways suggested above? Probably what we would see would be a child who:

Sits alone
Cries
Has many accidentally caused bumps and scratches
Rocks
Whines
Withdraws
Refuses to participate
Is inactive
Clings
Attacks others
Will not obey the teacher

Is overactive
Cannot concentrate
Is abusive
Runs away
Destroys property
Rejects limits
Eats voraciously

These children, as Tustin (1972) says about *autistic* children, "severely sap the caring person's confidence both by the violent feelings they arouse by their non-response and because care is repudiated. It is no wonder that when the parents of such children (particularly the mothers) come to helping agencies, they are doubtful about their capacity to be mothers, and are easily hurt by what is said to them particularly if it is implied that they have been 'bad' or inadequate mothers" (p. 154).

Next let us ask another question: What may have brought about the unhappy scene described? There are two sides to the parent–child equation: the parent, and the child. In addition, there may be the "fit" or "poorness-of-fit" between them, external realities that overshadow everything, and reciprocal interactions between the various factors.

On the parent's side of the equation, there may be any of a number of contributors. The parent may be immature, or in ill health. He or she may be suffering from drug abuse, depression, or a marriage to an alcoholic or to an abusive spouse. The pregnancy may have been unwanted. Or the parent may have his or her own agenda (e.g., to produce a "super baby" so as to validate the parent's competence through the infant's achievements). Some parents excite their babies in an effort to ward off their own feelings of boredom. Stern (1985) describes additional parental motivations as follows: "intrusive, overstimulating behavior on the part of the mother can arise from many causes: hostility, need for control, insensitivity, or an unusual sensitivity to rejection such that mother interprets each infant head aversion as a 'microrejection' and attempts to repair and undo it" (p. 195).

"Irritability in fathers," note Pedersen and Robson (1969), "is negatively correlated [to attachment] for boys" (p. 470). And finally, referring back to what Jackson and Todd wrote forty years ago, "children's problems in very many cases are a repetition of their parents' problems, in the sense that they originated in or were prompted by the parents' attitudes. More than that, the parents' problems can often be traced back to their relationship with their own parents. Thus, inevitably, similar symptoms tend to perpetuate themselves in several generations. . . ." (pp. 40–41).

As for the infant's contribution, there may be a difficult temperament, physical deformity, lethargy, or hyperactivity. Autistic rejection, including back-arching as a response to parental approach, is one characteristic of failure-to-attach children.

Poorness of fit is yet another determinant. We may find parental temperament, for example, not matching the temperament of the baby. Very different levels of intelligence may be yet another ingredient making for a poor fit. Motor coordination or pace of movement may be additional factors. It is important to note that a temperamental mismatch, if properly negotiated, does not have to be detrimental. Stern (1985) describes one such mismatch as follows:

> Eric is a somewhat bland infant compared to his more affectively intense mother, but both are perfectly normal. His mother constantly likes to see him more excited, more expressive and demonstrative about feelings, and more avidly curious about the world. . . . When he does show some excitement, mother encourages and even intensifies the experience just a little – not beyond his level of tolerance, usually – so that Eric experiences a higher level of excitement than he would alone. . . . This is generally pleasurable for the infant, as mother doesn't try to disrupt or redirect his experience. [p. 193]

External forces may be monetary concerns, for example, or difficult in-laws, or a landlord who threatens eviction, or a lease saying "no children" or "no noise." There may be adult- not child-determined cultural norms. Grossman and colleagues (1985), for example, conducted a cross-national study. The researchers paid home visits through the first year, then observed mothers and infants in the "Strange Situation" at 12 months. The authors found that

> in the Strange Situation a much higher percentage of the Bielefeld (German) sample was classified as Group A (avoidant) than the Baltimore sample (49% vs. 26%). We interpret this part of our findings with respect to the cultural values that we believe to be dominant in North Germany, where people tend to keep a larger personal distance. As soon as infants become mobile, most mothers feel that they should now be weaned from close bodily contact. . . . The ideal is an independent, nonclinging infant who does not make demands on the parents but rather unquestioningly obeys their commands. [p. 253]

Finally, there may be reciprocal factors. One clearly reciprocal factor may be a troubled multiplacement foster or adopted child together with a foster or adoptive mother who has high expectations or is unprepared in other ways. Although it is generally the mother who is hurt by the felt rejection, we have found that the father often plays a decisive role in determining the outcome. Referring to families of autistic children where the mothers are similarly stressed, Tustin (1972) states, "The father, in particular, can often give much-needed support to the mother" (p. 155).

Let us assume that these children behave as they do because they were never made to feel the way our initial infant was. Our initial infant experienced a joyful, beautifully synchronized parent–child interaction, which in turn allowed him to feel wonderful feelings about himself and about his world. Our second infant, by contrast, experienced attunement failure and a lack of joy. In consequence, his view of himself lacked appeal and confidence and his view of the world lacked respect and opportunity. Let us assume our task is to compensate this child for these deprivations. What might we do to enable him to feel better about himself and about others, and how might we go about doing this?

Compensation

Let us look back at the first list of playful parent–baby activities taking place in the delightful, cheer-filled nursery. Let us design a program in which emotionally deprived children would be provided these same joyful, physical, intensely personal experiences. And let us give all this in a playful setting where the adult is attuned to the child and where love is not conditional upon his providing a pleasing performance. Thus we would arrange for the structure of rhythmical, gentle singing, the challenging games of peek-a-boo, the intrusive excitement of nose beeps or soft puffs of air on the eyelids, and the nurturing swaddling and rocking in a blanket. We would give him all of these with the expectation that, over a period of time, our treatment will compensate him for his early crippling deprivations. This compensatory effort will be all the more effective, of course, if provided by a self-confident empathic adult (a parent under supervision, or a therapist).

Let us review the roles of structuring, challenging, intruding and nurturing now in the new context of compensation: although many structuring activities are also ensuring of safety, safety is by no means their only function. Structuring guarantees that the adult, not the child, is in charge. For many children, being in the presence of a take-charge adult is in itself reassuring. Jackson and Todd (1950) state, "The experience of being overwhelmed by one's emotions is an alarming one to an adult and must be very much more so to the child. A calm, gentle, but firm attitude on the part of the parent will be both reassuring and helpful . . . in teaching the child to control himself" (p. 37). For others, structuring assures the child that there is order in the universe, this being all the more necessary if his world is unruly and chaotic. The need for structure is not related to chronological age as much as it is to the child's experience of inner or outer disorder.

The challenging activities to be described are those that require a partnership, but do not require "good" behavior. Thus, we do not consider activities done alone to be a helpful kind of challenging, nor are those that demonstrate social maturity. It is not seen as therapeutically challenging for the child to write his name, clean his plate, or tie his shoelaces. Thumb, arm, or leg wrestling, in contrast, would be considered challenging, as would balancing books in a therapist–child relay race, or finding and identifying each other's toes hidden under a blanket.

Intrusion is quite appropriate for a child who is withdrawn or for one who is too rigidly structured. Intrusive activities, although not always welcome, are helpful for children who must constantly plan, organize, and count. For these children, intrusion offers adventure, variety, stimulation, and a fresh view of life. Intrusion introduces risk and a taste of the unknown. Intrusion allows a child to understand that surprises can be fun, and new experiences enjoyable. Because there is sometimes confusion as to the purposes and definition of intrusion (O'Connor 1991), it may be important to state here what intrusion is not. Intrusion should never be used as a means to another end, as, for example, to distract a child, to get him to comply, or to focus his attention on another activity. If a child is overactive, undirected, or overstimulated, it is structure that is used to calm him down and organize him, not intrusion. Indeed, children who suffer from agitated or chaotic behaviors or those who are easily overstimulated, such as "cocaine babies" or other children with central nervous system damage, are among the kinds of children for whom intrusion is definitely contraindicated.

Theraplay

Because of its play and bonding-enhancement properties, Theraplay (Jernberg 1979, 1991) has been found to be of particular value for children referred for problems of attachment (Schaefer 1991). Thus it is that children who are born prematurely, or are autistic (Jernberg 1979) or obsessive-compulsive (Jernberg 1979), or those who have been adopted (Jernberg 1991, Koller 1984) often find their way into Theraplay treatment. Thus it is also that problems of parental bonding and child attachment (e.g., foster parents, reclaiming birth parents, step-parents, etc.) lead families into this form of treatment. Theraplay's bonding and attachment-enhancing properties are a function of its design. Its treatment strategy is to replicate the early parent–infant relationship in all its aspects. These include the dimensions structuring, challenging, intrusion, nurturing, and playfulness all taking place within an atmosphere of empathic attunement and relaxed engagement. Just as a parent defines for the infant the boundaries of his world, the rules by which we live, what is safe and what is unsafe, so also does the Theraplay therapist provide the child the guidelines within which the therapy takes place. Just as a parent challenges the infant to stretch just a little beyond complacent comfort, so also does the Theraplay therapist. Just as a parent intrudes, delights, and surprises the infant, so also does the Theraplay therapist. And just as the parent nurtures, soothes, and comforts the infant, so does the Theraplay therapist.

It is noteworthy that Austin DesLauriers (1962), some of whose principles underlie the Theraplay (1979) method, in his work with schizophrenic (1962) and autistic children (1969) pioneered direct physical and active strategies, later termed by us *Intruding* and *Challenging*. When he lay down on the floor to bar a child's premature departure, for example, it might also be said that DesLauriers *Structured*. Going far beyond DesLauriers's early techniques, the staff of The Theraplay Institute (TTI) (1) formulated the four dimensions of Theraplay and included playfulness as a recent fifth, (2) conceived targeting a treatment plan specifically geared to the child's emotional level, (3) added the dimension *Nurturing*, (4) included parents as co-therapists, and (5) applied the notion *Empathy*.

Case Illustration: Successful Theraplay

Joey is an example of a child with a too-low threshold for stimulation – a child who is tactilely defensive. Joey was 4 when his parents brought him in for Theraplay. Joey's behaviors, as we saw them in our playroom, made it easy to understand why his mother could not provide her side, the parenting side, of the parent–child equation. Unlike the parent in our ideal nursery scene, Joey's mother was unable to structure or challenge, intrude or nurture, because whenever she approached Joey, he screamed. He screamed so loudly, in fact, that the neighbors protested. "All I could do was put him back in his cradle," his sobbing mother told us. Joey had been born hypersensitive to stimuli coming at him from either internal or external sources and showed pronounced hyperirritability in response.

It was easy to believe his mother's story and to understand her pain. Joey appeared for his first session, the Marschak Interaction Method (MIM) (Jernberg 1991, Jernberg et al. 1971, Marschak 1960, 1980) accompanied by his mother. The MIM is an evaluation method. It attempts to tap several dimensions of the parent–child relationship. These dimensions cover both the adult's ability to provide certain behavior and the child's ability to receive them. In addition to structuring, challenging, appropriate boundary maintenance, nurturing, attachment enhancing, empathy, and stress reduction, there is an eighth dimension: playfulness. These eight dimensions (Jernberg and Booth 1991) are a recent revision of Marschak's (1980) original four: promoting attachment, alerting to environment, guiding purposive behavior, and assisting in overcoming tension. It is this last revised dimension, that of playfulness, that often differentiates most clearly a wholesome relationship from a relationship that is flawed. It is our assumption that playfulness between parent and child is possible only when there is sufficient energy available, sufficient investment in one another, sufficient awareness of what each will find amusing, sufficient wish to please the other, sufficient spontaneity and freedom of spirit in each other's presence and mutual respect and responsiveness. In short, the two partners find joy in being in the company of one another. Genuine playfulness cannot be present when there is exploitation (e.g., when the task "Feed each other M&M's" is used by one partner to diminish the other), when either partner has a hidden agenda, when either feels the need to present a "false self," when there is bitterness, resentment, or rancor, or when one partner is too self-centered to be aware of or concerned with the other. It is difficult to be playful, of course, when one is feeling physically ill or emotionally depressed. It is just as difficult when one has been conditioned to expect a poor response. Asked to perform the Infant MIM task "Adult plays Peek-a-boo with child," one 8-month-old child's mother despairs, "It's just not going to work. It never works. He prefers to look for any other thing but he's just not interested in looking for his mother." With regard to the therapeutic use of parent–child observations, Stern (1974) notes that "examination and understanding of the actual, ongoing mother–infant interaction can and often should be considered one of the primary sources of clinical data for therapy" (p. 418).

As is typical for 4-year-olds, Joey sat with his mother side by side at a table (parents and much younger children perform the MIM with the infant sitting or lying on a mat or carpet). A strip of masking tape ran down the center of the table top to demarcate the territory of each of the two participants. Mother read aloud each printed index card, giving the instruction for the task ahead. The first task was "Take the two squeaky pigs out of Envelope #1. Give one pig to child. Keep one pig for yourself. Have the two pigs play together." Mother's pig gave one tiny squeak and Joey recoiled in horror, screaming a scream that would not stop. Mother proceeded to the next task, "Teach child something he does not know." Quite appropriately for a child Joey's age, Mother wanted to teach him to take off his boots. She leaned down to remove a boot, and again Joey issued a piercing scream protecting his face with his arms as though he were anticipating a beating (a fear, we are convinced, that was ill founded). Following this effort, Mother read aloud, "Play a familiar game together." She had barely approached Joey for "Patty cake" when he reverted once more to the blood-curdling scream. Next on the agenda was the task "Parent leaves room for a minute." By this time it was obvious that Joey was inconsolable. He wailed ever more loudly throughout the remainder of the MIM session. The following week, it was Father's turn to engage Joey in the MIM. His luck in doing so was no better than Mother's. In analyzing their videotapes, Phyllis Booth and I determined that these parents' efforts would have easily engaged any normal child. By the same token, any normal set of parents would have felt pained, inadequate, and rejected by a child who responded as Joey did. Therefore it seemed Joey's hypersensitivity had defeated both his parents' best attempts to promote attachment.

In the feed-back session that followed, both parents were apprised of our impressions. They were lauded for their noble efforts at engaging Joey and were told empathically how really bad it must feel to have to live with Joey's constant rejection. Both parents, but particularly Mother, reacted with appreciation and gratitude. We find it is mothers, even more than fathers, who have this reaction (Tustin 1972). Indeed, it is not unusual for mothers to verbalize, "Ah, at last somebody understands."

Joey showed up at The Theraplay Institute the following week for his first Theraplay session. He was accompanied by both parents. His screams were so loud, so ear-piercing, and so pervasive that he could be heard up and down the halls on his way to his appointment. Already upon his arrival his arms were raised to cover his face. When his arms were finally lowered, his hands shot up and covered his ears. His eyes were wide open and vigilant. A therapist and a trainee, Chuck West and Sue Papandrea, scooped him up from his chair in the waiting room, carried him joyfully between them down the corridor and began his first Theraplay session. They did so unhesitatingly and with confidence. Both parents sat with me on the other side of the viewing screen. Mother was anguished at the resistant behavior she witnessed in Joey. Sometimes she appeared too pained to watch. Father, at the outset, was disappointed in Joey's failure to achieve. Sometimes his harsh comments bordered on the punitive. Gradually it became Father, not Mother, however, who showed the greater interest in – or tolerance for? – observing and learning about what the two therapists were doing.

As Joey continued to scream, his therapists continued their therapeutic agenda. They always heard his protests and acknowledged that he was frightened and uncomfortable. Never for a minute, however, did they give in to the little "tyrant" who had defeated every baby sitter during his short life. His therapists never cajoled, reasoned, or backed off. They never "put him back in his crib." Instead, they reflected his pain and terror with a song that, matching his level of excitement, reached ever higher in pitch and volume. The song came to be known as the "NO! NO! Song." To the tune of "Twinkle Twinkle Little Star," it began: "I don't want to No! No! NO! I don't want to No! No! NO! No! No! No! No! No! No! NO! I don't want to, let me go! No! No! No! No! No! No! No! I don't want to! No! No! NO!" Joey stopped his screaming and his eyes opened wider. He studied his two therapists in amazement. Chuck held him in his lap while Sue touched a cup of water to his lips. It soon became apparent that Joey welcomed the mirroring of his mood, the understanding of his resistance, the quiet nurturing offered him, and the take-charge stance of his therapists who, in spite of all his protest, never retreated. Soon he calmed down.

In the following two sessions, Joey exhibited the kind of behavior we often find for a brief period in children as manipulative, aggressive, and domineering as Joey. As he lay cuddled into his therapists during these two sessions, Joey first appeared profoundly sad, then tears welled up in his eyes and spilled onto his cheeks. Eventually he began a deep, soft sobbing. In subsequent sessions, he lay calmly on Chuck's lap, solemnly gazing into both their faces and sucking hungrily while Sue fed him milk from a baby bottle. Five or six sessions later, the resistance had completely subsided and he was eager to come for his visits and to join his therapists in the Theraplay room. After about ten sessions, his near-phobic running away from the sight of the secretaries in the reception room had been replaced by an avid hovering over their typewriters, interested in watching them at work. By about the twentieth week these same secretaries, who at the beginning had declared their dread of his visits, were looking forward to the days he was due. "He looked so grotesque at the outset," one of them reported. "Now I think he's absolutely darling."

It was during session twelve that his therapists began doing adventurous activities with this child who, just a few weeks earlier, was still demanding order, slow pacing, and total predictability. (Although Theraplay therapists generally ignore such demands if the child issues them in the interest of maintaining control, therapists respect them in children whom we identify as having vestibular damage. Joey was one of these children.) By this session, however, Joey seemed ready to undertake the novel, to venture the exciting, and to take some risks. Chuck and Sue placed Joey on a blanket on the mat. Raising the blanket with Joey inside to ever greater heights, they gently swung it to and fro singing "Rock a bye baby in the tree top, when the wind blows the cradle will rock. When the bough breaks the cradle will fall, and that's when we'll catch you, cradle and all." On these final words, the therapists snuggled Joey deeper inside his blanket and gently lowered him into the lap of one of them. Joey requested, "More, More!" A few sessions later the challenge was increased yet further. In session fifteen, Joey was curled into a little ball in the arms of his dancing therapist, Chuck. As Chuck twirled around with Joey in his arms, Chuck sang "You can't have him, Sue." and added "This is *my* Joey and I want him *too* much." "Please, Chuck, please. Pretty please. Please with lots of sugar on it. Please give *me* a turn to have Joey." "Oh, all right Sue," Chuck agreed reluctantly, and with apparent carefree abandon he twirled once more and then tossed the Joey bundle to Sue. Sue caught him, looked adoringly into his face and commented on each gorgeous feature in it. Joey grinned. Chuck pleaded to get him back. They went through the same clowning demonstration and as Sue tossed him back to Chuck, Joey shrieked with glee. There were many more sessions, but in large part these were designed more to help Mother master the Theraplay strategy at home than because Joey still required the sessions with his therapists.

As we analyze Joey's treatment, we can see the replication of some of the playful activities we observed in our very first nursery scene. We can see the use of the nursery interaction dimensions: structuring, challenging, intruding, nurturing, and playfulness. We can see how these were carried out in an atmosphere of empathic attunement and playful engagement. We can also assume that Joey's view of himself and of the world must have gradually changed over this period. At the outset, he very likely thought of himself as vulnerable, incompetent, ugly, helpless and, above all, unlovable. He must have thought of the world as fearful, bewildering, unsafe, frightening, unempathic and, above all, unloving. Three months into his treatment his view of himself and of the world had changed. Clearly, he now viewed himself as worthy, fun, competent, curious, special, potent, adventurous and, above all else, lovable. Clearly, he now viewed the world as exciting, safe, pleasing, fun, trustworthy, attuned, helpful, caring, fascinating and, above all else, a loving place to be.

Other Child Therapy Procedures

In order to highlight the distinctive properties of Theraplay, it may be useful to compare it to other child treatment methods, through a consideration of the ways in which other kinds of therapists might undertake their efforts to help Joey. All of these sample sessions, are for the purpose of illustration and demonstration only, and are therefore caricatured and concentrated. No therapist will do with Joey, of course, exactly what he or she may have reported doing with another child.

Behavioral

If behaviorists M. H. Wolfe, T. Risley, or H. L. Mees were to do child therapy, the therapist might proceed as follows: he would aim to eliminate Joey's tantrum behavior by placing him in a room by himself when he had a tantrum. When the tantrum ceased he would allow Joey to come out and join him. Joey's parents and his teachers would be instructed to respond in the same manner whenever Joey had a tantrum at home or at school.

Client-centered

Permitting Joey to use whatever available playroom equipment there is, Virginia Axline accepts whatever Joey wishes to play out with it. All the while his therapist reflects, "You really are glad to be here today," "It makes you mad when things don't go right (like when the doll's legs won't bend to fit under that chair, right?)" and "You feel sad that our time's already almost up." Unlike when he is with his behavioral therapist, when he is with his client-centered one it is Joey, not his therapist, who takes the initiative. Unlike his psychoanalytic therapists, Joey's client-centered therapist makes no inferences, offers no interpretations, does not dwell on the past. Rather, she reflects only the emotions she observes in the here and now.

Family Systems

In a room with Joey and his two parents, Salvador Minuchin first aims to join the family, that is to become a participating member (Minuchin and Fishman 1981). In joining with Joey, who has his arms up as though guarding his face, Minuchin contributes his own arm to the cause, or else does the same to guard his own face.

Doing so, he quickly comes to experience himself, as do Joey's parents, as being yet one more object of Joey's tyranny. At this point he picks Joey up and lifts him so he is standing on a chair, towering above the others. "Is this about how tall he is with respect to his two parents?" Minuchin asks. In the discussion that ensues, Joey and both his mother and father come to understand the family dynamics. In time this will lead to an understanding of the marriage and of the role Joey plays in distracting his parents from focusing on one another.

Psychoanalytic

Recognizing Joey's severe fears of leaving his mother and being aware that "with very young children . . . the therapist must very often introduce variations in technique" (A. Freud 1946, p. 199), Anna Freud allows Mother to remain in the treatment room. This is not Freud's only deviation from the usual psychoanalytic abstinence. Since the demanding, the giving, and the receiving are much more important than what is demanded, given, or received she might give Joey a sweet or a favorite toy to tide him over the weekend so as to "enable him to contain his anxieties while continuing the analysis of them" (p. 196), sometimes "as an inducement . . . to carry on the analytic work" (p. 197) and sometimes as a "temporary expedient in order to enable the relevant material to be analyzed later" (p. 196). "At the beginning of treatment, Freud comes to an agreement with [Joey] about toys, for instance that the toys are for [Joey's] exclusive use in the treatment room and will be safely kept for him there" (p. 195). Eventually Mother is able to sit in the hallway just outside with the door ajar, and several months later she is told to remove herself to the waiting room. At first, Joey is permitted to stay with his mother in the waiting room. Whatever interpretations Freud offers him, she offers him out there. As Joey comes to understand his aggression toward his mother, he becomes more able to part from her. Then, as Joey becomes even more at ease in the treatment room he begins to play messily with clay and water, eventually splashing the dirty water on his therapist's dress. She interprets to Joey that dirtying her dress might be something he does to his mother to prevent her getting all dressed up to leave him for the evening. When particularly frustrated, Joey attempts to kick or bite his therapist. In response to his aggression, Anna Freud might tell him, "You want to bite me but you can't. You can bite the pillow and talk about being angry with me" (p. 201).

Melanie Klein might well see Joey's immediate impulse to run away as "a sign of a negative transference . . . [making it] imperative . . . so as to resolve this resistance that interpretation should begin as soon as possible," following an interpretation that takes his negative affects back to their original objects and situation. Joey calms down somewhat and returns to the treatment room. Klein then watches Joey, who is exerting particular effort to push a miniature horse inside a narrow toy wagon. She might interpret, "You are watching your Daddy's thingamajig fit inside your

Mummy's Regina [his words]." When Joey reaches for a toy truck and smashes it against the wall, she says, "That truck is your Daddy who doesn't let *you* put *your* thingamajig in her and you'd like to smash him for that." As the sessions progress, Joey eventually assigns Klein various roles and then plays out the interaction with each. By now he is using language to do so. "One of the conditions of a successfully terminated treatment," says Klein (1932), "is that the child, however young, should make use of language in the analysis to the full extent of his capacities" (p. 64).

Understanding Joey's hesitation to part from his mother in the waiting room, D. W. Winnicott (1977) allows Mother to enter the playroom with Joey, bringing along the clown doll Joey has brought from home. Once there, she sits on a couch in a part of the room distant from Winnicott and his toys. She is asked not to help in the process to follow. Joey sits close to her on the couch. In his corner, Winnicott begins to play with the toys. Soon he asks Joey to "Bring [BoBo] over to me. I want to show *him* the toys" (p. 9). In the process of doing so, Joey becomes fascinated with the toys and begins to disassemble, explore, reassemble, combine one toy with another, and comment on what he is doing. After a short time, Joey's mother is able to exit the therapy room, leaving the door ajar. For long periods Winnicott says nothing, yet Joey feels his caring, interested presence. After a time of engaged observation, tentatively, and using Joey's own language, Winnicott relates the theme of the play to a troubling experience, either within Joey himself or in relation to his environment. Many sessions after this first one, as Joey becomes more communicative, Winnicott draws with pencil on paper the first of a series of incomplete doodles. He and Joey then begin a round of taking turns, completing each other's squiggles (Winnicott 1971). As each completed squiggle emerges, Joey volunteers or Winnicott suggests its meaning just as he had done in the early sessions through Joey's use of the toys. He then interprets the symbolic meaning of Joey's play. Sometimes Joey assigns Winnicott himself to play roles. These may be roles depicting Joey's unacceptable impulses, fears, or wishes, or they may be specific people. Sometimes the plot starring Winnicott as protagonist reveals a dreaded or a longed-for outcome. Throughout, even when Joey foregoes his "false self" for a true self, he keenly experiences the Winnicott climate as a "holding" one-one in which the therapist is There with a capital "T."

Joey's session with Frances Tustin (1972) proceeds as follows: In his own locked drawer in the therapy room Joey finds the few simple toys that belong to him alone: some tame animals, some wild ones, family figures, paint, and crayons.

He removes some of these toys, and as he settles down to play with them his therapist interprets with words the actions that Joey is playing out. She labels the toy that runs over things "the cruel red tractor." She relates to the mother that the pull–apart toy that he breaks apart with vigor he "[tears] to pieces in his rage" (p. 161).

Finally, in addition to following some aspects of certain child therapists, Theraplay shares some features in common with those adult treatment approaches that have their roots in the mother–infant relationship. Masterson, Kohut, and Davanloo are three adult therapists who will therefore be given hypothetical consideration:

James Masterson (as spokesman for Margaret Mahler), focuses on how Mother's symbiotic attachment to him makes Joey experience "abandonment depression" whenever he attempts to attain normal individuation and separation. Indeed, so intense is Mother's need for Joey that he has managed to drive away every hired baby sitter over these four short years. In contrast, Masterson's expectations of him lead to a quite different approach to Joey. He makes it clear to him that infantile and self-defeating behaviors will not do. He makes it clear that he expects him to behave like any normal 4-year-old. Then, after Joey has accomplished a degree of self-activation, Masterson will allow Joey to "refuel." He will do this in the way mothers express interest in the toys their small children deposit in their laps while playing. Through "communicative matching," he will acknowledge Joey's newfound autonomy. In this process Masterson will contribute to Joey his own wisdom and his own view of whatever wholesome reality excites Joey at the moment.

In helping Joey with his damaged sense of self, Heinz Kohut, although not generally known as a specialist in child psychoanalysis, mirrors and validates what Joey is experiencing and, as a part of this, allows Joey the experience of idealizing Kohut.

Finally, were Joey to be scheduled for an appointment with Habib Davanloo (whose short-term dynamic psychotherapy has heretofore been used only with adults), their session might go something like this:
Joey and Davanloo sit with legs crossed, facing one another on the floor. Joey's eyes flee wildly about the room. Davanloo calls this to his attention. He might even call to Joey's attention his efforts to avoid eye contact as protecting him from experiencing intimacy. Whenever Joey tries to leave the scene physically, Davanloo confronts this effort at avoidance as well. Joey begins to cry loudly, in protest only at first. Then, perhaps sensing Davanloo's dedication to helping him, he begins deep, sad sobbing. At that moment Joey is experiencing his real emotions for the first time. Having manifested anxiety, guilt, and grief in the transference he then reenacts with his therapist, perhaps through attempted kicking and scratching, the underlying reactive sadism he feels toward the mother who abandoned him early to her own depressed withdrawal.
All of these therapies differ from Theraplay in the degree to which they

1. are serious rather than frivolous and playful
2. use dolls, toys, or other objects

3. ask questions
4. use verbalizations
5. focus on pathology rather than on health
6. allow the child to take the lead following the enunciation of basic playroom rules
7. discourage physical contact with the therapist
8. have no outlined agenda
9. discourage, when appropriate, rather than insist upon, regressive behavior
10. are not specifically geared to enhancing parent–child attachment.

Play Is Necessary

With its attendant pleasure and reciprocal joy, play affords infants the most direct – albeit not the only – avenue for enhancing their attachment to their care-givers. So primary is the need for play and so necessary is it for the formation, enhancement, and maintenance of attachment that even in the loving behavior between two adults, play has as its model the kinds of activities typical of the parent–infant dyad. To summarize, Winnicott (1990) writes, "On the basis of playing is built the whole of man's experiential existence" (p. 64).

References

Beckwith, L. (1985). Parent–child interaction and social-emotional development. In *Play Interactions: The Role of Toys and Parent Involvement in Children's Development*, ed. C. C. Brown and A. W. Gottfried, pp. 152–159. Skillman, NJ: Johnson & Johnson.

Biggar, M. L. (1984). Maternal aversion to mother–infant contact. In *The Many Facets of Touch*, ed. C. C. Brown, pp. 66–72. Skillman, NJ: Johnson & Johnson.

Bretherton, I. (1985). Pretense: practicing and playing with social understanding. In *Play Interactions: The Role of Toys and Parent Involvement in Children's Development*, ed. C. C. Brown and A. W. Gottfried, pp. 69–79. Skillman, NJ: Johnson & Johnson.

Brown, C. C., ed. (1984). *The Many Facets of Touch*. Skillman, NJ: Johnson & Johnson.

Brown, C. C., and Gottfried, A. W., eds. (1985). *Play Interactions: The Role of Toys and Parent Involvement in Children's Development*. Skillman, NJ: Johnson & Johnson.

Burlingham, D. T., and Freud, A. (1943). *War and Children*. New York: Ernst Willard.

Cicchetti, D. (1985). Caregiver–infant interaction: maltreated infants. In *Play Interactions: The Role of Toys and Parent Involvement in Children's Development*, ed. C. C. Brown and A. W. Gottfried, pp. 107–113. Skillman, NJ: Johnson & Johnson.

Cohn, J., and Tronick, E. Z. (1987). Specifity of infants' response to mothers' affective behavior. Paper presented at the meeting of the Society for Research in Child Development, Baltimore, MD., April.

Davanloo, H. (1990). *Unlocking the Unconscious*. New York: John Wiley & Sons.

DeCasper, A., and Spence, M. (1982). Prenatal maternal speech influences human newborns' auditory preferences. Paper presented at the 3rd Biennial International Conference on Infant Studies. Austin, TX.

DesLauriers, A. (1962). *The Experience of Reality in Childhood Schizophrenia.* New York: International Universities Press.

DesLauriers, A., and Carlson, C. F. (1969). *Your Child Is Asleep: Early Infantile Autism.* Homewood, IL: Dorsey.

Emde, R. N., and Sameroff, A. (1982). *The Place of Attachment in Human Behavior.* New York: Basic Books.

_____ (1989). *Relationship Disturbances in Early Childhood.* New York: Basic Books.

Emde, R. N., and Sorce, J. F. (1983). Rewards of infancy. In *Frontiers of Infant Psychiatry,* ed. J. D. Call, E. Galenson, and R. L. Tyson, pp. 17–30. New York: Basic Books.

Flint, B. M. (1959). *The Security of Infants.* Toronto: University of Toronto Press.

Fraiberg, S., Adelson, E., and Shapiro, V. (1975). Ghosts in the nursery: a psychoanalytic approach to the problems of impaired mother–infant relationships. *Journal of the American Academy of Child Psychiatry* 14:378–421.

Freud, A. (1946). *The Psycho-Analytical Treatment of Children.* London: Imago.

Greenough, W. T. (1984). Brain storage of sensory information in development and adulthood. In *The Many Facets of Touch,* ed. C. C. Brown, pp. 29–38. Skillman, NJ: Johnson & Johnson.

Grossmann, K., Grossmann, K., Spangler, G., et al. (1985). Maternal sensitivity and newborns' orientation responses as related to quality of attachment in northern Germany. In *Growing Points of Attachment Theory and Research,* ed. I. Bretherton and E. Waters, pp. 233–256. Monographs of the Society for Research in Child Development XX. Chicago: University of Chicago Press.

Jackson, L., and Todd, K. M. (1950). *Child Treatment and the Therapy of Play.* 2nd ed. New York: The Ronald Press Co.

_____ (1979). *Theraplay: A New Treatment Using Structured Play for Problem Children and Their Families.* San Francisco: Jossey Bass.

_____ (1988). Promoting prenatal and perinatal mother–child bonding: a psychotherapeutic assessment of parental attitudes. In *Prenatal and Perinatal Psychology and Medicine,* ed. P. G. Fedor-Freybergh and M. L. Vaness Vogel, pp. 253–266. Park Ridge, IL: The Parthenon Publishing Group.

_____ (1990). Attachment enhancing for adopted children. In *Adoption Resources for Mental Health Professionals,* ed. P. V. Grabe, pp. 271–279. New Brunswick, NJ: Transaction.

_____ (1991). Assessing parent–child interactions with the Marschak Interaction Method (MIM). In *Play Diagnosis and Assessment,* ed. C. E. Schaefer, K. Gitlin, and A. Sandgrund, pp. 493–515. New York: John Wiley & Sons.

Jernberg, A. M., Allert, A., Booth, P., and Koller, T. (1983). *Reciprocity in Parent-Infant Relationships.* Chicago, IL: The Theraplay Institute.

Jernberg, A. M., and Booth, P. (1991). *Revised Dimensions of the Marschack Interaction Method.* Chicago, IL: The Theraplay Institute.

Jernberg, A. M., Booth, P., Koller, T., and Allert, A. *Manual for the Administration and the Clinical Interpretation of the Marschak Interaction Method (MIM) Preschool and School Age.* Chicago, IL: The Theraplay Institute.

Jernberg, A. M., Wickersham, M., and Thomas, E. (1985). *Mothers' Behaviors and Attitudes toward Their Unborn Infants.* Chicago: The Theraplay Institute.

Klein, M. (1932). *The Psycho-Analysis of Children.* London: Hogarth Press.

Koller, T. K. (1984). *Guidelines for Teachers of Older Adopted Children: II.* Chicago: The Theraplay Institute.

Levenstein, P. (1985). Mothers' interactive behavior in play sessions and children's education achievement. In *Play Interactions: The Role of Toys and Parent Involvement in Children's Development*, ed. C. C. Brown and A. W. Gottfried, pp. 160–167. Skillman, NJ: Johnson & Johnson.

Main, M., and Weston, D. (1982). Avoidance of the attachment figure in infancy. In *The Place of Attachment in Human Behavior*, ed. C. M. Parkes and J. Stevenson-Hinde, pp. 31–59. New York: Basic Books.

Marschak, M. (1960). A method for evaluating child–parent interaction under controlled conditions. *Journal of Genetic Psychology* 97:3–22.

_____ (1967). Imitation and participation in normal and disturbed young boys in interaction with their parents. *Journal of Clinical Psychology* 23:421–427.

_____ (1980). *Parent–Child Interaction and Youth Rebellion*. New York: Gardner.

Minuchin, S., and Fishman, C. (1981). *Family Therapy Techniques*. Cambridge: Harvard University Press.

O'Connor, K. J. (1991). *The Play Therapy Primer: An Integration of Theories and Techniques*. New York: John Wiley & Sons.

Parkes, C. M., and Stevenson-Hinde, J., eds. (1982). *The Place of Attachment in Human Behavior*. New York: Basic Books.

Pedersen, F. A., and Robson, K. S. (1969). Father participation in infancy. *American Journal of Orthopsychiatry* 39:466–472.

Rauh, V., Nurcombe, B., Achenbach, T., and Howel, C. (1986). The mother–infant transaction program: an intervention for the mothers of low-birthweight infants. In *Infant Stimulation: For Whom, What Kind, When, and How Much?*, ed. N. Gunzenhauser, pp. 144–157. Skillman, NJ: Johnson & Johnson.

Reite, M. (1984). Touch, attachment, and health – is there a relationship? In *The Many Facets of Touch*, ed. C. C. Brown, pp. 58–65. Skillman, NJ: Johnson & Johnson.

Rose, S. (1984). Preterm responses to passive, active, and social touch. In *The Many Facets of Touch*, ed. C. C. Brown, pp. 91–100. Skillman, NJ: Johnson & Johnson.

Schaefer, C. E., ed. (1991). *Play Diagnosis and Assessment*. New York: John Wiley & Sons.

Seligman, M. P. (1991). *Learned Optimism*. New York: Knopf.

Stern, D. (1974). Goal and structure of mother–infant play. *Journal of the American Academy of Child Psychiatry* 13:402–419.

_____ (1985). *The Interpersonal World of the Infant*. New York: Basic Books.

Tustin, F. (1972). *Autism and Childhood Psychosis*. London: Hogarth Press.

Winnicott, D. W. (1971). *Therapeutic Consultations in Child Psychiatry*. New York: Basic Books.

_____ (1977). *The Piggle*. New York: International Universities Press.

_____ (1987). *Babies and Their Mothers*. Reading, PA: Addison-Wesley.

_____ (1990). *Playing and Reality*. 2nd printing. New York: Routledge, 1971.

Wolf, M. M., Risley, T., and Mees, L. H. (1964). Application of operant conditioning procedures to the behavioral problems of an autistic child. *Behavior, Research and Therapy* 1:305–312.

12

Relationship Enhancement

Louise F. Guerney

> The most important single influence in
> the life of a person is another person.
> —Paul D. Schaefer

Studies of infant bonding reveal that the quality of the relating that takes place between mother and child makes a major contribution to the child's ability to thrive both physically and emotionally (e.g., Broussard and Hartner 1970, Drotar and Echerle 1990). Nonorganic failure to thrive appears to stem from problems in the mother's skill at relating to the child appropriately. Absence of or limited reciprocal interaction between depressed mothers and their infants can lead to continued problems in individual functioning and in the children's ability to form other relationships (Weintraub et al. 1986).

The contribution of positive relationships to adjustment and interpersonal functioning is probably demonstrated no more dramatically than in the work of Garmezy (1986) on invulnerable children. He found that the presence of at least one supportive, caring person in the life of a youngster exposed to war, loss of total family, and other horrors could make the difference in maintaining positive mental health. Through relationships—first with the mother, then with other significant adults, siblings, and the interpersonal community—children learn about themselves, others, and even the physical world.

Harry Stack Sullivan (1947), the foremost interpersonal theorist, posited that our personalities are the sum total of our interpersonal response patterns and that we, in turn, elicit from others responses consistent with the patterns we present. From these patterns, good and poor relationships result, the latter constituting the basis for all psychopathology. According to Sullivan, and later Leary (1957), who expanded empirically on Sullivan's work, the patterns of responses we acquire are for the sole purpose of reducing intra- and interpersonal anxiety. Social learning theorists would explain these patterns of responses in terms of reinforcement, so that our relationship behaviors would be the result of what was experienced as rewarding. While anxiety reduction would be, in fact, negative reinforcement (the reward experienced when an aversive stimulus is removed), Sullivan/Leary did not use the concept of reinforcement.

267

It is not difficult to reconcile the two theoretical principles, however, by acknowledging that anxiety reduction and reinforcement work together to shape the ways in which we relate to each other. When patterns operating in important relationships – in the family, school, and so forth – generate unrewarding or anxious feelings for members, the relationships can become dysfunctional. For example, parents who respond primarily with hostility and punishment toward their children in turn pull aggressive and uncooperative responses from their children (Patterson 1982). When these children carry over the same responses outside the family, agents of schools and/or the community may attempt to intervene with the family. Their first step would be to look at the family relationships to determine in what way the child has been negatively influenced or trained to behave in socially unacceptable ways through the reciprocal response patterns used in the family. By one theory or another, lay persons and professionals alike tend to explain problems in terms of relationships, for instance, "His stepfather hated him," or "Her family was cold and distant." Our cultural belief that poor relationships with significant figures are at the root of emotional and behavioral disorders is so compelling, however, that even professionals need to be reminded that there are some disorders that are physically and neurologically based.

Without undue exaggeration, then, it is not inappropriate to define the task of psychotherapy – except where problems are known to be physically based – to be that of altering the client's relationship patterns so that the client can behave in ways that elicit rewarding and anxiety-reducing responses from others and, in turn, provide rewarding responses for those he relates to. This goal is no less applicable to child therapy. In fact, it would seem to be even more in keeping with the reasons for child treatment referrals. It has long been established that behavior problems are consistently the major reasons for child referrals. These problems consist primarily of the inability to cooperate, comply, and control the expression of aggression toward others and to get along with adults and other children. Social withdrawal, an obvious relationship problem, also ranks high as a referral reason. So, improving relationships is clearly a major task for the child therapist.

Behavioral approaches that do focus on parent–child relationships (e.g., Eyberg 1988, Patterson 1982) have been developed to try to address many specific, inappropriate behavioral interactions that occur in these relationships. Prevention programs that try to teach children appropriate responses for creating better relationships with peers, such as assertion programs (Borgen and Rudner 1981) and friendship building programs (Bierman 1989), are also found increasingly in schools and day care settings. But play therapy, of one model or another, has been for many years the most commonly used modality for dealing with children and their relationship problems. Play therapists, whatever method they use, not only treat children who have relationship problems, but must themselves establish nonproblematic relationships with the children to bring about improvements in their functioning. The centrality of positive, therapeutic relationships to successful outcomes in play therapy is generally accepted. Some theorists attribute positive therapeutic outcomes solely to this therapeutic relationship. Whether they share this singular view or credit other factors with change, all child therapeutic approaches would acknowledge the value of a positive child–therapist relationship for facilitating therapeutic gain and undergirding the techniques employed.

In this chapter, the goal will be to consider the play therapy process in regard to (1) improving the interpersonal relationships of children in all their contexts– family, schools, and so forth; (2) the process of establishing and optimizing the relationship between the child client and the play therapist; and (3) supporting evidence that play therapy does bring about relationship changes. Since group play therapy is offered most frequently when the primary need of child group members is to improve peer relationships, the above points will be considered in the context of group therapy as well. We will also include discussion of paraprofessionals and parents serving as therapists and the special issues involved with their assumption of the therapist role. While my own professional commitment is to the approach of Axline, derived from Rogers (Axline 1947, 1969), other approaches will also be presented so that the reader can develop a sense of the breadth of "play power" for changing relationships.

Theoretical and Empirical Considerations

Studies in Child Development

In 1971, researchers who asked how children learn to obey their mothers studied the relationship between maternal responsiveness, acceptance, and cooperation with their 9- to 12-month-old children, observing mother and child in an open-ended play situation in the family's own home. With children at this young age, obedience was defined as simple compliance to present, external signals. Infant obedience was associated with maternal expression of acceptance, cooperation, and sensitivity to infant's signals or, in other words, behaviors that promoted infant–mother harmony. Specific behaviors on the part of the mother to train, discipline, or control the baby's behavior did not increase the instances of infant compliance. The researchers (Stayton et al. 1971) concluded that a "disposition toward obedience emerges in a responsive, accommodating social environment without extensive training, discipline, or other massive attempts to shape the infant's course of development" (p. 1067).

More recently, other child development researchers investigated different variables in mother–child interactions that might contribute to child compliance with 4-year-old children and their mothers. The researchers studied the effects of training mothers in "Responsive Play," and observed their interactions with their children in comparison with a group of mothers who had not been trained. Mothers in the Responsive Play conditions were trained in the "Special Time Technique" (Parpal and Maccoby 1985), which places emphasis on responding positively and letting the child take the lead in the play. Mothers were instructed to avoid commands, asking questions, and making corrections. They were asked to practice this technique at home before being observed in the laboratory. Results indicated that *children whose mothers played using the Responsive Play technique reported significantly higher pleasure scores on a pleasure measure (nonverbal scale of emotion). The researchers (Lay et al. 1989) concluded that responsive parenting induces positive mood, which in turn mediates compliance. They suggest that the significance of their studies is that "behavioral interaction necessarily involves (or creates) an affective context and takes on an affective connotation. Moreover, the affective connotation and consequences of closely coordinated interactive play have significant implications for social learning and socialization" (p. 1410).

Both studies just described, in this author's view, support the hypothesis that a good relationship with the parent, with the positive, affective response it generates, *is* the underpinning of the child's desire to cooperate. Further, it would seem that cooperation is the child's response of choice when there is a good relationship with the parent. It can be extrapolated that noncooperation will result when children experience the parental relationship as nonrewarding, anxiety-producing, and/or too controlling.

Both studies cited established in a sound, empirical way that the specific behaviors of furthering the child, providing emotional support, and not interfering except where necessary, are consistently associated with child motivation to behave in a socially desirable way. Everyday wisdom lends additional credence to these observations. We have all learned at some point in life, particularly in inescapable situations such as in grade school, that we feel happier and more contented when the adult in charge behaves in an understanding and supportive way. We, in turn, are more likely to want to cooperate. When adults behave in an authoritarian way and simply impose without concern about the impact of their behavior upon us, we are more likely to conform superficially rather than fully participate and cooperate, or even find excuses not to conform. This folk wisdom was obviously not wasted on the early developers of play therapy methods. They emphasized the importance of the therapist being sensitive, caring, non–critical, and imposing only necessary restrictions. These features are generally recognized as being of great importance in all approaches and are at the base of the relationship-oriented therapies.

The Therapeutic Relationship

Until the time of Freud, there were no verbal therapies. The approach to the treatment of mental and emotional disorders was through physical approaches such as the use of magnets and hypnotism (Kanner 1948). Something was done to the patient by the therapist, and the notion of a relationship between therapist and patient was not considered a factor in the treatment. Verbal methods, on the other hand, fostered a relationship between therapist and client, requiring expressive participation by the client. But, in the early therapies, only the therapist could interpret the meaning of the client's expressions and thus was a most powerful authority upon whom the patient became very dependent. Resolving this dependence then became another relationship-oriented task for the therapist (A. Freud 1955).

For the first analytic play therapists (Kanner 1948, Klein 1948), play was viewed only as a means of demonstrating psychic conflicts for the purpose of interpreting them to the child. Relationship establishment through play and for facilitating the understanding of play was the contribution of Anna Freud to early play therapy methods. The importance of establishing and maintaining a therapeutic relationship with the play therapy client has remained a goal of most play therapies ever since.

Anna Freud (1955) – unlike her father and the earlier analysts who first developed play analysis for children – believed that play was a means of getting acquainted with the child, gaining his confidence, and getting the child to like her. Only after she had acquired information about the child from observing him play and obtaining information about his life, including the life history from the parents, did she attempt to try to understand the meaning of the child's play and interpret this to the child. At that point, the relationship would be sufficiently strong to assure the child that libidinous impulses would not drive away the therapist and that the therapist would support the child in helping to deal with such impulses (A. Freud 1955).

In the period between then and now, new relationship-based therapies have been developed. In this chapter, the major ones will be described in detail and the others mentioned in brief. The significant factor in each, however, is the belief that the relationship with the therapist is the major force responsible for therapeutic change.

Interaction of the Relationship and Playing

The unique qualities of the relationship may be most responsible for positive gains from play therapy. However, play is the medium in which the relationship is anchored, and as such we must view play as an integral, interactive part of the process of relationship building.

The exact contribution of play per se to the play therapy process has not yet been identified. It is obvious, however, that an adult who meets with a child in a play setting – the special world of childhood – is going to be perceived differently than other professionals. The trappings of the play setting spell out a different message than those of schools or professional offices. The child knows that this place is intended for play, and quickly learns that the adult intends to join in this activity to some degree. The adult enters the world of the child, and as such will be perceived as more of a peer of children than will other adults. An adult who shares in the child's games and play activities will be much better able to create a strong bond with that child than would a nonplaying adult. Children really like their play therapists, and therapists frequently remark on how much they enjoy playing with child clients.

What is it about playing together that promotes this strong bond? Some have referred to it as a "pleasure bond" resulting from sharing pleasures together. Certainly this is part of it, if only from a reinforcement perspective. We connect our pleasures with the people who are with us during those times. But it would seem that more than pleasure is derived from the play. Play sessions are a haven from reality in a sense. In fantasy play, the child can be mean, super-giving, supportive, aggressive, and destructive and the adult goes along with the child on those delightful excursions that permit the child to be what she needs to be at the moment. In my view, it is not just fun together that makes for the strong adult–child bond, but it is the sharing of the child's inner self with the adult in a play context. In fantasy play, the child can do what and be what he wants without ridicule or interference. Play provides an unreality to the child's expressions that makes it safer to deal with inhibited or unexpressed feelings. The person who shares in those explorations with the child takes on a very special meaning in the child's life. Play allows that to happen as it could not in other therapeutic modalities. The unreality of play protects us from owning the content any more than we are ready to own it. Even play that is more reality oriented, such as playing a structured game, protects us to some extent. We can think of it as only a game if we wish. With an accepting play therapist, losing a structured game does not threaten a child's status as it might with same-aged friends. Thus, the child can look at the meaning of the game and its outcome without threat. While some children lose poorly in the play sessions as well as in real life, they have the choice to take it less seriously, and with the therapist's acceptance can learn to do so in time, taking full advantage of the play quality to the game.

In all likelihood, the modality of play and the attitude of the therapist are both essential for a positive therapeutic relationship. Studies by Reif and Stollak (1972), and Stover and Guerney (1967) demonstrate that play with an untrained adult produces significantly less therapeutic change in children than play with an adult who is empathic, warm, and permits the child to lead. So, the therapist's positive behavior combined with the advantages of the play context seem to be the two essential factors that make play therapy powerful.

The Importance of the Therapeutic Relationship to All Play Therapies

Before turning our attention to relationship-based therapies, it is important to look at the place of the relationship with the play therapist in all therapies. It is almost impossible to describe a therapy of any sort without making note of the relationship. Few of the play therapies developed over the years fail to describe the importance of establishing rapport with the child at the outset of the therapy. However, beyond the development of initial rapport and, in time, the positive emotional attachment referred to by A. Freud (1955), the specific responses of the therapist contribute to relationship-building as well. By virtue of the different nature of the therapist's responses from those of most other adults in the child's life, whether these are contingency-related, reinforcing responses as in behavioral therapies, or nonevaluative ones, as in the relationship therapies, the interpersonal atmosphere they establish becomes a meta-communication with the therapist. As Marcus (1966) expressed it in describing the nonrelationship approach of Costume Play Therapy, "A trusting and meaningful relationship evolves from the ability to communicate understanding to the child, rather than from friendly playful activities as such" (p. 375).

Brady and Friedrich (1982), describing the training of play therapists, posit that play therapy follows Piaget's three developmental stages of play, and that the child's relationship with the therapist also follows the same developmental path, progressing over time along the "dimensions of intimacy, social complexity, perspective taking, and [increasing] the proportion of verbal materials to physical action" (p. 40). The therapist's behavior will be guided by the child's receptivity to the therapist's responses, and a genuine interactive process will ensue between the child and the therapist, which will be further shaped by the parameters of the play (Brady and Friedrich 1982).

In a discussion of therapeutic relationship, the phenomenon of transference should be mentioned. Transference feelings are positive and negative feelings of the client toward the therapist, believed to be transferred to her/him from feelings actually experienced with other significant figures, most often the parents. Transference is a concept developed in psychoanalysis. Methods for dealing with transference phenomena fill psychoanalytic writings. These feelings need to be resolved and separated from feelings specific to the therapist–client relationship. A. Freud (1955) argues that positive transference alone is the important part of transference when working with children.

Relationship Approaches in Play Therapy

While the relationship of the therapist to the child is recognized as an essential ingredient, ever present and making its contribution to what transpires in and results from the therapy in all approaches, relationship approach therapists take the therapeutic relationship still another step. They see the relationship with the therapist as the sine qua non of therapy. Catharsis, destructive and constructive play are important, but the play activities gain their full meaning only from the resulting response of the therapist. Play meanings are filtered and distilled through the reactions of the therapist. The relationship-oriented therapist does not merely passively permit or tolerate expression, but also verbally expresses acceptance by making empathic statements or reflections of feeling or comments on behavior and actions that let the child know that she is understood and accepted. For example, if the child were beating up a bop bag and calling it the names of family members, the therapist would not simply attend without comment. She would say something like, "You're really getting Billy (brother's name)" or, "You are so angry with Billy. You're really giving it to him today." In this way the child would know that both the behavior and the accompanying feelings were being accepted by the therapist. It is this acceptance of the child's desire, motives, feelings, and attitudes underlying the expression that makes the relationship approach different. The goal is to permit the child complete freedom of expression, with some limits on physical expression, so that she will release all she needs to release – be it the darkest and deepest of hitherto repressed feelings or positive expressions – without fear of criticism or rejection or threat to being fully valued by the therapist. The nonjudgmental, nonevaluative, that is, no negative feedback or praise (lest the child become eager to win approval or feel hurt when it is not given), behavior of the therapist makes it safe for the child to bring out in the open all conflicts and concerns. Such responses from an adult with whom the child has a positive attachment will permit the child to accept components of herself heretofore difficult to accept or even be aware of. Once accepted, the components can be managed positively, no longer needing to be repressed or otherwise defended against in some less than optimal way.

Axline/Rogers and Allen's Approaches

For those who are familiar with nondirective or client-centered or child-centered play therapy, the rationale provided above will be familiar as, in good part, the approach of Virginia Axline (1947, 1969). Axline derived this form of play therapy from the approach of her mentor, Carl Rogers, who developed client-centered therapy for adults (Rogers 1958). Rogers believed that all successful helping relationships – for child and adult clients – are characterized by the ability to understand the client's meanings and feelings, a sensitivity to the client's attitudes, and a warm interest without emotional overinvolvement. Rogers further believed that when acceptance was conditional, the client could not change or grow in the areas where the therapist could not accept the client. He saw the threat of external evaluation as a major impediment to therapy that stood in the way of the individual's arriving at his/her own self and socially responsible personhood. He believed that this was a danger even when the relationship was well established. Rogers's second revolutionary concept was his belief that the client, not the therapist, would know best what conflicts needed to be explored and the route to take through them.

The client-centered adult therapy of Rogers was radical, but its adaptation for children was a natural next step for a child therapist working in the Rogers theoretical framework, like Axline. While she and the other client-centered therapists interested in child therapy developed and researched the new approach with children, a contemporary was developing a receptive *zeitgeist* for the principles of the new therapy at the Philadelphia Child Guidance Center. Dr. Frederick Allen was the chief psychiatrist there, where he developed a widely accepted approach that extended the views of Anna Freud. Allen (1939) believed that change is made primarily through the therapeutic relationship. This relationship is not simply a necessary first step in order to make interpretations more palatable, as advocated by A. Freud. The quality of the relationship, which he believed should be a permissive one, determines the therapeutic outcome. A good therapeutic relationship respects the integrity of the child, has the capacity to accept the child as he is, and believes in the child's ability to work on his own problem. Allen wrote:

> I have no desire to impose my own standards upon a patient or to determine the specific attitudes toward which therapy will be directed. If I can create a relation in which the child or adult feels that he is accepted at the point he is in his own growth—rebellious, hostile, fearful, or what not—then that person has an opportunity to go ahead with those difficulties that are most concerning him. He is not kept busy defending himself against being "helped" and being remade. [p. 194]

It would seem that through a series of departures from Hug-Hellmuth, the first child therapist who introduced play into the therapy and relied entirely on interpretations (Kanner 1948), and described little interest in the relationship per se, the prevailing view of what made child therapy work had shifted to a conviction that the relationship was the primary factor. This view was advocated by both the leading child psychiatrist, Allen, and independently and contemporaneously by the leading child psychologist, Axline.

Not all therapies see the necessity for the therapist providing complete acceptance. Fair-play therapy, a method first described in 1979 by Peoples, views the therapeutic relationship as one that requires more natural responses from the therapist. Peoples (1983) believes that some of the behavior of children in permissive, child-directed play sessions is self-indulgent, irresponsible, and really difficult to accept, and should instead be responded to by the therapist in terms of the effect it produces. He maintains that the child can then become more responsible and see the therapy as a mutual endeavor, a more natural give-and-take situation. However, the therapist's responses remain socially appropriate, and empathy is still an important ingredient (Peoples 1983).

With their belief in the primacy of the relationship, all relationship therapists must face the same burning question: if the child develops a healthy, healing relationship with the therapist, in which the child can function interpersonally in a mature, appropriate way, how will the child be able to transfer these newfound abilities to different people and different circumstances outside of the play session? Allen answered the question by stating that he believed in the capacity of the child to assume responsibility for utilizing the therapeutic experiences in the relationships she establishes with others. The child "acquires in this relationship [with the therapist] a sense of self that gives him the capacity to relate himself to others and to grow" (Allen 1939, p. 197). Axline (1947) also saw the process arising from the relationship with the play therapist and extending beyond to others:

> As the child grows to accept himself, to grant himself the permissiveness to utilize all of his capacities, and to assume responsibility for himself . . . he applies this philosophy in his relationships with others so that he has a deep respect for people, an acceptance of them as

they are, . . . and a real belief in the integrity of the individual. . . . He places emphasis on a positive and constructive way of life. [pp. 28–29]

The concern with the specificity of relationship modification has resulted in a number of approaches that are directed toward bringing about positive changes in particular relationships. For example, relationships with absent parents have been addressed through the "Two Houses" approach of Kuhli (1979). Kuhli reports success in the use of the method with children who have experienced trauma in relation to family members. Children are presented with an "old house" where traumas may be reexperienced, then left behind there, and a "new house" to which more positive feelings can be connected with new adults and new living situations. Adoptive parent–child relationships have been addressed in play therapy relationship approaches by Jernberg (1979) and Ginsberg (1989).

Total reliance on the powerful therapist–child relationship to bring about all desirable interpersonal growth may not always be sufficient, although it is a necessary first step. Axline herself was a vigorous proponent of group play sessions, ideally in conjunction with individual play sessions. She believed that the combination facilitated the growth process, and when the problem was primarily social adjustment with other children, she felt that the group medium might sometimes be preferable when possible. She saw situations arising within groups that provided opportunities for children to work out their feelings about others *in situ*.

It is quite clear that, while both Allen and Axline attribute most gain in therapy to the relationship with the professional therapist in a one-on-one context, Axline and many others who followed her saw that relationship improvement might be, at least, bolstered when therapy is conducted in the context of relevant relationships.

Group Therapy

It is generally agreed that the advantage of the group format is to permit children to develop better relationships with peers, as well as the therapist, and to experience the kind of feedback possible only from peers. Since the development of play therapy, we have witnessed the rising success of the peer support and mutual support group movement based on the same principle of peer acceptance. In the therapeutic world, acceptance by peers, even around issues that do not involve peers – relationships with parents, institutional staff, and even the relationship of an individual to a health condition or disease – seems to have special powers that often are considered at least equal to those of professionals, at less cost.

Of course, children's play therapy groups, unlike some adult groups, do have an adult therapist. With larger groups (seven or more children), there are sometimes two. The therapist is the leader but, depending on the therapeutic model, the therapist shares more or less of her/his decision-making power with the children around the content and activities of the group. Regardless of the degree of control the therapist exercises over the agenda, the goal is always to create an atmosphere that permits group members to interact verbally and nonverbally. Because the group members do have a responsibility to each other as well as to the therapist, of necessity there must be behavioral guidelines and limits for interactions among members as well as in relation to the therapist. Antisocial and uncaring behaviors are usually controlled, and frequently become the focus of group discussion and attention as grist for the therapeutic mill. Group therapists judge progress in group relationships by how well the youngsters can interact among themselves without needing to "go through" the therapist. The new, unsure group member will need the therapist to provide a secure base until he is accepted by the group. Acceptance by the group may be the major gain for a child who has experienced problems with peer rejection or ignoring. However, therapists do not believe that group therapy is useful for young children or for children whose ego is so fragile or underdeveloped that they can not deal with a group. Children with a great need for adult nurturance can also fail to benefit from peer interactions. Many therapists use a group when they feel the child in individual therapy has already come to terms with adult figures, as symbolized by the therapist, and is ready to deal with peer relationships.

Ginott (1959, 1961), one of the early client-centered play therapists, did a considerable amount of work with children's as well as mothers' therapy groups. He recommended that children who have a "social hunger" for peer acceptance be placed into a group either after, or instead of, individual therapy (Ginott 1961).

Activity Group Therapy

Most widely recognized as a productive approach for preadolescents is Activity Group Therapy, described by its developer (Slavson 1947, Slavson and Shiffer 1974). In Activity Group Therapy, members share in activities popular to children of their ages. Often these are at first suggested by the therapist, chosen to permit parallel play as opposed to group play, because the members are not yet ready to relate as an entire group. When a greater maturity level is reached, group games will be chosen by either the therapist or group members. Stagnation at a level of group development would require the therapist to introduce activities designed to integrate members, or to add or subtract members to change the group's constellation.

The dynamics among group members must be carefully considered. The shy child who has become open and comfortable with an accepting adult therapist may clam up in a group of expressive peers. All group therapists seem to agree that groups function best when the dynamics of individual members are balanced between acting out and inexpressiveness. Ginott (1961) even went so far as to recommend that a child free of problems be placed in a group to serve as a model and to help normalize the other children.

In all groups, regardless of the theoretical base, the therapist must decide when to make therapeutic responses to an individual or to the group. Group members in time learn to do the same thing for each other, interpreting or empathizing, depending on the approach. Group problem solving is undertaken with the therapist as consultant. As in individual therapy, the group encourages expression and, at the same time, must impose limits on that expression to protect the psychological and physical safety of group members.

Consideration of what group therapy purports to do will provide the reader with a notion of what its potential might be to augment relationship development for children. The question must be raised as to whether the group method really accomplishes more than individual therapy for enhancing peer relationships. Controlled studies that place children randomly into group or individual therapy and compare progress in interpersonal development are lacking. We must recognize that success with the group approach has been reported only when (1) the therapist prefers the group approach to the individual approach, (2) it has been introduced to supplement individual therapy and the effects of both are not separated out, and (3) circumstances require that groups must be used to serve more children. Groups are likely to be employed for the latter reason in school settings, because children must function successfully in groups in classrooms, and therapy resources are usually limited.

Interestingly, some of the earliest empirical studies of psychotherapy were done with client-centered play therapy groups. Fleming and Snyder (1947) showed gains for a treatment group over a nontreatment control group, while Fisher (1953) and Moulin (1970) demonstrated the effectiveness of client-centered group therapy with groups of academic underachievers. Abramowitz (1976) examined more recent child group therapy outcome studies for all types of child treatment groups and concluded that the efficacy of group therapy for children was inconclusive. Only 28 percent of the groups, however, were play therapy groups of any type. Scrutiny of her tables shows that the results of the play therapy groups were superior to the results obtained for other types of child groups. Only two of the twelve play therapy approaches studied failed to yield at least some positive changes, whereas for other group approaches, including discussion groups, recreation therapy groups, and social skills training groups, only three out of ten groups showed positive changes. These results support the conviction of those who champion it, that group play therapy can achieve results even when groups are used out of necessity, and not solely as the approach of choice.

Parents as Play Therapists

A developing trend in the field that provides a response to some of the concerns about transfer and generalization of relationship gains from the therapist to the family is the use of parents as therapists. If parents serve as therapists, they are the ones who are accepting of the child's needs, empathic with the child's feelings, and able to place realistic limits on the child's behavior. Since relationship problems with the parents are a major reason for referral and are involved in many other kinds of problems as well, involvement of the parents would seem to reduce the extent to which the children must be able to reconceptualize themselves in relation to others. Instead of children having to learn that parents can also see them as acceptable and in turn accept them, parents are right there, demonstrating and living out the acceptance while serving as therapists. Progress in changing the relationship with the parent should be more certain and perhaps faster. Guerney and Stover (1971), working with parents as therapists, did in fact find this to be so in relation to expression of aggression. Children exhibited aggression in play sessions at an earlier point than with therapists (Guerney and Stover 1971).

Proponents of the use of parents as therapists point out many advantages, primarily the uniqueness and primacy of the child–parent relationship. Having the parents serve as therapists gives them new insights. Required as they are to assume the role of empathic, furthering therapists, they see their children from a different perspective. And, not only do they see the same behaviors differently, but they actually can observe different behaviors because their children can respond differently when the parents abandon their typical parenting behaviors.

When the parents are lacking in skills for communicating and managing the child's behavior, they learn to improve on these dimensions because the play therapist's ways of relating epitomize the good parent–child relationship. Baumrind (1967) has demonstrated empirically in a number of studies that parents who are warm, understanding, and supportive, but who insist upon and get age-appropriate behavior from their children, have the most socially competent children. These children establish good relationships with peers and with themselves in that they have high self-confidence in social as well as performance areas. The play therapist who, regardless of the approach, is understanding and accepting of the child while enforcing reasonable, unbending limits, really models the authoritative parent of Baumrind. So, while the parent is providing needed acceptance to the child in the therapy session the parent is learning a new way to parent that enables him or her also to behave differently outside of the play session. Parents can quickly see how the preferred responses they have been taught to use in the therapy situation can also apply elsewhere, and can generally make the transfer quite well.

There is still another advantage to having parents serve as the therapist. Children, too, can perceive their parents differently in the parent play session. To see that the parent is really a person with some depth – who can be tough with limits if need be, or permissive if there's no good reason not to be – is extremely enlightening to a child. It is possible for the child to learn that the parent has the basic capacity to be accepting. This knowledge can help the child diminish inappropriate ways of relating to the parent to try to get attention, power, or nurturance. Acceptance permits children to use more positive approaches in getting their needs met.

Play Approaches Using Parents as Therapists

Currently, there are a number of play approaches involving the use of parents, either exclusively or in some cases. Each of these will be presented in this section.

Child Relationship Enhancement Family Therapy (CREFT)

The first systematic effort to introduce parents into the play session as therapists – Filial Therapy, or as it has been more recently labeled, Child Relationship Enhancement Family Therapy (CREFT) – was developed by Bernard Guerney in the 1960s (Guerney 1964). However, scattered single case reports of parents playing with their children to relieve problems were reported in the literature prior to that. The first such account seems to be that of no other than Freud himself, in the case of Hans, in which Freud instructed and supervised the father on how to treat the child's phobia (Freud 1959).

Guerney and colleagues (Stover and Guerney 1967) developed training and supervision methods that permit parents to function effectively as play therapists using the Axline approach. Empirical studies have demonstrated not only that parents can carry out the role quite well (Stover and Guerney 1967) but that their children improve as much and as rapidly in play therapy as do children in more conventional treatments (Glass 1986, Guerney 1976, Wall 1979). Since CREFT includes all of the children in the family in addition to the target child and, where possible, both parents, the method is truly a variation on family therapy wherein family members learn skills for relating to each other in their ongoing relationships. First, empathic responding skills and limit setting are taught by the therapist through demonstration and much practice for use in the play sessions, held both at home and at the treatment site. Direct instruction is used for transfer and generalization to parents' roles outside, which comprises the last stage in the CREFT approach.

Advantages: One of the most powerful advantages of the CREFT approach is that assigning parents to this important role removes them from the underclass of parents whose child must receive treatment from professional therapists. Parents are trusted to carry out this task, albeit with an enormous amount of emotional and instructional support and reinforcement. But, in so doing, they are greatly empowered and in turn empower their children as well. No competition with a therapist exists for parents to deal with. As clinicians note, this can be quite destructive for the child and the therapist–child relationship. The child's gain is also the parents' gain. Parents relate to the therapists as their supervisors and consultants, giving parents a status of importance in their child's treatment and in the treatment team's structure.

Application: The CREFT approach has been used successfully with a variety of parents in the pursuit of one or both of two goals: to enhance the many functions of the parent–child relationship, and to ameliorate child problems. We are including under the parent–child relationship not only the more obvious affective aspects of the relationship – mutual positive feelings – but also the discipline and socializing functions of the parent. The control or action dimension of the relationship can influence the feeling components of the relationship as much as good feelings can influence discipline (Lay et al. 1989). Evaluation of the method has shown that changes do occur in these relationship aspects as well as on the affective dimension, thus supporting the validity of this goal (Ginsberg 1978, 1989, Glass 1986, Guerney 1976).

The efficacy of this method has also been demonstrated when the goal has been only to use the parent as a paraprofessional therapist and not specifically to enhance the parent–child relationship. Of course, just as children in play therapy become attached to the therapist, they also appreciate the parent in the therapist role, so that even good parent–child relationships become better. These kinds of improvements occur in children who have experienced physical traumas, illnesses and poor health, or loss of the nontherapeutic parent through death or divorce, and in adoptive and foster children (Cosner 1990, Ginsberg 1989). The goal in such instances is to have the parents serve as therapists, because parents can serve as ably when well-trained as professional therapists, with the added benefit of enhancing the parent–child relationship and/or preventing problems from developing in the relationship. The usual special regard that children feel for their play therapist goes to the parent and vice-versa. Rogers (1958) spoke of the mutual liking between therapist and client as the best single indicator of a well-established relationship and a progressing therapeutic process.

Involvement of parents in the therapeutic role can meet still another goal in the case of foster parents and adoptive parents. When children, especially those beyond infancy, enter a new family situation, both they and their parents face the special task of trying to create instant bonds that would have developed in the course of daily relating in birth families. Parent–child play sessions can accelerate the critical process of establishing trust and intimacy (Cosner 1990, Ginsberg 1990). The clearly caring, supportive stance of the play therapist in the safe atmosphere of the play session can counterbalance less-than-optimal everyday situations, and protect positive feelings from threat. For example, foster parents and adoptive parents often find themselves needing to teach older children who come into their family about basic personal care–behaviors mastered by other children years before–and/or about norms for relating to others, because the children either came from other cultures or dysfunctional families where they were not able to learn these basics. Parental efforts to retrain and to modify behaviors can be perceived by the children as rejecting and hypercritical. The play times together can be of enormous benefit in helping the children know that they are accepted even if some of their behaviors need to be modified. Baruch (1949) and Moustakas (1973) recommended play sessions on a regular basis for all families because of the value for children in experiencing pure acceptance by the most important people in their lives, and for the opportunity afforded to the parents to be understanding and accepting of their children. The daily nature of the chores of family living often are at odds with the relationship-building process. Such accepting play times may serve as a correction for this potentially erosive situation in all families.

Using the same rationale as outlined above for involving adoptive/foster parents, teachers have been employed as therapists for problem children in their classrooms. Improved teacher–child and peer relationships have resulted (Guerney and Flumen 1970, Kranz 1972).

Theraplay

While the approach is very different, with far more active leadership taken by the therapist for the purpose of stimulating the child and engaging him/her in appropriate fun, sharing, and nurturing, the Theraplay approach of Jernberg (1979) does include parents in some of its variety of formats. Parents and children are first assessed on behavioral measures – the Marschak Interaction Method (MIM) – to determine what areas of therapeutic activity are most needed (e.g., helping parent and child separate, become closer, and so forth). Therapists demonstrate to parents how to play and then include parents in interaction with their children as directed by the therapists. Parents also play at home using the same methods between sessions. Post-test scores on the MIM show changes in the desired direction in the parent–child interactions (Jernberg 1979).

Theraplay differs from other therapies described in this chapter in that the therapist actively attempts to make certain transactions occur based on what he or she recognizes as needed. These may be for intimacy development or for differentiation from adults. Theraplay is used very successfully with autistic children and mentally retarded children who need to be better able to draw upon their own abilities. While Theraplay therapists are very sensitive to the child's response to the therapist's initiations, they continue doing what they feel needs to be done until the child is able to respond in more mature, adaptive ways. The therapist's rule is anticipation of, not reaction to, what the child does.

Parent–child Interaction Therapy

Eyberg (1988) has developed a behavioral approach for the psychological treatment of the overt, externalizing behavior problems of preschool children. It emphasizes the quality of the parent–child relationship through a first phase of child-directed interactions in a play setting. A second phase of the treatment is added when the parent–child relationship appears to be optimal, as judged by observation and ratings. In this phase, the parents make specific demands for compliance, and use consequences if the child does not comply. With these two phases – one stressing the feeling dimension and the second the control dimension of the parent–child relationship – parents are prepared to transfer their new behaviors to the home. Positive changes in parental attitudes, reductions in child problem behaviors, and improved parent–child relationships have been demonstrated through this method (Eyberg 1988).

The Efficacy of Play Therapy for Improving Relationships

Changing relationships constitutes a major task of the play therapist and accounts for the majority of child treatment referrals, if one accepts the broader definition of relationship that includes the ability to comply with adult direction or discipline. Nonetheless, outcome research on play therapy to support its wide usage for bringing about desirable relationship changes is scant. Phillips (1985) notes, in an interesting article pointing out the lack of confirming empirical data in relation to play therapy, that the field suffers for a number of possible reasons from a lack of scientific rigor. As Phillips speculates, this might be (1) because play is not taken as a serious endeavor, even in the therapeutic context; (2) because of vague goals that are hard to quantify; or (3) because the field is predominantly clinical, with few empirical studies conducted, and those frequently yield equivocal results. Whatever the reason, we must recognize that clinical evidence is keeping the field alive and, for the most part, well.

We would be remiss not to cite research that at least partially supports the therapeutic value of play therapy. Since in this chapter we are concerned primarily with relationship effects, those will be the only ones referred to here. Studies showing change in academic performance, physical symptoms, and so forth, will be omitted unless a relationship component was also included in the inquiry.

Probably the most researched service to children is the Primary Mental Health Project (PMHP), created by Emory Cowen at the University of Rochester in the 1960s and now employed countrywide. Cowen and colleagues conducted many outcome studies examining program success (Weissberg et al. 1983). The major intervention of PMHP is Axline/Ginott play therapy conducted by specially trained school aides. PMHP researchers are interested in change in several developmental and performance areas, with an eye to preventing continued maladjustment in later school years. One scale of the major evaluation instrument deals with relationships. Generally, results on this instrument have been positive, although by no means unequivocally so. Differences in settings where the program is offered, research design and other technical variations make comparisons across studies difficult. Since clinical evidence is widely accepted as positive, the program continues to expand and thrive. The problem of clinical versus empirical evidence is a continuing one in the evaluation of services—methods that require much study independent of the treatments—before we can know which type of evidence is more valid (Mannerino and Derlak 1980).

Studies demonstrating gains in appropriate social behaviors, for instance, less aggressive or more prosocial, have been reported and valued by clinicians. Researchers raise questions about them, because the control groups and comparative treatment alternatives that could provide answers to troubling issues are rarely used. Whether simply giving one-on-one, valued, positive adult attention would have the same results as play treatments has not been fully resolved. However, Stover and Guerney (1967) were able to demonstrate that mothers simply playing with their children showed fewer child (and parent) positive changes in playroom relationship behavior than mothers using child-centered play with their children for equal periods of time.

Probably some of the earlier studies are most exemplary for meeting scientific criteria–those of Dorfman (1958) and Seeman and colleagues (1964)–which showed strong support for the child-centered approach of Axline (1947, 1969) in relationship improvement.

Guerney and Flumen (1970), in a well-controlled study involving behavior with raters blind to children's treatment category in the classroom, showed improvement in interpersonal behavior in elementary-school-aged children. Schmidtchen and Hobrucker (1978), using professional play therapists and both control and alternative treatment groups, found that client-centered play therapy was superior on interpersonal dimensions. Using the same type of rigorous design, but with parents as therapists in one group versus nonparent student therapists in the alternative treatment, Wall (1979) showed that both groups moved forward in relationship development, but the children playing with parents had greater relationship improvement with the parents. While their meta-analytic study of child treatment covered more than play therapies and evaluation of relationship variables, Weisz and colleagues (1987) were able to provide some support for the effectiveness of play therapy. So, when sound research has been conducted, evidence does emerge, with at least respectable frequency, that behind the smoke of enthusiasm for the play therapy modality, there is a flame–if not the proverbial fire–of empirical support for its efficacy.

Case Illustration of a Peer-Rejected Child

The following case illustrates the successful transfer of positive changes in individual play therapy with a parent therapist to improved relationships with peers in school and community settings.

H. was a 9-year-old, white, middle-class boy, the younger of two siblings. His sister was 16 years old. He was referred for treatment because he was an academic underachiever, did not participate in the classroom, and had no friends at school or in the neighborhood. In fact, H. was openly rejected by other neighborhood boys, who ridiculed and abused him. The summer prior to his referral, the boys had staged a "Let's drown H. day" at the community pool, during which they pushed his head under the water so vigorously and continuously that the lifeguard thought it prudent to pull him out. This rescue only added to H.'s plight of nonacceptance by his peers.

Basically, neither his parents nor his sister were rejecting of H., and they all tried to be supportive, offering suggestions, taking him for outings, and joining him up with groups that presumably would give him a chance to belong. His sister and father would become impatient with H., however. When his father tried to initiate a new learning or homework scheme that failed, both H. and the father would withdraw and feel defeated, which led to the father pulling back further. At the time of the referral, H.'s father had pretty much left trying to help his son to his wife, although he continued to support these efforts until proven ineffective, for example, by chauffeuring him to and from Boy Scout meetings. The parents felt miserable for their obviously unhappy and ineffectual child. The only step they took that appeared to be productive was getting H. a kindly tutor whose work did seem to allow him to move ahead slightly in school and raise his and the family's morale a bit. H.'s parents did not blame H. or anyone else. They saw the family caught in a web of negative incidents: by chance getting unsupportive teachers; by chance having neighbor children who excluded H.; and, by poor timing out of their control, having had to move into the area in the middle of the previous school year, saddling H. with a difficult transition. Earlier learning difficulties in the previous school had been dismissed by the teachers as the normal problems of left-handed boys.

Observation

As is our usual intake practice, H. and Mrs. S., his mother, were asked to spend thirty minutes playing together in a free-play situation observed by the supervising faculty member and two graduate students. Had H.'s father and sister been able to participate, they, too, would have been included in this observation. Neither one wished to be part of the observation nor, in the case of the father, of the parent–child treatment program. In the free play session, no demands are made of parent or child – only to play as they wish and to avoid contact with the camera, one-way vision mirror, and ceiling lights. Thus, rules imposed on the child come almost entirely from the parent, revealing parental anxieties about performance and need to control. Following the play of the child with the family member(s), a staff "child observer" takes over the play with the child to provide a contrast in how the child relates to a strange adult in the absence of the parent. In the meantime, the parent is interviewed about what transpired in the observation, about which the parent (but not usually the child) is fully informed in advance.

H. played imaginatively and actively during the play period with both his mother and the female child observer. He changed in no observable way when the observer replaced the mother. H. talked freely and well. He did not include either adult in his play except when he needed some help or information. He was not anxious, but did evidence much dependence and an avoidance of risk taking. He maintained his interest in the novel situation and appeared to have a thoroughly good time. It was noted, however, that H. had perceptual-motor problems, with poor large and small motor coordination.

While H. continued playing with the observer, Mrs. S. talked with the interviewer about the play session and referral issues. Various questionnaires were filled out in advance by parents and teacher, which were discussed. Follow-up on the observation explored H.'s poor perceptual-motor performance as well as his hesitation to undertake anything different without adult assistance. Exploration of the consistency of patterns across contexts was a goal here, along with an examination, with the parent's help, of what might be different from one situation to another.

H.'s mother revealed that H. always exhibited poor visual motor behavior and had had a history of poor motor development. He had always been considered slow-moving, clumsy, and sloppy – characteristics for which he was criticized by teachers and peers. School records revealed that his reading, math, spelling, and writing scores were well below grade level. Mrs. S. was told that our first priority was to determine whether H. might be learning-disabled and to deal with that before any psychotherapy recommendation.

A psychometric examination including auditory and visual learning processing tests revealed that H. was indeed quite impaired, although his verbal I.Q. was 120. The family was referred for remedial work for the learning disability, and the school was informed, in the hope that he would receive supplementary resource room help there. A recommendation was also made that psychotherapy, in the form of Filial Therapy (Child Relationship Enhancement Family Therapy), be undertaken to address the self-esteem problems acquired through years of underachieving and the subsequent ridicule heaped upon him by peers derisive of his school and athletic performances in games and on the playground.

Play Sessions

Since Mr. S. was not participating, Mrs. S. joined a group of other parents (in this case, all at-home mothers who met during the day) and followed the training pattern described in the section of this chapter on parents as therapists. Mrs. S. was a conscientious learner and scheduler of home play sessions. She conducted twenty-two sessions at home and seven observed sessions at the training site.

H. initially played in virtually the same way he had played in the intake play sessions. He continued to back off from anything that offered the slightest challenge and was constricted in his range and intensity of expression. As his mother became better able to address his feelings empathically, and he consequently felt accepted in the different situation, H. began to play more expansively. He frequently beat the bop-bag while chewing on the baby bottle and began to weave fantasies around his play. At first, they were clearly related to the play. For example, H. was beating up a boxer or villain, and sometimes he would wind up flat on his back on the floor drinking the baby bottle, having been spent from the fray. By the fourth session observed by the group (about the fifteenth home session, where he played similarly), H. departed from reactive fantasy to very planned, pretend play that he organized and directed. He began to include his mother in various roles that furthered his fantasies, and gave her decisive and assertive directions from which she was not to deviate. He became a powerful figure in each session who could control the entire world. In his final pretend play sessions, he repeated the fantasy he seemed to enjoy most: he was emperor of the universe and built heights where he would sit and rule (a chair on a table, for instance). He was totally in control and destroyed many an evil, disobedient subject. At the very end of his sessions, he had returned to reality play but was very much more assertive, demonstrated leadership, and in no way hesitated to tackle novel challenges. Usually, for safety's sake, we would not permit children to build structures like the "mountain" upon which H.'s emperor dwelled, but it seemed so important to H.'s progress to do a daring thing that we and his mother decided to allow H. to carry out this part of his drama.

Reports of his behavior in the neighborhood, the school, and in the family were dramatically different. Even though progress on improving his learning disabilities was slow, he was less hesitant about trying and did not engage in postponing, questioning, and dawdling behaviors, which he had done before when confronted with difficult material. His affirmation of self, gained from the playroom experiences, seemed to make it possible for him to be less avoidant, anxious, shy, and socially incompetent. His more confident, less dependent style seemed to be the major factor that accounted for his changed peer status. The parents had originally worried that having to leave the classroom to go to the resource center would make him even more different and more a target of ridicule, but behavior checklists by parents and teachers indicated that H.'s behavior had improved in every area, including peer acceptance.

The mother was a positive force in this dramatic change. She really had no vested psychological interest in H.'s being dependent and unassertive; she was reacting to the child's situation of incompetence basically due to his poor sensorimotor functioning and exacerbated by the secondary social problems resulting from inadequate performances. Her new knowledge that the problem was definable and to a certain extent treatable boosted her hopes and those of the whole family. Her important part in actually bringing about change through her ability to accept her son as "dictator," "emperor," "baby-bottle drinker," and so on, was a powerful message to H. Instead of being the family slob and boob, which is how he had depicted himself, he realized that he had greater potential, and his mother understood and accepted all of the behaviors he demonstrated in reaching that point.

While the same process probably would have occurred in a similar way with a professional play therapist, we believe that the mother's presence contributed to the transfer of H.'s new concept of self to situations outside of the playroom. Mrs. S. represented the outside social environment and was an important source of information about how he would be perceived there. Finally, the helplessness that the whole family experienced was overcome by the empowerment of the mother to help her son change and to acquire new powers for himself.

Relationships: The Ripple Effect

With the exception of the removal of intrapsychic symptoms, one might characterize all of the behavior change that results from child play therapy to be a process of interpersonal or relationship modification. Acting-out children become more compliant in relation to authorities, more obedient and overtly caring for their parents, and less aggressive toward their peers. Withdrawn children become less fearful of other people and better able to express themselves with them. Changes in relation to other people happen in large part because of the unique and positive nature of the relationship that the child has with the play therapist. By a yet uncertain process, the change carries over from the relationship with the therapist to relationships outside with similar figures, and then to peers and others. Clearly, some intervening processes must be present to make this happen. Allen (1939) and Axline (1947) would assume that it is the acceptance provided by the therapist that intervenes, which in turn becomes self-acceptance. When one accepts oneself, one no longer needs to behave inappropriately in social relationships or toward oneself. All of these explanations make inherent sense. Those who witness change in children resulting from the process know that it happens. Studies to support and explain it have been few, and their results sometimes equivocal.

Those of us who use play therapy operate on faith to a certain extent, but also know intuitively from our experience that we are involved in a powerful process—a unique therapeutic relationship. Alexander (1964) saw this therapeutic relationship in terms of its similarity to all genuine human relationships with one essential difference: the play therapist "gives undivided self completely to the child and is totally alert and sensitive to the child's feelings" (p. 257). Other realities intrude upon such dedication to the child in real-life relationships. Until we can learn to make daily relationships more like those in therapy, we will continue to depend upon therapists to improve children's relationships and help them carry the improvements over to the real world.

References

Abramowitz, C. V. (1976). The effectiveness of group psychotherapy with children. *Archives of General Psychiatry* 33:320–326.

Alexander, E. (1964). School-centered play therapy program. *Personnel and Guidance Journal* 43:256–261.

Allen, F. (1939). Therapeutic work with children. *American Journal of Orthopsychiatry* 4:193–202.

Axline, V. (1947). *Play Therapy.* Cambridge, MA: Houghton Mifflin.

———— (1969). *Play Therapy.* Rev. ed. New York: Ballantine Books.

Baruch, D. (1949). *New Ways in Discipline.* New York: McGraw-Hill.

Baumrind, D., and Block, A. (1967). Socialization practices associated with dimensions on competence in preschool boys and girls. *Child Development* 38:291–328.

Bierman, K. (1989). Improving the peer relationships of rejected children. In *Advances in Clinical Child Psychology,* vol. 12, ed. B. Lahey and A. Kazdin, pp. 53–84. New York: Plenum.

Bills, R. E. (1950). Non-directed play therapy with retarded readers. *Journal of Consulting Psychiatry* 14:140–149.

Borgen, W., and Rudner, H. (1981). *Psychoeducation for Children.* Springfield, IL: Charles C Thomas.

Brady, C., and Friedrich, W. (1982). Levels of intervention: a model for training in play therapy. *Journal of Clinical Child Psychology* 11:39–43.

Brock, G., and Coufal, J. (1985). Parent education as skills training. In *Handbook of Social Skills Training and Research,* ed. L. L'Abate and R. Milan, pp. 263–283. New York: John Wiley & Sons.

Broussard, E., and Hartner, M. (1970). Maternal perception of the neonate as related to development. *Child Psychiatry and Human Development* 1:16–25.

Cosner, R. (1990). *Foster and adoptive parents in filial therapy.* Paper presented at the Annual Convention of the American Psychological Association, Boston, MA, August.

Dorfman, E. (1958). Personality outcomes of client-centered child therapy. *Psychological Monographs* 72.

Drotar, D., and Echerle, D. (1990). The family environment in non-organic failure-to-thrive. *Journal of Pediatric Psychology* 15:479–489.

Eyberg, S. (1988). Parent–child interaction therapy: integration of traditional and behavioral concerns. *Child and Family Behavior Therapy* 10:33–45.

Fisher, B. (1953). Group therapy with retarded readers. *Journal of Educational Psychology* 35:356–360.

Fleming, L., and Snyder, W. (1947). Social and personal changes following non-directive group play therapy. *American Journal of Orthopsychiatry* 17:101–116.

Freud, A. (1955). *The psycho-analytical treatment of children.* New York: International Universities Press.

Freud, S. (1959). Analysis of a phobia in a five-year-old boy. In *Collected Papers,* pp. 149–289. New York: Basic Books.

Garmezy, N. (1986). Developmental aspects of children's responses to the stress of separation and loss. In *Depression in Young People,* ed. M. Rutter, C. Izard, and P. Read, pp. 297–324. New York: Guilford.

Ginott, H. (1959). Theory and practice of therapeutic intervention in child treatment. *Journal of Consulting and Clinical Psychology* 23:160–166.

———— (1961). *Group Psychotherapy with Children.* New York: McGraw-Hill.

Ginsberg, B., Stutman, S., and Hummel, J. (1978). Notes for practice: group filial therapy. *Social Work* 23:154–156.

Ginsberg, B. (1989). Training parents as therapeutic agents with foster/adoptive children using the filial approach. In *Handbook of Parent Training: Parents as Co-therapists for Children's Behavior Problems,* ed. C. Schaefer and J. Briesmeister, pp. 442–478. New York: John Wiley & Sons.

Glass, N. (1986). "Parents as Therapeutic Agents: A Study of the Effect of Filial Therapy." Unpublished doctoral dissertation, North Texas State University, Denton, TX.

Guerney, B. (1964). Filial therapy: description and rationale. *Journal of Consulting Psychology* 28:303–310.

———— (1976). Filial therapy used as a method for disturbed children. *Evaluation* 3:34–35.

Guerney, B., and Flumen, A. (1970). Teachers as psychotherapeutic agents for withdrawn children. *Journal of School Psychology* 8:107–113.

Guerney, B., Guerney, L., and Andronico, M. (1966). Filial therapy. *Yale Scientific Magazine* 40:6–14.

Guerney, B., and Stover, L. (1971). Filial therapy: final report to NIMH, Grant #1826401. University Park, PA: The Pennsylvania State University.

Guerney, L. (1983a). Client-centered (non-directive) play therapy. In *Handbook of Play Therapy,* ed. C. Schaefer and K. O'Conner, pp. 21–64. New York: John Wiley & Sons.

———— (1983b). Introduction to filial therapy. In *Innovations in Clinical Practice: A Sourcebook,* vol. 2, ed. P. Keller and L. Ritt, pp. 26–39. Sarasota, FL: Professional Resource Exchange.

Jernberg, A. M. (1979). *Theraplay.* San Francisco: Jossey-Bass.

Kanner, L. (1948). *Child Psychiatry.* Springfield, IL: Charles C Thomas.

Klein, M. (1948). *The Psycho-analysis of Children.* London: Hogarth.

Kranz, P. (1972). Teachers as play therapists: an experiment in learning. *Childhood Education* 49:73–74.

Kuhli, L. (1979). The use of two houses in play therapy. *American Journal of Orthopsychiatry* 49:431–435.

Landisberg, S., and Snyder, W. (1946). Nondirective play therapy. *Journal of Clinical Psychology* 2:203–213.

Lay, K. L., Waters, E., and Park, K. (1989). Maternal responsiveness and child compliance: the role of mood as a mediator. *Child Development* 60:1405–1411.

Leary, T. (1957). *Interpersonal Diagnosis of Personality.* New York: Ronald Press.

Mannerino, A., and Derlak, J. (1980). Implementation and evaluation of service programs in community settings. *Professional Psychology* 11:220–227.

Marcus, I. (1966). Costume play therapy. *American Academy of Child Psychiatry Journal* 5:441–451.

Moulin, E. (1970). The effects of client-centered group counseling play media on the intelligence, achievement, and psycholinguistics of underachieving primary school children. *Elementary School Guidance Counselors* 5:85–98.

Moustakas, C. (1973). *Children in Play Therapy.* Rev. ed. New York: Jason Aronson.

Parpal, M., and Maccoby, E. (1985). Maternal responsiveness and subsequent child compliance. *Child Development* 56:1326–1334.

Patterson, G. (1982). *Coercive Family Process.* Eugene, OR: Castalia.

Peoples, C. (1979). Fair play therapy: a new perspective. *Journal of Psychology* 102:113–117.

_____ (1983). Fair play therapy. In *Handbook of Play Therapy,* ed. C. Schaefer and K. O'Connor, pp. 76–94. New York: John Wiley & Sons.

Phillips, R. (1985). Whistling in the dark?: a review of play therapy research. *Psychotherapy: Theory, Research, and Practice* 22:752–760.

Reif, R., and Stollak, G. (1972). *Sensitivity to Children: Training and Its Effects.* East Lansing, MI: Michigan State University Press.

Rogers, C. (1958). The characteristics of a helping relationship. *Personnel and Guidance Journal* 37:6–16.

Schmidtchen, S., and Hobrucker, B. (1978). The efficacy of client-centered play therapy. *Proxis der Kinderpsychrologie and Kinderpsychiatrie* 1:64–66.

Seeman, J., Barry, E., and Ellinwood, C. (1964). Interpersonal assessment of play therapy outcome. *Psychotherapy: Theory, Research, and Practice* 1:64–66.

Slavson, S. (1947). *The Practice of Group Therapy.* New York: International Universities Press.

Slavson, S., and Shiffer, M. (1974). *Group Psychotherapies for Children.* New York: International Universities Press.

Smilansky, S. (1968). *The Effects of Sociodramatic Play on Disadvantaged Preschool Children.* New York: John Wiley & Sons.

Stayton, D., Hogan, R., and Ainsworth, M. (1971). Infant obedience and maternal behavior: the origins of stabilization reconsidered. *Child Development* 42:1057–1069.

Stover, L., and Guerney, B. (1967). The efficacy of training procedures for mothers in filial therapy. *Psychotherapy, Theory, Research, and Practice* 4:110–115.

Sullivan, H. S. (1947). *Conceptions of Modern Psychiatry.* Washington, DC: The William Alanson White Psychiatric Foundation.

Wall, L. (1979). Parents as play therapists: a comparison of three interventions into children's play. *Dissertation Abstracts International* 40:155B.

Weintraub, S., Winters, K., and Neale, J. (1986). Competence and vulnerability in children with an affectively disordered parent. In *Depression in Young People,* ed. M. Rutter, C. Izard, and P. Read, pp. 205–222. New York: Guilford.

Weissberg, R., Cowen, E., Lotyczewski, B., and Gesten, E. (1983). The primary mental health project: seven consecutive years of program outcome research. *Journal of Consulting and Clinical Psychology* 51:100–116.

Weisz, J., Weiss, B., Alicke, M., and Klotz, M. (1987). Effectiveness of psychotherapy to children and adolescents: a metanalysis for clinicians. *Journal of Consulting and Clinical Psychology* 55:542–549.

13

Play and Positive Emotion

Allyson I. Aborn

> Play seems to be a rather general accompaniment of life. Animals as well as humans play . . . one thinks generally of lightness, movement, and a feeling of pleasure associated with play. Even inanimate objects, organisms not capable of independent motion may, metaphorically, seem to play, as grasses that play in the wind, or light that plays across the sky. [Greenacre 1959, p. 62]

Neubauer (1987) writes, "Play has a special, unique place in psychic life, particularly in the world of the child" (p. 9). Many theorists have addressed the issue of play. Why does a child play? What is the function of play? Theories of play abound, for they are frequently a smaller segment of a larger theory of human behavior. As such, they are not mutually exclusive, but rather complementary. Different theorists focus upon different aspects of the play process, attempting to delineate, among others, the following issues: "Why *does* a child play? Where does the energy needed for play come from? What is the biologic function of play? Why is play what a child chooses to do? How does a child select a certain game or activity? What motivates a child to continue playing? What are the developmental consequences of play?" (Slobin 1976, p. 99).

In this chapter we purport to examine these questions from a very specific perspective: What is the role of "positive emotion" in play?

In the last decade, there has been a growing recognition of the significance of positive affective states. Researchers have noted that positively toned emotions are important in more effectively coping with stress; that when people feel good, their cognitive functioning expands; that they are more energized. We will look specifically at how the positive emotions are defined by different theorists. Then, what is the impact of the positive emotions upon the play of the child? What are the positive emotions created by play itself? Can these emotions be used therapeutically? If so, how?

The word *emotion* derives from the Latin verb *emovere*, "to move out," as one would move a crowd out of a forum or soldiers from an encampment. Implicit in this definition is the sense of an authoritative force engineering the movement of a passive mass. The mass is acquiescing to the movement, but not initiating the movement.

This literal translation of the Latin verb captures a vital characteristic of the concept of emotions: namely, that we experience ourselves as being *moved* by an emotion. This is a passive experience, as opposed to an experience in which we *will* an action to occur—or, to extend the contrast further, the feeling of *having* to do something because we are pressured by an external force. And so, intrinsic in the definition of emotion is the fact that we do not find ourselves acting out of habit or because of the requirements of the situation. We are not forced, either by ourselves or by others, to feel, for example, anger, sadness, fear, or joy.

"When we are moved by emotion we feel the desire to hit, hug, or whatever, even though our judgment may check this action. This is the paradox of emotional experience—we are passively being moved rather than acting, and yet this move-ment seems to be coming from within us," writes DeRivera (1977, p. 12). This is frequently expressed colloquially by such phrases as "falling in love," being "gripped by anger," "seized by fear," "torn by jealousy," "transported by joy," "subdued by grief," and so forth.

Joseph DeRivera developed his structural theory of the emotions in an attempt to integrate this paradox inherent in the definition of emotion (i.e., that an emotion passively moves us at the same time that it is a part of us). Most earlier theories of emotion were in some way related to instincts; instincts provide an impulsive force that passively moves us, and yet is part of our own bodies. Other theories related emotions to the perception of value in the individual's environment. Yet a third set of theories defined emotions as transformations of the relation between the person and his environment; the individual was seen as inseparable from the world in which he finds himself.

In DeRivera's (1977) structural theory,

> the experience of emotion reflects the transformation of our relation to the world . . . to the persons, objects, events and actions that are important to us. These transformations are the movements of emotion and each type of emotion (anger, fear, love) reflects a different kind of transformation. A transformation is not a passive reaction to a given stimulus situation, rather it is a *transaction* between the person and his environment, a way of organizing the relation between the person and the other so that the response itself gives meaning to the stimulus situation. [pp. 35–36]

It is the structure of the positive emotions that is the concern of this chapter; that is, the influence of these particular emotions upon the individual's relationship to his environment. This relationship is the focus of much of the child's play.

The Origin of Positive Emotions in Play

What, then, are these positive emotions that might occur in play? What are their derivatives? What sustains them in the process of play? How do they affect the quality and content of the play and how simultaneously does play affect these emotions?

We attempt to understand these questions by reviewing several major theories of play. The earliest attempts at an explanation of play are those that are biologically oriented. Herbert Spencer (Groos 1976a) postulated that animals far along on the evolutionary continuum do not require devotion of their full time and energy to the procuring of food. They therefore have surplus energy that can be directed into other activities. And yet, how does one determine that energy is surplus? Does this imply that when children, who usually have a great amount of energy, have nothing else to do, they play? Energy viewed this way is then considered to be surplus only if it is extended into play but not into work. Play is then considered fun time and by extrapolation becomes less important than work.

In response to this point of view, other theories within the biological framework evolved. Specifically, the "Erholungstheorie" (recreation theory) was developed by Lazarus, Colozza, and Groos in 1901 (Groos 1976b). They explained play as an opportunity for the restoration to the player of powers exhausted by work.

Karl Groos (1976a), who made extensive studies of primates at play, noted the appearance of playful activities in these higher orders, and saw this as biologically determined, but from a very different perspective than Spencer. He hypothesized that animals with complex forms of adaptation require play to practice behaviors for which inherited instinct may not be adequate. "Youth probably exists *for the sake of play*. Animals cannot be said to play because they are young and frolicsome, *but rather they have a period of youth in order to play;* for only by so doing can they supplement the insufficient hereditary endowment with individual experience, in view of the coming tasks of life" (p. 66). Play thus serves the purpose of developing an equipment of perceptual and motor patterns that in less-developed species are instinctively provided. It is, therefore, a learning experience, a practicum, as it were, of the physical, social, and symbolic skills necessary for survival in the adult world.

Freud addressed the phenomenon of play in numerous writings, among them: *Wit and its Relation to the Unconscious* (1905), *The Relation of the Poet to Daydreaming* (1912), *Totem and Taboo* (1919), *Beyond the Pleasure Principle* (1926), and *The Ego and the Id* (1923). Robert Waelder, in his 1933 paper entitled "Psychoanalytic Theory of Play," lucidly presents the Freudian theory of play. This is especially relevant to our area of concern, particularly as it addresses the role of the positive emotions in play.

Freud, quoted by Waelder (1933), states that children's games serve to elaborate material that has been experienced by the child: "Play is the gratification of a desire for pleasure . . . play deals with some portion of a pleasurable situation, or with some of the determinants of its realization; that in fact much of children's play is a manifestation of the pleasure principle" (p. 208).

Buhler makes the further distinction between pleasurable gratification and what he terms *functional pleasure,* pleasure experienced strictly in the pure performance of the playful activity, without regard to the success of the activity. *The joy of the play is in the activity itself.*

Although Groos's theory of play in higher animals as a period of *Vorubung* (preexercise) is one that was endorsed by Freud, Freud disagrees with Groos on the interpretation of repetition in play. He explains repetition, not only in terms of a practice for future life, but describes repetition on the basis of the pleasure involved in rediscovering and reexperiencing the familiar. In *Beyond the Pleasure Principle*, Freud (1922) looks in detail at the issue of play and repetition. The child gains from the repetition the reassuring knowledge of the stability of the world. "This does not contradict the pleasure principle; the reexperiencing of something identical is clearly in itself, a source of pleasure" (p. 45).

Yet, if this is so, how then does one adequately explain the reproduction by children in their play of actual experiences that are devoid of pleasure? Freud's position here is especially significant to the comprehension of the role of the pleasure principle in the repetition of symbolic games children create, as opposed to the practice games discussed by Groos.

Freud delineates certain games as the ego's attempt to repeat actively a traumatic event that was earlier experienced passively. These particular games are given preference at certain times and take on a fixed quality. The content of the games is unique and cannot be altered. These games have a characteristic course that cannot be explained in terms of Buhler's concept of functional pleasure. Waelder (1933) provides the following example: A child, traumatized in the past by a dentist, has a dental appointment. He returns home and immediately begins to "play dentist." The child plays at being a dentist repeatedly and very enthusiastically for several days; then the theme appears more rarely, is accompanied by less affect, and finally is no longer played. The intensity of the game and the affective content give the impression that the original experience itself has left an affective residue that is gradually assimilated by the child in the play. Once this has been accomplished the child no longer needs to recapitulate the original experience in play.

What is the pleasure of this play for the child? Freud (1922) postulates that such repetition goes beyond the pleasure principle. Although play resembles repetition compulsions, repetition in this instance is a positive experience, allowing the child to achieve mastery over a situation that in actual experience was too traumatic for the child to manage at the time that it occurred. "Play is a method of assimilating piecemeal an experience which was too large to be assimilated instantly . . . an event becomes traumatic because there is an onslaught of more events in a relatively brief interval of time than the immature organism could endure" (p. 46). This play, then, allows the child to provide a positive resolution by reconstructing a painful situation and becoming the master of it and not its victim.

Play, then, alleviates anxiety through its gradual assimilation. The child moves through the play from passivity to activity. The child provides himself with the opportunity to achieve mastery. The unique characteristics of play make this possible, for play occurs during a time of extraordinary malleability of both psychic and somatic material. It occurs at a time when the boundaries between reality and fantasy are unclear and changing, and this too contributes in permitting the abreaction of an experience in play.

Functional Pleasures of Play

Waelder holds that the central function of play is the gradual assimilation of anxiety. Yet this is only one of the functions of play. Much play serves simply to confirm or repeat positive, gratifying experiences, both for children and adults, in the manner postulated by Buhler. Simply put, play is fun.

Peller (1987) writes:

> All play brings wish fulfillment, pleasure, elation, a feeling of euphoria, well-being, a 'Spielrausch' . . . play is an attempt to compensate for anxieties and deficiencies, to obtain pleasure at a minimum risk of danger and or irreversible consequences. Play is a step toward sublimation . . . ego and id are on excellent terms in play. Play ceases to be play when the child loses his ability to stop *when he wants to do so* (italics added), when he becomes glued to one phase, one episode. Play has then become a phobic defense. [p. 180]

Anna Freud points out that the beginnings of the mechanisms of defense can be observed through play (Peller 1987).

Within the psychoanalytic framework, Peller has surveyed the impact of the dynamics of play, the motivations for play, and its changing form and style as the child matures. She uses this information, acquired through the observation of play activities of children of different ages, to understand more comprehensively the interdependence of libidinal and ego development.

Still other analysts explore other aspects of the functional pleasures of play, and expand upon Freud's basic hypotheses. According to Greenacre (1959), "Observing a baby 4–6 months old, kicking with his legs, making movements as though to push or to stretch, while he gurgles as though in a comfortably happy state, one cannot avoid the impression that there is some enjoyment in motion itself . . . not merely a release from anxiety and fear" (p. 70).

What is the role of playfulness, of the joy of play, in normal development? Moran (1987) describes playfulness as "a quality associated with lightheartedness and an empathic understanding by the parents of what the child feels . . . a pleasure-oriented flexibility . . . a natural response of parents to their young children's instinctive orientation to pleasure" (pp. 16–17). Moran perceives of parents as the mediators of their child's play, as permitting a pleasure-oriented flexibility that blurs the boundaries between reality and fantasy. In so doing, they provide the child with "necessary 'cushioning' in the move . . . from conformity to the pleasure principle toward conformity to the reality principle" (p. 27).

Studies in the field of mother–infant attachment indicate that early positive mother–infant interactions can serve as predictors of later secure attachments and later social competence. Observes Roggman (1991):

> Positive affect displayed in mother–infant play early in the first year is correlated with positive affect later in the first year . . . the integration of objects into mother–infant play with one-year-olds has been found to be related both to the developing social competence of the infant . . . and to the child's later cognitive competence. Furthermore, the sharing of toys and pretend play between mothers and toddlers is correlated with secure attachment relationships. [p. 13]

The earliest social play is generally initiated by the mother, or primary caretaker, and may include vocalizations, tactile contact, repetitions of certain behaviors, and exaggerated facial expressions. The infant responds with smiles and laughter. Roggman (1991) writes:

> The typical culmination of such face-to-face interactions is positive affect expressed by the infant. Evidently, the infant expects positive affect from the parent, too, because when parents are instructed to play in a depressed manner, infants stop playing. The goal of social play for both parent and infant, then, appears to be to sustain attention and to "delight one another." [p. 15]

The child's capacity for playfulness thus appears to be strongly based within the framework of this secure mother–child attachment. The infant experiences and learns the joy of play, the spontaneity of play in this very first play experience. Positive affect, which ensues from this experience, as well as being the creator of it, contributes to the child's endogenous sense of well-being, which then fosters increased capacity for social, emotional, and cognitive development.

Jean Piaget, in his extensive writings on child development, says relatively little about the emotional life of the child. The focus of his concern is primarily upon the growth of intelligence, which he considers the central developmental issue. He does, however, state that every intelligent act is accompanied by feelings, and that these feelings provide the energy that sparks intellectual growth. This is the area of Piaget's work that is most germane to our understanding of the role of positive emotions in the psychic life of the child. In explaining Piaget's view, Pulaski (1962) says, "Emotion is what makes intelligence dynamic, directed, ever seeking a better equilibrium; emotion and intelligence are two sides of the same coin" (p. 97).

Piaget perceives play as bridging the gap between the sensory-motor experience and the emergence of symbolic thought. He states that play is an indispensable step in the child's cognitive development.

Piaget further accepts, as does Freud, the mastery of conflict as a primary motivation for play. Just as Freud states that repetition is clearly a source of pleasure, so Piaget characterizes play as an activity in which assimilation predominates over accommodation: that is, the playing child is more engaged in adapting experience into his own construct than he is in changing his construct to meet the demands of reality and experience. Play becomes an assimilation of reality to the ego. As the child achieves mastery he experiences pleasure. The play then becomes fun. The fun is self-motivating and self-propagating. It is self-energizing, and allows the child to move to resolution by moving from a position of passivity to one of activity. Piaget (1962) states that the child uses both symbolic play (what he refers to as *ludic symbolism*) and imitation, a mimicking of his environment in his attempts to assimilate the world around him. For Piaget

the distinction (between fantasy play and imitation) lies in the smiles and signs of pleasure that accompany play, as opposed to the seriousness of the child's efforts to accommodate. When there is no longer an effort at comprehension, but merely assimilation to the activity itself . . . for the pleasure of the activity, that is play. [p. 148]

Based upon these premises, Piaget devises specific criteria for play. First, play can be an end in itself, whereas work and other nonludic activities involve a purpose that is not contained in the activity itself. Second, play is spontaneous, as opposed to the compulsions of work and the need for real adaptation. Third, and most critical to our understanding of the role of the positive emotions in play, Piaget avers that play is an activity that exists for pleasure. And yet, much of what we would categorize as work has no subjective end other than satisfaction or pleasure. Even so, it is not considered to be play. Piaget employs Freud's explanation of this difference by contrasting the *Lustprinzip* and the *Realitatsprinzip*. On one side is immediate compliance with the laws of reality, and on the other, adaptation to reality in which there is an element of satisfaction that is, however, subordinated to a kind of compliance or respect for what is objectively real.

Like Freud, Piaget (1962) does define certain games that are symbolic reproductions of painful occurrences that exist "beyond the pleasure principle." These games demonstrate that

Mere assimilation, in the form of repetition of an experienced event, even when such an experience was painful, is the primary factor in play and is more widespread than the pursuit of pleasure for its own sake . . . although play sometimes takes the form of repetition of painful states of mind, it does so not in order that the pain shall be preserved, but so that it may become bearable, and even pleasurable, through assimilation to the whole activity of the ego. [p. 149]

Piaget denotes the fourth characteristic of play as its relative lack of organization. The fifth is the equivocal freedom from conflicts in play. When conflicts do occur, the ego can be freed of them by compensation or by liquidation, whereas in serious activity conflicts are inescapable. Lastly, play can begin when incentives not contained in the initial action are included. These incentives depend upon the pleasure gained through unrestricted combinations or through symbolic imagination.

Erik Erikson (1950) follows the psychoanalytic tradition in considering symbolic games as being aimed at the mastery of conflicts. He writes, "I propose the theory that the child's play is the infantile form of the human ability to deal with experience by creating a model situation and to master reality by experiment and planning" (p. 222). Erikson's work on play disruption and the role of transference in treatment of children will be further discussed later in this chapter.

As stated at the outset, there is no definitive theory that explains our original question, "Why does a child play?" in a thoroughly comprehensive manner. We have touched here on several of the principal theorists and developmental frameworks. Two other theorists worthy of note are George Herbert Mead and Robert White.

Mead (1934) defined child's play in a more socially interactive model than that of the psychoanalytic school. He focused on the child's interaction with objects in his world as this enables the child to develop both a sense of self and a sense of the generalized other. Therefore, Mead believes that the child uses play to establish his own identity. By playing out social roles, and practicing adult roles, the child learns the social rules that regulate behavior, as well as learning "rule-bound behavior"; that is, the child learns to submit to rules even in those situations where his impulse would be to behave differently. This is an aspect of play only fleetingly addressed in the psychoanalytic literature.

White, as quoted by Slobin (1976), argues for the importance of play as stimulus-seeking behavior and combines it with the need of the child to learn physical and social skills:

> I have no intention to dispute what Erikson, among others, has shown about symbolism in child's play, and about erotic and aggressive preoccupations that lead to play disruption. But we lose, rather than gain, in my opinion, if we consider the child's *undisrupted* play, six hours a day, to be a continuous expression of libidinal energy, a continuous preoccupation with the family drama, *as if there could be no intrinsic interest* in the properties of the external world and the means of coming to terms with it. [p. 110, italics added]

An Examination of Positive Emotions

Having reviewed the work of the major theorists from the vantage point of exploring the role of the positive emotions within their theoretical construct of play, we turn now to a more specific examination of the positive emotions themselves.

Zuckerman (1980) reflects, "Certainly there must be some peculiar Calvinistic streak in modern psychology that accounts for our preoccupation with negative emotions, particularly the unholy trinity of *FEAR, ANGER, AND DEPRESSION* (FAD) . . . But, is FAD, or its absence, all there is to emotions?" (p. 71, italics added).

Until the last decade, content analyses of psychology textbooks indicated that approximately twice as much space was devoted to negative as to positive emotions. A partial explanation for this could well be that negative emotional states result in problems requiring therapeutic interventions. Yet, according to the research of James Averill (1980), this is a somewhat specious answer. His research indicates that there are fewer concepts in ordinary language that refer to positive as opposed to negative emotional states.

Within recent years, however, there has been a growing recognition of the significance of positive affective states (DeRivera et al. 1989), and a growing interest in a more discriminatory study of them.

In spite of this increased recognition, "positive emotion" typically is treated as a unitary state and labelled "happiness, feeling good, or positive mood state," without an attempt to discriminate between different positive affective experiences. This is in contrast to the study of negative emotions, where investigators distinguish between, for example, anger, sadness, and fear; between depression and anxiety; or between shame and guilt. [p. 1015]

Although it is widely felt that various terms for positive affect can be used interchangeably, DeRivera and colleagues (1989) share the view that different terms suggest distinctive emotions, and that these can be described and delineated in a scientifically systematic manner. It is their premise that "such distinctions may have important consequences for personal well-being, social relationships, cognitive processing and our understanding of emotion" (p. 1015). In 1988, they published such a study on the distinctions between the positive affects of elation, gladness, and joy.

Lindsay-Hartz (1981), developed the initial structural descriptions for these three affects, and it is upon these descriptions that DeRivera and colleagues developed their studies. In attempting to devise her structural descriptions, Lindsay-Hartz interviewed a sample population, asking each subject for a specific experience of two of the three emotions. The following are the structural definitions as provided by this research:

Elation occurs when a person suddenly finds that a wish involving the self has been fulfilled. The wish is not grounded in reality in that one does not actually expect such a fantasy to come true. Hence, when the event actually occurs, the person reports floating or feeling "lifted off the ground." The emotion gives rise to an impulse to jump up and down and a tendency to announce to others what has happened. . . . It was postulated that the emotion functions to allow the person to "realize" the wish, thus altering his or her self-image.

Gladness occurs when a hope, rather than a wish, is fulfilled. Hoping does not involve the fantasy inherent in wishing. Rather, it includes waiting for something that has a real possibility but presently is uncertain. Hoping also involves a dependence on someone or something with the power to provide what is needed. When the uncertainty is relieved and the goal achieved, the body becomes more relaxed and moves more freely. People report feeling more open and wanting to welcome others rather than hold back. It was postulated that gladness functions to strengthen the person's readiness to depend on others or events over which he or she has limited control.

Joy occurs when there is a mutual meeting between the person and another, in which the other is perceived as being unique. In contrast to elation, the body is in touch with reality and the psychological distance from others appears to decrease. Sensations also appear to be more acute. There is an impulse to celebrate the meaningfulness of the meeting and to include others in this celebration. It was postulated that this emotion functions to affirm the meaningfulness of life. [p. 169]

DeRivera and colleagues (1989) used the same basic structural description but a somewhat different methodology in attempting to distinguish between the three affects. In their first study, they asked the subjects to recall an experience of elation and others to recall gladness or joy. They devised substructures to distinguish among these experiences. In their second study they used their knowledge of the characteristics of the emotions to induce states of elation, gladness, and joy and then objectively measured these states.

DeRivera and colleagues' data confirmed clear structures for elation and gladness:

Elation is a distinct emotion that occurs in situations when events fulfill a personal fantasy. . . . Gladness describes a situation in which a hope is fulfilled . . . hence the subjects experienced relief and relaxation . . . the term Elation suggests a state of greater intensity, whereas Gladness suggests a quieter state and Joy a state that is more diffuse and passionate, with a longer duration. [p. 1020]

Although unable to confirm a "Joy" structure, the researchers were optimistic about the prospects of its establishment in the near future.

Based upon the aforesaid definitions and upon DeRivera's structural criteria, as well as upon our review of the theoretical literature, it is hypothesized here that the positive emotion most frequently experienced by children in play is that of gladness. The gladness situation requires fulfillment of a hope, which differs from the fantasy of a wish in that there is some realistic possibility of attaining the hoped-for goal. Feeling glad transforms the child in such a way that he can experience relaxation, following the initial anticipation of the desired goal, or the worry associated with being the passive participant in a final outcome. This relaxation causes the child to be more open and responsive to others. In addition, DeRivera (1989) has hypothesized that gladness allows the individual to accept his dependence on events or on external objects, when he is unable to control a situation. Therefore, gladness seems to increase the ability to hope, and the patience and freedom that go along with that ability. *The experience of this affect in play, then, allows the child to experience improved self-esteem; a sense of mastery and competence; and the freedom that evolves from realistic hope.*

In an experiment conducted more than forty years before DeRivera established his differentials in the characteristics of elation, gladness, and joy, Wally Reichenberg (1939) studied the influence of joyful emotions (here used generically to include all three positive affects) upon the quality of children's work. Reichenberg postulates that "children do better work under the influence of a joyful emotion, that satisfaction enhances and strengthens striving, and that joy provides *motivation in other unrelated activities*" (p. 186, italics added).

Reichenberg's experiment was as follows: each child, ages 10 and 11, was given a repetitious, nonstimulating task to perform until he was thoroughly tired of it (drawing lines on sheets of paper). A joyful experience was then introduced: a colorful treasure chest, replete with movable gadgets and locks, was given to the child. The child was then told that he could keep the treasures within the box if he could open it. The possibility of failure and the possibility of success aroused intense interest for the child. There was a trick to the box, so that the experimenter could unobtrusively make the box open if the child had any difficulty. The treasure chest contained toys and candy for the child to play with and keep. The child then returned to the original work task. In the control experiment, the work was the same, but instead of the treasure chest the child's break-time activity was the Struwe Cloud Pictures Test, which is a variation of the Rorschach.

Reichenberg determined that the opening of the treasure chest constituted a truly joyful experience for the child. This was ascertained firstly by the spontaneous remarks of the children during their play with the box and then again in their reports after the experiment. Reichenberg found that *the work task of the children was superior in quantity as well as in quality following the joyful experience. The joyful experience organized the play*, creating an improved tolerance of the demands of reality. The child derived new energy from this experience.

> A certain structure of the psychic systems has been built up which includes a certain state of tenseness and all efforts go towards maintenance of such tension. If a joyous emotion is created, the tension of the systems is no longer maintained. Under the influence of such an emotion, the psychic structure is broken up; the tension may find some outlet in overt behavior, and finally, a state of equilibrium results. . . . The whole system seems in a more fluid state. This fluid state permits the building up of new systems as soon as a new tension arises. In this fluid state there is a tendency to expand, the tension can be directed, new systems can be created, built up, differentiated. It is in such moments that the child seems ready to learn to approach new goals, old tasks with a better attitude, is willing to adjust; and that interaction between field and subject, subject and field, takes place. [p. 202]

Play and Cognition

More recently, there has been an upsurge of interest in the interaction of affective and cognitive processes in children, especially as this interaction is exhibited in play.

However, few systematic measurements have been devised for determining the nature of this interaction. Many researchers have developed independent indices and rating scales specific to their particular area of interest and the variables upon which they choose to focus. Researchers such as David Singer and Jerome Singer have been at the fore in advocating development of comprehensive measurement scales for cognitive/affective interactions in make-believe play. J. Singer (Singer and Singer 1976) stresses the importance of focusing upon very specific variables, and several of his studies give special attention to the variable of imagination. He also has developed a five-point rating scale for measuring positive affective expression, concentration, and mood. Yet most measures devised by other researchers do not focus primarily upon affective content themes in play. The exception to this is Sandra Russ (1987) who has studied intensively the various forms in which affective states are expressed in fantasy play and, subsequently, the cognitive integration of the affective material. To achieve this, Russ reviewed affective expression – both the actual experiencing of the affect and the expression of that feeling.

As has been previously elucidated, there is significant literature on the role of play in allowing for conflict resolution whose etiology is in prior trauma. There is significant literature on the role of catharsis in play, as well as significant data on the impact of cognition upon affect. Yet there is little definitive work on the role of the expression of both negative and positive emotion upon cognition.

The following studies are among these few, and are landmarks in the move toward the development of a more refined measurement system of the interaction between cognition and positive affect. Such a system would have significant implications for the role of play in treatment, especially in the assessment of the patient's capacity for conflict resolution and problem solving.

In 1972, Mischel and colleagues investigated the effects of affect upon cognition. Using preschool children, they attempted to determine the ability of their subjects to delay gratification based upon affectively positive or affectively negative cognitive distractions. As in Reichenberg's study, raters were carefully trained, observable behaviors were rigidly recorded, and the task clearly and simply explained to the subjects.

> The experimenter gave the subject instructions designed to encourage the child to generate his own thoughts and covert cognitive activities while waiting. He said, "Oh, while I'm gone you can think of anything that's fun to think of, for as long as you want to. Can you tell me something to think about that's fun?" (The experimenter paused for the child's examples and said, "Yes" no matter what the subject said.) The experimenter then added other examples: "You can also think about singing songs, or think of playing with toys or anything that is fun to think of." [p. 208]

This study determined that children waited longer for a reward when they were distracted by thinking of "fun things" than when they were thinking of either "sad things" or food rewards. "Delay of gratification . . . is longer when the cognitions were affectively positive distractions and shorter when the cognitions were affectively negative" (p. 210).

In accuracy of discrimination studies devised for preschool children in 1979, Masters and associates determined that "induced positive affective states influenced problem-solving and learning . . . they enhanced speed and accuracy. Negative affective states significantly retard learning" (Russ 1987, p. 150). It is to be noted that this is in contradiction to much of the literature presented earlier, in which the position was taken that any affective expression can be therapeutic and, ultimately, ego-enhancing if it can lead to conflict resolution.

In 1977, Lieberman studied the variable of playfulness, discussed earlier in this chapter. She focused her interest specifically upon the characteristics of spontaneity, humor, and joy. Her results indicate that her subjects (kindergarten children) performed at significantly higher levels on divergent thinking tasks than did nonplayful children. In other studies, Lieberman proposes the "existence of a playfulness dimension in early life which is a precursor of adult creativity" (p. 393). Lieberman's findings were much in keeping with those of Singer and Rummo (1973). These researchers assert that there is a correlation between playfulness and creativity in children. They also propose that the capacity for playfulness (as distinguished from the capacity of the child to play) is a precursor to the recombining of ideas in the adult creative process.

In exploring the affective content in fantasy play, it appears that affect may or may not accompany the content. As discussed previously, the psychodynamic position is that unresolved constriction in the affective fantasy sphere of the child's functioning could result in cognitive constrictions. Russ's studies in 1980 and 1982 were based upon this hypothesis. Her findings indicate that children able to reach primary process material through fantasy play performed better in school and were more creative in problem solving. Thus, the child's capacity to reenact conflict through play and the positive affect created by resolution of this conflict result in improved problem-solving skills for the child.

> The child gains access slowly to conflict laden material and plays it out until the conflict has been resolved. It is probable that *the working through process helps develop cognitive structure which further aids the child in assimilating future stressful events. In this way, how children handle affect partially determines cognitive structure and, therefore, functioning in a variety of areas.* [p. 151, italics added]

Despite the central role that this hypothesis holds in the psychoanalytic paradigm, there have been only limited systematic investigations of its veracity. In 1981, Barnett and Storm conducted such a study, based upon the Eriksonian model that play provides the child with a way of recapitulating difficult experiences and restoring a sense of mastery over the environment. This occurs through the reduction of anxiety and the ensuing development of positive affect (pleasure) in the resolution of the conflict.

Barnett and Storm's study induced a conflict situation in preschool children and then compared their subsequent play behaviors with a matched neutral group. Both the study and the control group were shown a film clip of a *Lassie* episode, in which Lassie and her master are forced to parachute from a plane during an electrical storm. They land on a cliff. Lassie's master is knocked unconscious, and Lassie rolls down the cliff to the water below. The film ends at this point. The film seen by the control group contains an additional segment in which Lassie is seen climbing out of the water and returning to her master, who has regained consciousness. Lassie and her master smile and hug as the film ends. The study included pre- and postphysiological and behavioral measures of anxiety and emotional upset of both the study group and the control group, as well as monitoring of the subsequent types and durations of play of both groups as they related to the source of the conflict. The study's findings corroborated its hypothesis: that play can serve as a medium through which children can successfully reduce the anxiety of an experienced trauma. Barnett and Storm (1981) declare that

> The data support the contention that children often initiate play experiences to cope with distress and accompanying anxiety encountered in their environment. Whether the strategy in play becomes one of replicating and hence controlling the unpleasant event, or of altering the outcome such that it becomes more desirable, *the result is the return to a more equilibrious state and the concomitant effect is pleasurable and positive.* [p. 173, italics added]

We have illustrated through the research of prominent theorists that positive emotions have an important effect upon the quality of the play experience, and that this has clear therapeutic implications. If current treatment modalities are capable of reducing negative affects, they should also be capable of increasing positive affects. These affects will not automatically appear, however, with the reduction of anxiety and inhibition. We should, perhaps, consider helping our patients move toward experiences that do not only disinhibit, but which *enhance* positive affect. "There is some power to 'positive thinking' and feeling . . . after anxiety is reduced to a tolerable minimum, positive affects can be powerful influences and may 'inoculate' the patient against recurrences of anxiety" (Zuckerman 1980, p. 9).

Case Illustration: A Boy Unable to Have Fun

The following synopsis of a study by Moran (1987) is a clinical example of the positive emotions evoked through play in the treatment setting.

Mrs. A. sought help for her problems with her son, William, age 5. At different times she had feared that he was mentally defective, brain-damaged, psychotic, hyperactive, and gifted. The first observations of Mrs. A.'s interaction with William showed her to intrude upon his play and to put a premium on achievement. The parents, both competent professionals, repeatedly expressed their need for William to do things that would reflect his high ability. At home, he was even provided with real tools instead of toy ones. Consequently, William regarded play as a task he was obliged to complete. "I will play tomorrow," he would say to his analyst in the early days of treatment.

Part of William's defensive maneuvers involved accumulating "reality" details and facts that were ineffective in the mastery of anxiety-arousing situations. In this accumulation of details and serious, sometimes frantic efforts to assemble props, William behaved very much as did his parents in their response to anxiety-arousing situations. Thus he repeatedly prepared games that he never came to play.

The defensive characteristics that William developed were well illustrated during his treatment by his consuming interest in certain books. These featured aggressive, masculine heroes, who, one assumed, provided William with a measure of vicarious gratification of his aggressive wishes. Being read to kept him in control of events, and to this extent reading was used as a resistance against anxiety-provoking material that might emerge if play were less structured. Consequently, his analyst had to devise ways to foster William's play so that she could gain access to his anxieties and conflicts. By providing him with admiration instead of explanations, allowing him to be passive instead of active, and recognizing his dependency needs, the therapist provided relief to William. She told him that although he felt he had to do something in treatment, there was nothing he really must do, and this permissive attitude gradually freed the boy, who began to work at his own slow pace.

Play became a pleasure instead of a burden as William began to delight in the escapades of naughty Anthony, the storybook character who splashed water about. The therapist's acceptance of the mischievous boy in the story enabled William to permit himself to identify with his pranks. For the first time in analysis, he involved himself in fantasy play, which provided real excitement and pleasure. His parents observed that at home, William's play had become "joyous." They described his slightly naughty, pleasure-filled ploys as "naughty but charming."

Subsequently, William began to paint more freely. He turned a feather from his Indian headdress into an Indian pen and "wrote" invisibly. He was playful and confident that the invisible writing could not fall short of anyone's expectations. His therapist praised his work/play and helped him to consolidate his new-found freedom. By building up an atmosphere in which fantasies and their derivatives became acceptable to his therapist, then to himself, and finally to his parents, William became able to bring fears and fantasies to treatment where they could be analyzed.

William exhibits here what Erikson (1950) refers to as "play disruption," defined as "the sudden and complete or diffused and slowly-spreading inability to play" (pp. 475–476). William's emotional conflicts have become so intense that they are discharged both into the play and into the transferential relationship with the therapist.

And so, the role of the positive emotions in the treatment setting is twofold: the therapist enables the play to occur; once the child experiences the positive affects secondary to play, he has increased energy and capacity to cope with the underlying conflicts. Reichenberg (1939) writes:

> The child, experiencing joy, a very positive feeling, projects this feeling as a vector, a positive valence, to the entire psychological field. This gives a chance to introduce objects or concepts into his psychological field, which immediately share in this general positive value of the environment. [p. 201]

References

Arlow, A. (1987). Trauma, play, and perversion. *Psychoanalytic Study of the Child* 42:31–43. New Haven, CT: Yale University Press.

Averill, J. (1980). On the paucity of positive emotions. In *Assessment and Modification of Emotional Behavior: Advances in the Study of Communication and Affect,* ed. K. R. Blankstein, P. Pliner, and J. Polivey, pp. 7–45. New York: Plenum.

Barnett, L. A., and Storm, B. (1981). Play, pleasure, and pain: the reduction of anxiety through play. *Leisure Sciences* 4:161–175.

DeRivera, J. (1977). A structural theory of the emotions. *Journal of Psychological Issues.* Monograph 40, v. 10, #4. New York: International Universities Press.

DeRivera, J., Possell, L., Verette, J. A., and Weiner, B. (1989). Distinguishing elation, gladness, and joy. *Journal of Personality and Social Psychology* 57:1015–1023.

Erikson, E. (1950). *Childhood and Society.* New York: Norton.

_____ (1977). *Toys and Reasons: Stages in the Ritualization of Experience.* New York: Norton.

Freud, S. (1922). *Beyond the Pleasure Principle.* London: Hogarth.

Greenacre, P. (1959). Play in relation to creative imagination. *Psychoanalytic Study of the Child* 14:61–80. New York: International Universities Press.

Groos, K. (1976a). The play of animals: play and instinct. In *Play–Its Role in Development and Evolution,* ed. J. Bruner, A. Jolly, and K. Sylva, pp. 65–67. New York: Basic Books.

_____ (1976b). The play of man: teasing and love play. In *Play–Its Role in Development and Evolution,* ed. J. Bruner, A. Jolly, and K. Sylva, pp. 68–83. New York: Basic Books.

Jacobson, E. (1946). The child's laughter. *Psychoanalytic Study of the Child* 2:39–60. New York: International Universities Press.

Lewin, B. D. (1950). *The Psychoanalysis of Elation.* New York: Norton.

Lieberman, J. N. (1967). A developmental analysis of playfulness as a clue to cognitive style. *Journal of Creative Behavior* 1:391–397.

Lindsay-Hartz, J. (1981). Elation, gladness, and joy. In *Conceptual Encounter: A Method for the Exploration of Human Experience,* ed. J. DeRivera, pp. 162–224. Washington, DC: University Press of America.

Mischel, W., Ebbe, E. B., and Zeiss, A. R. (1972). Cognitive and attentional mechanisms in delay of gratification. *Journal of Personality and Social Psychology* 21:204–218.

Moran, G. (1987). Some functions of play and playfulness: a developmental perspective. *Psychoanalytic Study of the Child* 42:11–29. New Haven, CT: Yale University Press.

Neubauer, P. B. (1987). The many meanings of play. *Psychoanalytic Study of the Child* 42:3–9. New Haven, CT: Yale University Press.

Ostow, M. (1987). Play and reality. *Psychoanalytic Study of the Child* 42:193–203. New Haven, CT: Yale University Press.

Peller, L. E. (1954). Libidinal phases, ego development, and play. *Psychoanalytic Study of the Child* 9:178–198. New York: International Universities Press.

Piaget, J. (1962). *Play, Dreams and Imitation in Childhood.* New York: Norton.

Pulaski, M. A. S. (1971). *Understanding Piaget.* New York: Harper & Row.

Reichenberg, W. (1939). An experimental investigation on the effect of gratification upon effort and orientation to reality. *The American Journal of Orthopsychiatry* 9:186–204.

Roggman, L. A. (1991). Assessing social interactions of mothers and infants through play. In *Assessing Play Diagnosis and Treatment,* ed. C. E. Schaefer, K. Gitlin, and E. Sandgrund, pp. 13–41. New York: John Wiley & Sons.

Russ, S. W. (1987). Assessment of cognitive affective interaction in children: creativity, fantasy, and play research. In *Advances in Personality Assessment,* vol. 6, ed. J. Butcher and C. Spielberger, pp. 141–155. Hillsdale, NJ: Lawrence Erlbaum.

Singer, D. L., and Rummo, J. (1973). Ideational creativity and behavioral style in kindergarten-age children. *Developmental Psychology* 8:154–161.

Singer, J. L., and Singer, D. (1976). Imaginative play and pretending in early childhood: some experimental approaches. In *Child Personality and Psychopathology,* vol. 3, ed. A. David, pp. 69–112. New York: John Wiley & Sons.

Slobin, D. I. (1976). The role of play in childhood. In *The Therapeutic Use of Child's Play,* ed. C. E. Schaefer, pp. 95–117. New York: Jason Aronson.

Sroufe, L. A., and Wunsch, J. P. (1972). The development of laughter in the first year of life. *Child Development* 43:1326–1344.

Waelder, R. (1933). Psychoanalytic theory of play. *Psychoanalytic Quarterly* 2:208–224.

Waters, E., Wippman, J., and Sroufe, L. A. (1979). Attachment, positive affect, and competence in the peer group: two studies in construct validation. *Child Development* 50:821–829.

Zuckerman, M. (1980). To risk or not to risk: predicting behavior from negative and positive emotional states. In *Assessment and Modification of Emotional Behavior: Advances in the Study of Communication and Affect,* ed. K. R. Blankstein, P. Pliner, and J. Polivy, pp. 71–94. New York: Plenum.

14

Mastery of Childhood Fears

D'Arcy Lyness

This chapter places normal childhood fears within a developmental context and shows how play activity serves the child's striving for growth and wholeness. Erikson's (1950) model is used as a conceptual framework.

Play is a central resource for the child. It is the child's natural means of expression and learning. Play activity gives form to the child's experiences. It provides a forum for the exploration of strengths as well as fears.

Childhood fears are associated with normal growth and development. Play allows the child to express particular fears and, at the same time, is a vehicle for mastering them. Play is a spontaneous activity used by the child to master normal as well as situational fears. The expressive and manageable aspects of play are especially gratifying for the child. As basic developmental challenges are explored and progressively resolved, the child experiences a sense of mastery.

Case study examples are presented here to illustrate the value of play in the clinical setting. Play is an essential tool for the clinician who works with children. It can be used by the clinician for a twofold purpose: to recognize the child's specific fears, and to assist the child in his movement toward resolution.

Normal Childhood Fears and Expression through Play

Erikson conceptualized a series of progressive developmental issues, focal points of the child's unfolding experience. Each stage involves particular developmental challenges. In the best of circumstances, the child actively explores and resolves these challenges. How the child handles and resolves them has long-term consequences in terms of his sense of self and relationships with others.

Erikson's model defines each developmental stage as having two end-points. One point enhances the child's functioning and growth. The other has a detrimental effect; it impedes healthy functioning. The young child experiences issues related to basic trust versus mistrust, autonomy versus shame and doubt, initiative versus guilt, and industry versus inferiority. A child's resolution of each challenge is successful when it enhances healthy functioning.

Normal childhood fears and anxieties emerge during each developmental challenge. Observation of the child's play activity reveals age-related themes and fears. Specific play behavior characterizes each stage, and demonstrates the child's normal attempts at mastery.

Strangers! The Infant's Fear of the Environment

To the infant, the world is full of new experiences and stimuli. With an infant's limited frame of reference, many stimuli are overwhelming. The infant's adaptive response to these perceived dangers is fear. Erikson (1950) has defined the infant's primary task as establishing a sense of basic trust versus mistrust in the physical and interpersonal environment. The infant is sensitive to the immediate physical environment. His sense that the environment is stable, predictable, safe, and nurturing promotes a sense of trust. In an unpredictable or unresponsive environment, the infant's potential for basic trust can be supplanted by a perception of the world as threatening and dangerous.

Infants process their world through sensorimotor faculties (Piaget 1954). Not surprisingly, the infant's fears are grounded in concrete sensate experience. Normal fears during the first year of life include fear of loud noises, fear of falling, which is manifest as a startle response to sudden movement, and fear of strangers (Schachter and McCauley 1988).

Play during infancy takes the form of sensorimotor exploration. The infant plays with his own hands and feet and gains gradual control of their movement. He reacts with joy to certain strong visual stimuli such as bright color or mother's face. Repetitive manipulative play, such as shaking a rattle, strengthens the infant's sense of being able to predict and understand the environment. Recognition of patterns consistently seen, heard, and felt brings a sense of mastery and trust.

In an interactive context, mother's play with the infant involves touch, visual cues, and vocalization. This early mother-initiated play assists in bonding and expression of love. The infant may also initiate play with mother. In play, the infant explores the boundaries between self and mother (Winnicott 1971). This activity solidifies the infant's sense of being able to engage, predict, and control mother. In a similar way, peekaboo play delights the infant who is mastering a sense of permanence, especially as it applies to the mother. Mother becomes a reliable source of protection and satisfaction.

Accompanying the attachment to mother is a developing fear of being without her. This is known as *separation anxiety*. Separation anxiety begins in infancy and may persist until about age 3. Fear of separation is expressed in a variety of forms. The earliest manifestation of separation anxiety is stranger anxiety, which presents at about 8 months of age. At this stage of development the child has learned to distinguish the known from the unknown, the familiar from the unfamiliar. The emergence of stranger anxiety signals mastery of an important developmental task. The child is now able to recognize and distinguish stimuli – sensory and emotional – that have been stable and consistent in his world.

The Dark! The Toddler's Fear of Separation and Loss of Love

During the second and third years of life, a toddler's primary concern shifts to issues of autonomy and control. Erikson (1950) describes the developmental challenge of this age as autonomy versus shame and doubt. At this stage of development, the toddler has the cognitive and emotional awareness of being separate from parents. Because of the child's achievements – walking and emergent language – independence assumes psychosocial importance.

The toddler uses new skills to regulate his separation fears with the compelling urge to seek independence. The physical ability to move about independently enables him to initiate physical separation from loved ones in order to experiment with issues of distance and closeness.

Separation fears may take the form of fear of the dark. The toddler may use extended bedtime routines to keep the parents present, delaying separation. Hide-and-seek and you-chase-me interactions between mother and toddler are common games. While this play resonates with the earlier interaction of dropping and retrieving toys, new developmental skills provide the child with an expanded sense of self and possibility.

The toddler initiates play interactions that involve separation and reunion. Control and repetition are important aspects of this play. In contrast to the infant's interactive play, the toddler's hide-and-seek play moves toward reunion. The child finds he can control the separation himself, and by doing so masters fears of abandonment and bolsters courage for times when he may be left alone in the future.

In the normal developmental sequence, the toddler must learn to regulate bodily functions and modify the expression of impulses. Toilet training occurs during this time. Limits and boundaries between the self and the loved one are explored. The child complies with parents' wishes in order to maintain their love and approval. Fear of loss of love develops as the toddler attempts to meet parental expectations. A successful resolution of this stage involves two things: the child's ability to establish and maintain appropriate autonomy, while at the same time maintaining an awareness of parental safety and protection. The safety provided by parental limits reinforces the child's growing sense of self-control. The child wants to feel separate and distinct, yet connected and understood. Healthy resolution enables the toddler to feel proud and loved.

Other boundaries between the self and the not-self are processed. The toddler's fears of flushing the toilet or of water going down the drain illustrate his concern with boundaries between self and product. The toddler's sense of his own power and control is so tentative that he imagines disappearing by being flushed or washed away with his product.

The toddler's new task of learning to control bodily functions is also reflected in his play. Playing with messy things such as mud, sand, and paint assists in mastering the developmental task. These materials are symbolically gratifying, while at the same time socially accepted and approved ways of being messy.

Scary Monsters! The Preschooler's Fear of Injury

The child's growing sense of trust and safety, coupled with heightened feelings of control and independence, pave the way for curious exploration. Erikson (1950) conceptualized the child's task during this stage as initiative versus guilt. As curious strivings lead to successful excursions into the unknown, the child's sense of initiative is reinforced. To the extent that the child's natural curiosity is curtailed, and his efforts to make magical wishes come true are ridiculed, the child experiences guilt and vulnerability.

The body and its integrity are important in maintaining a show of strength as the child ventures into his expanding world. Separation fears have been largely resolved; the child's fears of aggression and injury assume central importance. By 3 years of age, the child has developed the capacity for symbolic thought and a rudimentary ability to perceive cause and effect. His fears manifest in new ways because of his ability to imagine and fantasize. His own aggression is projected and symbolically transformed into monsters that threaten to eat him up. Fantasy expands his fear of the dark into fear of the ghost that will jump out of the dark place. His fears of monsters, ghosts, and witches are intensely experienced. The preschooler has not yet developed the cognitive skills of the older child who can reassure himself that there's no such thing in real life.

Issues of trust and safety in the environment are being explored at a new level. The preschooler may fear big dogs or animals, perceiving them as potential aggressors. Gradually, fear of strangers has subsided, although shyness with new people may develop. Although the preschooler no longer cries at the sight of the doctor's white coat, fear during the medical visit is still present. Earlier fear of the doctor was a form of stranger anxiety. The preschooler's worries about the doctor are rooted in the fear of injury, and the egocentric belief that being hurt, even by the doctor's needle, is a punishment for being bad.

The child's play reflects his newly acquired ability for symbolic thought and imagination. During this stage, the child's magical beliefs not only allow new expression of fears, but also new mechanisms for mastering them. The preschooler's play involves wishes, magical beliefs, and imitation. Play at being mommy, daddy, Superman, the baby, or a puppydog allows expression for many ideas and issues. In terms of his fears, the child engages in play that allows him to be the doctor, the scary monster, or the superhero. The preschooler takes particular delight in scaring others. Hide-and-seek play of toddlerhood now evolves into a playful interaction in which the child jumps out from a hiding place to surprise and "scare" the parent.

Aspects of the child's fear of injury may be expressed through pretend play in which the child has a broken arm, or is repeatedly "killed" and magically restored to life. The child may play at being "hurt" and then "all better." By wearing lots of bandages, the preschooler reassures himself that any injury can be fixed.

This stage prepares the child for future endeavors in which success is contingent upon curiosity. Positive experiences lead to active participation in school and a sense of enjoyment in the learning process. Creativity is fostered during this stage. Imagination is used to explore possibilities and perceptual realities. A sense of his body as resilient and whole allows the child to move into the next stage with confidence.

Robbers and Bad Guys! Fear of Conscience During Early School Age

Between the ages of 6 and 10, the child's interest is primarily in exploring his role within the peer group. With accumulated physical, cognitive, and social skills, the child is ready to venture beyond the familiar bounds of the family and into the larger social arena of the peer group. The child is interested in discovering what he can accomplish or make by using all his abilities. His role, in fact, is largely defined by his abilities.

Erikson (1950) described the developmental theme of this stage as industry versus inferiority. The child wants to join in and be accepted, to feel capable and measure up, to be industrious and produce objects that demonstrate skill. Refined fine motor skills, coupled with cognitive abilities, enable the child to print his name, color within the lines, and "make something" with paper and scissors. These products are a source of great pride. With developing gross motor skills, the child can ride a bike, jump rope, bat a ball, and swim. These exciting abilities promote a sense of boundless possibilities of what the child can do. Differences become important for the first time as he compares himself to other children. The child with physical limitations may be perceived by others as inferior, and be ostracized. Children who are limited in their ability to demonstrate fine motor coordination, reading, intelligence, or athletic skills will be vulnerable to a sense of inferiority.

The early school-age child moves away from the family and into the new, uncharted territory of the social environment. Remnants of earlier fears accompany this movement. With the child's growing sense of the real world, robbers and kidnappers embody lingering fears of separation, punishment, and a sense of vulnerability. He still believes that what he thinks or wishes may come true. He also feels guilty about bad thoughts and bad behavior, and fears punishment that may result when he disobeys his developing conscience. Keeping and sharing secrets provide a means of expressing a personal sense of self. The child demonstrates new-found modesty about secret or private body parts. Secrecy is also reflected in his attitude toward his own thoughts. He can have secret thoughts and keep those thoughts from others.

Play during this time revolves around developing abilities. Bike riding, running, jumping, and climbing characterize the early part of this stage. In terms of expression of fear, play themes reflect not so much the child's fear itself, but his response to the fear, especially his efforts to keep fears at bay. Organization has become the child's primary means of deferring anxiety. The development of ritual play reflects the child's attempts to organize thoughts and affects. During play, the child tests fears and tries to master them. Examples of play of this nature include "Dare and double dare," "Prove there's no such thing," "Step on a crack and break your mother's back." Group play involves structured games with rules. The play form during this stage demonstrates the child's central interest in the peer group, the importance of adherence to rules, and a developing sense of fair play.

Features of Play that Promote Mastery of Fears

Play is inherently pleasurable for the child. The child is the master of his play. Play activity, in and of itself, can be therapeutic for the child. Wolpe (1958) uses the term *reciprocal inhibition* to refer to the phenomenon that certain states are mutually exclusive. Anxiety and relaxation cannot be experienced at the same time. Play activity can provide a means of comfort and pleasurable distraction for the fearful child. Morris and Kratochwill (1983) describe the application of this principle in the treatment of fearful children. When two stimuli are systematically coupled, the presence of a stronger positive stimulus will change the child's experience of a fear-provoking negative stimulus. Thus, play and its elements can be used as a means of systematic desensitization for the fearful child.

In addition to being naturally pleasurable, a central function of play is the gradual assimilation of anxiety (Erikson 1950, Waelder 1932). Play has a number of particular features that promote mastery of the child's fears. It allows the child to move from a passive to an active role. This is especially important to the child who has already felt victimized by the object of his fear. Play presents the child with opportunities to explore developmental themes and gives concrete expression to several defense mechanisms that are particularly effective in helping the child to master his fears (Freud 1966, Peller 1952). These include repetition, identification, denial, and projection.

Repetition

Repetition promotes familiarity, predictability, and mastery. It allows new skills to be exercised and consolidated. The infant will shake a rattle until he has satisfied his need to predict and control the sound produced by his activity. Eventually, his repetition of the particular behavior will decrease as assimilation occurs (Piaget 1962).

The process of repetition and assimilation occurs in many types of play. The toddler engages mother in the same game of hide-and-seek and repeats the play until the separation fear is mastered. Repetition of fantasy play is common among 4-year-olds. As developmental issues are resolved, the specific playful repetition decreases and is eventually given up.

Four-year-old Matt created a fantasy play in which he played the role of Peter Pan. Every day at nursery school, he recruited his favorite "Wendy" and re-enacted a scene in which Peter saves Wendy from Captain Hook. Although other children wanted to join in the play, Matt would have no part of it. He only wanted that particular schoolmate to play Wendy, and he would take no role other than Peter. The lines were repeated the same way each time. Eventually, after many performances, the play was abandoned and forgotten. Sometime after his 5th birthday, Matt remarked to his mother, "Remember when I was only 4 and I used to play Peter Pan? It was my favorite game when I was a little boy."

Identification

Play enables the child to assume various roles. The child can be a monster, a villain, or a growling tiger. Play provides the child with an opportunity to replay a fearful experience from a stronger position. He is the active doer rather than the one being done to. Through identification into a more powerful role, the child can undo a traumatic experience and develop resources for the next time he finds himself in the fear-provoking situation (Peller 1952). Anna Freud (1966) provided the well-known example of the "ghost-girl." In order to ensure that she didn't encounter a ghost imagined to be lurking in the hallway, the little girl moved through the hallway making the gestures and sounds of a ghost. As long as she *was* the ghost, the ghost couldn't frighten her.

A 5-year-old boy I met in the hospital playroom was scheduled for surgery the following morning. We were playing with medical play kits; he was performing surgery on a doll and intermittently giving me a few needles. Quite casually, he gave expression to the process of his play and how it helped him master his fear.

"I'm not afraid of monsters anymore," announced the boy surgeon, "and do you know why?"

"Why?"

"Because I was Freddy Krueger for Halloween last year, and he's the scariest monster in the universe, that's why."

"And now, you're the doctor."

"Yeah," he replied, wiping my arm with an alcohol prep. "Hold still, you're getting a few more needles so I can be ready for tomorrow."

Denial

Expanding imagination allows the child to elaborate on experiences for the purpose of mastery. In play, the child can disavow aspects of reality that he finds unpleasant or unacceptable. He can change reality to suit his own purposes; he can pretend to possess attributes that enable him to enjoy a sense of power over his fear. In play, he can be bigger, braver, stronger. Through denial in fantasy play, the child can change elements of a reality-based situation he has experienced. Characters or content can be changed to transform the fear-provoking experience and create a happy outcome.

Joanne's parents had recently divorced. Her father had moved to an apartment nearby. Although Joanne had regular visits to his new home, her parents were aware that the changes in the family caused Joanne considerable distress.

Joanne's favorite playthings were her doll house and the family of dolls that fit inside it. Her parents bought her a second small doll house to represent father's new apartment. They hoped it would help Joanne understand the new arrangements. They showed Joanne how the father doll could be placed in the new doll house. Later, Joanne quietly removed the father doll and placed him in the old doll house. Her play consisted of arranging the family of dolls together in the old doll house. She pretended the new doll house was a neighbor's home where a little girl lived with two parents.

Projection

In play, the child can attribute aspects of his own role to another, such as a doll or imaginary playmate. In this way, the child can indulge wishes or express fears that he dare not acknowledge in his current status.

The child can project his mischievous nature onto an imaginary playmate without fear of loss of approval. He can gratify his need for an extra measure of protection or nurturing by projecting it onto the baby in his play.

Five-year-old Danny was working on his fears of the dark. Trying to be brave, he told his mother he was no longer afraid. Danny insisted, though, that his stuffed dog Pinky be tucked in beside him each night. "Pinky's awfully scared of the dark," Danny told his mother. "He likes to sleep very close to me so he's not afraid." One night while Danny was walking upstairs to bed, his parents saw him clutching Pinky tightly. "Are you scared, Pinky?" Danny asked in a low tone. He continued, "I'm right here. There's nothing to be scared of."

When Fears Are Excessive

Fears that significantly compromise the child's healthy functioning are considered excessive. A 5-year-old with excessive separation fear cannot leave mother in order to attend school. The 10-year-old who is still afraid of the dark risks the ridicule of his peers. His fearfulness engenders a sense of inferiority and compromises his ability to exercise new skills.

Excessive fear may be the remnant of unsuccessfully resolved developmental conflicts. Normal fears are expressed and resolved through play as issues emerge during each developmental stage. Developmental issues are not always resolved in a growth-promoting way, due to a number of factors. Inadequate environmental support of the child, psychosocial trauma, or limited resources on the part of the child are common reasons for failure to achieve adequate resolution of developmental issues. Consequently, the child gets stuck in a certain theme that he is unable to master alone.

Particular psychosocial situations can foster excessive fear. Birth, death, divorce, moving, and hospitalization are examples of situations that can heighten specific fears at any given stage. Regardless of the age at which it occurs, moving to a new neighborhood can reawaken the child's fear of separation and his concern with environmental stability. Separation fear is intensified when the young child enters school. Hospitalization is a situational stressor that presents challenges involving many themes simultaneously. Depending on the age and developmental level of the child, the hospital experience may trigger excessive fear of bodily injury or mutilation, fear of separation or abandonment, and fear of loss of control or loss of parental love.

Excessive fear is expressed in the child's play in several ways. These include difficulties in engaging in the play form; inability to leave the play form behind; repetitive, nonproductive play; or expression of fears that are developmentally inappropriate.

Difficulty Engaging in the Play Form

Like all activities, play has form and structure. The particular nature of the play evolves with the child's developing skills and abilities (Peller 1952). A hallmark of healthy play is the flexibility of the child to move in and out of various possibilities. By age 3, the child should be able to utilize imagination and fantasy to assume roles and be an active participant in his play. The child with excessive fear may demonstrate constriction within the play form, difficulty assuming an active role, or less flexibility in exploring the possibilities provided by various mechanisms of the play.

Inability to Leave the Play Form Behind

By the time the child enters school, play activity carries a sense of time. Play has a beginning, a middle, and an end. The healthy child is able to leave the play form behind, reenter his everyday reality and assume his normal identity. The child with excessive fear will demonstrate a problem in breaking away from the form of the play.

Repetitive Nonproductive Play

Sometimes the child's attempts at mastery are ineffective. He may be unable to resolve a particular issue and may experience a compulsion to repeat activities over and over. Repetitive nonproductive play is characterized by the child's frustrated attempts to resolve the play toward a satisfying outcome.

Developmentally Inappropriate Fears

Childhood fears are associated with developmental issues and are normally resolved as each stage is mastered. Lingering fears, unresolved in the normal developmental sequence, may hinder later emotional endeavors. The 10-year-old who is afraid of the dark demonstrates fear that should normally have been resolved at an earlier stage. An 8-year-old who is afraid to play group sports because he might get hurt demonstrates poor resolution of a normal developmental fear.

Play Therapy for Excessive Fear

In the clinical setting, the excessively fearful child utilizes the therapist's assistance in making productive use of play. Play can be used in a preventative capacity with the child facing a potentially traumatic experience. In the case of excessive or situational fear, the child often requires the assistance of the clinician to move the play form forward and promote a satisfying closure. The therapist can provide structure and support, introduce possibilities for resolution, or present new mechanisms to the child who is stuck.

The utility of play therapy with fearful children has been demonstrated in the clinical setting (Harvey 1975). Although play therapy interventions have yet to be subjected to rigorous scientific inquiry, several studies suggest its effectiveness. Studies have compared the fearful child's response to free play with his response to specific thematic play therapy. Thematic play with young children entering school was found to decrease their separation fears more effectively than nonthematic play (Milos and Reiss 1982).

In the hospital, specific play therapy interventions were more effective in resolving children's hospital fears than simply talking about hospital experiences and fears, or engaging in free nonthematic play (Rae et al. 1989). In recognition of the benefits of play therapy for ill and injured children, many hospitals provide play therapy opportunities for their pediatric patients. Play therapy remains a central tool for the psychotherapist who works with children. Following are several examples illustrating the role of play as both a diagnostic and a therapeutic tool. The four primary fears discussed above are respectively illustrated by the case examples below.

Clinical Examples

Marvin: A 7-Year-Old with Excessive Separation Fear

Marvin was a 7-year-old who was brought to therapy because of his excessive fearfulness at bedtime. He slept with his mother and demanded that she go to sleep when he did. Without her, he was too fearful to stay in bed alone. He was also afraid of the dark and refused to go alone to the bathroom for fear of monsters or spooks. Marvin felt ashamed that his younger cousin called him "Big Baby." His classmates teased him for talking in a babyish voice.

History revealed that Marvin's mother had a severe postpartum depression that lasted on and off for the first 18 months of his life. She required several hospitalizations, and Marvin endured lengthy separations from her. Marvin experienced another loss at age 5, when his parents separated and his father left home.

In therapy, Marvin played at being a "big, strong wrestler," but announced his role rather unconvincingly in his baby voice. "No monster would mess with me because I am the biggest and the strongest." Although the therapist recommended that Marvin begin to sleep in his own room, the mother was unable to relinquish her protective role at bedtime.

Eventually the parents reconciled, and the father returned home. Together, the parents were able to follow the recommendation of the therapist to help Marvin sleep in his own bed. For a while, he needed his mother to stay until he fell asleep. If he awakened alone during the night, he would panic and run out of the room, calling for her. After several weeks of sleeping in his own bed, Marvin developed a greater sense of mastery and security. He began to alter his role in play to a more effective one. He no longer used the baby voice when he proclaimed, flexing his muscles, "I am a big, strong wrestler. But my Daddy is even bigger and stronger. Any monsters try to mess with *me,* and I'll tell my Daddy. He'll show them!"

This case illustrates the presentation and resolution of a developmentally inappropriate fear. Because he endured lengthy separations from his mother, Marvin's normal separation fear extended beyond the time of normal resolution. Marvin endured painful separations from his mother during critical years when the issues of trust and security would normally have been addressed and resolved. Father's absence further interfered with the adequate resolution of normal fears, resulting in extended infantile behavior. Marvin acted like a baby and talked in baby talk. His half-hearted attempts to become a "wrestler" failed to resolve the problem. Success in the wrestler role would have meant that he would have to act like a big boy and cease sleeping with Mother, a step he was not ready to take. Stuck in a double bind until Dad came home, Marvin's play reflected the dilemma. His role play of the manly wrestler demonstrated his desire to be powerful, but his baby voice and demeanor kept him safe and dependent. With the return of his father, the family dynamic changed, allowing him to risk sleeping in his own bed. His subsequent play behavior reflected his new-found confidence.

Shawn: A 3-Year-Old Experiencing Fear of Loss of Love

Shawn had just turned 3 when he was hospitalized with a fractured leg. He was confined to his bed with the leg in traction. For the first several days of the hospitalization, he wet the bed. This caused him great distress and considerable discomfort since he needed to be moved each time the sheets were changed. Reminded to use the urine bottle that hung at his bedside, he cried in protest and frustration. When the nurse came in to ask him if he needed to use the bottle, he offered a vehement "No!" and tried to keep his already wet sheets a secret.

Confronted with the wet sheets, Shawn said, "Rafael did it!" referring to his stuffed toy. "I only pee in the big toilet. I can do it all by myself. My mom likes it that way." He went on to describe his toileting accomplishments in detail and his mother's proud response. Asked about the urine bottle, he replied with frustration, "I *told* you, my mom doesn't *like* me to pee in a bottle. She only likes me to pee in the big toilet, and I only pee in the big toilet because I'm big."

Shawn projected the unacceptable behavior of bedwetting onto his stuffed toy. He expressed the fear that he would lose his mother's love and approval if he stopped exercising the new toileting skills that made her so proud. The intervention was to teach Shawn that a big boy at the hospital can learn to use the bottle all by himself. Reframing the use of the urine bottle so that it became a developmental accomplishment, the therapist helped Shawn to find a new way to gain love and approval, and at the same time to gain a sense of mastery and control over the hospital environment.

Richard: A 5-Year-Old Experiencing Fear of Bodily Injury

Richard was a playful and imaginative 5-year-old boy whose chronic illness required frequent blood tests. He had been stoic and cooperative for several years. Lately, though, he had developed a fear that the needle might break off in his arm, or that there might be another injurious consequence during the blood test. Richard's fear intensified his experience of pain and made it difficult for the doctor to locate a "good" vein.

In the hospital playroom, Richard busied himself fixing everything. His favorite activity was wearing a play tool belt and proclaiming himself "Mr. Fixit. I can fix anything good as new." He also enjoyed pretending to invent new ways to make something "different and better than before."

In a playful session, Richard's fear about needles was explored with the therapist. Richard said he supposed that his veins would not give their blood because they were afraid. When they became afraid, they got cold and thin, and nearly disappeared. "Probably trying to hide from the doctor," he thought. Asked what might make the veins feel better, he replied, "A trip to the beach." He supposed that if the veins were warm, they could feel happy and relaxed, and they would "come right up to the top and give their blood."

A hypnotherapy intervention utilized the theme of his play and his coping strategy to be in control and fix everything. Guided imagery was used to teach Richard how to warm up and cool down his arm. He sent his arm to the beach to lie in the warm sunshine or take a swim in cool ocean water. His ability to control his body temperature by using his imagination increased his confidence. In subsequent visits, Richard warmed up the arm, made sure it was relaxed and ready, and allowed the doctor to draw the blood.

This case illustrates how play can be used for diagnostic purposes. Observation of the spontaneous themes that emerge during play can assist the therapist in understanding the child's conflict, strategy for coping, and attempts at mastery. The therapist can incorporate this information into the design of an intervention.

Richard's fear of needles expressed his feelings of physical vulnerability. His fear was developmentally appropriate; fears of bodily injury are normal during the preschool years. But Richard's chronic illness heightened his sensitivity to this conflict. Having experienced many painful procedures, Richard had developed a perception that his body was somehow damaged.

By projecting his fear onto the arm, Richard could distance himself from the fear. He assumed the role of a competent protector, "Mr. Fixit," who could make sure the arm would be good as new. Richard's special strength, his imagination, was reinforced through the hypnotherapy intervention. By using the power of his imagination he was able to maintain control over his body and he began to feel more powerful than vulnerable.

Davey: A 10-Year-Old Experiencing Fear of Conscience

A 10-year-old boy began therapy with presenting problems of restless sleep, nightmares, and bed wetting. These symptoms had their onset shortly after he was in a car accident with his stepfather. Davey's stepfather had sustained severe head trauma and died.

In therapy sessions, Davey drew detailed pictures of baseball and football players, all of which had strong emphasis on the protective headgear worn. He had memorized statistics of the players' performances, and recited them whenever he drew. He was organized, perfectionistic, and liked to do each picture the same as the last.

During one of the sessions, he asked, "Is there any such thing as Bloody Mary?" He revealed that his friend had told him of a ritual-type game that involved looking in a mirror, turning around three times, and saying, "I don't believe in Bloody Mary." The lights are then blinked a prescribed number of times, and when the player looks in the mirror, he will see that the angry and bloody face of Bloody Mary has appeared. Davey had been dared by his friend to play the game, but he had not mustered his courage to do so. He did not want to take the chance that Bloody Mary really would appear and would be angry with him for saying she wasn't real. There was a curse attached, which Davey felt meant that one would be haunted by Bloody Mary forever.

Therapy goals focused on helping Davey explore his fears. As the therapy progressed, he was able to produce a painting of Bloody Mary, but was so frightened by the completed painting that he could barely look at it. With the therapist's support he was able to look at the painting, and began to talk about the car accident. He cried as he described seeing the bloody head of his stepfather in the car. Subsequent therapy sessions focused on the relationship he had with his stepfather, including his ambivalence and resentment. Davey felt guilty for past bad feelings toward the stepfather. He also wondered if God had taken the stepfather in response to his own occasional wishes that he would go away.

Working through his grief and guilt, Davey was intent on facing his fear, concretely expressed in the Bloody Mary game. With the therapist standing behind him, he performed the ritual in front of a mirror. His anxious laughter followed as he saw what created the illusion. "It's my face, looking scared! There's no Bloody Mary! Whew!"

This case illustrates the importance of the concrete aspects of play to the child. Play gives expression to abstract feelings that are otherwise difficult for the child to recognize and verbalize. Davey's fear of conscience resonated with play that involved rituals and the forbidding consequences of bad thoughts and bad feelings. He introduced the "Bloody Mary" game, asking for the therapist's help in facing his fear of a concrete object. Through this type of concrete play activity, Davey could comfortably master his fears without having to address directly the more powerful images of the terrible car accident. Even after the therapeutic work was done, the boy still needed to confront his fear concretely in the play to prove to himself that he was safe and unharmed. Davey's ability to perform the ritualized play was concrete proof that he had mastered his fear.

What Play Reveals

Childhood fears are associated with normal stages of growth and development. These fears are typically explored and resolved in a sequential order. Play is the child's natural means of expression and learning. The child uses play to express and master fears. The child uses imagination, cognitive skills, and physical abilities to become an active participant in play. Characteristic play behavior may be observed at each developmental stage. The form of play reflects the child's developing abilities. The theme of play reflects the developmental issue.

Play is especially useful to the child because it gives concrete form to experiences and feelings the child finds difficult to verbalize. Play itself provides particular mechanisms that foster mastery. The form of play signals the child's advancement to the next developmental stage. It also reveals the child's difficulty in overcoming certain fears. Play can be used as a clinical tool by the therapist for diagnostic purposes as well as a means for intervention.

References

Erikson, E. H. (1950). *Childhood and Society.* New York: Norton.

Freud, A. (1966). *The Ego and the Mechanisms of Defense.* New York: International Universities Press.

Harvey, S. (1975). Play for children in hospital. *International Journal of Early Childhood* 7:185–187.

Milos, M. E., and Reiss, S. (1982). Effects of three play conditions on separation anxiety in young children. *Journal of Consulting and Clinical Psychology* 50:389–395.

Morris, R. J., and Kratochwill, T. R. (1983). *Treating Childrens' Fears and Phobias: A Behavioral Approach.* New York: Pergamon.

Peller, L. (1952). Models of children's play. *Mental Hygiene* 36:66–83.

_____ (1954). Libidinal phases, ego development, and play. *Psychoanalytic Study of the Child* 9:178–198. New York: International Universities Press.

Piaget, J. (1954). *The Construction of Reality in the Child.* New York: Basic Books.

_____ (1962). *Play, Dreams and Imitation in Childhood.* New York: Norton.

Rae, W., Worchel, F., Upchurch, J., and Sanner, J. (1989). The psychosocial impact of play on hospitalized children. *Journal of Pediatric Psychology* 14:617–627.

Schachter, R., and McCauley, C. (1988). *When Your Child Is Afraid.* New York: Simon & Schuster.

Waelder, R. (1932). Psychoanalytic theory of play. *Psychoanalytic Quarterly* 2:227–298.

Winnicott, D. W. (1971). *Playing and Reality.* London: Tavistock.

Wolpe, J. (1958). *Psychotherapy by Reciprocal Inhibition.* Stanford CA: Stanford University Press.

15

Game Play

Steven Reid

Game playing is a universal and natural human activity that has been a part of nearly all civilizations since earliest recorded history. Games are widely viewed as forms of amusement, but they also have a significant role in development and adaptation to the environment. The dual nature of games is readily observable in the play of both children and adults, in which enjoyment and a sense of seriousness exist side by side. It is the duality of game play that distinguishes it from the kind of unstructured play that appears earlier in the ontology of the human organism and that offers unique possibilities for psychotherapeutic intervention.

The terms *games* and *play* have different meanings in the play therapy literature. Play is seen as a voluntary, spontaneous, pleasurable activity with no particular endpoint or goal. In therapy with children, play constitutes, on some levels, a substitute for verbalization, fantasy expression, or free association. Thus, in a play therapy room one sees toys and materials that encourage fantasy expression and symbolic play, such as dolls, puppets, doll houses, art supplies, molding clay, sand, and water. One of the most critical therapeutic ingredients of play is its pretense, which allows for the release of painful psychic material that would ordinarily be too difficult for a child to express consciously.

Games typically referred to in the play therapy literature include board games, card games, street games, and fine and gross motor games. Organized sports, math and logic games, video games, and recreational games have not yet found a niche in play therapy. Games differ from play in many respects, but also share several characteristics, two of which include enjoyment and pretense. Games are meant to be fun and also to be separate from real life. The phrase "playing a game" contains two meanings, one describing the intrinsic pleasure of play, the other the "as if" quality of play.

Yet games focus much less on imagination and pretending than free play does. Games typically involve competition, a challenge to apply one's skills to win. Compared to free play, games require more in terms of emotional control, intellect, and social skills. Furthermore, games have rules that restrict and define the behavior of the players. The form and style of game play parallels "real life" much more than free play, which is more open-ended with much more variability and flexibility permitted in behavior and role definition. The high level of freedom inherent in free play allows the participant to express impulses and manipulate reality much more readily than in game play.

Another defining characteristic of game play is its inherent social nature. Games usually require interaction between two or more players. A minimum requirement for participation in most games is to play with other people in a self-controlled, cooperative fashion. Play, on the other hand, often involves interaction, but certainly does not require it. Children involved in sensorimotor or pretend play, in fact, often find sharing of the activity restrictive.

The purpose of this chapter is to elucidate the singular therapeutic properties of game play by reviewing the history of selected games, presenting the theoretical and developmental foundations of game play, highlighting therapeutic ingredients found in games, and illustrating the use of games in clinical practice.

Historical and Theoretical Foundations

Games are ubiquitous in modern society and have been throughout history. Archaeological and cross-cultural studies have found that most recorded cultures developed, or inherited from ancestors, an enormous variety of games. In 1891, Stewart Culin, a young archaeologist and ethnologist, was asked to prepare an exhibit of the games of the people of the world for the 1893 Chicago World's Fair. In his investigations, he found the subject to be too vast, so he chose to concentrate on the Aborigines of North America. He continued his work after the World's Fair and subsequently published the book *The Games of the North American Indians* in 1907. The book contains 846 pages and 1,112 illustrations, and catalogues an amazing number of dice games, guessing games, hoop and stick games, ball games, and counting games.

Many games can be traced to prehistoric times and appear to have had a direct correlation to survival and adaptation. Ball playing is probably the oldest known game. Prehistoric man played throwing games with sticks, bones, and stones. As early as 2050 B.C., women were depicted playing ball on Egyptian murals and on hieroglyphics. The theoretical rationale for the emergence of ball games lies in the practice of throwing objects in order to improve coordination and accuracy for the killing of prey. Another explanation of early ball throwing, and other games that involve repeated exchanging of items among players, involves practicing the act of sharing resources, which has obvious survival value (Sutton-Smith 1961). Yet another reason for the development of ball games can be found in the rhythm and repetition involved in playing catch with a ball, which has a relaxing effect on the players (Wood and Goddard 1940). This last hypothesis is important, because it suggests that a purely recreational activity evolved from one that had more serious and instrumental characteristics.

Tag is another ancient game thought to have been played in prehistoric times.

Tag evolved from a spiritual ritual of touching objects made of wood or stone to ward off evil spirits or break spells. This ritual then led to a belief that one could pass on, or contract, evil spirits by touching another human being. Today, the fundamental aspect of tag remains, where one touch from a finger spreads the evil of being "it" from one person to another.

Blindman's Bluff is thought to be derived from ancient rites of human sacrifice in prehistoric religions. The game has a sadistic quality in that one person in a group is blindfolded and victimized by others. In Greece, about 2,000 years ago, the game was played by boys and was called Muinda, or Brazen Fly. One boy was blindfolded while his playmates whipped him with papyrus husks until one of them was caught. The game evolved into Blindman's Bluff and was popular in England during Elizabethan times. However, it retained an aggressive aspect in that the blindfolded person was gently hit with a knotted hood or rope. The game developed a sexual quality as fondling replaced hitting, but this was then prohibited by the Victorians. Today, the game is much less violent and sexual, and also much less popular.

One can see that many of our present-day childhood games have roots in ancient cultures. Early play theorists attempted to explain the enduring aspects of games by employing biological or genetic concepts. For example, Groos (1898) developed the Instinct-Practice Theory, in which game play is viewed as instinctive and instrumental in the practice of essential behavior patterns important in later adult life. His theory was based on observations of the play of both animals and humans, and focused on the similarity between play behavior and real life activities of humans and the development of survival skills of animals.

Whereas game playing subsequently failed to fit the definition of instinct, the notion of practicing behaviors necessary for survival has been preserved in current theoretical formulations of game play. Many theorists have suggested that repeated exposure to and play with games occupies a central role in the socialization of children (e.g., Avedon and Sutton-Smith 1971, Piaget 1962). Essential components of socialization, including self-discipline, problem solving, emotional control, and adoption of leader and follower roles, are prominent features of game playing (Serok and Blum 1983).

While it is clear many games originated for the practice of adaptive behaviors, current forms of ancient games are more often played strictly for amusement. For example, playing cards originated in ancient India and were designed to teach military strategies to young nobles. Unlike chess, checkers, and backgammon, which were also developed to teach military strategy, cards have two different red armies and two different black armies, allowing for more intricate military maneuvers as well as a greater number of possible participants in the game. Presumably, the colors black and red were chosen because they were the first two colors recognized by humans (Wood and Goddard 1940). In ancient times, a variety of symbols and personifications were portrayed on the faces of cards, including natural forces (wind, fire, air), military resources, and soldiers and officers of differing military ranks.

Card playing reached the modern age soon after cards arrived in Europe. In medieval times, cards were brought back from the Orient after the Moorish invasion of Spain and the return of the Crusaders from their trek in the Near East. Soon after, cards became identified with the royal court – in fact, the face of King Henry VII is preserved on all four kings in the traditional deck of cards. Identification with military strategies diminished and were replaced by concepts of monetary power and worth. Card playing proliferated and is now one of the most popular forms of game play. Today, card playing retains an emphasis on intellectual strategy and competition, but it has no direct survival value and is not connected to teaching of military strategy.

Several theorists explain the concept of amusement in game playing by emphasizing the purely recreational and pleasurable aspects of play. The Surplus-Energy Theory (Mitchell and Masson 1948) is based on the view that all play is simply the release of excess energy. In this theory, play is viewed as being random and noninstrumental. In the Recreational Theory (Mitchell and Masson 1948), play is not viewed as a form of release, but as a means of regaining energy that has been depleted through work. Thus, the intellectual may find rest and relaxation by playing a game involving physical movement, and a laborer, by playing a game involving mental skill.

These two views of game play were developed during the time of the Industrial Revolution, when the concepts of work and play were sharply defined. The theories highlight essential elements of recuperation and release of physical energy that, in addition to practice of adaptive behaviors, help the human organism adjust to environmental conditions. Freud's psychoanalytic theory (Strachey 1962) was also developed around the end of the nineteenth century, and includes a discussion of a theory of play in which the concept of catharsis is prominent. Catharsis is similar to the energy-release notion except that it refers to discharge of emotional or psychic energy, not necessarily physical energy. Freud theorized that the fundamental process of personality development was the inhibition and repression of basic drives, a process that results in pent-up tension. This tension must then be discharged in socially acceptable ways, one of which is game playing. The cathartic theory of game play thus offers an interpretation of Blindman's Bluff as a release and displacement of aggressive and sexual drives, especially as it was played in Greek and English cultures.

We see from Freud's view of play and games that the content of these activities reflects basic emotional states and tensions found in the individual participants. One may extend this view to include society as a whole, wherein, hypothetically, games of a particular culture would mimic the prevailing psychological concerns and conflicts of its members. Evidence from cross-cultural studies of game play provides some indirect support of this hypothesis. For example, games of chance predominate in cultures associated with environmental uncertainty and unpredictability, those in which food supplies, climate, settlements, and so forth are highly variable (Sutton-Smith and Roberts 1971). Games such as tag, hide and seek, and red rover (central person games), on the other hand, could represent anxiety about exercising social independence. Research has shown that in cultures in which central person games predominate, there exists a significantly greater concern with independence training during childhood, as well as a greater tendency for the adolescent child to leave his or her own kinship group to marry among relative strangers, than in those cultures in which central person games do not exist or are not prominent (Sutton-Smith 1971). Some modern games were developed as a direct result of anxieties resulting from social pressures. Monopoly, for instance, a game involving acquisition of wealth through real estate, was created during the Great Depression in the 1930s.

Freud (Strachey 1962) also highlighted the notion of mastery as a motivating force in game play. In his view, game playing involved not only the expression of impulses (primary process) but also the mastering of anxiety (secondary process). Peller (1954) further explicated the id and ego processes involved in play. She viewed game playing to be a step toward sublimation of basic impulses, in that all play implies moving from a passive, receptive role to an active one. Only small quantities of anxiety can be mastered in play, whereas anxiety of high intensity disrupts play. According to Peller, games become an important vehicle for the resolution of the aggressive feelings characteristic of the oedipal period.

Mitchell and Masson (1948) theorized that games contain aggression because fighting is a natural, spontaneous response to certain life situations. Fighting releases strong emotions aroused by physiological responses to threatening stimuli. With the development of civilized society came laws and social taboos against uncontrolled fighting. Play and games were created by humans to provide acceptable outlets for anger and hatred, derivatives of the basic fight response.

Although games differ in the level of competition and often contain elements of cooperation, nearly all modern games involve some form of contest, which by itself is a symbolic expression of aggression. The highest level of symbolic aggression is found in games in which one opponent directly attacks another, such as by capturing or neutralizing an opponent's piece (e.g., checkers, chess). Only a few games other than organized sports have retained overt aggression, such as "King-of-the-mountain" and "Flinch" (the latter involves one person hitting another if the other moves in response to the pretend action of hitting). Nevertheless, Redl (1958) argued that aggression, power, and dominance/submission exist in all games. Sutton-Smith (Sutton-Smith and Roberts 1971) has called games "models of power" (p. 79) by which children and adults learn socially acceptable ways to succeed over others. Many games establish a hierarchy of dominance, such as those requiring that a leader be designated and that the other players follow the leader. Games and game playing have become a central metaphor in the sociology literature for the understanding of social conflict. The competition found in games is analogous to the naturally occurring conflicts of interest in business, political, and interpersonal interactions (Schlenker and Bonoma 1978). Game theory has been used to study the evolution of territoriality and mate selection in animals, and cooperation and antagonistic behavior in humans (Maynard-Smith 1984).

As societies have become more complex and sophisticated, the interdependence between people has increased. An individual's actions can affect a large number of people and, at the same time, one's own well-being depends in large part on the actions taken by others. The evolution of game playing has paralleled this trend. Games that are simple, physical, and overtly aggressive have given way to those that are more complex and civilized. As part of this trend, modern game playing has seen the burgeoning of board games.

Board games typically involve a higher level of interpersonal communication, cooperation, and shared decision-making than other forms such as street games, card games, or physical games. Board games emphasize intellectual skills such as forethought and judgment, and downplay physical skills such as strength and endurance. Board games provide a flexible medium for the creation of new games, and alteration of the rules of existing games. This type of flexibility is applicable to the complex and ever-changing modern world.

In summary, games have throughout history served a dual purpose in providing amusement and enjoyment as well as several important functions important to the survival and adaptation of human beings. These functions include recuperation, catharsis, sublimation or adaptive expression of aggression, intellectual development, and various elements of socialization. All of these have been exploited in the use of games in psychotherapy. Before discussing the therapeutic ingredients of game playing in greater detail, we will first examine game playing from a developmental point of view.

Developmental Perspective

Major theories of play view this vital activity as dynamic and subject to changes in form, style, and range over the course of human development. These theories have a remarkable similarity in terms of the developmental progression of play. In most major theories, earliest forms of play in infants and toddlers are seen to reflect the emergence of a primitive sense of self and the narcissism characteristic of the first stage of psychological development. During these early years, play is dominated by egocentric bodily movements. In the preschool years, children's play is believed to reflect growing concerns about their relationships with significant adult figures. As such, preschool play is characterized by symbolic, dramatic forms in which strong feelings and magical thinking predominate. As children enter the elementary school years, play becomes increasingly realistic and complex, involving interpersonal interactions and situations that gradually approximate real-life social phenomena.

Playing of games, defined as they are in the play therapy literature as rule-governed, organized social activities, emerges somewhere between 5 to 8 years of age. This critical developmental transition has been explained in terms of changes in or acquisition of new cognitive, emotional, and social capacities.

Piaget (1962) ties the transition from symbolic play to game play to the development of a higher order of cognitive development characterized by logical thinking, problem solving, and interest in quantifying the environment. A child entering this new stage of cognitive development has greater perception of reality, and therefore prefers more realistic, goal-oriented games typical of those played by adults.

Peller (1954) links the emergence of game playing to the reduction of oedipal preoccupations. Oedipal play is marked by the processes of idiosyncratic fantasy and magical thinking, and the content of oedipal play often involves the basic triangle (Freud 1923). Through dramatic play, children can fantasize about putting themselves in the place of envied adults or release tensions related to frustration of oedipal wishes. Resolution of oedipal strivings is achieved through identification with an adult figure, and is reflected in a shift in interest from fantasy play to games that parallel life in the adult world. Game playing also facilitates identification with peers of the same sex, which helps loosen oedipal ties.

Social theorists have emphasized that game playing reflects the growing child's readiness to band together with equals, not only for camaraderie, but for help in facing the authority of the adult world. Mead (1934) discusses the parallel between the rules governing behavior in games, and laws and codes of conduct that exist in the adult world. Parten (1932) studied the social play of preschoolers and found that their social play becomes increasingly complex, progressing through stages of solitary, parallel, associative, and cooperative play. Research on cooperation in play has found that it emerges as early as 22 months (Ross and Kay 1980) but does not become a critical ingredient in play until middle childhood (Stoll et al. 1968, Zigler and Child 1956). Many writers have stressed the importance of games in the socialization process. Serok and Blum (1983) describe games as mini-life situations in which the basic elements of socialization – rule conformity, acceptance of the norms of the group, and control of aggression – are integral components of the process of play.

Game playing, particularly the adoption of roles within games, has been linked to identity development in children. Baumeister (1986, 1987) postulated that children's identities develop and expand over time through three self-definition processes. The simplest form of self-definition, called assigned component (Type I), involves the passive acquisition of stable features of identity. Early recognition of self as having a certain gender, belonging to a particular family, and having specific physical characteristics, are examples of assigned component identity development. The individual does nothing to acquire these identity features; they are passively acquired, and remain constant throughout life.

Type II self-definition is called single transformational, and involves a discrete change in identity based on meeting a particular set of criteria. Although these components of identity are not passively acquired, many are universal milestones in a child's development that are not self-selected. Learning to walk or ride a bike and entering school are examples of criterial transformations. Furthermore, Type II self-definition occurs throughout the lifespan as people acquire new aspects of identity, such as by joining a social organization, becoming a psychologist, or getting married. In Type II self-definitional processes, the identity is stable until the transformation takes place, and is stable afterward.

A third process of self-definition, Type III, is labeled hierarchical, and involves identity acquisition based on external, quantifiable, hierarchical dimensions. Such roles are based heavily on an individual's competence, and are subject to many alterations and refinements. They permit precise and extensive comparisons among individuals, and are continually subject to change. Seeing oneself as wealthy, famous, intelligent, successful, or important among peers is an example of the hierarchical process of self-definition.

Baumeister suggests that the role structures in children's games reflect the progression of identity development from more stable, passively acquired roles to those that are externally defined, based on competence, and unstable. In a 1988 study by Baumeister and Senders, 339 children, ranging in age from 2½ to 15 years, were asked to identify their favorite games from a list of forty-nine. These games were previously evaluated and categorized on the basis of their role structure as follows: (a) Type I games, consisting of "Simon Says," house, "Mother May I," Candyland, Doctor, and others in which a player adopts a single, stable role throughout the game, (b) Type II games, consisting of tag, dodgeball, hide-and-seek, Blindman's Bluff, and others in which players change roles as part of the game, usually between two fundamental roles, and (c) Type III games, consisting of basketball, Monopoly, baseball, chess, and others in which players change or identify with several roles or adopt sub-roles. In many Type III games, each player takes and holds one continuous role and simultaneously switches among sub-roles. In baseball, for example, a player's team membership remains constant, but the player rotates between several sub-roles: batter, fielder, runner, and so forth.

The study involved children selecting their own favorite games, and teachers identifying games that were popular among the students in their classes. The results of this study suggest that role structure of games does parallel identity development. Table 15–1 below illustrates the pattern.

These findings indicate that games involving the single enactment of preassigned, stable roles were favored by young children in the symbolic play stage of development. These games are noncompetitive and not directed toward a specific goal. Theoretically, these games help affirm the preschooler's growing awareness of stable features of his identity. Children in the early latency stage prefer games that involve role switching among a few roles that are more complex and less directly representative of important people in a child's social world. Preadolescent and adolescent children prefer competitive games based on competence that allow for more variation in role structure.

The developmental progression to competitive games involves a transitional step in which competitive games are played, but in which the demand and threat of the contest are diluted by reliance on luck to decide the outcome. Chance-based competitive games are preferred by children 6 to 9 years of age (Type II age range),

Table 15-1. Mean Start-Up Ages

Structural Dimensions	Teachers' Ratings
Role definition	
Assigned, stable role	3.1
Single transformation	6.0
Hierarchical	8.1
Role switching	
Constant role	4.1
Switching roles	5.5
Constant role, switch subroles	8.1
Competition	
Noncompetitive	3.3
Chance-based competition	4.9
Skill/strategy competition	7.4

Adapted from Baumeister & Senders, "Identity Development and the Role Structure of Children's Games." *Journal of Genetic Psychology,* 1988, 150:19–37. Used by permission.

as found in the study by Baumeister and Senders. Such games enable children to experiment with new and different roles without requiring them to cope strategically and skillfully with opposition. In this stage of development, children's identities are in flux, as they are just beginning to make comparisons against their peers as a basis of self-definition (Ruble 1983). It is not until late childhood that identity and self-definition come to focus on issues of competence and measurement against peers, in which the self becomes increasingly equated with performance (Erikson 1968).

Therapeutic Ingredients of Games

The versatility of games has been exploited by psychotherapists in helping children resolve emotional conflicts. In this section, aspects of games that have particular relevance for therapeutic work are identified and elaborated.

Therapeutic Alliance

Games are nonthreatening and familiar to children, thus providing an important medium for establishing rapport. They are such an enjoyable part of children's lives that even the most resistant child will be drawn to game play in the therapy context.

The therapist as well as the child plays the game – this has the effect of relaxing the adult–child boundary and rendering the therapist more human to the child. Many children enter therapy with a negative attitude because the decision to enter into a helping situation is usually made by their parents, not themselves. Children with poor ego strength may feel intense pressure being alone with a therapist in an unfamiliar office. Games can help these children feel more comfortable and engage them in a working relationship.

Diagnosis

Earliest uses of games in therapy focused on their projective value. Observing *how* a child plays the game, as well as the content of his verbalizations during play, provides important insight into the child's personality structure. Gardner (1986) elucidates typical responses of children having a variety of maladaptive personality characteristics, including passive-dependency, egocentrism, social isolation or psychosis, antisocial behavior, obsessive-compulsive symptoms, and neurologically based learning disabilities.

To illustrate, a passive-dependent child may constantly ask for help or advice, or may lose a game on purpose to please the therapist; an antisocial child may overemphasize winning and have trouble accepting defeat. The therapist will also readily observe the intellectual strengths and weaknesses of the child playing a game, as nearly all games require intellectual effort. The cognitive capacities and thinking styles of children are important to ascertain when formulating therapeutic interventions such as psychoanalytic interpretations or cognitive restructuring.

Although the diagnostic use of games remains a subjective clinical procedure vulnerable to therapist bias and individual perceptions, there have been efforts to develop standardized measures of psychological functioning using games. One example is the Kiddie Formal Thought Disorder Story Game developed by Caplan and Sherman (1991). This game involves analysis of cognitive and linguistic properties of children's stories, and use of a scale based on established criteria for diagnosis of formal thought disorder.

Pleasure

Game playing in naturally occurring contexts is understood to promote emotional growth. Games are natural and enjoyable activities and have special significance for children who have difficulty experiencing pleasure, such as withdrawn or autistic children. The pleasurable aspect of game playing relates not only to nurturing oneself but also to nurturing others. Playing a game in which participants clearly experience fun is a reciprocal process. In therapy, the child not only gives himself pleasure, but also has been instrumental in giving pleasure to the therapist, who also enjoyed the game. This giving process results in the feeling of being needed, useful, and wanted.

Communication

A game, by definition, is separate from reality. One is free from the restraints and pressures of daily life when playing a game. Games invite the relaxation of defenses that would normally inhibit expression of feelings, thoughts, beliefs, and attitudes in normal social intercourse. The bounds of self-expression might be limited by the process of game play, which often invokes practical discussion of rules, concentration on strategy, and attentiveness toward the actions of other players. Yet the positive outcome of this process is the resultant communication *between* the players. A certain level of cooperation and mutuality of purpose is inherent in game play. As children relax and lose themselves in the game, their defenses relax and they often begin to talk about feelings and ideas that are important to them. Frey (1986) and Gardner (1986) discuss points of departure, in which the players leave the game to discuss psychological issues expressed during game play.

Fantasy

Games often expose children to novel situations that lead to the development and expression of creative energies. Games provide ambiguous stimuli and allow for a variety of responses. Many relatively new therapeutic board games focus on fantasy expression, for example, Our Game (Vlosky 1986).

Catharsis

A certain type of expression, catharsis, is also often elicited by the process of game playing. Strong feelings of anger, resentment, frustration, and jealousy can be discharged within the safe confines of a game. In particular, negative feelings a child may have about his parents or other adult figures will be more easily expressed in a game situation. This is true because the therapist is an adult and therefore a representative of the adult world. From a psychoanalytic viewpoint, game play can facilitate the development and working through of transference by promoting cathartic expression of emotion.

Sublimation

Games provide more opportunities for sublimation of instinctual or forbidden urges than free play, by virtue of their higher degree of structure and role definition. For instance, a child's sexual or aggressive impulses might be channeled into increased concentration and effort to win the game. Typically, therapeutic board games have a variety of adaptive responses and solutions to conflicts readily available, which the child must consider. These outcomes might not otherwise have been within the child's awareness, and can actually lead to more adaptive resolution of emotional conflicts.

Insight

Game play often reveals unhealthy behavioral patterns on the part of the child client. The task of the therapist is to bring these patterns into the child's awareness. One advantage of games is that the therapist is also a player, and so can first model for the child a response indicating self-awareness, such as "Oh, I keep blocking my own path to home!" This kind of response sets the tone for self-examination. Another advantage of games is their separation from real life. A negative self-evaluation within the confines of game behavior is less threatening than one made in reference to real life behavior. Gradually, the therapist can help the child become aware of behavioral patterns that generalize from the game context to the child's larger world.

Reality Testing

Games are realistic forms of play that contain rules that are analogous to societal norms. In order to participate, players implicitly reach a consensus on the meaning of the rules and the game procedures. Games are played by at least two people, necessitating a certain amount of cooperation, agreement upon rules, and shared objective perception of reality. Game players cannot change the rules at will or use imagination to manipulate the course of the game to fit individual wishes. For all of these reasons, game play enhances reality testing. Distortion of reality is seen in the form of cheating and denial of events (e.g., insisting that the number on the die was different than that observed by other players). The therapist can gently insist upon playing in a realistic fashion and reinforce more adaptive and realistic game responses.

Ego Enhancement

The competitive nature of games demands concentration, impulse control, and self-confidence. Games invoke the processes of the ego and superego to a greater extent than those of the id, and therefore call upon the player to deal with anxiety, which is the primary task of the ego. Anxiety regarding competition, self-esteem, power, helplessness, and risk taking is often aroused by a game, especially when played with an adult, as is often found in a therapy context. Games provide opportunities for the child in treatment to confront and master uncomfortable feelings. In the pretend situation found in a game, children are more willing to experiment with new behaviors and to accept direction given by adults. The process of learning how to play a game, and of improving one's performance and outcome (i.e., winning) also provide children with experiences that increase self-confidence and a sense of mastery.

Cognitive Growth

Intellectual skills, such as concentration, memory, anticipation of consequences, reflectivity, creative problem solving, and logical thinking are all called upon by various games. Games have found a place in classroom instruction and remedial education because they provide an enjoyable and nonthreatening medium for learning of cognitive skills. Learning of new behaviors, self-reflection, and self-understanding are cognitive processes that are essential to emotional development in and out of the therapeutic relationship.

Socialization

Learning to get along with other people is a critical challenge that occurs throughout the lifespan. Problems such as aggression, social inhibition, and social isolation are common among children referred for psychotherapy. Games appear to have particular relevance for conduct-disordered and delinquent youth, whose problems are thought to stem from a failure in the socialization process. Games offer opportunities to experience depersonalized sources of authority in the form of the rules and structures that define the games, as well as positive peer pressure for socialized behavior. By playing games, children are also sensitized to the aversive consequences of rule-violating behaviors. Within the process of naturalistic game play, rule violators are generally stigmatized or forced to offer an apology, or at least an admission of guilt, to remain in the game. Learning the consequences of socially unacceptable behavior is an important socialization process. So too, is learning how to deal with aggressive and competitive feelings in an appropriate manner. The rules of games require children to compete and assert themselves within certain limited boundaries. Group norms exist that dictate how winners and losers should behave in relation to one another. Subjecting oneself to the control or command of others is also a part of many games. This process is analogous to learning to deal with others in the real world who are more powerful than oneself.

Types of Games

Several different classification schemes for games have been developed. The classifications developed by Sutton-Smith and Roberts (1971) are based on what determines who wins. Three types of games are distinguished: (1) games of physical skill, in which the outcome is determined by the players' motor abilities; (2) games of strategy, in which cognitive skill determines who wins; and (3) games of chance, in which the outcome is accidental.

Physical Skill

Games of physical skill can be further divided into gross-and fine-motor games. Gross-motor games are usually not suitable for a therapy office or room. Furthermore, they may encourage acting out, instead of verbalization, of feelings and emotions. Despite these disadvantages, they have been employed in play therapy. Schachter (1974, 1984, 1986) has developed a series of physical interactive games, which he calls Kinetic Psychotherapy, to treat a range of adjustment difficulties and depression in children. According to Schachter, these games are particularly useful for facilitating the expression of certain emotional reactions that are otherwise difficult to elicit without the release function of movement. Gross-motor games have also been used for treatment of children with deficits in self-control (Kendall and Braswell 1985, Shapiro 1981).

Fine motor games include Tiddly Winks, pick-up sticks, Operation, Perfection, darts, battling tops, penny hockey, and so forth. These games are usually highly competitive, have easily explained rules, and are particularly useful for evaluating a child's impulse control and general level of ego integration (Bow and Goldberg 1986).

Strategy

The outcome of strategy games depends primarily on the cognitive skills of the contestants. There are innumerable strategy games available today, but some of the most widely cited in the play therapy literature include Connect Four, checkers, most card games, Chinese Checkers, and Uno, among others. Advantages of strategy games include their amenability to being played by two people in an office, and the opportunities provided to observe the child's intellectual strengths and weaknesses. Strategy games also permit the expression of aggression in symbolic form without the physical arousal associated with physical games. A possible disadvantage of strategy games is that they require activation of ego processes including concentration and intellectual effort. Depending on one's clinical orientation, these ego processes may enhance or detract from the therapy process.

Chance

Games of chance include bingo, roulette, a few card games (e.g., War), Candyland, and Chutes and Ladders, among others. Pure chance games, except for adult gambling, tend to be on a simple level and are therefore useful as an introduction to game playing. This notion is consistent with the empirical finding that young children's earliest game preferences are those in which winning depends primarily on chance (Baumeister and Senders 1988). A real therapeutic advantage of chance games is that they neutralize the adult's superiority in intellect, experience, and skills. On the other hand, children often lose interest in games that do not require use of strategy or skill.

Other game classification schemes have been developed. Spates (1976) views childhood games as representative of social norms and success strivings. He places games in terms of their sociological significance into three major classes: competitive games, aggressive games, and acquisitional games. While the meanings of the first two classes of games are self-evident, the latter category, acquisitional games, is linked to the concept of wealth. Wealth and monetary power are attached to specific material goods such as possessions and money. Many games have as their chief emphasis the winning of symbolic material goods and principal roles of the possessor and the dispossessed. The critical feature of such games is the objective of acquiring a part of the opponent's collection that he has put up as stake. Examples of such games are many, and include Monopoly, marbles, flipping coins or cards, War, and Risk. The notion of classifying games according to their acquisitional nature is consistent with the theoretical view of games as models of social power.

Recent advances and innovations in the use of games in play therapy has wrought new methods of classifying games. Rabin (1983) and Varenhorst (1973) categorize games on the basis of the amount of rules and type of activity emphasized (cognitive, behavioral, or both). In their book *Game Play: Therapeutic Use of Childhood Games* (1986), Schaefer and Reid classify games with respect to the therapeutic emphasis or objective of the game. These groupings include communication games, problem-solving games, ego-enhancing games, and socialization games.

Communication Games

The central focus of communication games is to promote self-expression and communication. Communication between child and therapist is considered to be critical to the success of therapy. Many children, however, are reluctant to disclose their thoughts, feelings, and fantasies, and few accept the notion that such disclosure would be beneficial to them. Games provide a nonthreatening activity through which the therapist and child can communicate. Certain games greatly facilitate self-expression, such as therapeutic board games including the Ungame (Zakich 1975), Imagine (Burks 1978), Social Security (Burten 1976), Talking, Feeling, and Doing Game (Gardner 1973), and The Story Telling Card Game (Gardner 1988). There has been a recent explosion of development of therapeutic board games; to illustrate, perusal of a recent copy of the play therapy catalog, *Childswork Childsplay*, finds a listing of over fifty such games.

In order to foster a nonthreatening, permissive atmosphere in the therapy situation, most communication board games are designed with a reduced emphasis on competition, skill, and strategy, concomitant with an increased focus on cooperation as well as rewards for self-expression. Thus, a player advances along the path or receives tokens or chips for just expressing his feelings or thoughts. The correctness of responses is typically not evaluated or directly rewarded in communication board games.

Most communication games encourage self-expression on different levels, ranging from projection of fantasy material to statements of beliefs and moral judgments, creating a high amount of flexibility in terms of steering the game play to ensure the child's continued involvement along the way. The Feeling Cards in the

Talking, Feeling, and Doing Game, for instance, contain questions designed to range from threatening to mildly anxiety-provoking to very nonthreatening.

Therapeutic board games also usually encourage actual expression of feelings or behaviors rather than just talking about feelings or behaviors. Thus, in a game of Social Security, one may draw a card with the instruction to make a sad face or to jump up and shout. The purpose of these game features is to encourage a relaxation of ego controls to allow for free expression of feelings and thoughts.

Some communication games were created specifically to promote expression of deeper unconscious psychological material. One such game is the Story Telling Card Game, developed by Gardner. This game is similar to the projective assessment instrument, the Thematic Apperception Test, in that clients are encouraged to create stories based on pictures. Gardner made a game of this activity by employing twenty-four picture cards portraying common scenes (e.g., living room, classroom, kitchen, backyard, etc.), fifteen human figurines, chips, an arrow spinner, and dice. Players use the spinner to get chips or select from one of several categories of cards, use the dice to determine how many figurines may be used, and are rewarded with chips for telling a self-created story and the lesson or moral of the story. The stories provide points of departure for a wide variety of therapeutic interchanges between client and therapist. Other games designed to promote fantasy expression include Our Game (Vlosky 1986), and Lifestories and Conversations, listed in the *Childswork Childsplay* catalog.

Problem-Solving Games

Problem-solving games are those that help individuals deal with specific problems such as divorce, dysfunctional family communication, academic underachievement, and hyperactivity. These types of games reward logical thinking and problem solving by surrounding them in an atmosphere of play, enjoyment, and challenge. In recent years, many original therapeutic board games have been developed based on this premise. These games tend to be highly structured, cognitively oriented activities that incorporate behavioral strategies to provide incentives for participation and involvement in the problem-solving process. Among therapeutic board games listed in the *Childswork Childsplay* catalog are several problem-solving games including: Assert with Love, the Stress Management Game, the Anxiety Management Game, the Self-Esteem Game, Say No To Drugs Game, Study Smart, Coping and Decisions, Divorce Cope, Play It Safe With SASA (sexual abuse), Scruples for Kids, and Beautiful Place (environmental awareness).

Ego-Enhancing Games

This category refers more to a particular use of games than to a specific set of games themselves. Ego-enhancing games typically include relatively simple, well-known games such as checkers, card games, target games, Sorry, Connect Four, Trouble, and so on. Use of these games is based on the assumption that children feel more comfortable and derive more enjoyment from familiar games. The use of these games to enhance ego functioning is predicated on the competitive, challenging aspects of game playing. Competitive games require children to apply their skills to win the game. The child is faced with playing against an adult who is superior in intelligence and experience. As a result, feelings of competition, aggressiveness, trust, and helplessness are often expressed by children in therapy. The diagnostic information compiled during game play can be used to understand the child's psychological functioning and to guide therapeutic interventions.

Socialization Games

Socialization games take advantage of the inherent social-interactive nature of games, as well as the developmental readiness of older children to engage in social play. Socialization games usually take place in a group therapy situation. Socialization games can be used as part of highly structured, behavioral-based programs designed to shape and reinforce a variety of adaptive social behaviors. Other therapists use socialization games in a less structured format. For example, Serok (1986) describes the use of repeated game play sessions in the treatment of juvenile delinquents. Specific socialization processes practiced in game play include self-discipline, cooperation, socialized competition, leadership–followership, emotional control, problem solving, and conforming to generalized rules.

Clinical Applications

Use of play and games in child psychotherapy was begun by child analysts such as Anna Freud and Melanie Klein to lure children into therapy and to promote fantasy expression. Formal game playing was not widely discussed in the child psychotherapy literature before the 1950s. Loomis's (1957) article on the use of checkers in therapy marked the first significant work on the therapeutic value of game playing. Loomis regarded game playing as a medium for expression of unconscious conflict, in particular resistance. Meeks (1970) and Beiser (1979) further espoused the projective value of game playing. They viewed it as a projection in particular of the relationship between the players involved. Components of the working relationship between therapist and child, including resistance, transference, and countertransference, are more readily expressed within the confines of game play than in conscious discourse between therapist and child.

Traditional psychodynamic child psychotherapy has incorporated games into the therapy process, albeit in a limited context. In their discussions of game playing in child psychotherapy, Gardner (1969, 1975, 1986) and Levinson (1976) emphasize that games tend to elicit only certain types of projection of unconscious material, namely, those associated with the child's relationships with significant adults.

Bettelheim (1972) and Berlin (1986) discuss games in terms of their value in eliciting conflicts regarding helplessness, power, and aggression.

Gardner (1986) cautions that formal games have less intrinsic projective value than many other play media. Instead of promoting relaxation of ego controls, games activate the ego by challenging the participant to apply his skills to win the game. Whereas a child's abilities and personality are readily projected in game play, deeper unconscious conflicts are not.

It seems that the traditional use of games in therapy has been adjunctive, that is, as a tool to reduce resistance, enhance communication, and provide a projective screen for diagnosis and treatment. Even therapeutic board games are generally viewed as tools to open up lines of communication. Broadly speaking, within this framework, game play by itself is not considered therapeutic. Nevertheless, there has been an increase since the early 1970s in the application of games to special problems and settings. As part of this trend, the process of game playing is often viewed as therapeutic, not adjunctive. A positive aspect of the increased specialization of game play therapy is an increase in empirical efficacy research. The following segment provides a sampling of recent developments in game play therapy in which some evaluative research has been conducted.

Divorce

Epstein (1986) describes his creation and utilization of two games for children of divorce, the Children's Feedback Game and the Could This Happen Game. These games are used as part of 3-month group therapy programs for children who have experienced the divorce of their parents. In the Children's Feedback Game, children learn to take the role of peers, give and receive feedback, share, and take turns. These skills are thought to enhance the group interaction process underlying the Could This Happen Game. In this game, the children are divided into two teams that compete with each other. Hypothetical stories are presented, and children are asked to consider the probability of events in the story occurring in real life. The stories are innocuous to begin with, then gradually approximate situations, events, and conflicts relating to divorce and its effects on family members. Points are won for realistic guessing and for discussion of feelings relating to the story. Positive outcomes in therapy have been found for children who played these games.

The Changing Family Game (Berg 1982, 1986) is a board game incorporating cognitive-behavioral principles to help children cope with the problems of divorce. The game involves moving from start to finish by answering questions on cards. The questions cover a range of divorce-related concerns, including peer ridicule and avoidance, paternal blame, maternal blame, self-blame, fear of abandonment, and hopes of reunification. Cards also cover issues regarding single parenting and visitation. An efficacy study on the Changing Family Game found that the adequacy of solutions children offer to problems improves over game-playing sessions (Berg et al. 1985).

Impulsivity/Acting Out

Swanson (1986) discusses the use of two games within a cognitive-behavioral framework to help children reduce impulsive responding and increase attention to task in classroom settings. The game of Beat the Clock, adapted from the television game show by Shapiro (1981), involves the child outlasting the clock by remaining on task until the alarm sounds. The child earns chips by remaining on task, whereas chips are removed for going off task. The child has the opportunity to earn chips for each game that is played, and the chips can then be exchanged for a small prize.

The Stop and Think Game, as described by Kendall and Braswell (1985), is a vehicle for learning the self-instructional model of self-control. The game is especially effective when used in conjunction with fine motor games such as pick-up sticks, according to Swanson (1986). First, the therapist models stopping to think and asking questions to oneself (self-instruction) before initiating a turn in the game. Then, the child is encouraged to stop and ask questions as well. Again, chips are used to reward successful self-instruction and problem solving. Because of their behavioral structure, both the Beat the Clock and the Stop and Think games are amenable to empirical research regarding their effectiveness.

Bow and Goldberg (1986) describe the use of games with a fine motor component as being particularly helpful for children with self-control deficits. The process of repetitive play and support and guidance from the therapist enables the child in therapy to master his impulses in at least one setting with one set of materials. Shapiro (1981) catalogues a number of games and activities designed to help children learn self-control.

The Good Behavior Game, developed by Barrish and colleagues (1969), has been found to be effective in reducing inappropriate and disruptive behavior of students in the classroom (Barrish et al. 1969, Harris and Sherman 1973, Medland and Stacknick 1972). The concept of the Good Behavior Game is simple: a class is divided into teams based upon the inappropriate behavior they exhibited most frequently during baseline recording sessions. Each inappropriate behavior displayed by a team member is recorded by a mark on the blackboard in the team's designated area. If the team's total marks at the end of the session do not exceed the criterion specified by the teacher, the team receives the agreed-upon reinforcement. The sense of competition engendered by the forming of teams provides additional motivation for children to control their inappropriate behavior. A recent study found the Good Behavior Game to be dramatically effective in reducing a variety of inappropriate behaviors of emotionally disturbed children in a special education class (Salend et al. 1989).

Games have also been applied to more severe behavior disturbances such as chronic aggression. Researchers have found that traditional cognitive and behavior programs have been less effective with children exhibiting severe behavior problems (e.g., Bugental et al. 1977, Sprafkin and Rubenstein 1982). A recent study (Dubow et al. 1987) found that a control condition consisting of game play with cards and board games, directed by an adult leader, was more effective in reducing aggression than cognitive and behavior interventions. This serendipitous result was attributed to the intrinsic motivating factor of winning a game against a peer, a goal seen as being more immediate and real than the rewards offered by the opposing interventions.

Social Isolation/Inhibition

Much has been written about the benefits of game play for teaching social skills, not only for preschool children just learning to interact with peers (Opie and Opie 1976, Ross 1982), but also for older, unsocialized, or delinquent children and for retarded adolescents and adults (Foxx et al. 1983, Hurff 1981).

Recent developments in this area include the adaptation of the format of Trivial Pursuit to teach social and community living skills to adolescents and adults with developmental disabilities (Nochajski and Gordon 1987). Game questions were revised to tap knowledge regarding basic components of socialization and independent living. An efficacy study found that the game improved performance of subjects in community living skills.

Another study found that repeated play of a cooperative game between two children, one identified as a social isolate, dramatically increased the level of cooperative play and number of social interactions initiated by the inhibited child (Johnson et al. 1981). An interesting finding is that the target child's cooperative play increased only with those children with whom she played the experimental game.

Fear of Medical Procedures

Over the last three decades, play has increasingly been used to help prepare children for medical interventions, including hospitalizations, surgery, and diagnostic testing (Azarnoff 1986), with positive results found in several empirical studies (Chan 1980, Ferguson 1986, Rie et al. 1968). However, hospital-based play programs are often inadequate to prepare children because of staff shortages (Schrader 1977). Further, the play programs may not be suitable for older children, who are likely to reject the idea of playing with dolls or puppets, the traditional play materials for preparation for medical intervention (Klinizing and Klinizing 1977).

In light of these issues, Henkens-Matzke and Abbott (1990) developed the game Hospital Windows, a medically oriented, educational activity designed to increase knowledge and decrease fears of young children regarding common health care practices and procedures. The game has real photographs of medical procedures and involves the opportunity to touch real medical equipment. An initial study found favorable results in terms of reducing fears and increasing knowledge about medical procedures.

Case Illustration: An Encopretic Boy

John, a 10-year-old boy, was referred for chronic encopresis. Extensive medical testing had all but ruled out physiological causes to his problem. He developed the habit of soiling at age 5, well after he had established bowel control and independent toileting. His parents reluctantly sought psychological help at the advice of his pediatrician and gastroenterologist.

John presented as a quiet, adultlike, emotionally constricted, and depressed child. He initially showed no interest in game play. He talked about his problem willingly but with a detached intellectualism. He explained that his soiling – his "accidents" – only happened when he was outside playing a game such as baseball or soccer with his friends. He would become so engrossed in the activity that he didn't even realize he had soiled. Yet it was clear from our early discussions that John was actively suppressing strong feelings associated with his problem. When pressed to discuss his feelings about his parents finding soiled underwear and their subsequent negative reactions, as well as the punishments that followed, he expressed feigned indifference.

Realizing that my first task was to facilitate his expression of emotions, especially anger, I asked John if he wanted to play a game with me. He hesitated but then agreed and chose the game Uno, which we played exclusively for a number of sessions. John's style of play was quite colorless and devoid of emotional involvement. He was extremely polite and gracious in defeat as well as victory. To encourage affective expression on his part, I exaggerated my emotional responses during the game. When I lost, which was infrequently, I appeared to be momentarily angry and shocked that I could be beaten by a young child, and even engaged in silly behaviors like sticking out my tongue at him or throwing the cards when I lost to try to get him to relax his controls somewhat. I feigned a strong desire to beat him and became excited whenever I did well during game play.

John slowly began to join this game within the game and become more animated and expressive. At first, his affective expressions remained at the verbal level (e.g., "Oh, come on, I stink!"). Finally, he began to let real emotion slip through after losing the last of six games in a row. He let some hurt show on his face, threw his cards down, and said he wouldn't play any more. I verbally reflected his anger and he said it wasn't fair of me to play so hard to beat a child. For the first time, I felt that he had let his actual child self show through.

John's affect changed after this session. He appeared much more relaxed and eager to play games when he entered the therapy room. His mother related that he now talked about really liking therapy and looking forward to the hour, whereas previously he resisted going. John now showed more interest in playing different games. After experimenting with Candyland, Simple Object Bingo, Trouble, Connect Four, Mastermind, Sorry, and checkers, he settled on Trouble and Simple Object Bingo. Both of these games are primarily based on chance with a minimal amount of strategy needed to win. These games seemed for John to neutralize my superiority in strategy and allow for more fairness in our competition.

As it turned out, the equality of competition permitted John to express other conflicts. John was a good player and had little trouble playing on the same skill level as I did. Our contests were very even, with both of us winning about the same amount of time. Yet I noticed that he stopped himself from beating me on several occasions in order to let me win. In addition, he seemed sheepish and self-conscious upon beating me. After noticing this pattern, I asked him about it. He denied making self-defeating moves, but I insisted that he did let me win and that he should stop it immediately. I told him that it was insulting to me. I called his behavior reverse cheating. This seemed to surprise John; he then admitted to letting me win in order to make me feel better. He jokingly said that he didn't want "to make me angry."

I suggested that he was afraid to win. I explained that maybe he was afraid that I would disapprove, reject, or otherwise become angry at him for beating me. This led to a discussion of fear of anger. I steered our conversation to John's experiences at home. He related with some bitterness that his parents get angry with him all the time, but that every time he gets mad, he gets punished by having to stay in his room. When asked about what makes them the most angry, John said that his soiling makes them furious. We talked about ways in which his mother and father express anger. I asked John to role play angry reactions expressed by either of his parents. He appeared to enjoy this exercise and the catharsis it brought.

After this significant session, I made a point of reminding John in a teasing, playful way not to give me any help during game play, and that if he did I would then *really* get angry. A few times I caught him handicapping himself and expressed my irritation. My rationale for this intervention was to give John an opportunity to experience adult anger in a controlled setting in which he could assimilate and master his own anxiety related to being the object of anger.

John's affect during sessions became much better. He was much more animated and expressive. At home, however, his behavior took a turn for the worse. His parents reported that he had become oppositional and would talk back to them frequently, even being belligerent at times. I had a session with the parents and explained the importance of allowing John to possess and express anger, not just positive feelings. I interpreted his belligerence as the first clumsy attempts on his part to stand up to his parents and express his displeasure or discontent about certain issues. I asked them to consciously make an effort to recognize and show acceptance of *all* of John's feelings. While they should not accept inappropriate behavior, they should acknowledge in a nonjudgmental manner the negative feelings underlying the behavior.

The parents also related to me that John had not had an encopretic episode since beginning therapy four months ago. While he had had similar periods of normal bowel activity in the past, once for as long as ten months, the parents were quite hopeful that this most recent period represented the beginning of the end of his soiling pattern. Unfortunately, over the next 6 months John had two or three episodes. I worked closely with the parents at these times to help them control their anger and reproachful reactions toward John. It became clear that John's mother had much more difficulty than his father in letting go of her anger toward him. I suggested to them that John substituted soiling for more adaptive methods of expressing normal feelings of anger and resentment any child has at times for his parents.

John did not disclose to me in session that he had a soiling episode. However, I told him that his parents had told me. This visibly upset him, and throughout the next few sessions he verbalized hostile feelings toward them, especially his mother. I noticed that John often made a raspberry sound with his mouth to express displeasure toward his mother. I began to imitate this sound and then join in his verbal thrashing of his parents. I expanded on this by making the sound and then saying "Yeah, poop on them." This amused John, and he repeated this phrase often.

Over the following sessions I gradually geared, by interventions, toward making the connection between the sound John made in therapy and his actual soiling at home. I sensed that John would not accept this interpretation outright, so I focused on his need to express anger toward his parents because he never is allowed to get angry in front of them. Eventually, John made the connection on his own.

This case illustrates the value of games in establishing a rapport with a child in therapy and in facilitating the expression of angry, hostile, and fearful feelings. The games became a projective screen onto which John transferred from his family life a significantly conflictual relationship pattern. Finally, game playing helped maintain John's interest in therapy and in working through his difficulties.

The Spectrum of Games

Games have many characteristics that make them suitable and effective tools for enhancing the process of child psychotherapy. The functions of game play include recuperation, catharsis, sublimation or adaptive expression of aggression, intellectual development, and various elements of socialization. Game playing, the main activity of childhood, is particularly relevant to children over the age of 5, when concerns about competence and social interaction become prominent. Game play in a therapy setting provides experiences of pleasure and fosters communication and self-expression, reality testing, and insight, and strengthens cognition, socialization, and self-control. The number and type of therapeutic games have expanded tremendously over the past 20 years. Therapists can now choose among games targeted for specific problems including divorce, low self-esteem, social isolation, fear of medical procedures, poor impulse control, anxiety and stress, and aggressiveness.

References

Avedon, E. M., and Sutton-Smith, B. (1971). *The Study of Games*. New York: John Wiley & Sons.

Azarnoff, P. (1986). Preparation with medically-oriented play. In *Medically-Oriented Play for Children in Health Care: The Issues*, pp. 221–240. Santa Monica, CA: Pediatric Projects.

Barrish, H. H., Saunders, M., and Wolf, M. M. (1969). Good behavior game: effects of individual contingencies for group consequences on disruptive behavior in a classroom. *Journal of Applied Behavioral Analysis* 2:119–124.

Baumeister, R. F. (1986). *Identity: Cultural Change and the Struggle for Self*. New York: Oxford University Press.

——— (1987). How the self became a problem: a psychological review of historical research. *Journal of Personality and Social Psychology* 52:163–176.

Baumeister, R. F., and Senders, P. S. (1988). Identity development and the role structure of children's games. *Journal of Genetic Psychology* 150:19–37.

Beiser, H. R. (1979). Formal games in diagnosis and therapy. *Journal of Child Psychiatry* 18:480–490.

Berg, B. (1982). *The Changing Family Game*. Dayton, OH: Cognitive-Behavioral Resources.

——— (1986). Cognitive-behavioral intervention for children of divorce. In *Game Play: Therapeutic Use of Childhood Games*, ed. C. Schaefer and S. Reid, pp. 111–138. New York: John Wiley & Sons.

——— (1991). *Childsworth Childsplay Catalog*. Philadelphia: Center for Applied Psychology.

Berg, B., Hickey, N., and Snyder, L. (1985). *The changing family game: efficacy of cognitive-behavioral intervention of children of divorce.* Paper presented at the meeting of the Midwestern Psychological Association, Chicago, IL, September.

Berlin, I. (1986). The use of competitive games in play therapy. In *Game Play: Therapeutic Use of Childhood Games,* ed. C. Schaefer and S. Reid, pp. 197–214. New York: John Wiley & Sons.

Bettelheim, B. (1972). Play and education. *School Review* 81:1–13.

Bow, J. N., and Goldberg, T. E. (1986). Therapeutic uses of games with a fine motor component. In *Game Play: Therapeutic Use of Childhood Games,* ed. C. Schaefer and S. Reid, pp. 243–256. New York: John Wiley & Sons.

Bugental, D. B., Whalen, C. K., and Henker, B. (1977). Causal attributions of hyperactive children and motivational assumptions of two behavior change approaches: evidence for an interactionist position. *Child Development* 48:874–884.

Burks, H. F. (1978). *Psychological Meanings of the Imagine! Game.* Huntington Beach, CA: Arden.

Burten, R. (1976). *Social Security.* Anaheim, CA: The Ungame Company.

Caplan, R., and Sherman, T. (1991). Kiddie formal thought disorder rating scale and story game. In *Play Diagnosis and Assessment,* ed. C. Schaefer, K. Gitlin, and E. Sandgrund, pp. 169–202. New York: John Wiley & Sons.

Chan, J. (1980). Preparation for procedures and survey through play. *Pediatrician* 9:210–219.

Dubow, E. F., Huesmann, L. R., and Eron, L. D. (1987). Mitigating aggression and promoting prosocial behavior in aggressive elementary schoolboys. *Behavioral Research Therapy* 25:527–531.

Epstein, Y. M. (1986). Feedback and could this happen: two therapeutic games for children of divorce. In *Game Play: Therapeutic Use of Childhood Games,* ed. C. Schaefer and S. Reid, pp. 159–186. New York: John Wiley & Sons.

Erikson, E. (1968). *Identity: Youth and Crisis.* New York: Norton.

Ferguson, R. V. (1986). Medically-oriented play: the need for research. In *Medically-Oriented Play for Children in Health Care: The Issues,* ed. P. Azarnoff, pp. 292–317. Santa Monica, CA: Pediatric Projects.

Foxx, R. M., McMorrow, M. J., and Schloss, C. N. (1983). Stacking the deck: teaching social skills to retarded adults with a modified table game. *Journal of Applied Behavior Analysis* 16:167–170.

Freud, S. (1923). *The Ego and the Id.* London: Hogarth.

Frey, D. (1986). Communication boardgames with children. In *Game Play: Therapeutic Use of Childhood Games,* ed. C. Schaefer and S. Reid, pp. 21–40. New York: John Wiley & Sons.

Gardner, R. A. (1969). The game of checkers as a diagnostic and therapeutic tool in child psychotherapy. *Acta Paedopsychiatrica* 36:142–152.

———— (1973). *The Talking, Feeling, and Doing Game.* Cresskill, NJ: Creative Therapeutics.

———— (1975). *Psychotherapeutic Approaches to the Resistant Child.* New York: Jason Aronson.

———— (1986). The game of checkers in child therapy. In *Game Play: Therapeutic Use of Childhood Games* ed. C. Schaefer and S. Reid, pp. 215–232. New York: John Wiley & Sons.

———— (1988). *The Story Telling Card Game.* Cresskill, NJ: Creative Therapeutics.

Groos, K. (1898). *The Play of Animals.* Trans. E. Balkwin. New York: Appleton.

Harris, V. W., and Sherman, J. A. (1973). Use and analysis of the "Good Behavior Game" to reduce disruptive classroom behavior. *Journal of Applied Behavior Analysis* 6:405–417.

Henkens-Matzke, A., and Abbott, D. A. (1990). Game playing: a method for reducing young children's fear of medical procedures. *Early Childhood Research Quarterly* 5:19–26.

Hurff, J. M. (1981). Gaming technique: an assessment and training tool for individuals with learning deficits. *American Journal of Occupational Therapy* 35:728–735.

Johnson, T. J., Goetz, E. M., Baer, D. M., and Green, D. R. (1981). The effects of an experimental game on the classroom cooperative play of a preschool isolate. *Revista Mexicana de Analisis de la Conducta* 1:37–48.

Kendall, P. C., and Braswell, L. (1985). *Cognitive-Behavioral Therapy for Impulsive Children.* New York: Guilford.

Klinizing, D. R., and Klinizing, D. G. (1977). *The Hospitalized Child: Communication Techniques for Health Personnel.* Englewood Cliffs, NJ: Prentice-Hall.

Levinson, B. M. (1976). The use of checkers in therapy. In *The Therapeutic Use of Child's Play,* ed. C. Schaefer, pp. 383–390. New York: Jason Aronson.

Loomis, E. A. (1957). The use of checkers in handling certain resistances in child therapy and child analysis. *Journal of the American Psychoanalytic Association* 5:130–135.

Maynard-Smith, J. (1984). Game theory and the evolution of behaviour. *The Behavioral and Brain Sciences* 7:95–125.

Mead, G. H. (1934). *Mind, Self, and Society.* Chicago: University of Chicago Press.

Medland, M. B., and Stacknick, T. J. (1972). Good behavior game: a replication and systematic analysis. *Journal of Applied Behavior Analysis* 5:45–51.

Meeks, J. (1970). Children who cheat at games. *Journal of Child Psychiatry* 9:157–174.

Mitchell, E. D., and Masson, B. S. (1948). *The Theory of Play.* New York: Burns.

Nochajski, S. B., and Gordon, C. Y. (1987). The use of Trivial Pursuit in teaching community and independent living skills to adults with developmental disabilities. *American Journal of Occupational Therapy* 41:10–15.

Opie, I., and Opie, P. (1976). Street games: counting out and chasing. In *Play–Its Role in Development and Evolution,* ed. J. S. Bruner, pp. 96–113. New York: Basic Books.

Parten, M. B. (1932). Social participation among preschool children. *Journal of Abnormal and Social Psychology* 27:243–269.

Peller, L. E. (1954). Libidinal development as reflected in play. *Psychoanalysis* 3:3–11.

Piaget, J. (1962). *Play, Dreams, and Imitation in Childhood.* New York: Norton.

Rabin, C. (1983). *Towards the use and development for social work practice.* Unpublished manuscript.

Redl, F. (1958). The impact of game ingredients on children's play behavior. *Proceedings of the Fourth Conference on Group Processes* 4:33–81.

Rie, H. E., Boverman, H., Grossman, B. J., and Ozoa, N. (1968). Immediate and long-term effects of intervention early in prolonged hospitalization. *Pediatrics* 41:755–764.

Ross, H. S. (1982). The establishment of social games among toddlers. *Developmental Psychology* 18:509–518.

Ross, H. S., and Kay, D. A. (1980). The origins of social games. In *Children's Play,* ed. K. Rubin, pp. 29–53. San Francisco: Jossey-Bass.

Ruble, D. (1983). The development of social comparison processes and their role in achievement-related self-socialization. In *Social Cognition and Social Behavior: Developmental Perspectives,* ed. E. T. Higgins, D. Ruble, and W. Hartup, pp. 162–188. New York: Cambridge University Press.

Salend, S. J., Reynolds, C. J., and Coyle, E. M. (1989). Individualizing the good behavior game across type and frequency of behavior with emotionally disturbed adolescents. *Behavior Modification* 13:108–126.

Schachter, R. S. (1974). Kinetic psychotherapy in treatment of children. *American Journal of Psychotherapy* 28:430–437.

_____ (1984). Kinetic psychotherapy in the treatment of depression in latency age children. *International Journal of Group Psychotherapy* 34:83–91.

_____ (1986). Techniques of kinetic psychotherapy. In *Game Play: Therapeutic Use of Childhood Games*, ed. C. Schaefer and S. Reid, pp. 95–107. New York: John Wiley & Sons.

Schaefer, C., and Reid, S., eds. (1986). *Game Play: Therapeutic Use of Childhood Games*. New York: John Wiley & Sons.

Schlenker, B. R., and Bonoma, T. V. (1978). Fun and games: the validity of games for the study of conflict. *Journal of Conflict Resolution* 22:7–38.

Schrader, E. S. (1977). Hospital tours for well-children help them to cope. *Journal of Operating Room Nurses* 26:13.

Serok, S. (1986). Therapeutic implications of games with juvenile delinquents. In *Game Play: Therapeutic Use of Childhood Games*, ed. C. Schaefer and S. Reid, pp. xxx–xxx. New York: John Wiley & Sons.

Serok, S., and Blum, A. (1981). Therapeutic uses of games. *Residential Group Care and Treatment* 1:3–14.

Shapiro, L. E. (1981). *Games to Grow On*. Englewood Cliffs, NJ: Prentice-Hall.

Spates, J. (1976). Sociological overview of games. In *Street Games*, ed. A. Milberg, pp. 286–290. New York: McGraw-Hill.

Sprafkin, J., and Rubenstein, E. A. (1982). Using television to improve the social behavior of institutionalized children. In *Prevention in Human Services: Rx Television: Enhancing the Preventive Impact of TV*, ed. J. Sprafkin, C. Swift, and R. H. Ross, pp. 200–221. New York: Haworth.

Stoll, C. T., Inber, M., and James, S. F. (1968). *Game Experiences and Socialization: An Exploration of Sex Differences*. Baltimore: Johns Hopkins Press.

Strachey, J., ed. (1962). *The Standard Edition of the Psychological Works of Sigmund Freud*. Vol. 1. London: Hogarth.

Sutton-Smith, B. (1961). Cross-cultural study of children's games. *American Philosophical Society Yearbook* 426–429.

_____ (1971). Play, games, and controls. In *Social Control*, ed. J. P. Scott, pp. 84–100. Chicago: University of Chicago Press.

Sutton-Smith, B., and Roberts, J. M. (1971). The cross-cultural and psychological study of games. *International Review of Sport Sociology* 6:79–87.

Swanson, A. J. (1986). Using games to improve self-control deficits in children. In *Game Play: Therapeutic Use of Childhood Games*, ed. C. Schaefer and S. Reid, pp. 233–243. New York: John Wiley & Sons.

Varenhorst, B. B. (1973). Game theory, simulations, and group counseling. *Educational Technology* 13:40–43.

Vlosky, M. (1986). *Our Game*. Broomfield, CO: Transitional Dynamics.

Wood, C., and Goddard, G. (1940). *The Complete Book of Games*. Garden City, NY: Doubleday.

Zakich, R. (1975). *The Ungame*. Anaheim, CA: The Ungame Company.

Zigler, E., and Child, I. L. (1956). Socialization. In *Handbook of Social Psychology*, ed. G. Lindzey and E. Aronson, pp. 210–248. Reading, MA: Addison-Wesley.

Afterword

It is obvious in examining the different schools of play therapy that no single approach has all the answers. Accordingly, one needs to select play methods that meet the needs of the individual case. The more knowledgeable therapists are of curative factors that cut across the schools, the better able they will be to apply interventions that work for the particular child. Such an integrative, eclectic approach seems best for meeting the needs of clients with markedly different problems and diagnoses. By approaching play therapy from an integrative framework, one is more likely to apply a comprehensive treatment plan combining therapeutic factors for optimal effectiveness.

There has been a neglect of attention to therapeutic factors by play therapists. Previous attempts to list or classify these factors are lacking. This is surprising, since the identification of common factors across therapeutic modalities is one of the most significant trends in the field of psychotherapy. A greater understanding of common factors will assist therapists to become more aware of why they do what they do in play therapy. Emerging theories of play therapy need to recognize the role of therapeutic factors and their underlying mechanisms of action.

A listing of therapeutic factors in play therapy must be somewhat arbitrary at this point. Knowledge of this subject is in the beginning phase, and uncertainty remains about boundaries and taxonomy. The fact that this is the first book to delineate the common factors points to the distance to go before the factors are fully understood and amenable to therapeutic control. There is a pressing need for more research on the reliability and validity of the therapeutic factors. In particular, we need to know which clients benefit the most from each specific factor. Research on play therapy must move beyond a narrow outcome focus (does it produce change?) to an investigation of process variables (what specific aspects of play result in the improvement?).

—Charles E. Schaefer

Index

Developmental factors (*continued*)
  catharsis and, 118–122
  communication, therapeutic value of
      play, 51
  competence, developmental play, 66–68
  game play, 13, 328–331
  imagery and, 193–195, 201–202
  metaphoric teaching, 230
  normal, play and, 2–3
  normal fears, 309–314
  play and, 1–2, 45
  play types, communication, 43–44
  relationships
      enhancement of, theoretical and
          empirical considerations,
          269–270
      establishment of, resistance, dynamics
          underlying, 20
      resistance and, 24–27
      role play, play indicators and remedial
          play activities, summary table,
          174–175
      symbols, reading of, communication,
          53
Developmental play (competence), 66–68
  motor play, 66–67
  object play, 67
  social play, 67–68
  socio-dramatic play and language skills,
      68
Developmental-supportive play,
      abreactive-enactment and, links
      between, 156–160
Diagnosis
  game play, therapeutic content of, 332
  resistance, developmental factors and,
      26–27
Differentiation subphase, role play, clinical
      case examples, 180–181
Direct observations, image measurement
      and fantasy production, 197
Disabled child, mediated play, competence,
      71–72
Dispositions, of play, problem solving,
      85–86
Divergent thinking skills, creative problem
      solving, 83–84

Divorce
  game play clinical applications, 340
  imagery, case examples, 213–214
Drama therapy, imagery,
      psychotherapeutic applications,
      211–213
Dreams
  image measurement and fantasy
      production, 200
  imagery and, 192

Educational settings, imagery applications
      in, 214–216
Ego, play definition, 42
Ego enhancement
  game play, therapeutic content of, 334
  games for, description and
      developmental effects of, 338–339
Eidetic images
  imagery and, 191–192
  psychotherapeutic applications, 206
Elation, positive emotion, 299
Emotion. *See also* Positive emotion
  catharsis
      overview of, 107–109
      play therapy factor, 8
  communication
      awareness of child and, 47–48
      therapeutic value of play, 51–52
  symbols, reading of, communication,
      53
Emotional release. *See* Catharsis
Empathy, role play as tool for development
      of, 183–184
Encopresis, game play clinical case
      illustration, 343–345
Enjoyment. *See also* Positive emotion
  communication, awareness of child and,
      47
  play definition, 42–43
  play therapy factor, 12
Environment
  catharsis, developmental perspective and,
      119–120
  problem solving, 86–87
Existential play therapy, described, 4

Relationship enhancement *(continued)*
    child-centered approach, 274–276
    group therapy, 276–278
    overview, 273–274
    parents as therapists, 278–282
    play therapy factor, 11–12
    ripple effects and, 287–288
    theoretical and empirical considerations,
      269–273
    developmental studies, 269–270
    playing and, 271–272
    therapeutic relationship, 270–273
Relationship establishment, resistance,
    dynamics underlying, 19–20
Relaxation therapy, imagery,
    psychotherapeutic applications,
    202–203
REM sleep, image measurement and
    fantasy production, 200
Repetition, fears, play features which
    promote mastery of, 314–315
Repression, catharsis, theoretical issues,
    109–110
Resistance, 17–40
    clinical case examples, 32–38
    clinical practice techniques, 27–31
    Color-Your-Life technique, 29–31
    family word association game, 31
    hidden puppet play, 27–28
    puppetry and ventriloquist figures, 28
    storytelling techniques, 28–29
    developmental factors and, 24–27
    dynamics underlying, 17–24
    combining play and therapy, 22–23
    initial contact, 20–22
    overview, 17–18
    relationship establishment, 19–20
    therapist's personality, 18–19
    therapist's role in play, 23–24
    overcoming, play therapy factor, 5–6,
      38–39
Rigidity, symbols, reading of,
    communication, 54
Robbers and bad guys, normal fears,
    313–314
Role development, game play,
    developmental factors, 329–330

Role play, 167–188
    clinical case examples, 177–183
    autism, 178
    differentiation subphase, 180–181
    object constancy, 181–183
    rapprochement, 181
    symbiosis, 178–180
    communication, significance of play,
      44–45
    defined, 167
    empathy development and, 183–184
    historical foundations, 168–169
    new skills acquisition and, 184–186
    object relations theory, 169–177
    autistic and symbiotic phases, 172
    object constancy, 176–177
    overview of, 169–172
    separation-individuation subphases,
      172–173, 176
    play indicators and remedial play
      activities, summary table, 174–175
    play therapy factor, 9–10
Rules
    game play, play therapy factor, 13
    play types, communication, 44

Selective attention and openness, problem
    solving, play and creativity link,
    91–92
Self, personality contrasted, 121
Self-expressive communication. *See*
    Communication
Self-image
    of infant, attachment formation, 246–253
    role play, object relations theory and,
      171–172
Self-instruction techniques, imagery,
    psychotherapeutic applications, 205
Self-projection, therapist's personality,
    resistance, dynamics underlying, 19
Self-realization, relationship enhancement,
    play therapy factor, 12
Self-report measures, image measurement
    and fantasy production, 197–199
Sensorimotor play, play types,
    communication, 43–44